Higher Learning

Reading and Writing about College

edited by

Patti See, Student Services Coordinator

Bruce Taylor, Professor of English

University of Wisconsin–Eau Claire

Prentice
Hall

Upper Saddle River, New Jersey 07548

Library of Congress Cataloging-in-Publication Data

Higher learning : reading and writing about college / [compiled by] Patti See, Bruce Taylor.
    p. cm.
    ISBN 0-205-28789-1
    1. Readers—Education, Higher. 2. Universities and colleges—Problems, exercises, etc.
3. Education, Higher—Problems, exercises, etc. 4. Readers—Universities and colleges. 5.
English language—Rhetoric. 6. Academic writing. 7. College readers. I. See, Patti. II.
Taylor, Bruce, 1947 Feb. 19-

PE1127.E37 H54 2001
428.6—dc21

00-025096

Acquisitions Editor: Sande Johnson
Managing Editor: Mary Carnis
Director of Manufacturing and Production: Bruce Johnson
Manufacturing Manager: Ed O'Dougherty
Assistant Editor: Michelle Williams
Marketing Manager: Jeff McIlroy
Marketing Assistant: Barbara Rosenberg

Prentice-Hall International (UK) Limited, *London*
Prentice-Hall of Australia Pty. Limited, *Sydney*
Prentice-Hall Canada Inc., *Toronto*
Prentice-Hall Hispanoamericana, S.A., *Mexico*
Prentice-Hall of India Private Limited, *New Delhi*
Prentice-Hall of Japan, Inc., *Tokyo*
Pearson Education Singapore Pte. Ltd.
Editora Prentice-Hall do Brasil, Ltda., *Rio de Janeiro*

Credits are listed on page 337, constituting a continuation of the copyright page.

10 9 8 7 6 5 4 3
ISBN 0-205-28789-1

Contents

One ~ Where We're Coming From: Leaving Other Lives 1

Two ~ School Daze: Life in the First Year 63

Three ~ Student Affairs: Friends and Lovers 133

Four ~ Teacher, Teacher: Will This Be on the Test? 213

Five ~ Been There, Done That: Looking Forward, Looking Back .. 299

Appendix ~ Critical Thinking Points on Selected Films 335

Preface

"

*Higher Learning provides students and teachers a vehicle
to explore, reflect on, and perhaps even discover issues
about ethnic, class, age, gender, and sexual diversity.*

"

Imagine entering a foreign country where you understand just enough of the language to communicate but cannot quite grasp the customs or the etiquette of the land. Imagine you had to learn the culture of that country without anyone showing or telling you how. This is what going to college is like for many first-year students.

Higher Learning: Reading and Writing about College presents imaginative literature—fiction, poetry, and creative nonfiction—that appeals to students and teachers because it is written from their point of view. It is literature that allows them to see how their individual experience fits into the culturally and historically diverse traditions and perspectives of university life.

Avid readers—students, teachers, and lifelong learners—know literature is the one place a person is never alone. This collection allows readers to discover people just like them, as well as people sometimes so different from them to be almost, at least at first, unimaginable. Students can watch these people struggle with problems and challenges, most of which never appear in any college catalogue or on any class syllabus. Though universities provide an array of student support systems, there are some aspects of university life that new students must work through mostly on their own. Character, maturity, and experience will be as essential to success as high school class rank or SAT scores. Alienation, isolation, and loneliness will be as much of a challenge as English Composition or Calculus.

Many college texts for first-year students focus on time management, critical thinking, active reading, and lecture and text note taking. These survival skills are the nuts and bolts of college success. This collection, written by people who have "been there and done that," displays the whole machine chugging along in all its imperfect glory. These readings provide good and bad examples, some broader views and alternative takes of individual experiences, parables of the admirable, cautionary tales, and funny stories.

College students, especially first-year students, often feel isolated on campuses. The degree to which students feel a "connectedness" to a university, a sense of place and a way of fitting in that many teachers and administrators by now take too much for granted, leads to how well the students perform, in fact whether or not they complete a degree. *Higher Learning* offers some of the "inside" stories of college life, addressing the difficult issues that students face in their transition to college. It also provides students and teachers a vehicle to explore, reflect on, and perhaps even discover issues about ethnic, class, age, gender, and sexual diversity.

How to Use This Book

Reading and writing questions are provided as a part of the text and should be read before and after reading each piece of literature, as a way to get readers involved in the kind of close and active reading done at the college level. In addition to providing prompts for class discussion, Critical Thinking Points, offered before and after each piece under the categories of *As You Read*, *After You've Read*, and *Some Possibilities for Writing*, accomplish the following objectives:

❦ provide a focus for each reading

❦ help readers formulate their own questions while they read

❦ provide a historical and/or cultural context for the reading

❦ create a forum for reader response, analysis, and critical reflection

❦ promote creative writing and expository responses that connect readings to students' personal lives

❦ provide prompts for informal and formal writing assignments, such as journal entries, class presentations, collaborative group writing projects, and research papers

❦ make connections between readings and other classic pieces of literature that are easily found in most college libraries

Each chapter of *Higher Learning* focuses on a particular stage of college life.

Chapter One, "Where We're Coming From: Leaving Other Lives," explores the aftermath of surviving 12 years of formal education, the personal and cultural influences that affect making the decision to go to college, the possibility of teaching oneself, and how to find and follow the future that awaits us.

Chapter Two, "School Daze: Life in the First Year," delves into personal examples of coping with such dilemmas as roommates, failing grades, balancing home and school, applying course work to real lives, meeting professors' expectations, and sifting through advice and models to find the most appropriate and valuable ones.

Chapter Three, "Student Affairs: Friends and Lovers," looks at issues of first love, virginity, rape, AIDS, sexual discovery, homosexuality, romantic breakups, and platonic friendships. These pieces demonstrate just how difficult it is to try to establish equal respect between and among the sexes given the various roles that social expectations play in gender relationships.

Chapter Four, "Teacher, Teacher: Will This Be on the Test?" probes the always complex relationship between students and teachers, as well as between professors themselves and the university system. This section helps students see teachers as people with many of the same ongoing concerns and challenges that the students face every day.

Chapter Five, "Been There, Done That: Looking Forward, Looking Back," shows it is never too late to look ahead, offering pieces that explore life after graduation and the advantage of hindsight when offered by people who have survived what today's students are trying to get through.

"Some Films for College Lives" are listed at the end of each chapter to complement the sections with a popular culture perspective that explores the depiction of college in cinema since 1927. An appendix offers critical thinking points about the films.

There are many larger college issues that require additional reflection and analysis, perhaps in the form of extended research. *Further Suggestions for Writing*, a list of prompts at the end of each chapter, accomplishes the following objectives:

❦   creates a forum for analysis of academic and social issues at college

❦   synthesizes topics from chapter readings

❦   provides prompts for traditional rhetorical strategies in persuasion /argumentation, comparison/contrast, cause/effect, and classification.

Our goal in providing this book is that students will not only be motivated to read, but they will be moved to reflect and write about their own experiences, their campus, their college life in general, and the world around them.

Acknowledgments

We wish to thank the Network for Excellence in Teaching and the Office of University Research at the University of Wisconsin–Eau Claire for their grant support throughout researching and writing this book, as well as the Academic Skills Center and the Department of English for their clerical support.

Thank you to our reviewers who saw our book in various stages: Lee Rademacher, Purdue, Calumet; Bob Nelson, Rutgers University; Margaret Pobywajlo, University of New Hampshire at Manchester; Jan Norton, Missouri Western State College; Karan Hancock Gier, University of Alaska–Anchorage; Rodney Keller, Ricks Community College; Kathryn Lowe, University of Evansville; Anne Lundquist, Guilford College; Karen L. Reinhart, Spokane Community College; Adrian R. Levitt, Seton Hall University; and Alison Valerian, Seton Hall University.

We are indebted to Meredith Weber for her thorough research as a graduate assistant. Special thanks to Jim Thornton and Karen Taylor for typing, proofing, and making suggestions. This book would not be possible without Frank Smoot. Finally, thanks to the students in UW-Eau Claire's Collegiate Bridge Program and College Writing Courses who were our first audience.

Chapter One

Where We're Coming From: Leaving Other Lives

College is the place to explore different people, languages, cultures, lifestyles, ideologies, and livelihoods. The selections here examine a variety of times and places and will help you begin to realize how geographic area, family size, religious affiliation, ethnic background, and any other outside influences affect who and what any individual becomes.

This chapter will explore —

- Overcoming stereotypes and prejudices
- Sacrifices that are sometimes made in order to attend college
- Various reasons for going to college
- Formal education that does or does not prepare students for adult life
- What it means to be "self-educated" and the values of learning on one's own
- The benefits of planning for a future or waiting for your future to find you

Incurring My Mother's Displeasure
from The School Days of an Indian Girl

Zitkala-Sa

"

Thus, homeless and heavy-hearted, I began anew my life among strangers.

"

Critical thinking points: As you read

1) What are some clues as to the era?

2) The language and tone of this essay are very formal. Why might that be so?

3) Speculate on what causes prejudice among ethnic groups. What are some stereotypes, past or present, of Native Americans?

In the second journey to the East I had not come without some precautions. I had a secret interview with one of our best medicine men, and when I left his wigwam I carried securely in my sleeve a tiny bunch of magic roots. This possession assured me of friends wherever I should go. So absolutely did I believe in its charms that I wore it through all the school routine for more than a year. Then, before I lost my faith in the dead roots, I lost the little buckskin bag containing all my good luck.

At the close of this second term of three years I was the proud owner of my first diploma. The following autumn I ventured upon a college career against my mother's will. I had written for her approval, but in her reply I found no encouragement. She called my notice to her neighbors' children, who had completed their education in three years. They had returned to their homes, and were then talking English with the frontier settlers. Her few words hinted that I had better give up my slow attempt to learn the white man's ways, and be content to roam over the prairies and find my living upon wild roots. I silenced her by deliberate disobedience.

Thus, homeless and heavy-hearted, I began anew my life among strangers.

As I hid myself in my little room in the college dormitory, away from the scornful and yet curious eyes of the students, I pined for sympathy. Often I wept in secret, wishing I had gone West, to be nourished by my mother's love, instead of remaining among a cold race whose hearts were frozen hard with prejudice.

Zitkala-Sa (1876–1938) was a Sioux Indian. "Incurring My Mother's Displeasure" appeared in the *Atlantic Monthly* in 1900. It is a part of her larger work, *The School Days of an Indian Girl.*

During the fall and winter seasons I scarcely had a real friend, though by that time several of my classmates were courteous to me at a safe distance.

My mother had not yet forgiven my rudeness to her, and I had no moment for letter-writing. By daylight and lamplight, I spun with reeds and thistles, until my hands were tired from their weaving, the magic design which promised me the white man's respect.

At length, in the spring term, I entered an oratorical contest among the various classes. As the day of competition approached, it did not seem possible that the event was so near at hand, but it came. In the chapel the classes assembled together, with their invited guests. The high platform was carpeted, and gayly festooned with college colors. A bright white light illumined the room and outlined clearly the great polished beams that arched the domed ceiling. The assembled crowds filled the air with pulsating murmurs. When the hour for speaking arrived all were hushed. But on the wall the old clock which pointed out the trying moment ticked calmly on.

One after another I saw and heard the orators. Still, I could not realize that they longed for the favorable decision of the judges as much as I did. Each contestant received a loud burst of applause, and some were cheered heartily. Too soon my turn came, and I paused a moment behind the curtains for a deep breath. After my concluding words, I heard the same applause that the others had called out.

Upon my retreating steps, I was astounded to receive from my fellow students a large bouquet of roses tied with flowing ribbons. With the lovely flowers I fled from the stage. This friendly token was a rebuke to me for the hard feelings I had borne them.

Later, the decision of the judges awarded me the first place. Then there was a mad uproar in the hall, where my classmates sang and shouted my name at the top of their lungs; and the disappointed students howled and brayed in fearfully dissonant tin trumpets. In this excitement, happy students rushed forward to offer their congratulations. And I could not conceal a smile when they wished to escort me in a procession to the students' parlor, where all were going to calm themselves. Thanking them for the kind spirit which prompted them to make such a proposition, I walked alone with the night to my own little room.

A few weeks afterward, I appeared as the college representative in another contest. This time the competition was among orators from different colleges in our state. It was held at the state capital, in one of the largest opera houses.

Here again was a strong prejudice against my people. In the evening, as the great audience filled the house, the student bodies began warring among themselves. Fortunately, I was spared witnessing any of the noisy wrangling before the contest began. The slurs against the Indian that stained the lips of our opponents were already burning like a dry fever within my breast.

But after the orations were delivered a deeper burn awaited me. There, before that vast ocean of eyes, some college rowdies threw out a large white flag, with a drawing of a most forlorn Indian girl on it. Under this they had printed in bold black letters words that ridiculed the college which was represented by a "squaw." Such worse than barbarian rudeness embittered me. While we waited for the verdict of the judges, I gleamed fiercely upon the throngs of palefaces. My teeth were hard set, as I saw the white flag still floating insolently in the air.

Then anxiously we watched the man carry toward the stage the envelope containing the final decision.

There were two prizes given, that night, and one of them was mine!

The evil spirit laughed within me when the white flag dropped out of sight, and the hands which furled it hung limp in defeat.

Leaving the crowd as quickly as possible, I was soon in my room. The rest of the night I sat in an armchair and gazed into the crackling fire. I laughed no more in triumph when thus alone. The little taste of victory did not satisfy a hunger in my heart. In my mind I saw my mother far away on the Western plains, and she was holding a charge against me.

1900

Critical thinking points: After you've read

1) Was it easy to feel empathy for the narrator? Why or why not?

2) In what ways is Zitkala-Sa "homeless"?

3) Read or reread Booker T. Washington's selection from Up from Slavery. *How is Zitkala-Sa's experience at college similar to Washington's? How is it different?*

4) Historically, learning "the white-man's ways" has separated Native Americans from their heritage. Why would the narrator physically and spiritually separate herself from her people in order to go to college? What are some details from the story that show this?

Some possibilities for writing

1) Imagine what happens when the narrator finally returns to her tribe. Write the reunion scene between Zitkala-Sa and her mother.

2) Recall a time when you purposely disobeyed your parents. What circumstances led to this? Write about the moment you knew you would go against their wishes. What was the outcome?

3) The narrator feels isolated from her classmates because of their prejudice. Have you ever felt isolated from classmates, friends, or family? Write a scene describing your isolation or someone else's.

4) Though the author is given the respect of her classmates when she wins the oratorical contest, she still feels the loss of her mother. Choose another character from your reading, from popular culture or from your own experience who is torn between home and school, and compare Zitkala-Sa's experience to that character's.

5) Research the number of Native Americans at your university. Seek out a Native American student and interview him or her about individual experiences of adapting to college. How does that student's experience compare to Zitkala-Sa's experience?

6) *Research and write a brief report about the Dawes Act (or General Allotment Act) of 1887. How do the philosophical and political implications of this act further your understanding of the memoir?*

an excerpt from
Up from Slavery

Booker T. Washington

The sight of it seemed to give me a new life. I felt that a new kind of existence had now begun — that life would now have a new meaning. I felt that I had reached the promised land, and I resolved to let no obstacle prevent me from putting forth the highest effort to fit myself to accomplish the most good in the world.

Critical thinking points: As you read

1) What are some clues to the time and place?

2) The author had no idea where Hampton was or how much tuition cost. What circumstances might have led the author to have such a desire to go to college?

3) Pay attention to the tone, mood, and attitude of the author. What specific details lead you to believe what you do about that tone, mood, and attitude?

4) Recall a time when you felt proud of yourself for learning, simply for the sake of acquiring knowledge. What led to this?

   Notwithstanding my success at Mrs. Ruffner's I did not give up the idea of going to the Hampton Institute. In the fall of 1872 I determined to make an effort to get there, although, as I have stated, I had no definite idea of the direction in which Hampton was, or of what it would cost to go there. I do not think that any one thoroughly sympathized with me in my ambition to go to Hampton unless it was my mother, and she was troubled with a grave fear that I was starting out on a 'wild-goose chase.' At any rate, I got only a half-hearted consent from her that I might start. The small amount of money that I had earned had been consumed by my stepfather and

Booker T. Washington (1856–1915) was an American educator who urged blacks to attempt to uplift themselves through education and economic advancement. He was born in Franklin County, Virginia, the son of a slave. From 1872 to 1875, Washington attended a newly founded school for blacks, Hampton Normal and Agricultural Institute (now Hampton University). In 1879 he became an instructor at Hampton. The school was so successful that in 1881 Washington was appointed principal of a black school in Tuskegee, Alabama (now Tuskegee University).

the remainder of the family, with the exception of a very few dollars, and so I had very little with which to buy clothes and pay my travelling expenses. My brother John helped me all that he could, but of course that was not a great deal, for his work was in the coal-mine, where he did not earn much, and most of what he did earn went in the direction of paying the household expenses.

Perhaps the thing that touched and pleased me most in connection with my starting for Hampton was the interest that many of the older coloured people took in the matter. They had spent the best days of their lives in slavery, and hardly expected to live to see the time when they would see a member of their race leave home to attend a boarding school. Some of these older people would give me a nickel, others a quarter, or a handkerchief.

Finally the great day came, and I started for Hampton. I had only a small, cheap satchel that contained what few articles of clothing I could get. My mother at the time was rather weak and broken in health. I hardly expected to see her again, and thus our parting was all the more sad. She, however, was very brave through it all. At that time there were no through trains connecting that part of West Virginia with eastern Virginia. Trains ran only a portion of the way, and the remainder of the distance was traveled by stage-coaches.

The distance from Malden to Hampton is about five hundred miles. I had not been away from home many hours before it began to grow painfully evident that I did not have enough money to pay my fare to Hampton. One experience I shall long remember. I had been travelling over the mountains most of the afternoon in an old-fashioned stage-coach, when, late in the evening, the coach stopped for the night at a common, unpainted house called a hotel. All the other passengers except myself were whites. In my ignorance I supposed that the little hotel existed for the purpose of accommodating the passengers who traveled on the stage-coach. The difference that the colour of one's skin would make I had not thought anything about. After all the other passengers had been shown rooms and were getting ready for supper, I shyly presented myself before the man at the desk. It is true I had practically no money in my pocket with which to pay for bed or food, but I had hoped in some way to beg my way into the good graces of the landlord, for at that season in the mountains of Virginia the weather was cold, and I wanted to get indoors for the night. Without asking as to whether I had any money, the man at the desk firmly refused to even consider the matter of providing me with food or lodging. This was my first experience in finding out what the colour of my skin meant. In some way I managed to keep warm by walking about, and so got through the night. My whole soul was so bent upon reaching Hampton that I did not have time to cherish any bitterness toward the hotelkeeper.

By walking, begging rides both in wagons and in the cars, in some way, after a number of days, I reached the city of Richmond, Virginia, about eighty-two miles from Hampton. When I reached there, tired, hungry, and dirty, it was late in the night. I had never been in a large city, and this rather added to my misery. When I reached Richmond, I was completely out of money. I had not a single acquaintance in the place, and, being unused to city ways, I did not know where to go. I applied at several places for lodging, but they all wanted money, and that was what I did not have. Knowing nothing else better to do, I walked the streets. In doing this I passed by many food-stands where fried chicken and half-moon apple pies were piled high and made to present a most tempting appearance. At that time it seemed to me that I would have promised all that I expected to possess in the future to have gotten hold of one of those chicken legs or one of those pies. But I could not get either of these, nor anything else to eat.

I must have walked the streets till after midnight. At last I became so exhausted that I could walk no longer. I was tired, I was hungry, I was everything but discouraged. Just about the time when I reached extreme physical exhaustion, I came upon a portion of a street where the board sidewalk was considerably elevated. I waited for a few minutes, till I was sure that no passers-by could see me, and then crept under the sidewalk and lay for the night upon the ground, with my satchel of clothing for a pillow. Nearly all night I could hear the tramp of feet over my head. The next morning I found myself somewhat refreshed, but I was extremely hungry, because it had been a long time since I had had sufficient food.

As soon as it became light enough for me to see my surroundings I noticed that I was near a large ship, and that this ship seemed to be unloading a cargo of pig iron. I went at once to the vessel and asked the captain to permit me to help unload the vessel in order to get money for food. The captain, a white man, who seemed to be kindhearted, consented. I worked long enough to earn money for my breakfast, and it seems to me, as I remember it now, to have been about the best breakfast that I have ever eaten. My work pleased the captain so well that he told me if I desired I could continue working for a small amount per day. This I was very glad to do. I continued working on this vessel for a number of days. After buying food with the small wages I received there was not much left to add to the amount I must get to pay my way to Hampton. In order to economize in every way possible, so as to be sure to reach Hampton in a reasonable time, I continued to sleep under the same sidewalk that gave me shelter the first night I was in Richmond. Many years after that the coloured citizens of Richmond very kindly tendered me a reception at which there must have been two thousand people present. This reception was held not far from the spot where I slept the first night I spent in that city, and I must confess that my mind was more upon the sidewalk that first gave me shelter than upon the reception, agreeable and cordial as it was.

When I had saved what I considered enough money with which to reach Hampton, I thanked the captain of the vessel for his kindness, and started again.

Without any unusual occurrence I reached Hampton, with a surplus of exactly fifty cents with which to begin my education. To me it had been a long, eventful journey; but the first sight of the large, three-story, brick school building seemed to have rewarded me for all that I had undergone in order to reach the place. If the people who gave the money to provide that building could appreciate the influence the sight of it had upon me, as well as upon thousands of other youths, they would feel all the more encouraged to make such gifts. It seemed to me to be the largest and most beautiful building I had ever seen. The sight of it seemed to give me a new life. I felt that a new kind of existence had now begun — that life would now have a new meaning. I felt that I had reached the promised land, and I resolved to let no obstacle prevent me from putting forth the highest effort to fit myself to accomplish the most good in the world.

As soon as possible after reaching the grounds of the Hampton Institute, I presented myself before the head teacher for assignment to a class. Having been so long without proper food, a bath and change of clothing, I did not, of course, make a very favourable impression upon her, and I could see at once that there were doubts in her mind about the wisdom of admitting me as a student. I felt that I could hardly blame her if she got the idea that I was a worthless loafer or tramp. For some time she did not refuse to admit me, neither did she decide in my favour, and I continued to linger about her, and to impress her in all the ways I could with my worthiness. In the meantime I saw her admitting other students, and that added greatly to my discomfort, for I felt, deep down in my heart, that I could do as well as they, if I could only get a chance to show what was in me.

After some hours had passed, the head teacher said to me: "The adjoining recitation-room needs sweeping. Take the broom and sweep it." It occurred to me at once that here was my chance. Never did I receive an order with more delight. I knew that I could sweep, for Mrs. Ruffner had thoroughly taught me how to do that when I lived with her.

I swept the recitation-room three times. Then I got a dusting-cloth and I dusted it four times. All the woodwork around the walls, every bench, table, and desk, I went over four times with my dusting-cloth. Besides, every piece of furniture had been moved and every closet and corner in the room had been thoroughly cleaned. I had the feeling that in a large measure my future depended upon the impression I made upon the teacher in the cleaning of that room. When I was through, I reported to the head teacher.

She was a 'Yankee' woman who knew just where to look for dirt. She went into the room and inspected the floor and closets; then she took her handkerchief and rubbed it on the woodwork about the walls, and over the table and benches. When she was unable to find one bit of dirt on the floor, or a particle of dust on any of the furniture, she quietly remarked, "I guess you will do to enter this institution." I was one of the happiest souls on earth. The sweeping of that room was my college examination, and never did any youth pass an examination for entrance into Harvard or Yale that gave him more genuine satisfaction. I have passed several examinations since then, but I have always felt that this was the best one I ever passed.

I have spoken of my own experience in entering the Hampton Institute. Perhaps few, if any, had anything like the same experience that I had, but about that same period there were hundreds who found their way to Hampton and other institutions after experiencing something of the same difficulties that I went through. The young men and women were determined to secure an education at any cost.

1901

Critical thinking points: After you've read

1) *Washington learns some important lessons on his journey to Hampton. What are they?*
2) *Washington says about a reception for him in Richmond, "This reception was held not far from the spot where I slept the first night I spent in that city, and I must confess that my mind was more upon the sidewalk that first gave me shelter than upon the reception, agreeable and cordial as it was." What might such a statement say about Washington's personality?*
3) *Washington says of his first assignment from the head teacher, "The sweeping of that room was my college examination, and never did any youth pass an examination for entrance into Harvard or Yale that gave him more genuine satisfaction. I have passed several examinations since then, but I have always felt that this was the best one I ever passed." Why was this so important to him?*
4) *Washington says of first seeing Hampton, "I felt that I had reached the promised land." Why was education so important to him? Do you feel it is as important for you?*

Some possibilities for writing

1) *Write a scene in which Washington, who is sleeping under the boardwalk on his way to Hampton, meets a man who attends college. Or, write a scene between Washington and another African-American man who has no aspirations for college.*
2) *Find* Up from Slavery *and read Chapter 8, "Teaching School in a Stable and a Hen-House." After reading the piece, compare/contrast and comment on Washington as a student and a teacher.*
3) *Contact your school's Admissions Office or Dean of Students Office to find out the number of African-American students at your university. Are there any student groups specifically for African-American students? Interview an African-American student about his or her experiences at college. Keep in mind that one student's experience does not represent that of all African Americans on campus, but how does the individual experience compare to yours?*

Raising My Hand

Antler

> **"**
>
> How often I knew the answer / And the teacher (knowing I knew) /
> Called on others I knew (and she knew) / had it wrong.
>
> **"**

Critical thinking points: As you read

1) Think of a time when you knew the answer and the teacher called on someone else. How did you feel? Did this situation affect you differently when you were younger?

2) How would you characterize Mrs. Hamma's attitude toward her students? What details in the story led you to this?

3) In what ways does this piece work as a poem? Could it have been written as a story? What changes would have to be made?

One of the first things we learn in school is
    if we know the answer to a question
We must raise our hand and be called on
    before we can speak.
How strange it seemed to me then,
    raising my hand to be called on,
How at first I just blurted out,
    but that was not permitted.

How often I knew the answer
and the teacher (knowing I knew)
Called on others I knew (and she knew)
    had it wrong!

Antler (b. 1946) is the author of *Factory* (City Lights) and *Last Words* (Ballantine), winner of the Walt Whitman Award and a Pushcart Prize. He has poems in over eighty anthologies including *Earth Prayers, A New Geography of Poets*; *Reclaiming the Heartland: Lesbian & Gay Voices from the Midwest*; and *American Poets Say Goodbye to the 20th Century*.

How I'd stretch my arm
    as if it would break free
    and shoot through the roof
    like a rocket!
How I'd wave and groan and sigh,
Even hold up my aching arm
    with my other hand
Begging to be called on,
Please, me, I know the answer!
Almost leaping from my seat
    hoping to hear my name.

Twenty-nine now, alone in the wilds,
Seated on some rocky outcrop
    under all the stars,
I find myself raising my hand
    as I did in first grade
Mimicking the excitement
    and expectancy felt then,
No one calls on me
    but the wind.

1990

Critical thinking points: After you've read

1) *Have you ever known a student like the narrator? What were some of your reactions to him or her? Were you ever such a student? How did your classmates react to you?*
2) *Did the rule "raising my hand" prepare the author for his life in the wilderness? Why or why not?*
3) *Antler talks about one of the basic "rules" of formal education — raising one's hand to speak. Make a list of other rules you've learned, from elementary school through high school. What rules now seem silly and outdated?*
4) *What are some of the reasons a teacher might not call on a student with a raised hand?*
5) *Have you ever known the answer to a question but did not raise your hand? What were some of the reasons you didn't?*

Some possibilities for writing

1) *Speculate about what questions the narrator is thinking of answering when he raises his hand at the end of the poem. Once you have a list of questions, consider what some of the possible answers might be. Make a list of those.*

2) *Choose one of the rules you've recorded above. Write at least a page about how you continue to use that rule or how you never use that rule now. For instance, being quiet when someone else is speaking is a rule most of us learned in kindergarten (or before) and continue to obey throughout our lives. Or in fourth grade you had to ask to use the bathroom, but you don't usually need to do that as an adult.*
3) *Read or reread Walt Whitman's "When I Heard the Learn'd Astronomer." Compare and contrast it to Antler's poem. What does each seem to be suggesting about teaching? What does each seem to be suggesting about learning?*
4) *Below are lines from Section 2 of Walt Whitman's "Song of Myself." After reading them, write a response to Antler's poem as it might be written by Whitman.*

> Have you reckon'd a thousand acres much? have you reckon'd the earth much?
> Have you practis'd so long to learn to read?
> Have you felt so proud to get at the meaning of poems?
>
> Stop this day and night with me and you shall possess the origin of all poems,
> You shall possess the good of the earth and sun, (there are millions of suns left,)
> You shall no longer take things at second or third hand,
> Nor look through the eyes of the dead, nor feed on the spectres in books,
> You shall not look through my eyes either, nor take things from me,
> You shall listen to all sides and filter them from your self.

The English Lesson

Nicholasa Mohr

———— 66 ————

Adult Education offered Basic English, Tuesday evenings from 6:30 to 8:00, at a local public school. Night customers did not usually come into Rudi's Luncheonette until after eight. William and Lali promised that they would leave everything prepared and make up for any inconvenience by working harder and longer than usual, if necessary.

———— 99 ————

Critical thinking points: As you read

1) Have you ever struggled to learn a second language? What was most difficult about it for you?

2) In what ways is Mrs. Hamma condescending toward her students? How might she feel if she realized this?

3) Why are some English-speaking people often intimidated by groups of people speaking another language? Is that the case for Mrs. Hamma?

"Remember our assignment for today everybody! I'm so confident that you will all do exceptionally well!" Mrs. Susan Hamma smiled enthusiastically at her students. "Everyone is to get up and make a brief statement as to why he or she is taking this course in Basic English. You must state your name, where you originally came from, how long you have been here, and . . . uh . . . a little something about yourself, if you wish. Keep it brief, not too long; remember, there are twenty-eight of us. We have a full class, and everyone must have a chance." Mrs. Hamma waved a forefinger at her students. "This is, after all, a democracy, and we have a democratic class; fairness for all!"

Lali grinned and looked at William, who sat directly next to her. He winked and rolled his eyes toward Mrs. Hamma. This was the third class they had attended to-

———

Nicholasa Mohr is a writer from New York City. Her fiction for both young readers and adults often features Puerto Rican characters in urban settings, such as the El Barrio section of New York where Mohr was born. She won a 1981 American Book Award from the Before Columbus Foundation for *Felita* (1979); her other books include *El Bronx Remembered: A Novella and Stories* (2nd edition, 1986), *Rituals of Survival: A Woman's Portfolio* (1985), and *Nilda: A Novel* (2nd edition, 1986).

gether. It had not been easy to persuade Rudi that Lali should learn better English.

"Why is it necessary, eh?" Rudi had protested. "She works here in the store with me. She don't have to talk to nobody. Besides, everybody that comes in speaks Spanish — practically everybody, anyway."

But once William had put the idea to Lali and explained how much easier things would be for her, she kept insisting until Rudi finally agreed. "Go on, you're both driving me nuts. But it can't interfere with business or work — I'm warning you!"

Adult Education offered Basic English, Tuesday evenings from 6:30 to 8:00, at a local public school. Night customers did not usually come into Rudi's Luncheonette until after eight. William and Lali promised that they would leave everything prepared and make up for any inconvenience by working harder and longer than usual, if necessary.

The class admitted twenty-eight students, and because there were only twenty-seven registered, Lali was allowed to take the course even after missing the first two classes. William had assured Mrs. Hamma that he would help Lali catch up; she was glad to have another student to make up the full registration.

Most of the students were Spanish-speaking. The majority were American citizens — Puerto Ricans who had migrated to New York and spoke very little English. The rest were immigrants admitted to the United States as legal aliens. There were several Chinese, two Dominicans, one Sicilian, and one Pole.

Every Tuesday Mrs. Hamma traveled to the Lower East Side from Bayside, Queens, where she lived and was employed as a history teacher in the local junior high school. She was convinced that this small group of people desperately needed her services. Mrs. Hamma reiterated her feelings frequently to just about anyone who would listen. "Why, if these people can make it to class after working all day at those miserable, dreary, uninteresting, and often revolting jobs, well, the least I can do is be there to serve them, making every lesson count toward improving their conditions! My grandparents came here from Germany as poor immigrants, working their way up. I'm not one to forget a thing like that!"

By the time class started most of the students were quite tired. And after the lesson was over, many had to go on to part-time jobs, some even without time for supper. As a result there was always sluggishness and yawning among the students. This never discouraged Mrs. Hamma, whose drive and enthusiasm not only amused the class but often kept everyone awake.

"Now this is the moment we have all been waiting for." Mrs. Hamma stood up, nodded, and blinked knowingly at her students. "You may read from prepared notes, as I said before, but please try not to read every word. We want to hear you speak; conversation is what we're after. When someone asks you about yourself, you cannot take a piece of paper and start reading the answers, now can you? That would be foolish. So . . ."

Standing in front of her desk, she put her hands on her hips and spread her feet, giving the impression that she was going to demonstrate calisthenics.

"Shall we begin?"

Mrs. Hamma was a very tall, angular woman with large extremities. She was the tallest person in the room. Her eyes roamed from student to student until they met William's.

"Mr. Colón, will you please begin?"

Nervously William looked around him, hesitating.

"Come on now, we must get the ball rolling. All right now . . . did you hear what I said? Listen, 'getting the ball rolling' means getting started. Getting things going, such as —" Mrs. Hamma swiftly lifted her right hand over her head, making a fist, then swung her arm around like a pitcher and, with an underhand curve, forcefully threw an imaginary ball out at her students. Trying to maintain her balance, Mrs. Hamma hopped from one leg to the other. Startled, the students looked at one another. In spite of their efforts to restrain themselves, several people in back began to giggle. Lali and William looked away, avoiding each other's eyes and trying not to laugh out loud. With assured countenance, Mrs. Hamma continued.

"An idiom!" she exclaimed, pleased. "You have just seen me demonstrate the meaning of an idiom. Now I want everyone to jot down this information in his notebook." Going to the blackboard, Mrs. Hamma explained, "It's something which literally says one thing, but actually means another. Idiom . . . idiomatic." Quickly and obediently, everyone began to copy what she wrote. "Has everyone got it? OK, let's GET THE BALL ROLLING, Mr. Colón!"

Uneasily William stood up; he was almost the same height standing as sitting. When speaking to others, especially in a new situation, he always preferred to sit alongside those listening; it gave him a sense of equality with other people. He looked around and cleared his throat; at least everyone else was sitting. Taking a deep breath, William felt better.

"My name is William Horacio Colón," he read from a prepared statement. "I have been here in New York City for five months. I coming from Puerto Rico. My town is located in the mountains in the central part of the island. The name of my town is Aibonito, which means in Spanish 'oh how pretty.' It is name like this because when the Spaniards first seen that place they was very impressed with the beauty of the section and —"

"Make it brief, Mr. Colón," Mrs. Hamma interrupted, "there are others, you know."

William looked at her, unable to continue.

"Go on, go on, Mr. Colón, please!"

"I am working here now, living with my mother and family in Lower East Side of New York City," William spoke rapidly. "I study Basic English por que . . . because my ambition is to learn to speak and read English very good. To get a better job. Y — y también, to help my mother y familia." He shrugged. "Y do better, that's all."

"That's all? Why that's wonderful! Wonderful! Didn't he do well, class?" Mrs. Hamma bowed slightly toward William and applauded him. The students watched her and slowly each one began to imitate her. Pleased, Mrs. Hamma looked around her; all together they gave William a healthy round of applause.

Next, Mrs. Hamma turned to a Chinese man seated at the other side of the room.

"Mr. Fong, you may go next."

Mr. Fong stood up; he was a man in his late thirties, of medium height and slight build. Cautiously he looked at Mrs. Hamma, and waited.

"Go on, Mr. Fong. Get the ball rolling, remember?"

"All right. Get a ball rolling . . . is idiot!" Mr. Fong smiled.

"No, Mr. Fong, idio*mmmmmmm!*" Mrs. Hamma hummed her m's, shaking her head. "Not an — It's idiomatic!"

"What I said!" Mr. Fong responded with self-assurance, looking directly at Mrs. Hamma. "Get a ball rolling, idiomit."

"Never mind." She cleared her throat. "Just go on."

"I said OK?" Mr. Fong waited for an answer.

"Go on, please."

Mr. Fong sighed, "My name is Joseph Fong. I been here in this country United States New York City for most one year." He too read from a prepared statement. "I come from Hong Kong but original born in city of Canton, China. I working delivery food business and live with my brother and his family in Chinatown. I taking the course in Basic English to speak good and improve my position better in this country. Also to be eligible to become American citizen."

Mrs. Hamma selected each student who was to speak from a different part of the room, rather than in the more conventional orderly fashion of row by row, or front to back, or even alphabetical order. This way, she reasoned, no one will know who's next; it will be more spontaneous. Mrs. Hamma enjoyed catching the uncertain looks on the faces of her students. A feeling of control over the situation gave her a pleasing thrill, and she made the most of these moments by looking at several people more than once before making her final choice.

There were more men than women, and Mrs. Hamma called two or three men for each woman. It was her way of maintaining balance. To her distress, most read from prepared notes, despite her efforts to discourage this. She would interrupt them when she felt they went on too long, then praise them when they finished. Each statement was followed by applause from everyone.

All had similar statements. They had migrated here in search of a better future, were living with relatives, and worked as unskilled laborers. With the exception of Lali, who was childless, every woman gave the ages and sex of her children; most men referred only to their "family." And, among the legal aliens, there was only one who did not want to become an American citizen, Diego Torres, a young man from the Dominican Republic, and he gave his reasons.

" . . . and to improve my economic situation." Diego Torres hesitated, looking around the room. "But is one thing I no want, and is to become American citizen" — he pointed to an older man with a dark complexion, seated a few seats away — "like my fellow countryman over there!" The man shook his head disapprovingly at Diego Torres, trying to hide his annoyance. "I no give up my country, Santo Domingo, for nothing," he went on, "nothing in the whole world. OK, man? I come here, pero I cannot help. I got no work at home. There, is political. The United States control most the industry which is sugar and tourismo. Y — you have to know somebody. I tell you, is political to get a job, man! You don't know nobody and you no work, eh? So I come here from necessity, pero this no my country —"

"Mr. Torres," Mrs. Hamma interrupted, "we must be brief, please, there are —"

"I no finish lady!" he snapped. "You wait a minute when I finish!"

There was a complete silence as Diego Torres glared at Susan Hamma. No one had ever spoken to her like that, and her confusion was greater than her embarrassment. Without speaking, she lowered her eyes and nodded.

"OK, I prefer live feeling happy in my country, man. Even I don't got too much. I live simple but in my own country I be contento. Pero this is no possible in the situation of Santo Domingo now. Someday we gonna run our own country and be jobs for everybody. My reasons to be here is to make money, man, and go back home buy my house and property. I no be American citizen, no way. I'm Dominican and proud! That's it. That's all I got to say." Abruptly, Diego Torres sat down.

"All right." Mrs. Hamma had composed herself. "Very good; you can come here and state your views. That is what America is all about! We may not agree with you, but we defend your right to an opinion. And as long as you are in this classroom, Mr. Torres, you are in America. Now, everyone, let us give Mr. Torres the same courtesy as everyone else in this class." Mrs. Hamma applauded with a polite light clap, then turned to find the next speaker.

"Bullshit," whispered Diego Torres.

Practically everyone had spoken. Lali and the two European immigrants were the only ones left. Mrs. Hamma called upon Lali.

"My name is Rogelia Dolores Padillo. I come from Canovanas in Puerto Rico. Is a small village in the mountains near El Yunque Rain Forest. My family is still living there. I marry and live here with my husband working in his business of restaurant. Call Rudi's Luncheonette. I been here New York City Lower East Side since I marry, which is now about one year. I study Basic English to improve my vocabulario and learn more about here. This way I help my husband and his business and I do more also for myself, including to be able to read better in English. Thank you."

Aldo Fabrizi, the Sicilian, spoke next. He was a very short man, barely five feet tall. Usually he was self-conscious about his height, but William's presence relieved him of these feelings. Looking at William, he thought being short was no big thing; he was, after all, normal. He told the class that he was originally from Palermo, the capital of Sicily, and had gone to Milano, in the north of Italy, looking for work. After three years in Milano, he immigrated here six months ago and now lived with his sister. He had a good steady job, he said, working in a copper wire factory with his brother-in-law in Brooklyn. Aldo Fabrizi wanted to become an American citizen and spoke passionately about it, without reading from his notes.

"I proud to be American citizen. I no come here find work live good and no have responsibility or no be grateful." He turned and looked threateningly at Diego Torres. "Hey? I tell you all one thing, I got my nephew right now fighting in Vietnam for this country!" Diego Torres stretched his hands over his head, yawning, folded his hands, and lowered his eyelids. "I wish I could be citizen to fight for this country. My whole family is citizens — we all Americans and we love America!" His voice was quite loud. "That's how I feel."

"Very good," Mrs. Hamma called, distracting Aldo Fabrizi. "That was well stated. I'm sure you will not only become a citizen, but you will also be a credit to this country."

The last person to be called on was the Pole. He was always neatly dressed in a business suit, with a shirt and tie, and carried a briefcase. His manner was reserved but friendly.

"Good evening fellow students and Madame Teacher." He nodded politely to Mrs. Hamma. "My name is Stephan Paczkowski. I am originally from Poland about four months ago. My background is I was born in capital city of Poland, Warsaw. Being educated in capital and also graduating from the University with degree of professor of music with specialty in the history of music."

Stephan Paczkowski read his notes carefully, articulating every word. "I was given appointment of professor of history of music at University of Krakow. I work there for ten years until about year and half ago. At this time the political situation in Poland was so that all Jewish people were requested by government to leave Poland. My wife who also is being a professor of economics at University of Krakow is of Jewish parents. My wife was told she could not remain in position at University or remain over there. We made arrangements for my wife and daughter who is seven years of age and myself to come here with my wife's cousin who is to be helping us.

"Since four months I am working in large hospital as position of porter in maintenance department. The thing of it is, I wish to take Basic English to improve my knowledge of English language, and be able to return to my position of professor of history of music. Finally, I wish to become a citizen of United States. That is my reasons. I thank you all."

After Stephan Paczkowski sat down, there was a long awkward silence and everyone turned to look at Mrs. Hamma. Even after the confrontation with Diego Torres, she had applauded without hesitation. Now she seemed unable to move.

"Well," she said, almost breathless, "that's admirable! I'm sure, sir, that you will do very well . . . a person of your . . . like yourself, I mean . . . a professor, after all, it's really just admirable." Everyone was listening intently to what she said. "That was well done, class. Now, we have to get to next week's assignment." Mrs. Hamma realized that no one had applauded Stephan Paczkowski. With a slightly pained expression, she began to applaud. "Mustn't forget Mr. Paczkowski; everyone here must be treated equally. This is America!" The class joined her in a round of applause.

As Mrs. Hamma began to write the next week's assignment on the board, some students looked anxiously at their watches and others asked about the time. Then they all quickly copied the information into their notebooks. It was almost eight o'clock. Those who had to get to second jobs did not want to be late; some even hoped to have time for a bite to eat first. Others were just tired and wanted to get home.

Lali looked at William, sighing impatiently. They both hoped Mrs. Hamma would finish quickly. There would be hell to pay with Rudi if the night customers were already at the luncheonette.

"There, that's next week's work, which is very important, by the way. We will be looking at the history of New York City and the different ethnic groups that lived here as far back as the Dutch. I can't tell you how proud I am of the way you all spoke. All of you — I have no favorites, you know."

Mrs. Hamma was interrupted by the long, loud buzzing sound, bringing the lesson to an end. Quickly everyone began to exit.

"Good night, see you all next Tuesday!" Mrs. Hamma called out. "By the way, if any of you here wants extra help, I have a few minutes this evening." Several people bolted past her, excusing themselves. In less than thirty seconds, Mrs. Hamma was standing in an empty classroom.

William and Lali hurried along, struggling against the cold, sharp March wind that whipped across Houston Street, stinging their faces and making their eyes tear.

In a few minutes they would be at Rudi's. So far, they had not been late once.

"You read very well — better than anybody in class. I told you there was nothing to worry about. You caught up in no time."

"Go on. I was so nervous, honestly! But, I'm glad she left me for one of the last. If I had to go first, like you, I don't think I could open my mouth. You were so calm. You started the thing off very well."

"You go on now, I was nervous myself!" He laughed, pleased.

"Mira, Chiquitín," Lali giggled, "I didn't know your name was Horacio. William Horacio. William Horacio. Ave María, so imposing!"

"That's right, because you see, my mother was expecting valiant warrior! Instead, well" — he threw up his hands — "no one warned me either. And what a name for a Chiquitín like me."

Lali smiled, saying nothing. At first she had been very aware of William's dwarfishness. Now it no longer mattered. It was only when she saw others reacting to him for the first time that she was once more momentarily struck with William's physical difference.

"We should really try to speak in English, Lali. It would be good practice for us."

"Dios mío . . . I feel so foolish, and my accent is terrible!"

"But look, we all have to start some place. Besides, what about the Americanos? When they speak Spanish, they sound pretty awful, but we accept it. You know I'm right. And that's how people get ahead, by not being afraid to try."

They walked in silence for a few moments. Since William had begun to work at Rudi's, Lali's life had become less lonely. Lali was shy by nature; making friends was difficult for her. She had grown up in the sheltered environment of a large family living in a tiny mountain village. She was considered quite plain. Until Rudi had asked her parents for permission to court her, she had only gone out with two local boys. She had accepted his marriage proposal expecting great changes in her life. But the age difference between her and Rudi, being in a strange country without friends or relatives, and the long hours of work at the luncheonette confined Lali to a way of life she could not have imagined. Every evening she found herself waiting for William to come in to work, looking forward to his presence.

Lali glanced over at him as they started across the wide busy street. His grip on her elbow was firm but gentle as he led her to the sidewalk.

"There you are, Miss Lali, please watch your step!" he spoke in English.

His thick golden-blond hair was slightly mussed and fell softly, partially covering his forehead. His wide smile, white teeth, and large shoulders made him appear quite handsome. Lali found herself staring at William. At that moment she wished he could be just like everybody else.

"Lali?" William asked, confused by her silent stare. "Is something wrong?"

"No." Quickly Lali turned her face. She felt herself blushing. "I . . . I was just thinking how to answer in English, that's all."

"But that's it . . . don't think! What I mean is, don't go worrying about what to say. Just talk natural. Get used to simple phrases and the rest will come, you'll see."

"All right," Lali said, glad the strange feeling of involvement had passed, and William had taken no notice of it. "It's an interesting class, don't you think so? I mean — like that man, the professor. Bendito! Imagine, they had to leave because they were Jewish. What a terrible thing!"

"I don't believe he's Jewish; it's his wife who is Jewish. She was a professor too. But I guess they don't wanna be separated . . . and they have a child."

"Tsk, tsk, los pobres! But, can you imagine, then? A professor from a university doing the job of a porter? My goodness!" Lali sighed. "I never heard of such a thing!"

"But you gotta remember, it's like Mrs. Hamma said, this is America, right? So . . . everybody got a chance to clean toilets! Equality, didn't she say that?"

They both laughed loudly, stepping up their pace until they reached Rudi's Luncheonette.

The small luncheonette was almost empty. One customer sat at the counter.

"Just in time," Rudi called out. "Let's get going. People gonna be coming in hungry any minute. I was beginning to worry about you two!"

William ran to the back to change into his workshirt.

Lali slipped into her uniform and soon was busy at the grill.

"Well, did you learn anything tonight?" Rudi asked her.

"Yes."

"What?"

"I don't know," she answered, without interrupting her work. "We just talked a little bit in English."

"A little bit in English — about what?"

Lali busied herself, ignoring him. Rudi waited, then tried once more.

"You remember what you talked about?" He watched her as she moved, working quickly, not looking in his direction.

"No." Her response was barely audible.

Lately Rudi had begun to reflect on his decision to marry such a young woman. Especially a country girl like Lali, who was shy and timid. He had never had children with his first wife and wondered if he lacked the patience needed for the young. They had little in common and certainly seldom spoke about anything but the business. Certainly he could not fault her for being lazy; she was always working without being asked. People would accuse him in jest of overworking his young wife. He assured them there was no need, because she had the endurance of a country mule. After almost one year of marriage, he felt he hardly knew Lali or what he might do to please her.

William began to stack clean glasses behind the counter.

"Chiquitín! How about you and Lali having something to eat? We gotta few minutes yet. There's some fresh rice pudding."

"Later . . . I'll have mine a little later, thanks."

"Ask her if she wants some," Rudi whispered, gesturing toward Lali.

William moved close to Lali and spoke softly to her.

"She said no." William continued his work.

"Listen, Chiquitín, I already spoke to Raquel Martinez who lives next door. You know, she's got all them kids? In case you people are late, she can cover for you and Lali. She said it was OK."

"Thanks, Rudi, I appreciate it. But we'll be back on time."

"She's good, you know. She helps me out during the day whenever I need extra help. Off the books, I give her a few bucks. But, mira, I cannot pay you and Raquel both. So if she comes in, you don't get paid. You know that then, OK?"

"Of course. Thanks, Rudi."

"Sure, well, it's a good thing after all. You and Lali improving yourselves. Not that she really needs it, you know. I provide for her. As I said, she's my wife, so she don't gotta worry. If she wants something, I'll buy it for her. I made it clear she didn't have to bother with none of that, but" — Rudi shrugged — "if that's what she wants, I'm not one to interfere."

The door opened. Several men walked in.

"Here they come, kids!"

Orders were taken and quickly filled. Customers came and went steadily until about eleven o'clock, when Rudi announced that it was closing time.

The weeks passed, then the months, and this evening, William and Lali sat with the other students listening to Mrs. Hamma as she taught the last lesson of the Basic English course.

"It's been fifteen long hard weeks for all for you. And I want you to know how proud I am of each and every one here."

William glanced at Lali; he knew she was upset. He felt it too, wishing that this was not the end of the course. It was the only time he and Lali had free to themselves together. Tuesday had become their last evening.

Lali had been especially irritable that week, dreading this last session. For her, Tuesday meant leaving the world of Rudi, the luncheonette, that street, everything that she felt imprisoned her. She was accomplishing something all by herself, and without the help of the man she was dependent upon.

Mrs. Hamma finally felt that she had spent enough time assuring her students of her sincere appreciation.

"I hope some of you will stay and have a cup of coffee or tea, and cookies. There's plenty over there." She pointed to a side table where a large electric coffee-pot filled with hot water was steaming. The table was set for instant coffee and tea, complete with several boxes of assorted cookies. "I do this every semester for my classes. I think it's nice to have a little informal chat with one another; perhaps discuss our plans for the future and so on. But it must be in English! Especially those of you who are Spanish-speaking. Just because you outnumber the rest of us, don't you think you can get away with it!" Mrs. Hamma lifted her forefinger threateningly but smiled. "Now, it's still early, so there's plenty of time left. Please turn in your books."

Some of the people said good-bye quickly and left, but the majority waited, helping themselves to coffee or tea and cookies. Small clusters formed as people began to chat with one another.

Diego Torres and Aldo Fabrizi were engaged in a friendly but heated debate on the merits of citizenship.

"Hey, you come here a minute, please," Aldo Fabrizi called out to William, who was standing with a few people by the table, helping himself to coffee. William walked over to the two men.

"What's the matter?"

"What do you think of your paisano. He don't wanna be citizen. I say — my opinion — he don't appreciate what he got in this country. This a great country! You the same like him, what do you think?"

"Mira, please tell him we are no the same," Diego Torres said with exasperation. "You a citizen, pero not me. Este tipo no comprende, man!"

"Listen, you comprendo . . . yo capito! I know what you say. He be born in Puerto Rico. But you see, we got the same thing. I be born in Sicily — that is another part of the country, separate. But I still Italiano, capito?"

"Dios mío!" Diego Torres smacked his forehead with an open palm. "Mira" — he turned to William — "explain to him, por favor."

William swallowed a mouthful of cookies. "He's right. Puerto Rico is part of the United States. And Sicily is part of Italy. But not the Dominican Republic where he been born. There it is not United States. I was born a citizen, do you see?"

"Sure!" Aldo Fabrizi nodded. "Capito. Hey, but you still no can vote, right?"

"Sure I can vote; I got all the rights. I am a citizen, just like anybody else," William assured him.

"You some lucky guy then. You got it made! You don't gotta worry like the rest of —"

"Bullshit," Diego Torres interrupted. "Why he got it made, man . . ."

As the two men continued to argue, William waited for the right moment to slip away and join Lali.

She was with some of the women, who were discussing how sincere and devoted Mrs. Hamma was.

"She's hardworking . . ."

"And she's good people . . ." an older woman agreed.

Mr. Fong joined them, and they spoke about the weather and how nice and warm the days were.

Slowly people began to leave, shaking hands with their fellow students and Mrs. Hamma, wishing each other luck.

Mrs. Hamma had been hoping to speak to Stephan Paczkowski privately this evening, but he was always with a group. Now he offered his hand.

"I thank you very much for your good teaching. It was a fine semester."

"Oh, do you think so? Oh, I'm so glad to hear you say that. You don't know how much it means. Especially coming from a person of your caliber. I am confident, yes, indeed, that you will soon be back to your profession, which, after all, is your true calling. If there is anything I can do, please . . ."

"Thank you, miss. This time I am registering in Hunter College, which is in Manhattan on Sixty-eighth Street in Lexington Avenue, with a course of English Literature for beginners." After a slight bow, he left.

"Good-bye." Mrs. Hamma sighed after him.

Lali, William, and several of the women picked up the paper cups and napkins and tossed them into the trash basket.

"Thank you so much, that's just fine. Luis the porter will do the rest. He takes care of these things. He's a lovely person and very helpful. Thank you."

William shook hands with Mrs. Hamma, then waited for Lali to say good-bye. They were the last ones to leave.

"Both of you have been such good students. What are your plans? I hope you will continue with your English."

"Next term we're taking another course," Lali said, looking at William.

"Yes," William responded, "it's more advance. Over at the Washington Irving High School around Fourteenth Street."

"Wonderful." Mrs. Hamma hesitated. "May I ask you a question before you leave? It's only that I'm a little curious about something."

"Sure, of course." They both nodded.

"Are you two related? I mean, you are always together and yet have different last names, so I was just . . . wondering."

"Oh, we are just friends," Lali answered, blushing.

"I work over in the luncheonette at night, part-time."

"Of course." Mrs. Hamma looked at Lali. "Mrs. Padillo, your husband's place of business. My, that's wonderful, just wonderful! You are all just so ambitious. Very good . . ."

They exchanged farewells.

Outside, the warm June night was sprinkled with the sweetness of the new buds sprouting on the scrawny trees and hedges planted along the sidewalks and in the housing project grounds. A brisk breeze swept over the East River on to Houston Street, providing a freshness in the air.

This time they were early, and Lali and William strolled at a relaxed pace.

"Well," Lali shrugged, "that's that. It's over!"

"Only for a couple of months. In September we'll be taking a more advanced course at the high school."

"I'll probably forget everything I learned by then."

"Come on, Lali, the summer will be over before you know it. Just you wait and see. Besides, we can practice so we don't forget what Mrs. Hamma taught us."

"Sure, what do you like to speak about?" Lali said in English.

William smiled, and clasping his hands, said, "I would like to say to you how wonderful you are, and how you gonna have the most fabulous future . . . after all, you so ambitious!"

When she realized he sounded just like Mrs. Hamma, Lali began to laugh.

"Are you" — Lali tried to keep from giggling, tried to pretend to speak in earnest — "sure there is some hope for me?"

"Oh, heavens, yes! You have shown such ability this" — William was beginning to lose control, laughing loudly — "semester!"

"But I want" — Lali was holding her sides with laughter — "some guarantee of this. I got to know."

"Please, Miss Lali." William was laughing so hard tears were coming to his eyes. "After . . . after all, you now a member in good standing . . . of the promised future!"

William and Lali broke into uncontrollable laughter, swaying and limping, oblivious to the scene they created for the people who stared and pointed at them as they continued on their way to Rudi's.

1977

Critical thinking points: After you've read

1) *How are the students' introductions of themselves a true reflection of their personalities? Does this come through because of or in spite of the language difference?*

2) *Why do William and Lali wait till the last night of class to mimic Mrs. Hamma? Is this scene funny to anyone but them? Why or why not?*

3) *Does William and Lali's desire to improve their English skills remind you of the drive for knowledge experienced by other characters in this collection? Who are they? How are the experiences alike? How are they different?*

4) *Are there English as a Second Language classes offered in your home community? Are they offered in the area surrounding the university you attend? What ethnic backgrounds do the adult students represent?*

5) *Explore the relationships between William and Lali, and Rudi and Lali. How are the relationships different? What does Lali share with William that she doesn't share with her husband?*

Some possibilities for writing

1) *Imagine William and Lali ten years in the future. What has become of them? Or, choose one of William and Lali's classmates and imagine him or her ten years in the future.*
2) *How do the lives of Mrs. Hamma's students compare to your life as a college student? What obstacles do her students face that you do not? How are your lives similar? What strengths and/or resources do you have that they might not have, or vice versa?*
3) *Diego Torres holds an opposing view from the rest of the members of the class concerning citizenship. Which of these views seems to make the most sense to you? Why?*
4) *"English Only" instruction, as opposed to bilingual education, is a major controversy in many parts of the United States. Evaluate the opposing views on either side of this issue, then choose one side and support it.*
5) *Although the inscription on the Statue of Liberty reads, in part, "Give me your tired, your poor, your huddled masses at your teeming shore," immigration has always been a controversial issue in the history of the United States. What is the current attitude and/or policies toward immigration? Write a report to deliver to your class.*

Miss Rinehart's Paddle

Jeri McCormick

"

the other side of power

"

Critical thinking points: As you read

1) Were you the kind of student who got into trouble or the kind who did everything right?

2) The poem is saturated with violent images. What are some of them?

> The long hard rumor
> had hit us years before
> but there was nothing we could do
> to fend sixth grade off.
> One September morning
> we filed into Miss Rinehart's room
> to face the thick glasses,
> heavy oxfords, spit curls.
>
> The weapon occupied
> her middle drawer
> and was rarely used on girls,
> though Betty Jo got five whacks
> for her haphazard map of Brazil —
> the Amazon all smeared and off-course,
> Rio de Janeiro inland by inches.
>
> I sat through six months
> of imagined failures,
> ended up a jittery stooge
> with all *A*'s, the best parts in plays

Jeri McCormick (b. 1934) lives in Madison, Wisconsin, teaches creative writing at senior centers and elderhostels. Her poems have appeared most recently in *Poetry Ireland Review*, *Cumberland Poetry Review*, and *Rosebud*. Her book of poems, *When It Came Time*, was published in 1998 by Salmon Publishing Ltd. in Ireland.

and only now wonder
about the other side of power.

1991

Critical thinking points: After you've read

1) *What might the author mean when she calls herself "a jittery stooge / with all A's, the best parts in plays"? What leads her to say this?*
2) *The author says, "and only now wonder / about the other side of power." What makes her feel guilty? What might the "other side of power" be?*
3) *What did you feel as you read this poem? Was it painful, funny, or sad to read? What made it so?*
4) *Recall elementary or junior high teachers who were especially "mean." What made them mean? What did you fear about them?*
5) *Read or reread Antler's "Raising My Hand," and compare and contrast it to McCormick's poem. What are some similarities between the two poets' experiences? What are some differences?*

Some possibilities for writing

1) *Many of us have memorable episodes from elementary school or junior high classrooms that changed the way we feel about teaching and/or learning. Recall an episode. What makes it a memorable moment? What changes did the event lead to?*
2) *Talk to your parents and grandparents about their experiences in school. Write an essay comparing your experience in school to that of your parents or grandparents.*
3) *The "old school" of teaching believed that instilling fear in children kept them in line and a good swat once in a while was appropriate. Research corporal punishment in schools. When did it become illegal for public school teachers to hit students? Some people believe that children would have more respect for adults if teachers were allowed to spank or paddle. Argue for or against corporal punishment.*
4) *Physical discipline is rarely practiced much anymore in this country. What other kinds of discipline do teachers and/or school systems employ? Which do you think are the most effective?*
5) *In 1998, an elementary school teacher was arrested for assault after cutting her fourth-grade student's fingernails. The teacher repeatedly asked the girl's mother to cut the long, painted nails because they were a distraction to the girl and her classmates. At what point should teachers use "force" to gain students' attention? Has our nation gone too far in respecting the rights of children? Argue for teachers' rights or students' rights.*

an excerpt from

The Day I Became an Autodidact: And the Advice, Adventures, and Acrimonies That Befell Me Thereafter

Kendall Hailey

"

Why do people think you have to leave home to become an adult, happy human being?

"

Critical thinking points: As you read

1) *Journal entries are often personal, spontaneous accounts. In what other ways is this piece like a journal?*
2) *Watch for contrasts between the author and her friend Julie. What might be some of the differences between a formal college experience and learning on one's own?*
3) *What stengths, tools, or circumstances does Hailey have that allow her to become an autodidact?*

Hailey set out to record in her journal the day-to-day results of an unconventional choice: quit school in tenth grade to become an "autodidact," what she says is "a swell word for one who is self-taught." Her parents, both writers, supported her choice to get a head start on "reading everything ever published."

Julie Reich has gotten over her college depression. I got a letter addressed to Kendall Hailey, bum, filled with news of men and wine coolers.

Kendall Hailey (b. 1966) says, "I would like to be a writer all my life for two reasons. First, because I seem to have a lot of concerns and worries and passions that can be truly answered only on paper. And secondly, because I feel I owe such a great debt to all those I have read and listened to, who have kept me such great company, and I would like to try to repay them by giving as much of myself as they gave of themselves, inadequate though the repaying will be." *The Day I Became an Autodidact: And the Advice, Adventures, and Acrimonies That Befell Me Thereafter* was published in 1988 by Delacorte.

Dear Kenny,

First I'll answer your question:
Q. So, are you a lot smarter by now?
A. Yes. Tons.

Classes Update:
English I has turned out to be an exact repeat of ninth to twelfth grades. Well, maybe I'll remember the stuff this time. I understand <u>rien</u> of French III. We're supposed to speak all in French, and eighty-five percent of the class understands and I, along with the other fifteen percent, keep quiet. Art history is faintly interesting, and I have not understood enough of calculus to tell you anything about it.

Now, on to a more interesting subject: men.
Number one: freshman; lives down the hall; left-handed, like me; blond hair; excellent dancer. Problem, has girlfriend. Depression sets in.
Okay, here's Number Two: Senior. He asked me to dance at a frat party and we danced for at least seven songs, then we stopped and he said he wanted to dance later, but I haven't seen him since. He told me he thought I was a good dancer twice. I don't remember exactly what he looked like because he's about six feet tall and I had trouble looking up at his face for long periods of time. I memorized his jacket, though. Problem self-evident . . . no hope.

Besides my men-problems (they are no longer boys), I'm okay. My last letter probably sounded depressing, but I like it better now than I did then. I'm getting into the swing of things. I got drunk two nights ago. I talked to my mom yesterday. And she asked me if people drink at the parties. I said, "What do you think?" Then she asked me if I'd tried anything so I told her I had wine coolers (one third wine, two thirds 7-Up). I didn't tell her I had four of them and went to sleep feeling nauseous. Anyway . . . have fun studying Rome, if you can.

Love, Julie

•

Why do people think you have to leave home to become an adult, happy human being?

I talked to Julie Reich the other day. She called me long distance and the last thing she said was, "Kendall, do you think I'm still the same?"

I mean there she is, independent, breaking away, and she asks me that. I told her to drop out and come live with us. Some might say that her initial period of unrest is necessary to eventually become a stronger, better person, but in a world where I could be struck down tomorrow, I'm not going to spend one moment being lonely without an emotion-back guarantee that I'll be better for it.

You can't say something like this without being eyed as a Brontë girl in the making, but I love my family and I don't ever want to be without them. A line from George's letter said,

I see in you much youth that will lift as soon as you can relate to people your own age who also love what you love and you will be you instead of the daughter, the sister, the niece, granddaughter, etc.

But what I want in my life are more of these roles, not fewer. We are made up of who we love, so the more people I love, the more complete, the more I, I will be. This was his last paragraph:

See, you are shy. And you are sheltered. And you are suspicious. And a little bit fearful. But so is everyone. But going off on your experience into newness will eliminate all that. I guess what I'm saying is either go away to college or go away to explore. But move. You have it in you to nest and hide out and stay protected and the reason for this letter is to beg you to begin the journey in your mind that soon you will begin in your life. Move figuratively and literally.

He's right when it comes to shy, sheltered, suspicious and fearful, I am a little of all four, but as far as moving, I'll let Eudora Welty answer for me. I don't suppose I ever read a book as slowly as I did *One Writer's Beginnings*. I would read each line again before going on to the next, but the last were my favorites: "As you have seen, I am a writer who came of a sheltered life. A sheltered life can be a daring life as well. For all serious daring starts from within."

There is my friend Julie Reich, away from home, in a new city, surrounded by people her own age, and scared to death in the middle of her four safe subjects. While here I am, surrounded by five safe people, writing as many different things as I can (from novel to play to screwball comedy to mystery) and reading the same way (from James to Juvenal to John Van Druten) and feeling so courageous. As if the world is not some place far off I have to conquer, but sitting right next to me in my other armchair, waiting for me to take another poke at it.

So I hope I won't sound like a coward when I say that I think George is wrong, that in my view what I've done takes a lot more guts than to head for a "small college" as he advises, though not at first glance and not at first. I didn't have to face the little terrors of leaving home and finding new friends and adjusting to new ways. And I don't yet have to face the huge terror of making enough money to provide the food, shelter, and clothing I have always taken for granted. But I do have to face a certain kind of terror, life with no schedules and free periods and tests to break it up and show me what to do with it.

I have been given the chance to live my own best life, but no instructions were included with the chance. So I haven't been exactly sure how to do it or if my efforts have been any good. I certainly don't know who I am the way I did in school. I don't suppose one is ever as secure as one is in school because there are such easy standards. An *A* is the best and if you get an *A*, then you're the best. And if you get all *A's*, then you couldn't possibly be doing more with your life. In the life I've been living, it hasn't been as clear as that.

It's funny, when people go to college, they often have a hard time adjusting at first, but everyone advises them to stick to it. With autodidacts, the period that's hard is after the newness of freedom has worn off, and you begin to wonder what you should be doing with this freedom. But even if the struggle to get the most out of my freedom is sometimes hard for me, I don't want to stop struggling.

I know that for certain now. I've seen too much of life, and even if I haven't loved all I've seen, I've loved being able to see so much. I don't ever want the days to slip together in some terrible way and I'll look back and life will be gone. I want to feel something every day, even if occasionally it happens to be a little mystery. Even if at times I feel a little lost, I want to find my own way.

•

I got the most heartbreaking letter from a college friend today. Ever since I had known her she wanted to be an actress, and so after graduation, when I was afraid I would not see her again, I wrote to tell her what a wonderful actress I thought she was.

She wrote today that she did not get into the acting school she wanted to, so she is giving up her dream of being an actress. It takes so little to destroy a dream.

I sometimes look at adult people and wonder how they could have ended up so sad, and yet here I am at the formation of what may be some very sad lives. We are changed people once we let go of what we hope for.

Most of my dreams are pretty silly, but I will not let go of one of them, no matter how much of what is laughingly referred to as "real life" gets in the way. As Ruth Gordon said, the key to success is: Don't Face Facts . . .

•

My grandparents are celebrating Thanksgiving with us. I think that after being with me, they are now primarily thankful for my cousins Alexis and Mimi, who will both soon be off to college.

My grandmother Janet said to me, "If you don't stop reading all these books, you're going to be over-educated. I think you should go to college."

I fear many things, but I've never yet feared over-education. I really do think it's last on my list of things to worry about.

It's so odd, too, that this remark should come from Janet, since she makes great works a part of daily life better than anyone I know. She's always taking a course in some aspect of literature, history, or art.

I pointed out that she, too, was in danger of being overeducated, but Janet said she had spent all these years trying to make up for dropping out of Vassar to attend art school in Italy two years before graduation.

She's read more than anyone I know and is one of the few adults I can discuss great literature with because she is one of the few adults who reads it now instead of having read it fifty years ago. I wonder if any of those dames who graduated in Vassar's Class of 1934 have read *The Divine Comedy* in the last ten years. My grandmother has. And I am as proud of her education as she is worried about mine.

My grandfather Earl is more baffled than worried. A couple of weeks ago he sent me these articles about the Constitution that had been sent to all the members of his law firm. He wrote that perhaps I might find them educational. I was very touched at his unexpected broadening of my studies.

Though the broadening of my education was another point of contention. My grandparents worry that I might turn out lopsided concentrating on history and literature, and pretty much ignoring science and math. But I pointed out that college wouldn't necessarily correct that. A friend of mine about to graduate from Yale has yet to take a science or math course, and many such progressive colleges no longer force a student who's happy with the humanities to take math or science.

People are always arguing in favor of college, that you are made to read things you would never read on your own, but it's hard to take joy in the things we are made to read. And I think following the path of what really interests us will eventually branch out into all knowledge. After all, the Greeks led me to Isosceles and his triangle and the Romans led me to Pliny the Elder and his *Natural History*, unnatural though it was.

I think I finally persuaded the grandparents that I will not make a total mess of things, but they would be more persuaded if I told them this on a postcard from Stanford.

And I do feel for them. My grandfather was the first person in his family to go to college. His father thought he was very foolish to leave the farm. But he knew he had to, the same way I know I don't have to.

1988

Critical thinking points: After you've read

1) *Is it realistic that many high school graduates would opt for a life of intellectual exploration like Hailey? Why or why not?*

2) *Read or reread Andrew Hicks' "My First Week at Mizzou." How are the pieces similar? How are they different?*

3) *College is often a vehicle for students to explore — through reading or personal encounters — experiences they wouldn't stumble upon on their own. Hailey says, "It's hard to take joy in the things we are made to read." Do you take as much pleasure in "forced" experiences? Why or why not?*

4) *Hailey writes, "Why do people think you have to leave home to become an adult, happy human being?" In what ways has American society adapted this criteria for being "grown up"?*

5) *Read or reread Jennifer Sheridan's "Carmen" and/or Cristina Salat's "50% Chance of Lightning." Compare and contrast the relationship between Hailey and Julie to that of Carmen and Kate in "Carmen" or Robin and Malia in "50% Chance of Lightning."*

Some possibilities for writing

1) *Could you be an autodidact? What topics or areas of interest would you explore on your own if you had the time and money? Make a list. Why have you chosen what you have?*

2) *Hailey says, "We are made up who we love, so the more people I love, the more complete, the more I, I will be." Do you agree with her? Why or why not? How are you made up (or not) of the people you love?*

3) *Hailey quotes Eudora Welty: "For all serious daring starts from within." Do you believe this is true? Why or why not? Recall a time when you were "daring." Did it start from within, or was it prompted by external sources? Write about that experience.*

4) *Hailey writes, "My grandfather was the first person in his family to go to college. His father thought he was very foolish to leave the farm. But he knew he had to, the same way I know I don't have to." Was there ever a time in your life in which you intuitively knew you had to do something, even though your friends and family may not have agreed with your decision? How did you handle the situation, and what, if anything, did you learn from that experience?*

5) *Find and read Chapter Two of Eudora Welty's* One Writer's Beginning. *Why might Hailey be attracted to a person with such a life?*

6) *Find and read the essay "Self Reliance" by Ralph Waldo Emerson. How do you think Hailey would respond to that essay? Why do you think the way you do?*

In High School I Majored in Shop

Peter Martin

"

They told us / assembly lines were / forever.

"

Critical thinking points: As you read

1) What are some stereotypes of students who take shop classes in high school?
2) What are some stereotypes of success for Americans, especially for men?
3) Who is the "they" in this poem? Who is the "us"?
4) What is the difference between a job and a career? Which do you hope to have?

They told us
assembly lines were
forever. That
assembly lines
never stopped.
They showed us
filmstrips about
happy couples
with children
and Dad coming home
with his lunch bucket
happy, greeting
his children on
bended knee,
setting his lunch bucket
on the driveway pavement
of his new ranch-style
home. This

Peter Martin (b. 1950) is a probation and parole agent. He has also been a factory worker, bartender, teacher, and construction worker. A fourth printing of his chapbook, *Licking My Wounds*, was released in 1997.

was living,
they said.
And we believed them.

1987

Critical thinking points: After you've read

1) Why might the verb tense of this poem be important?

2) Why do you think the image of the "lunch bucket" is repeated twice within such a short poem?

3) What are some of the things people mean when they say "The American Dream"? What does that have to do, if anything, with this poem?

4) In what ways might this poem lead someone to decide on going to college?

Some possibilities for writing

1) Change the title to "In High School I Majored in Art" or "Gym" or "English" or "Computer Science" or "Business," and write your own description.

2) Write a letter to one of your parents or grandparents describing how and why you want your career and lifestyle to be the same as or different from theirs.

3) If you have ever worked on an "assembly line" or a similar type of job, record some of your memories and experiences.

4) Read or reread Michael Lancaster's "The Eyes of Chickens." Discuss the attitudes about males, masculinity, and how to decide on a future — if one can decide at all — that Lancaster's story shares with this poem.

5) Compare and contrast the Technical Colleges with the more traditional four-year colleges in your state. Some of the things you might want to consider are "mission" statements, enrollments, admission requirements, faculty preparations, costs, and job placements after graduation.

50% Chance of Lightning

Cristina Salat

❝

Well, what's the point of being gay if I'm never going to be with anybody?

❞

Critical thinking points: As you read

1) *Watch for the different responses Robin and Malia have toward college. What are they?*
2) *Were you eager to apply to and go to college like Malia, or not quite ready to leave home like Robin? Why?*
3) *Speculate about how Robin's mother died. What details in the story led you to that theory?*
4) *Are the people you know more like Malia (concrete goals, even down to the type of car she hopes to drive) or more like Robin (abstract wishes, such as simply "be happy")? Are you more like Malia or Robin? In what ways?*

"I wonder if I'll ever have a girlfriend." Robin stamps her sneakers against the wet pavement, tired of waiting.

Malia laughs. "Is that all you think about?"

"Well, what's the point of being gay if I'm never going to be with anybody?" Robin shifts the big umbrella they are sharing to her other hand. Fat silver drops of rain splatter above the plastic dome. She wishes the bus would run on time for once.

"Independent women. We vowed, remember? No guy chasing," Malia says.

Robin shoots Malia a look.

"Or girl chasing," Malia adds quickly.

"You can't talk," Robin says, trying not to feel each strand of her hair as it frizzes. "You have someone."

"That's true." Malia smiles.

Cristina Salat is an author, the founder of Shark Productions Independent Films, and an urban-born Black German Indian. Her work has been published by Bantam Books, Children's Television Workshop, and HarperCollins.

Robin looks at the gray, wet world through her clear umbrella. It's hat weather. Black baseball hat and hair gel. She uses both, but nothing really helps on damp days like this. "It's silly to worry how you look. Rain can make you alive if you let it!" Robin's mother used to say. She loved stormy weather almost as much as Robin didn't.

"It's Friday! How come you're so quiet?" Malia asks. "You're not obsessing about your hair, are you? It looks fine. I'd trade you in a second . . . so don't start in about my perfect Filipino hair!" She grins, reading Robin's mind.

Robin can't help smiling. They've known each other a long time.

"Guess what!" Malia changes the subject. "Tomorrow is me and Andrew's six-month anniversary. That's the longest I've ever gone out with anybody."

Robin sighs. "You guys will probably get old together." And I'll be the oldest single person on the face of the planet, she thinks gloomily.

Malia's forehead wrinkles into a slight frown. "No. I'm leaving. I can't wait to get out of here." A large electric bus lumbers to the curb and stops with a hiss. "I sent my applications out yesterday. NYU, Bryn Mawr, Hampshire, and RIT, in that order," Malia says as she boards.

They squeeze onto the heated bus between packed bodies in steaming overcoats. The bus lurches forward.

"Where did you decide?" Malia asks, grabbing onto a pole near the back.

Robin shrugs.

Malia raises one eyebrow. "It's almost Thanksgiving. You are still going to try for NYU and Hampshire with me, aren't you?"

"I guess," Robin says. "I haven't had time to decide anything yet." It's not like she hasn't been thinking about it.

College catalogs are spread across the floor of her bedroom. All she has to do is figure out where she wants to spend the next four years of her life. New York? Massachusetts? Zimbabwe? There's an endless stream of choices.

"You better make time," Malia says. "You shouldn't wait until the deadlines."

"Give me a break, okay?" Robin stares past the seated heads in front of her.

"Cranky, cranky." Malia elbows Robin's arm.

A woman wipes one hand across a steamed window for an outside view and pulls the bus cord. She vacates her seat and Malia and Robin squeeze past someone's knees to claim it. With Malia balanced on her lap, Robin turns her head toward the window and watches the city swish by. She tries to picture herself next fall, suitcases packed, excited to be going. She's almost eighteen; she should want to leave home. A new room. New city. New friends.

I can't leave, not yet! The air in the bus is thick and warm; it's hard to breathe enough in. Outside the window, sharp edged buildings and signs fly past. Robin's head feels light and disconnected. She presses her face against the cold glass. She doesn't have to leave. She can apply to San Francisco State or USF right here in the city. Or she won't go at all. Malia's mom didn't go to college. Robin's dad didn't go either, but he wants her to. "You're smart, like your mother," he's always saying. But what if she doesn't want to go?

It's okay, Robin repeats to herself. No one can make me.

Outside the window she watches a small, mixed terrier approach the curb, sniffing the ground. Its fur is wet and matted, standing up in points. The dog steps into the stilled, waiting traffic. Robin scans the sidewalk for the dog's person. Don't they know it's dangerous to let their puppy wander into the street?

Robin stares through the window, her mind racing. Maybe it's lost. She could help. She could get off the bus and . . . A car honks loudly. Something inside her shrinks up. Malia's weight is heavy on her lap. The dog looks up and scampers back to the curb as traffic surges and the bus rumbles forward. Robin cranes her neck. She should get off, before it's too late. But she can't.

"What is it?" Malia asks, feeling Robin's shift.

Robin forces herself to lean back in the seat and breathe slowly. She's being stupid. The dog won't get run over. Its owner is probably just down the block.

They hang their jackets over the chair in Malia's small, neat room and Robin drops her baseball cap onto the desk.

"You want to see my list of goals?" Malia asks. "I read in *New Woman* if you know exactly what you want, you're more likely to get it." She hands Robin an open, spiral-bound note-book and drops next to her on the bed.

Malia Manansala

Goals for Now
Get into a good college, far away
Major in computer science or business
Get another part-time job for clothes, makeup, etc.
Have fun!

Eventually
Dressy job where I make a lot of money and get respect
Nice apartment with classy things
Old BMW or jeep Cherokee (depending where I live)
Great friends
Marry someone loyal, sexy, and successful

"Money." Robin shakes her head. "Even if we get scholarships, we're going to be paying off college loans forever."

Malia nods. "That's why I need a big career. I'm not going to suck up to some man for money. You should make a goal list," she suggests, handing over a pen. "I need a snack."

Robin flops onto her side. Why not? At the top of a clean page, in slow, careful letters, she writes:

<u>Goals</u>

Figure Out Who I Am
Be Proud Of Myself
Fall in Love
Do Something Good

Robin frowns at her list. How does Malia know exactly what she wants?

"Hand it over." Malia comes back into the room with a tray of hot cocoa and microwaved pork buns.

"Okay, but it's not like yours."

"Do something good?" Malia makes a face. "Can you be more specific?"

"Hey, I didn't pick on your list!"

"I don't get it. When you want to do something, you just do it. This year you start telling everyone, 'I'm a lesbian, deal with it.' Why can't you be like that about college?"

"It's different," Robin says, thinking, I didn't tell everyone. My mother never got to know. Her mom drove a red Ho CRX with African pendants dangling from the rearview mirror. She took the highway a lot, to avoid city traffic. Route I South. Robin yanks her mind away.

"You are going to do more with your life than just be a lesbian, aren't you?" Malia prods.

Robin gets to her feet, shaking the damp bottoms of her baggy jeans away from her ankles. "Can I borrow something dry?"

"Come on. Seriously. What kind of job do you want?" Malia sounds like Robin's mom and dad used to — always excited about plans.

"I don't know. Something to help people," Robin says, looking through the closet.

"Peace Corps? Lawyer? Social worker?" Malia suggests.

"No," Robin says, a faded memory seeping into her mind. She used to play medicine woman when she was little, healing stuffed toy rabbits and her plastic Ujima dolls with bowls of grass-flower soup. "I always pictured myself in a fun office," she tells Malia, "where people or animals would come when they didn't feel well."

"You want to be some kind of doctor!" Malia enthuses.

Robin shakes her head. Playing medicine woman was a kid thing. "You know I can't stand blood and guts." Robin focuses her attention in the closet, taking out a black lace top and black leggings.

"How about a therapist? You could help people's minds."

"And listen to people complain all day?" Robin asks as she changes.

Malia sighs, shutting the notebook. "Well, what do you want to do tonight? I told Andrew I'd call him by four. Oh, I forgot! My mother and the jerk are going out after work. They won't be home till late. Do you want to have a party?"

"Yes!" Robin says. "Go rent some movies. I'll call for a pizza and invite everybody."

Andrew arrives first with a soggy Safeway bag tucked into his aviator jacket.

"Hey, Robbie!" he says, unpacking jumbo bottles of root beer and 7UP on the living-room table.

The doorbell rings again. Robin runs to let in Malia's friend Dan, who has brought his sister, Cybelle — a junior — and another girl. Malia has plenty of friends. Most of them are at least part Filipino.

Being a mix (African and Polish), Robin doesn't care who her friends are. She only has a few anyway, though she knows lot of people. When her mother died at the end of sophomore year, nobody knew what to say, so they acted like nothing happened. Robin still hangs out with the same people, but just because it's something to do; not because she cares.

When Malia returns from the video store, fifteen people are sprawled on the couch and floor with paper plates of mushroom and garlic pizza.

"Party woman," Andrew teases Malia, leaning down for a kiss. "You're soaked."

"It was only drizzling when I left. Sorry I took so long. I couldn't decide!" Malia takes two video cassettes out of a plastic bag. "I got a vampire movie and *The Best of Crack-Up Comedy*."

"I love vampires!" Cybelle adjusts one of the five rhinestone studs on her left ear. "Let's get scared first."

"Go change," Andrew tells Malia. "I'll set up the movie." He nudges her toward the bedroom.

Robin watches, wondering if anyone will ever care like that about her. For some reason the wet dog she saw from the bus pops into her mind. Nobody cared enough to keep it safe.

"Hi. You're Robin Ciszek, right?" A white girl in ripped jeans and a "Save the Planet" sweatshirt sits down next to Robin on the couch. "I read your article in the school paper! I'm April, Cybelle's friend. I never thought what it feels like to be gay until I read your essay. Do you know a lot of gay people, or was the story mostly about you?" April's slate colored eyes are wide and curious.

Robin takes a big bite of pizza. It's still hard to believe she wrote an article about being gay and submitted it to the school paper. She must have been crazy.

"I hope you don't mind me asking," April says quickly. "I'm just interested."

"The story's mostly about me," she tells April. "I don't know a lot of other gay people."

"I guess you will next year," April says. "My sister goes to UC Berkeley, and she says there's like three different gay groups on campus."

Robin feels her shoulders clench up. Is college the only thing anyone can talk about? Of course, it'll be worth it to be out of high school just to get away from the stupid notes guys are taping on her locker door: ALL YOU NEED IS A REAL MAN and ROBIN C. AND MALIA M. EAT FISH.

"Personally, I'm glad I don't have to think about college for another year," April continues.

"Really? Why?" Robin asks, surprised.

April looks away, embarrassed. "It's dumb. I have this cat. I don't want to leave her."

"Guess what I brought!" Cybelle calls out as Andrew dims the living-room light. She takes a half-full bottle of brandy from her tote bag.

"I'll have a little of that," Malia says, coming back into the room in overalls and a fluffy white sweater. "To warm me up."

"Quiet — it's starting," Gary yells from the easy chair as a bold, red title flashes across the television screen.

"I want to sit on the couch," Tara giggles. "Move over, Danny."

April moves toward Robin to make room for another person. Her hip rests against Robin's. The couch armrest presses into Robin's other side.

"Oh, hold me, Andrew!" Cybelle teases Malia as eerie music fills the darkened room. Malia laughs.

April's leg relaxes against Robin's. Out of the corner of one eye, Robin looks at the girl sitting next to her. April is watching the screen. Robin's thigh sizzles.

Robin nonchalantly eases sideways until their arms and legs are touching. A faint scent of perfume tinges the air. April doesn't move away. Robin's whole left side buzzes. She sinks into the couch, holding her breath. It would be so amazing if —

If what? Just because this girl liked the article doesn't mean she's interested. Robin moves her leg away, mad at herself. On screen, a shadowy figure suddenly whirls around and grins evilly. April leans softly against Robin.

Warm drops of sweat trickle down Robin's side. The room feels dark and red. Robin could reach out, take April's hand, trace one finger over the knuckle bumps and pale, freckled skin. . . .

Halfway through the vampire movie, Robin has to go to the bathroom, bad. She is tempted, but restrains herself from squeezing April's leg as she gets up.

Away from everyone, she splashes cold water on her face, smiling. Could April really be interested? I could go back and sit away from her to see if she follows me.

Feeling hot and wild, Robin unlocks the door. It doesn't budge. She pulls harder, leaning backward, and opens it a foot.

"Hi, Robin." Cybelle grins, peeking around the corner.

"What's with you? Get away from the door," Robin says.

"Okay." Cybelle runs one hand through her porcupine patch of short, black hair. "C'mere. I want to ask you something." Cybelle pulls Robin into Malia's room. She shuts the door without flicking on the light.

"Smell my breath," she says, leaning close.

A warm rush of brandy air tickles Robin's face.

"I can't go home wasted. Do I smell like pizza or alcohol?" Cybelle asks. Her lips touch the side of Robin's mouth.

"What are you doing?" Robin asks.

Cybelle nuzzles Robin's face, tracing her lips along Robin's. "Don't you like me? Kiss me back."

Robin's heart stutters. Is this for real? Cybelle slides one hand under Robin's hair and grips the back of her neck, kissing harder.

I've wanted this for so long, Robin thinks, awkwardly moving her arms around Cybelle. It's weird not being able to see. Robin touches sharp shoulder blades through the thin cotton of Cybelle's turtleneck.

I should have helped that dog. The thought scuttles into Robin's head. Why is she thinking about that now!

Cybelle sucks on Robin's lower lip. I should have gotten off the bus and helped. I could have taken it to the pound, or home. Why didn't I do something?

Cybelle's small tongue slides into Robin's mouth. Why am I doing this? I've seen Cybelle around school and never wanted to. She's got a boyfriend. She'll probably tell everyone, "I made out with the lesbian at Malia's house," for a laugh.

Robin shifts sideways. "I have to go."

"What?"

"I'm going back to the living room." Robin feels for the wall switch and flicks on the light.

Cybelle blinks. "How come? It's okay. Nobody misses us." She smiles and tugs on Robin's arm, moving closer.

"I want to see the rest of the movie," Robin says, pulling away. It's a lame excuse, but what else can she say? "I want to kiss somebody I'm really into, and you're not it"?

Cybelle stops smiling and drops Robin's arm. "Oh sure," she laughs. "You're scared! Writing that story and you don't even know what to do! What a joke." She yanks open the door and walks out before Robin can respond.

Robin follows Cybelle to the living room and watches her take the small, open spot on the couch next to April. She glares at the back of Cybelle's spiked head. Who does she think she is? I don't have to make out if I don't want to!

Whirling around, Robin heads back to the bedroom and jams her feet into her sneakers.

"You okay?" Malia asks, coming in.

"Sure." Robin doesn't look up.

"Are you leaving? What's going on?"

"Nothing I want to talk about right now." Robin zips up her jacket. They walk to the front door. Robin flings it open. She can't wait to be outside.

"Call me tomorrow, okay? Hey." Malia grabs Robin's jacket.

Robin looks back over her shoulder. "What?"

"We're best buddies forever, right?"

If Malia moves to New York and Robin stays here . . . Nothing's forever.

"Sure," Robin says, looking away.

Malia smiles and reaches out for a hug. "I'm sorry you didn't have a good time. Let's go shopping tomorrow morning, just you and me. Okay?"

As soon as Robin steps away from Malia's house, she realizes she's forgotten her baseball cap. Angrily, she pops open her umbrella. It doesn't matter. There's a bus stop at the corner and she's just going home.

Water drops drum against the plastic shield above her head as cars zip by, their rubber tires splashing against wet asphalt. Robin glares at each car that passes. She will never own one. What if that dog got run over? She should have helped. A bolt of light illuminates the night. Robin looks helplessly down the empty street for a bus. She hates being out alone after dark, even when it's not very late.

Whenever someone worried, her dad used to say: "There's a fifty-fifty chance of something good happening." Robin's mother loved that saying. Her father hasn't said it much lately. It's hard to believe in good stuff when you're dealing with the other fifty percent. At least she ended the thing with Cybelle. That's something. Robin might want experience, but she's not desperate.

Thunder swells, filling the night. Robin cranes her neck, looking down the street. No bus. So it's fifty-fifty. Should she wait here, hoping no weirdos show up and bother her before the bus comes, or should she start walking in this lousy weather? Her parents used to take walks in the rain. They were nuts
. . . but happy.

Robin starts to walk. A sharp wind whips by, threatening to turn her umbrella inside out. Okay, why not? She has nothing to lose. Robin clicks the umbrella shut. Rain falls cold against her face and settles onto her thick hair, expanding it. She walks fast, with the wooden umbrella handle held forward, staying near the streetlamps. Water trickles down her face and soaks into her clothing. She licks her lips. The rain tastes strangely good.

When she reaches the place where she saw the dog, Robin stops and studies the black road. A few torn paper bags. No blood or fur. It could be dead somewhere else. Or it could be off foraging in a garbage can or sleeping under a bush.

I'm sorry I didn't get off the bus to see if you needed help, she thinks. Next time I will. I hope you're safe. But maybe the dog didn't need help. Maybe it wasn't even scared. Maybe it was totally pleased to be out exploring and taking care of itself. Robin decides to picture the terrier that way.

From down the block a bus approaches, grumbling to a stop a few feet ahead. Robin hurries over. As the doors squeal open, she looks behind at the dark, empty street. She is afraid, but she doesn't want to be. Slowly, Robin turns away.

It is a long walk home under the wide, electric sky.

At the warm apartment on Guerrero Street, Robin finds her father asleep on their living-room couch. A paperback novel is spread open across his chest and his glasses are pushed up onto his forehead. Standing over him, dripping onto the brown shag rug, Robin feels tender and old. She removes his glasses and places the book on the glass coffee table, careful not to lose his page.

In her room, Robin drops her wet clothing to the floor and changes into an old set of flannel pajamas. Then she sits down at her drafting-table desk. Nothing's forever, and that's just the way it is. Moving college applications aside, she lifts two thick San Francisco phone books from the floor.

Robin thumbs through the thin A-L yellow pages slowly. There is something she can do. Something right.

Attorneys, Automobile . . . Bakers, Beauty . . . Carpets, Collectibles . . . Dentists, Divers . . . Environment . . . Florists . . . Health. Health clubs, health and diet, health maintenance, health service. A boxed ad catches Robin's eye.

Holistic Health Center
Dedicated to the well-being of body and mind
Licensed: nutritionists, massage therapists, acupuncturists
Courses in herbal healing, yoga, natural vision, Tai Chi

Medicine without blood and guts. Smiling to herself, Robin reaches for some loose-leaf paper and a pen. There's a new life out there, waiting for her. She just has to find it. She moves A-L aside and flips open M-Z. By ten p.m. three loose-leaf pages are filled with numbers and addresses. At the top of the first page, she writes: Call for info.

Robin stretches and climbs into bed with her new list. She rubs the soles of her bare feet against the chilled sheets. Maybe life is like rain. Alive if you let it be; lousy and depressing if you don't. She rolls onto her stomach. Under the information for the Shiatsu Institute, the College of Oriental Medicine, and the School for Therapeutic Massage, she writes: Tell Malia to get April's number from Dan. Call her?!?!?!

1994

Critical thinking points: After you've read

1) Malia thinks if people know exactly what they want, they're more likely to get it. Do you believe this is true? Why or why not?

2) Compare Robin's and Malia's lists of goals. Who do you think is more likely to be satisfied? Can you judge this simply from someone's goals? Why or why not?

3) Why do you think Robin doesn't get on the bus when it stops for her? What does the dog seem to represent to Robin? What details in the story led you to that?

4) Why do you think Robin "acts" on her future at the end of the story? Why might it be appropriate for Robin to find her future in a phone book rather than a college catalogue?

5) Robin thinks of her father's saying: "There's a fifty-fifty chance of something good happening." Why might the title become "50% Chance of Lightning"?

6) Robin "comes out" in an article in the school newspaper, yet she's never had a sexual experience with a woman. Why do you suppose she isn't interested in Cybelle's advances?

Some possibilities for writing

1) *Make two lists of your goals: one abstract like Robin's and one concrete like Malia's. For instance, an abstract goal would be "work with people," while a concrete goal that is an extension of that would be "get a degree in elementary education."*

2) *There are advantages and disadvantages to having a life's plan like Malia does. Make a list of advantages concerning having your goals and life mapped out. Now make a list of disadvantages concerning having your goals and life mapped out.*

3) *Robin is harassed with notes on her locker after her article in the school newspaper. Recall a time when you were teased for your ethnic background, sexual preference, or simply the way you talked or walked or something you did. Write about your experience.*

4) *Write a scene depicting Robin and Malia at their ten-year high school reunion. What do they look and act like? Are they still friends? What kinds of careers do they have? Have they achieved their goals?*

5) *Contact your Dean of Students or Residence Life Office to find out what types of support are available for gay, lesbian, or bisexual students on your campus. Research student organizations that offer an outlet for these students. Deliver a report to your class on your findings.*

Somewhere in Minnesota

Peter Klein

"
your dark eyes focused
on a brilliant future.
"

Critical thinking points: As you read

1) *Because of poetry's condensed nature, every word is important. What details give you an idea of what the poem might mean?*
2) *Why might Klein have written his poem without punctuation? What effect does it have on the reader? On the poem?*
3) *Why might the lines end where they do? How would the poem be different if the lines were longer or shorter?*

somewhere in Minnesota
there is a photograph
mailed from denver
to an uncle in duluth
who left it in a diner
on a table by the salt
it marked a woman's place
in a drugstore fiction
where it lay for years
until her freshman son
found it told his friends
the subject was his steady
then threw it in a lake
this picture was of you
your mortar board smile
gleaming softly beneath

Peter Klein (b. 1960) wrote this poem while a student in college.

the photographer's light
your dark eyes focused
on a brilliant future.

1979

Critical thinking points: After you've read

1) *What might the author mean by such phrases as "your mortar board smile" or "your dark eyes focused / on a brilliant future"?*
2) *Who do you think the "you" is in this poem?*
3) *What are some other objects that might stand for similar things as the photo seems to in this poem?*
4) *How do the places in which the photo ends up contribute to your reading of the poem? What do these places have in common?*

Some possibilities for writing

1) *Have you ever been in a relationship that ended badly? Were you the one who left or who was left? Write a scene that shows rather than tells what went wrong with the relationship.*
2) *Page through your own high school yearbook. Write a brief impression of the memories the pictures call to mind. Be as specific as you can in communicating these impressions.*
3) *Look at your parents' or grandparents' high school graduation photos and write about the people then compared to the people as you know them now.*
4) *Find yearbooks in your college library from ten or twenty years ago or longer. What seemed to be different about the people and the university then? What seems to be still the same?*
5) *Rewrite "somewhere in Minnesota" as a short story. Add scenes for each brief episode in the poem.*

The Eyes of Chickens

Michael Lancaster

───── **66** ─────

At that point in my life I was pulled in two directions. One was college, though I had no idea what to study. The other was diesel mechanics and learning to drive trucks. The summer months were time to figure things out, to 'get my head straight,' as Irene used to say, and I spent as many hours staring into hazy images of the future as I did on the chores Billy outlined over breakfast.

───── **99** ─────

Critical thinking points: As you read

1) One technique fiction writers often use is to include recurring images that subtly tie scenes together. Notice all of the references to blood in this story. Why do you think this is so?

2) Look for references and allusions to chickens throughout the story. Why is the chicken an appropriate animal for this story?

3) How does the first-person point of view contribute to the effectiveness of the story? In what ways would the story be different if it were written in the third-person?

The summer after high school I lived with my oldest sister and her husband on the apple-rich slopes of the Yakima Valley, moving sprinklers and working odd, dusty jobs in exchange for room and board. The arrangement was her idea — she'd left home when I was young and now she wanted to know me. I saw it as a chance to move away from my parents without being alone in the world.

At that point in my life I was pulled in two directions. One was college, though I had no idea what to study. The other was diesel mechanics and learning to drive trucks. The summer months were time to figure things out, to "get my head straight," as Irene used to say, and I spent as many hours staring into hazy images of the future as I did on the chores Billy outlined over breakfast.

Michael Lancaster (b. 1959) was born in Ellensburg, Washington. He now lives in Missoula, where he earned a master's degree in creative writing from the University of Montana. His short fiction has been published in several literary journals including *CutBank* and *Talking River Review*.

I was killing time one morning, leaning against the fence tossing feed to the chickens, when Billy appeared out of nowhere. Before I could make excuses about not working on the pump, Billy grinned. He rested his arms on the fence rail, his elbow nudging mine. He nodded toward the nervous hens, scratching the dirt for food.

"Think they've figured out we're just waiting to eat 'em?"

"I don't think they're that smart," I said.

Billy tapped a can of Skoal against his index finger, squeezed a dark clump and wadded it beneath his lip. He smiled, and brown tobacco clung to his teeth. This was the man my big sister married.

Billy looked straight ahead, squinting as if he saw something off in the distance. All I saw was the green canopy of apple trees rising to the irrigation ditch, then more orchards shimmering up the far side until the hill got too steep to irrigate and the slope grew tan with sagebrush and range grass. Billy farmed apples. He'd had some hard years lately — frost and hail; soft prices when his crop was good — and he was down to eighty of the original two hundred acres his father had left him.

"There's a cockfight at Ben Palmer's place tonight," Billy said. He had a habit of pausing between thoughts, and I waited for him to go on.

"Oscar's got a bird he's going to fight. Says he'll help pick my bets if I drive him. Can't keep that piece-of-shit Buick running." Billy looked at me and grinned. "You wanna come along?"

If I'd given it any thought, I would've said no, but the sudden invitation took me by surprise. Billy had helped me with my car a couple times and we went fishing once on the Yakima, but that was about it. The only things we had in common were my sister and his house. Irene and I, on the other hand, were hitting it off pretty well. She told me stories from before I was born, when Dad was drinking and Mom was trying to shut out the world, and I remembered what I could from my own childhood, stories that didn't seem interesting to me. She drank in every word. We were getting to be friends, she and I. She wanted me and Billy to be friends too.

"Sure," I told him. "Never been to a cockfight before."

The screen door slammed behind Billy Junior and Sarah. "Lunch time! Lunch time," they shouted. Billy couldn't help smiling when he saw them racing toward us. Irene leaned out the doorway. She had red hair, like me, and she wore it long.

"Lunch is on the table, guys," she called.

Billy scooped his finger through his lip and flung the black wad to the ground. Then he picked up the kids, one in each arm, and carried them into the house.

By early evening I was beginning to wonder if Billy had forgotten. I had the hood up on my car, but wasn't really working on anything. I'd slipped out after dinner to avoid getting caught in the middle of an argument about cockfights — which were illegal in Washington, Irene reminded us. Billy told her it was my idea, that he had mentioned the cockfights and I'd asked to come along. When Irene raised her eyebrows and looked at me, I'd muttered, "Why not?"

The sky had faded from afternoon cyan to a hazy pale blue. Billy ran the sprinkler on the grass every night, and the slow chut-chut-chut and drum roll return, again and again exactly the same, washed all thoughts from my head and left me with a sudden ache of sadness. I didn't know why. I wanted to stay home, keep Irene company, or at least go back inside and tell her good-bye. Instead, I stayed where I was, listening to the sprinkler, feeling the chill of evening air nudging into the shade. When I saw Billy coming I pulled off a spark plug wire and pretended to study it. He was dressed in his good jeans, a white cowboy shirt with pale blue checks, and the straw cowboy hat with the pheasant-hackle band he wore on trips to town. I thought about running inside for a better shirt.

"We've got to pick up Oscar down at the ghetto," he said.

We drove to the migrants' quarters, a row of stucco boxes a half-mile down the gravel road. Oscar was squatting in his doorway beside a wooden box with holes in its lid. Oscar's shirt had rhinestone snips down the front and sleeves ripped off at the shoulders. His green baseball cap looked sat on. Billy and I waited in the cab, our elbows out the windows. Three little boys trotted doglike through the dust that hung in front of the truck.

"I'm having a talk with my fighter," Oscar said, patting the box. "This bird is feeling lucky. He has the heart of a warrior."

"Good," said Billy. "Load him up and let's go."

Oscar wedged the cage between the wheel well and the cab and rode up front with me and Billy. I got stuck in the middle, and when Billy shifted gears, I had to slide my knees against Oscar's leg. Neither of them gave me room, and I felt like a kid riding with my shoulders pulled up and my knees pressed together.

To get to Ben Palmer's we cut through Toppenish with its Old West storefronts and headed south on Wapato Road, past beet fields and vineyards and acre after acre of the cockeyed poles and taut strings that green hops shimmied up. We left pavement and followed rutted wheel tracks through an apple orchard until we came to an unpainted wooden building the size of a garage. Cars and pickups were parked wherever there was space around the building and in the tall grass between the trees, and we pulled off as close as we could get. A boy in a jeans jacket stood just outside the open door. He looked no older than me. The sun hadn't been down five minutes, but the air already felt cool, and I could smell the grass. The light from the building was unnaturally bright, and as we walked toward it I saw men framed by the doorway, some standing, some sitting on bales of hay, their smallest features vivid: a gleam of gold tooth, a tufted arch of eyebrow, a patch of red flannel on dark, weathered skin.

The boy in the jeans jacket stopped me with a hand on my arm. "Ten dollars," he said. Billy gave him a twenty for the two of us, and we followed Oscar through the crowd until we found a place to stand near the wall. Beside me a man held a fighting cock under his arm and lashed a shining curved blade just above the chicken's foot. Two other men stood by very close.

One pointed at the blade, said something in Spanish, and the handler corrected a loop.

Billy went to find Ben Palmer, and Oscar slipped off in the crowd. I leaned against a post and hoped I didn't look nervous. In the corner behind me, a man sold cans of beer and homemade tacos. In the center of the room, bales of hay were arranged two-high in a circle broken by an opening just wide enough to walk through. A fluorescent tube hung down, and the dirt in the ring was swept smooth.

I'd expected the room to be filled with wild cackles and bloody feathers, but the only thing going on was a dice game. I watched from behind the bales while a young man rolled, took bets, then rolled again. He showed his palms to the bettors and scooped up their money He shrugged and rolled once more.

I was about to go stand by Billy, but before I could move, the man with the dice climbed out of the ring and two other men walked in cradling chickens. They lifted the birds over their heads, and people started shouting and pointing, making bets. The handlers thrust the birds toward each other until their beaks almost touched and the chickens struggled to break free and fight. Released, the birds went at each other. They rose together in a flapping blur, fell to the ground apart, then started toward each other again, meeting and rising in a flurry, and when they came down this time one bird stood above the other, but I saw no blood.

The handlers picked up their birds, and I assumed the fight was over. But the owner of the limp chicken lifted it like a conch shell and blew into the feathers on its back, just above the tail. Then he plucked out a curved tail feather that spiraled to the ground and he lowered the bird once more. The other handler watched all this and without expression released his bird. It ran to the weakened chicken, rose above it, and found flesh with the blade. Blood puddled in the dust.

There wasn't much clapping or whooping as the men settled their bets, but I looked over at Billy and he and Ben Palmer were sitting next to each other on a bale laughing, and Oscar was standing behind them laughing too. I decided to find out how much they'd won and maybe figure out from Oscar how to place a bet.

Something came over Billy's face when he looked up and saw me, but he recovered his smile, and I smiled too.

"Ben," Billy said, "this is Irene's brother, Martin." We shook hands, and Ben Palmer glanced at Billy, then back at me.

"Get yourself a beer, son. Enjoy yourself." He looked over my shoulder toward the crowd, and I wasn't sure if he was still talking to me when he said, "Anything you can't find, just ask."

"Look," Billy said, leaning so close I could smell Skoal and beer on his breath. "I'm going to step outside with Ben for a while. Why don't you stay here. Bet on some fights. Oscar'll help you." He dug into his pocket and pulled out two twenties. "Here," he said, "consider this a bonus." Billy wove through the crowd and walked out the open door where he and Ben Palmer disappeared in the darkness.

Oscar laid his hand on my shoulder. "Soon it will be my rooster's turn," he said. "Put your money on him."

I squeezed through a couple men to get near the ring for Oscar's fight. The betting happened quickly and in Spanish, so I hung on to the money Billy gave me. Oscar took long, slow strides around the ring, holding his chicken in both his hands as if it were precious and delicate. He raised it above his head, then he and the other handler shoved the birds together so they almost tangled beaks, and they struggled fiercely to get at each other. Oscar smiled as he released his chicken.

The birds rose together three times without damage. They looked more like dancers than fighters, and people started yelling for action. "C'mon, Oscar," I shouted. I felt like I had an interest. I looked around the room for Billy. He wouldn't want to miss this. I stood on my toes to see over the heads in the crowd. The yelling stopped and I turned back toward the ring to see Oscar's chicken rumpled on the dirt, wings outstretched, twitching.

I worked my way along the bales until I reached the door. Standing in the smoky light of the building, I couldn't see a thing outside. I started to wish I had stayed home with my sister and let Billy come here alone. I imagined her in front of the television, her legs curled beneath her. Whenever Billy went to town for a beer, Irene would entertain the kids with projects, baking and decorating cookies, building bird houses from milk cartons. And once Billy Junior and Sarah were in bed, Irene and I played backgammon or watched TV. Sometimes I wanted to ask her questions — not about our parents and growing up but about Irene's life now, raising Billy's kids, living on the farm. Are you happy? Do you wish you'd done things differently? Is it too late for a change? But I'd look at her unworried face and decide not to chance it. In the mornings after his nights out, Billy would have little appetite for breakfast, but he'd manage to eat a couple cookies, dipping them in his coffee while he sat red-eyed at the table watching the rest of us gobble bacon and eggs. Back in the ring, another fight had started. I walked outside, into the cool night air.

The boy who took our money when we arrived was still at the door. I said "Howdy" as I walked past. He grunted and nodded. I worked through the darkness around the corner of the building, feeling my way over uneven clumps of grass and dirt. The sky was just on the blue side of black, and shadows fused the apple trees into a solid dark form.

I walked toward a small square of light. As I came closer, I could make out the hunched shape of a trailer at the edge of the trees and the shadows of several men shuffling at the bottom of the steps. The door opened and I saw a man in cowboy boots and a cowboy hat tucking in his shirt and fixing his belt. He walked down the metal steps, and another man went in: Billy.

Someone grabbed my elbow, an old man with a pocked face who asked me something in Spanish. I shook my head and he leaned close, nodding toward the trailer. He repeated whatever it was he'd asked, still gripping my arm. I tried to shake free but his hand clamped tighter, and finally I let him lead me to the trailer. He called out to the men.

"Hombre," was the only word I understood, and the men in the line laughed. The old man pushed me into the cluster of others and they grabbed ahold. There was no use struggling, and they passed me from one to another toward the front of the line, cackling with laughter.

I climbed the steps and looked down at their faces. The men shouted, crowding. They prodded me toward the door, poking as if I were a farm animal they intended to buy, and I kicked wildly in their direction, but this only brought more laughter. They wouldn't back off, and there was only one place for me to go. I had a good idea what I'd find in the trailer. I slipped in as quickly as I could and pulled the door closed. I could hear their laughter muffled through tin walls.

I stood in the first of two rooms divided by a doorless threshold. A kerosene lamp threw quivering light on the trailer's grimy walls. Sitting cross-legged on the floor before me, nestled in a bed of quilted blankets, was a round Mexican girl with a puffy face and one blackened eye. She was naked, and one nipple was bleeding. In the fold of skin beneath her belly an indigo bruise spread like oil. She didn't look at me, didn't speak. A smell, thick and wet like honey and blood, rose from the nest of blankets. I knew if I stayed I would vomit.

In the other room, shadows and sounds of movement. Billy's pheasant-hackled cowboy hat lay on the floor.

When I opened the door, the men let me pass. They jeered me, but they seemed tired of their game and anxious to get inside themselves. No one put a hand on me.

I worked my way to the edge of the ring and squeezed onto a bale beside a man in a straw hat. Two cocks eyed each other, their handlers pacing behind them like referees. I looked for Oscar, but I saw only unfamiliar faces intent on the chickens fighting in the dust. I expected a hand on my shoulder any minute, to be discovered and thrown out the door. But few of the men took their eyes off the cockfight long enough to look at me, and those who did showed no more expression than if they'd glanced at a mirror and seen their own image.

After a couple more fights, Billy swung onto the bale beside me. I didn't say anything, kept my eyes on the ring.

"Win any money?" Billy asked. I turned my head toward him but not far enough to meet his eyes. Billy was quiet for a minute, then he said, "We've got to wait for Oscar."

"What's he doing?" I asked.

"He's outside."

"Out in the trailer?"

Billy hesitated. "Oscar doesn't think about nothing but chickens. He's outside talking to some joker about buying a new bird. What about you? You have yourself a little visit out back?"

I didn't answer, and finally Billy said, "Of course not. Didn't think you would."

So we sat on the bales and watched chickens fight while we waited for Oscar. I kept my eyes on the ring and my jaw clenched. In one fight, a large chicken was pitted against one much smaller, but the smaller bird got a lucky slice in their first pass. The handlers picked up the birds and talked low to them. But when they put them back down on the dirt, the bigger chicken turned its back and cowered, covered itself with its wings. People started to laugh and jeer. The handler picked up the big chicken and wiped blood from its beak. But when he put it down, the cock cowered once more. It wouldn't fight. The men laughed hard at this. The handler was unable to smile.

Billy laughed along with the other men, who seemed to think this bird that wouldn't fight to the death was the funniest thing they'd seen. The handler carried his bird from the ring. The man looked straight ahead, unwilling to meet eyes with anyone in the crowd. But the bird he carried looked around at everything, eyes open, surprisingly calm.

Before the next fight, Oscar slipped onto the bale next to Billy as if he had never left.

"You ready, Oscar?" Billy asked.

"Sure." He fetched his empty cage from a corner of the room.

Billy said, "Let's go."

We headed for the truck as bored and casual as if we'd just walked out of a movie. We used the light from the doorway behind us to keep from stumbling into things, and I suddenly realized that what had happened was over and Billy was already thinking about the morning weather and tomorrow's chores.

"Hey, Billy," I heard myself say. He stopped and turned around, his eyebrows raised. I wasn't sure what I was going to say next. I wanted to deck him. I wanted to rush him, drive him to the ground with my shoulder and beat him until he couldn't take any more. Instead, I reached into my pocket and pulled out the forty dollars. I crumpled the bills and dropped them on the ground.

"Keep your money," I said, my voice trembling.

Billy's face was calm, amused. He slowly reached down to pick up the money, and while he was bent over I tackled him.

We rolled in the wet grass, and I drew back my fist, but before I could swing at him Billy popped me in the eye, a short, hard punch I didn't see coming. That one punch was all it took to stop me. Kneeling in the grass, I held my face in my hands and rocked back and forth.

"God damn it, Martin," I heard Billy say, "What'd you go do a dumb-ass thing like that for?"

My cheekbone felt puffy, unfamiliar, like a lip after the dentist. I was afraid if I tried to say anything I'd start to cry, and that would be the worst thing that could happen. I wished Billy and Oscar would leave. But when I opened my eyes I saw Billy's and Oscar's boots.

"You all right?" Billy asked.

I didn't answer.

"What the hell got into you anyway?"

They stood there, waiting. I still didn't say anything. Finally, I picked myself up and faced the two men.

"You'll have a shiner," Oscar said.

"At least I didn't hit you in the mouth. Probably would have broke some teeth. Jesus. You'll have a mouse, but you'll live."

Without another word he and Oscar walked toward the truck with the same nonchalance as before. I didn't have any choice but to follow.

Driving toward home Billy was silent, but I could feel the restlessness in his shoulder pressed against me. The sky was black and salted with stars. I got the feeling they'd have things to talk about if I weren't there.

We let Oscar out at the ghetto, the truck door slamming hollow as Billy pulled away, the two of us alone in the cab. Billy was still quiet, still staring out the windshield, but staring like he felt eyes on him. Just then a jackrabbit jumped into the beam and somehow zigzagged ahead of us without getting hit, disappearing into the dark brush at the side of the road.

"Jesus criminy," Billy said, swerving to miss it. He looked over at me and smiled. "What are you going to tell Irene?"

I didn't answer. After a second, Billy took another quick look my way. Then he looked back at the road, his eyes small and dark.

"I know what I'd do," he said. He jerked another look at me and the truck bounced through a rut. He looked back and forth between me and the road. His tiny eyes didn't blink. They looked like the eyes of a chicken.

"Anything could have happened tonight. Those Mexicans get drunk and they're liable to swing at anybody."

I didn't say anything, and Billy put his eyes back on the road, his hand tight at the top of the wheel, the green light of the dash shining weakly across his face. I could see my sister's children in his jawbone. I saw the resemblance in the curve of his lips. I still didn't say anything, and Billy began to smile.

I rolled down the window and put my face in the breeze, the soothing crunch of tires on gravel wrapping me like a blanket, the rumble of the cab carrying me back to the house where my sister waited, her children in their beds dreaming. I felt strangely calm. I put my hand out on the mirror. The wind blew back my hair. There wasn't enough light to make out my features, but I kept looking in the mirror, and the wind rushed by.

When we reached the house a light was burning. My sister met us at the door in her slippers and robe. She touched my swollen eye and asked what happened, pure concern in her voice. She led me to a kitchen chair and sliced the cellophane from a package of steaks. She covered my eye with meat. It was heavy and smelled of blood, but the cold felt good and I believed I could feel the pain being pulled from my flesh.

Only then did she speak again: "Somebody want to tell me what happened?"

Most of the decisions that have shaped my life I made in an instant, without much thought of their consequences. I've never been sure of the forces that have led me to either speak my mind or shut up, to act or sit back and let things happen. One thing leads to another—but which things? And to where? I chose college that summer over diesel mechanics more from a distaste for grease than a hunger for knowledge. That led to a desk job, soft and secure. And I made choices about the kind of man I'd become, although I didn't realize it at the time. Or maybe I didn't have a choice at all, other than to watch who I was unfold before me, through actions I was destined to take.

Sometimes, when I replay that night, it's me who answers my sister. I tell her about Billy and the girl in the trailer, how I got my black eye. I promise Irene that I'll keep Billy off her back if she decides to pack her bags and gather her children. After all, I tell her, you're my sister. We're family. Blood.

And for a minute I feel good. Until I remember myself holding the cold meat on my face, not saying a word, looking with my good eye at my sister's husband, and waiting for him to invent the story we would use in place of the truth.

1994

Critical thinking points: After you've read

1) *Why does Martin cover for his brother-in-law? What truth does he "rewrite"?*
2) *If Martin told the "truth" to his sister in the last scene, how would it "reshape" his future?*
3) *What if Martin had been a girl? In what ways would this story have been different?*
4) *Martin realizes that all of his choices — made in an instant "without much thought of their consequences" — have molded the person he has become. Do you think that is true for all of us? How is it true for Martin? For you?*

Some possibilities for writing

1) *Rewrite the last scene between Martin and his sister Irene. This time, Martin tells the truth.*
2) *Martin makes his decision to go to college — "more from a distaste for grease than a hunger for knowledge." Is this true of college-bound students you know? Write an essay exploring the various factors and experiences that led you to apply to college.*
3) *Read or reread Peter Martin's "In High School I Majored in Shop." Compare Martin's perspective on building a future to that of the narrator in Martin's poem. How are their attitudes similar and/or different?*
4) *Find the short story "I Want to Know Why" by Sherwood Anderson in* Winesburg, Ohio *(1919). Compare and contrast it to this story.*
5) *This type of story is often referred to as an "initiation" story. Find out what elements usually make up this type of story, and write an analysis of this story as an initiation.*

Further Suggestions for Writing — "Where We're Coming From"

1) What kinds of changes do you think your being away at college will make for your family and/or your friends at home? Write about some of them.

2) What do you expect to miss the most about high school. What do you expect to miss the least? Why?

3) What kind of high school student were you? Write about the traits you would like to keep as a college student as well as those you would like to change and why this is so.

4) Recall a time when you were thrust into a situation in which you did not quite fit in, such as moving to a new neighborhood or starting at a new school. Describe your experience. How does it compare to starting college?

5) Totally new experiences may create a sense of physical exploration that parallels a mental exploration. Recall some recent experience that was new, different, foreign, and perhaps even frightening. As you record that experience, reflect on what you learned, how your preconceptions changed, or how it was strange or mysterious. What ideals gradually dawned on you?

6) Think of your high school — a team organization, group of friends. Write about one of the most important problems this group faces. Write a letter that proposes some specific solutions for this problem.

7) If you participated in athletics programs in high school or college, write an essay describing what that activity did or did not teach you. If you participated in any other organized programs, write an essay describing what that involvement did or did not teach you.

8) For some college students, especially first-year students, it is much easier to look back on past successes and good memories from high school rather than to look forward to future goals. Is this true for you? What obstacles do you think you must overcome before you look forward to the next stage of your life?

9) Some people believe we often learn in different ways than our mothers and our fathers did. Write an essay that examines and illustrates this theory from your personal experience.

10) Most people want to succeed at what they do, and college is no exception. Why and how much do you want to succeed at college? What does success at college mean for and to you?

11) If you could be known for anything right now, what would that be? What would you like to be known for in ten years? In fifty years? Why?

12) Recall a time in your life when you didn't feel "normal." What led to experiencing that? How did you get past it?

13) Were you ever teased for not knowing an answer in class or not getting a joke

one of your friends told? How did you react? How did you feel? Write a scene describing your experience.

14) *Choose the person in your life who most often gives you helpful advice. Write an essay describing the types of advice he or she has given you.*

15) *Choose the person in your life who most often gives you poor advice. Write an essay describing the types of advice he or she has given you.*

16) *Think of a time when you lacked the verbal skills you needed to communicate effectively. It may have been a college interview, writing a letter to a friend, or expressing your ideas in class. Write about how it made you feel and how you coped with the problem.*

17) *Think of some significant accomplishment in your life. Write about how curiosity, discipline, risktaking, initiative, and/or enthusiasm contributed to that accomplishment. Were there other qualities that contributed as well? Write about them also.*

18) *Identify a talent you have or information you possess that is unique, such as tap dancing, scubadiving, or how to make maple syrup. Write at least a page about why this is important to you and why others should know about it.*

19) *Visit your college learning center and interview tutors or staff about the causes of test anxiety. Research some ways to alleviate test anxiety.*

20) *Interview two or three experienced students about their first year. What kinds of pressure and problems did they have? How did they handle them? Seek their advice on things you are concerned about.*

21) *Prepare for a crucial situation that is likely to happen to you as a college student this semester. Imagine exactly what might happen and write a description of it. Explain why this situation is likely to be so crucial. Include all the possible outcomes from the best to the worst, and figure out what you might do to prepare for the situation before it occurs.*

22) *Why do students care what other students think? Write an essay called "Peer Pressure Among College Students."*

23) *What cocurricular activities do you plan to pursue in college? How do these activities relate to your academic or career plans?*

24) *Choose a campus organization you are thinking about joining and investigate it. Prepare a written report on this organization to deliver to the class.*

25) *If you are new to the town your school is in, or even if you are not, find something interesting, odd, or unique about that town and present your findings to the class as a report.*

26) *Visit your campus Ecumenical Center. What services are provided that offer spiritual support to students?*

27) *Go to an on-campus event of any kind that you have never experienced before, such as a symphony, a ballet, a poetry reading, or a debate. The possibilities are endless. With an open mind, summarize, describe, and/or evaluate it. Do you think you would ever attend another event of this kind? Why or why not?*

What kinds of things to you think you would need or would like to know more about in order to appreciate or understand another event like this?

28) *Why do some students drop out of college?*

29) *Choose one of your responses to "Some possibilities for writing" in this section and do further research on some aspect of the topic you addressed in your narrative. Write about how and why this new information would have improved your previous effort.*

Selected Films — "Where We're Coming From"

American Graffiti (1973, USA). The action takes place over one typical night for a group of high school graduates. Cowritten and directed by George Lucas (the auteur behind the *Star Wars* trilogy). Comedy. 110 min. PG

Baby, It's You (1983, USA). A Jewish girl and a Catholic boy come of age against a working-class background in the late '60s. Written and directed by John Sayles. Comedy/Drama. 105 min. R

Breaking Away (1979, USA). Oscar winner (for best original screenplay) about a teen just out of high school searching for his identity through bicycle racing. Filmed on location at Indiana University. Comedy/Drama. 100 min. PG

Class (1983, USA). Two prep school roommates come up against class differences and a salacious secret neither one is fully aware of. Comedy/Drama. 98 min. R

Dead Poets Society (1989, USA). Set in the '50s. Unorthodox prep school English teacher Robin Williams inspires his students to love literature. Oscar for best original screenplay. Drama. 128 min. PG

Fast Times at Ridgemont High (1982, USA). Based on the factual book by Cameron Crowe, who returned to high school as an adult masquerading as a student for a year. Film debuts of Forest Whitaker, Eric Stoltz, Anthony Edwards, and Nicolas Cage. Comedy. 90 min. PG

Just Another Girl on the IRT (1993, USA). A quick, sassy girl from the projects has designs on a med school career until her accidental pregnancy postpones her plans. A debut for both the lead actor (Ariyan Johnson) and director (Leslie Harris). Special Jury Award at Sundance Film Festival. Drama. 96 min. R

Mystic Pizza (1988, USA). Three young women of blue-collar Portuguese descent work in a pizzeria in the coastal town of Mystic, Connecticut, and one dreams of going to Yale. Romantic comedy. 104 min. R

Noa at Seventeen (1982, Israel). Set in the '50s. Against the backdrop of the newly formed and turbulent Israeli homeland, a middle-class family debates school versus kibbutz for their daughter. In Hebrew; subtitled. Drama. 86 min.

October Sky (1999, USA). Based on the memoir *Rocket Boys* by Homer H. Hickam Jr., this true story begins in 1957 with Russia's historic launch of the Sputnik satellite. Homer sees Sputnik as his cue to pursue a fascination with rocketry, but winning the science fair is his only ticket to college and out of life in this West Virginia coal mining town. Drama. 108 min. PG

Risky Business (1983, USA). With his parents out of town, entrepreneurial Tom Cruise decides to spend the lull while waiting to hear from colleges dancing in his underwear and organizing a prostitution ring. By the time he gets to college, he's a wiser man. Comedy. 99 min. R

Rushmore (1999, USA). In this charmingly eccentric sleeper, Max Fischer — a frantically overactive 10th grader at Rushmore Academy — edits the school newspaper and yearbook; serves as president of the French Club, German Club, Chess

Club, and Astronomy Club; captains the fencing and debate teams; and directs the Max Fischer Players, for whom he writes and produces plays about police corruption, inner-city violence, war, and other epic subjects. Comedy. 133 min. R

Say Anything . . . (1989, USA). A young kickboxer falls for the smart girl. She's college bound; he's maybe not. Comedy/Drama. 89 min. PG-13

Stand and Deliver (1988, USA). A class from an East L.A. barrio commits to taking the Advance Placement Test in calculus, inspired by their dedicated, tough-love teacher (James Edward Olmos). Drama. 105 min. PG

For Critical Thinking Points on these films, see Appendix (p. 335).

Chapter Two

School Daze:
Life in the First Year

Many first-year students often walk around in a daze—sleep deprived, homesick, stuck in the kid-in-a-candy-store syndrome, or feeling like a castaway in a strange land. All of the pieces in this section focus on the sometimes humorous, sometimes very serious experiences that make up the first year of college.

This chapter will explore —

- Transitions to dorm life
- Interaction between students and college support staff
- How to relate course work to personal lives
- Establishing a balance between school and home life
- A variety of ways to experience college

A Day in the Life Of . . .

Greg Adams

"

REWIND.

"

Critical thinking points: As you read

1) What do you expect the poem to be about from its title?
*2) Why is this a poem and not a short story or a diary entry? What specifically
   makes this a poem?*
3) What are some of the narrator's personality traits? How do you know that?

8:04 a.m., Kleenex, lamp
light, Irish Spring, Pert
Plus, boxers, pants, shirt,
Malt-O-Meal, milk, vitamin.

parking lot, bridge, college
algebra, Burger King, hot chocolate,
short story, bridge, parking
lot, keys, stereo, guitar.

local news, frozen chicken, instant
potatoes, salt, butter,
milk, aspirin, Rolaids, rented
video, beer, popcorn, Kleenex.

beer, more beer, salt, burnt
kernels, credits, STOP, Close
Up, mint floss, sleep sofa, allergy
pill, lights, REWIND.

1994

Greg Adams (b. 1970), a songwriter and poet, is currently working as a newspaper editor.

Critical thinking points: After you've read

1) *What might the details in the poem say about the narrator's personality? How might brand names, such as Irish Spring, Pert Plus, and Rolaids, reflect who and what a person is?*
2) *Which of these details seem to particularly reflect college life? How might that contribute to your reading of the poem?*
3) *Imagine you could ask the narrator, "So, how was your day?" What do you think he would say? Why?*
4) *Why do you think there are no verbs in the poem? What effect does that have on the poem?*

Some possibilities for writing

1) *Rewrite the poem so it is pertinent to your day. Include specific details in the way that the author does.*
2) *Try the above again, but this time make it about a day in your life when you were in high school.*
3) *Write about some part of your daily routine — getting up, going to bed, walking the dog, driving to work — the more mundane the better, as seen by a disinterested, objective third person. Try as hard as you can not to* tell *the reader what you want them to know, but* show *them with concrete details.*
4) *The same as above but as observed by a person who wants the reader to like or to dislike you. Or, as observed by a person who wants the reader not to trust you. Or, from your own point of view, which reflects a particular state of mind such as happiness, depression, joy, or boredom. Try as hard as you can not to* tell *the reader what you want them to know, but instead* show *them with concrete details.*

Ten Commandments for a College Freshman

Joseph McCabe

66

College is a new beginning, a clean slate. . . . Burn your bad bridges. No one at college knows about that soiled baggage you've been carrying.

99

Critical thinking points: As you read

1) What clues you to the era in which this was written? What advice seems dated to you? What advice seems still pertinent to college students?

2) The father asks of his son, "Give me your ideas on what to scrap and what to keep." What is your response to this? What are the five most important commandments to you? Why? What are the two most important ones to you? Why?

3) This piece was written in the form of a letter. What are some qualities of a letter that make this piece effective? How would this work differently if it were simply "Ten Commandments for Freshmen" and not a part of a personal letter from father to son?

4) What kinds of advice were you given before you came to college? Which advice will be the easiest for you to follow? Why? Which advice will be the hardest for you to follow? Why?

Dear J.B. —

   . . . As you know I am asked from time to time to talk to high school students about college and how to prepare for it. Do you think something like the following would be helpful? I'm thinking of calling it: Ten Commandments for a College Freshman. Give me your ideas on what to scrap and what to keep.

I. Thou Shalt Plan to Succeed.

Does this seem as obvious as the need for a quarterback on the football team? I don't mean *hope* to succeed. I mean that success in college will be much more likely

Joseph McCabe (b. 1912) is an ordained minister in the United Presbyterian Church and trustee of the Princeton Theological Seminary and Herbert Hoover Presidential Library. His books include *Your First Year at College* (Westminster, 1967) and *Reason, Faith, and Love* (Parthenon, 1972).

if you really draw up a schedule of hours for study, work, and play. Lay out your day and your week. Get in the habit in high school. This will be the secret of getting things done in college and enjoying the whole experience.

II. Thou Shalt Handle Freedom Responsibly.

No one is going to tell you when to get up, go to eat, study, or go to bed. It's amazing that so many survive, and, of course, many don't. Freedom such as a student has at college is devastating for that freshman who has little sense of responsibility. You've got to get set for freedom; it isn't doing what comes naturally.

III. Thou Shall Spread the Joy of Learning.

Learning is an exciting adventure as you have already discovered in the best of your high school courses. Beware those who are "sent" to college, for they will be taking the attitude that education is the enemy of fun. Beware the cynics. They're on every campus and their refrain runs like this, "Poor food, dorm is like a jail, dull professors, slobby team, why did you come here?" You will sometimes wish they would take their budding ulcers or sour stomach elsewhere. But if it's an education you're after, you'll get it, and you will enjoy the process.

IV. Thou Shalt Scale Down Those Reports on the Sex and Liquor Bit.

Not every co-ed takes the pill as routinely as most takes aspirin, and the extracurricular is not a perpetual beer bust. Most fellows on campus are still looking for the girl they want to marry, and it isn't going to be the b********** who was quick to bed. When you read of students getting bombed on booze, remember you're getting a minority report.

V. Thou Shalt Plan to Commit Fun — and Often.

The world of academia has two extremes. There's the playboy who can't get a book open or the body to the library and there's the grind who never lives it up at all. You should expect to go on a real study binge, but the bookworm learns less than the fellow who knows how to make learning the leitmotif and still plays with abandon. American adults don't know how to play at all. Did they unlearn it in college?

VI. Thou Shalt Know at Least One Professor or One Dean Personally.

Even at the risk of seeming to make yourself a bore! But much more likely you will be welcomed as a student mature enough to relate to a mature person, and that will set both of you up. Invite him to the Union for coffee and he'll flip inwardly — but he'll go and he will be delighted by the invitation. At the small college this kind of relationship should come about readily, but often it doesn't. All the best universities are striving to make it happen more often. You can do this one yourself, and then say (but not to the prof or the dean), "This lowly freshman has solved the most pressing problem facing higher education in America today!" And you will be right.

VII. Thou Shalt Be Concerned.

But not simply with war on the other side of the world and the social causes of our day. Keep informed, and do what you think is right about these. But what about the cook, the maid in your dorm, the campus maintenance crew, and the night watchman? Just say, "We students appreciate you," and someone will go through the day as though it were Christmas.

VIII. Thou Shalt Be Selective.

Paper, yearbook, student government, fraternity and sorority, dances, ball games, bull sessions, dates, causes, movies, etc., etc., . . . the whole works! If you make them all, you're a bust; and if you miss them all, you're a dud. Don't spread yourself so thin that they would never miss you if you didn't show. But do choose a few, get involved, and get that good part of a college education which no classroom can ever provide.

IX. Thou Shalt Strive to Keep Healthy.

All that psychosomatic stuff has real substance. It isn't sin, it's lack of sleep that ruins so many college careers. Phys ed is required and that will get the body exercised, but there's no requirement that you eat sensibly and keep hours conducive to vigor. You will see many students just too jaded to play well or to study at all.

X. Thou Shalt Forget and Remember.

Take some time to sit down with yourself and recall those things of which you are ashamed and sorry — and then forget them. College is a new beginning, a clean slate, and all that. Burn your bad bridges. No one at college knows about that soiled baggage you've been carrying. Remember those relationships which have made life good. They were clean and decent, and to think of them is a lift. As a freshman, look back at those relationships which brought lasting joy and seek them again. Life is the fine art of forgetting — and remembering.

Well there they are, J.B. What's missing and what needs to be said better? If you forget them all, do remember the love of all of us here.

— Dad

1963

Critical thinking points: After you've read

1) The author talks about "soiled baggage" someone might bring to college. What kinds of things might he be talking about? How might someone "burn" their "bad bridges" ?
2) The author talks about "that good part of a college education which no

classroom can ever provide." What kinds of things do you think he is talking about, and what might be "good" about them?

3) *McCabe says, "American adults don't know how to play at all. Did they unlearn it in college?" Do you believe this is true? Why or why not? Speculate on the cultural influences that might allow a person to make this statement, especially in 1963. Is it true of present-day adults? Why or why not?*

4) *How does the father mask his advice to his son? How might the son respond to this letter? How would you respond if you received this from one of your parents?*

5) *There are both "do's" and "do not's" in McCabe's letter. What are some other common themes throughout these ten commandments?*

Some possibilities for writing

1) *The father asks, "What's missing and what needs to be said better?" What do you think? Rewrite this letter incorporating your thoughts.*

2) *Since 1963, what has changed in the world and at college? Incorporate those changes into an update of this letter from your contemporary perspective.*

3) *McCabe says, "You've got to get set for freedom; it isn't doing what comes naturally." Write about your first few weeks of "freedom" at college. How did you react to your freedom? Did you "get set" for it as the author advises? In what way?*

4) *Write a letter to your parents titled "Ten Commandments for the Parents of a College Freshman." Include both do's and do not's.*

5) *Choose one of the pieces of advice in this selection and try to convince someone that it is particularly good or bad advice.*

6) *Choose one of the pieces of advice in this selection and write at least a page that illustrates and/or explains how and why it is good or bad advice.*

7) *Research college Web sites and find more "advice columns" for college students. How do McCabe's ten commandments compare to the other advice pieces you've found?*

My First Week at Mizzou

from Another Year in the Life of a Nerd

Andrew Hicks

---- 66 ----

I have only one class on Fridays, the omnipresent Spanish class, so that leaves plenty of time for leisure, studying, and keeping up on letter correspondence. . . . Okay, you got me, I slept all afternoon.

---- 99 ----

Critical thinking points: As you read

1) Pay attention to the tones and the attitudes of the journal. What elements of the writing contribute to these tones?

2) One of the first things writers should consider is their "purpose" and "audience." What do you think the purpose and audience of this piece are? What elements lead you to think the way you do?

3) Recall your experience of first coming to campus. How is your experience different from Hicks' experience? How is it similar?

4) What are some of the stereotypes you associate with nerds? Why? Does the narrator conform to or violate any of these? Is he really a nerd?

August 22, 1995

The first day of the end of my life. Yes, the college experience has begun for your favorite nerd and so far it hasn't been that much different from the high school experience, except that I am now completely independent, miles from home and — oh yeah — stone cold drunk. No, of course I'm not. That statement was incorrect. I'm actually *fall-down* drunk. That last statement was also incorrect, as I've obviously never been drunk in my life. I've been exempt from peer pressure thus far in my life, except for the time those guys got me hooked on phonics, a habit I haven't been able to break since. Still, who knows what will happen to me now that I'm stuck

As of 1999, Andrew Hicks (b. 1978) was a senior and journalism major at the University of Missouri–Columbia. Andrew traces his ostracism from popular society to the age of 5, when he was moved up to first grade after a month of kindergarten. "Apparently, I was finger painting and taking naps on a higher level than the other kids." Andrew's four "Years in the Life" comedy diaries have garnered critical praise from *Netsurfer Digest* and *The Web*.

on the grounds of a large state university, open and susceptible to all forms of temptation. I may even convert from the original "Star Trek" to "Star Trek: The Next Generation."

Dorm life, obviously, is my first experience of living in close quarters with another person, if you don't count the year and a half I was shacked up with "Golden Girl" Estelle Getty. I'd be remiss if I didn't take up valuable space in the book berating my roommate, but he's actually a pretty nice guy. A quiet guy, too. Keeps to himself. At least that's what the neighbors will tell the police after he kills me in my sleep. Think I'm being paranoid? Then you haven't seen the stack of *Soldier of Fortune* magazines, the poster of the Army guy carrying an automatic gun, the American flag hanging over the bed. Now are you starting to see the scenario? I own several Japanese electronic products, including the laptop computer I'm typing this on. What if this militant patriot decides to make sure I never buy foreign again? Still, he's probably just a normal American teenager, hence the Kathy Ireland poster on the wall. Of course, she's fully-clothed, so maybe he's not so normal after all.

At least my roommate passed one TV compatibility test, the one that asks "Do you like 'America's Funniest Home Videos'?" I could never voluntarily share a room with someone who found Bob Saget amusing. I still have to see about a second TV compatibility test, this one concerning late-night talk show hosts. As far as I'm concerned, there are two kinds of people in the world, the Letterman people and the Leno people. I've only met one Conan person in my life, but this was a McCluer student named Sumar who had continuing flashbacks to Woodstock '94, so that tells you something. My family and I are all staunch Letterman men, but of course my two best friends are Leno people, so what good does that test do? See, I've been here one day and already my theories on life are falling apart.

August 24, 1995

Today was the first day of classes. My first class on Mondays, Wednesdays and Fridays doesn't start until 10:40, but since I made no attempt to conceal that fact from my employers, I had to get up bright and early this morning to serve people their heart attacks.

The one good thing about getting up at 6:30 is that there aren't any other people using the showers. As you may imagine, with an ample body like mine, I'll never be president of the Public Showers Fan Club. I am grateful that there are stalls to separate the showers, but I still sometimes accidentally reveal too much, as evidenced a few days ago, when somebody said, "Hey, that pasty white shower curtain has a crack in it." Of course it wasn't a shower curtain, but I didn't tell the guy that.

The stalls are only shoulder high, so even though certain parts are strategically concealed, you still have to make small talk with the other people in the shower room. I've already found out saying "nice penis" doesn't cut it as far as small talk goes. And I've also found out, darn the luck, that coed dorms don't mean coed showers. *Animal House*, you lied to me!

At 10:40 I was off to Spanish class, which I had thought would be my first challenging Spanish class. After all, it had taken both ounces of my brain power to test into Spanish 2 during the Summer Welcome. Once I got to class, though, and heard the jocks and frat boys saying *"Como . . . uh . . . my llama . . . uh . . ."* I canceled any previous thoughts regarding the degree of difficulty.

My other class today was an Honors class regarding the study of the book of Revelation and other apocalyptic literature, a subject I've always found fascinating, to the point where I've actually watched the 1973 Christian movie *A Thief in the Night* more than once. Enduring a movie that bad more than once should automatically save anyone's soul from hell.

Even though the University policy states that instructors can't do anything but discuss the semester syllabus (syllabi, in the plural) on the first day, but both classes did assign homework. For the Revelation class I have to walk up to complete strangers on the street and record their opinions on how the world would end, which isn't exactly a casual icebreaker for conversation. I might as well be asking them to imagine their sweet grannies burning in hellfire for all eternity.

August 25, 1995

I went to my remaining three classes today and, let me tell you, it ain't gonna be that hard for me this semester. Part of that stems from the fact that my English class centers strictly on autobiographical writing. See what I mean? All I ever do is write about myself. If only the class had been even more specific and focused on humorous autobiographical writing, I would have been set for life. But I'm sure the instructor has a sense of humor. You should have seen the suspenders he was wearing.

Three of my "instructors" are full-fledged professors, not bad for freshman courses at a large state school. The other two instructors are ambitious grad students, including my Spanish teacher, who insists on the annoying habit of speaking in Spanish all the time. She said yesterday that if you want to be good at playing football, you play football. And if you want to be good at speaking Spanish, you speak Spanish. Or something like that. I'm not sure about the exact explanation because she said it in Spanish. See, it's a no-win situation. Excuse me, *es un no-gana situacion*.

Psychology class should prove to be interesting for the mere fact that it consists of over 500 students. I have a sneaking suspicion I'm the only person in the class and the other 499 were just extras brought in for an experiment to see how I would react to the crowd. I was clever enough to anticipate that scenario and decided to throw off the results by jumping up and down, yelling "Mickey Mouse is in my pocket! You can't have him! None of you! Stand back, I have a light saber!" What I didn't anticipate was the appearance of the Mizzou police five minutes later to haul me away.

Last night we had a meeting of all the guys in my dorm. Seeing all the people I live with all at once made one thing perfectly clear to me — I have to keep my door locked at all times. As far as roommate relations go, there have been no significant developments. The guy just doesn't talk. And he keeps putting up more of the gun/military posters, the latest featuring a skull with criss-crossed guns, reading "Mess with the best, die like the rest." Oh yeah, one more thing — I haven't been sleeping too well either.

August 26, 1995

I have only one class on Fridays, the omnipresent Spanish class, so that leaves plenty of time for leisure, studying and keeping up on letter correspondence. . . . Okay, you got me, I slept all afternoon. I think I was entitled, though, after getting up at 6:30 this morning to work in the dining hall. I am gradually getting the hang of proper food-handling procedures, as today I only contaminated the food with two deadly bacteria instead of the usual three.

My first dining hall shift was a barbecue picnic at the football field, where — it has been constantly mentioned — the Astroturf has been replaced by real grass. What they didn't mention was that we were serving the Astroturf on buns with barbecue sauce for dinner. Apparently, all the rules about hygiene outlined at the orientation meeting don't apply to outdoor meals. The swarm of flies swimming in the cole slaw clued me in to that fact. Towards the end of the evening, the flies had actually constructed a miniature waterslide leading into the cold slaw and were taking turns sliding down the damn thing.

This is the first Friday night here on campus and I imagine there's plenty of drinking going on. I myself have had two pitchers of Brita filtered water, so watch out! You can tell I've loosened up out here. I used to drink only tap water, but the water here has so much lead in it there's a pencil sharpener attached to the sink.

It's been an exciting Friday night for me. A trip to the laundry room and the computer lab in the same evening. I thought the computer lab would be fairly empty due to it being Friday night and all but the first time I went in the computers were all in use. "Why aren't you people out getting drunk?" I demanded. "Leave the computer room to dorks like me who have nothing better to do." But no one budged. Oh well, I can always come back later to coerce preteen girls over the Internet.

August 29, 1995

Although there's not much spiritual conviction to be found in most Mizzou students (their philosophy in life centers more around "two boobs and a brewski" than the Bible), there are still quite a few Christian organizations on campus, many of which go to great lengths to attract students' attention. Today, for example, there was a street preacher yelling at the top of his lungs at one intersection about "fornication" and "hay-ell," with the traditional evangelist flair, the kind of college student who would be more at home at Oral Roberts University than a large state school.

As I was walking past this spectacle, I overheard a girl commenting. She was a Jim Morrison–worshiping vampire clone with purple hair and a nose ring. She said three words concerning the street preacher: "That guy's weird." I considered stopping and pointing out the full irony of the girl's comment but decided against it.

My week at Mizzou has proven to me that there are quite a few people out there who stretch the bounds of "normal," whatever that may be defined as. Today in my Revelation course a group of students reported back on their interviews with people about their opinions on the world's end. Although most respondents did have the traditional Rapture / Tribulation / Antichrist / Armageddon beliefs or the naturalistic science-geek perspective of the earth ending due to "cyclical forces," there were some that just couldn't be classified.

One person thought the earth would literally shrink to one-eighth its original size and people would have to push each other off into space to retain their position, until the only people left were murderers whom God would cast into hell. Of course, this guy's brain has probably shrunk to one-eighth its original size. . . . Another person, a Black power advocate, said that, due to negligence by white supremacists, the ozone hole would widen, giving all white people skin tumors. Only people of African origin would survive. I think this guy must have graduated from McCluer.

The professor then told us of a book manuscript with conclusive proof that the world would end on November 14, 1999, to which one person responded, "Do we get off class for it?" A humorous exchange I had nothing to do with but nevertheless felt compelled to transcribe so maybe I can sell it to *Reader's Digest* one day.

1995

Critical thinking points: After you've read

1) Why would/does anyone keep a journal? What do you think would be some of the advantages of doing so?

2) What might be some of the differences between keeping a journal for yourself or "going on-line" with one? Pay attention not only to what you would say but how you would say it.

3) Imagine the author reading his journal some ten or twenty years in the future. What do you think he will think and/or feel about it then?

Some possibilities for writing

1) Create or recreate your own journal of your first few days of classes.

2) Imagine you are one of the characters that appears in this journal and rewrite one or more of the scenes from that character's point of view.

3) Write about the funniest incident that happened to you since getting to campus. Now write about the saddest or most disappointing incident.

4) Read or reread Jennifer Hale's "Hunters and Gatherers." Compare and contrast Hicks' personality to Hale's. Is she a "nerd"? Why or why not? Can only males be nerds?

5) Research the characteristics of your Freshman class. After finding out as much as you can about such things as race, ethnicity, financial background, high school class rank, and ACT or SAT scores, write a profile of the class.

6) *The same as above, but consult the most recent on-line edition of the* Chronicle of Higher Education *and write a report on how your school's profile compares to that of other universities.*

an excerpt from
Diary of a Freshman

Charles Macomb Flandreau

"

I was careful not to say that I had failed or flunked, or hadn't passed, as that was not the impression I wished to convey.

"

Critical thinking points: As you read

1) What is a "double entendre"? How is this technique used in this piece?
2) Pay attention to the attitude and tone of the advisor and the student. What do you think each was trying to accomplish?
3) This scene took place on a college campus almost one hundred years ago. What are some things that are still true of college students? What are some things that are still true of advisors and administrators?

My advisor is a young man and seems like an appreciative, well-disposed sort of person (he offered me a cigar after I had sat down in his study), so I didn't have any difficulty in telling him right off what I had come for.

"I've heard from my hour examinations," I said, "and I find that I have been given *E* in all of them." (I was careful not to say that I had failed or flunked, or hadn't passed, as that was not the impression I wished to convey.)

"We have met the enemy and we are theirs," he answered pleasantly. "Yes, I heard about that," he went on, "and I hoped you would come in to see me." Then he waited awhile — until the clock began to get noisy — and at last he glanced up and said —

"What was it doing when you came in? It looked like snow this afternoon." But I hadn't gone there to discuss meteorology, so I ignored his remark.

"I can scarcely think I could have failed in everything," I suggested.

"It *is* somewhat incredible, isn't it?" the young man murmured.

Charles Macomb Flandreau (1871–1938), born in Minnesota, was a newspaperman, a writer, and a Harvard graduate who wrote memoirs of his college days "embodied" in a series of satiric stories found in *Harvard Episodes* (1897) and *Diary of a Freshman* (1901).

"I never stopped writing from the time an examination began until it stopped," I said.

"What did you think it was — a strength test?" he asked brutally.

"I told all I knew."

"Yes," he acknowledged; "your instructors were convinced of that."

"And I don't think I got enough credit for it. If I had the books here, I feel sure I could make this plain."

"Well, let's look them over," he answered readily; and much to my astonishment he went to his desk and brought back all my blue-books.

I confess I hadn't expected anything quite so definite as this, but I tried to appear as if I had hoped that it was just what might happen. We sat down side by side and read aloud — first an examination question (he had provided himself with a full set of the papers) and then my answer to it.

"Explain polarized light," he read.

"The subject of polarized light, as I understand it, is not very well understood." I began; at which my adviser put his hands to his head and rocked to and fro.

"If you don't mind," I said, "I think I'd rather begin on one of the others; this physics course is merely to make up a condition, and perhaps I've not devoted very much time to it; it isn't a fair test." So we took up the history paper and read the first question, which was: "What was the Lombard League?" My answer I considered rather neat, for I had written: "The Lombard League was a coalition formed by the Lombards." I paused after reading it and glanced at my adviser.

"It was a simple question, and I gave it a simple answer," I murmured.

"I'm afraid you depreciate yourself, Mr. Wood," he replied. "Your use of the word 'coalition' is masterly."

"But what more could I have said?" I protested.

"I don't think you could have said *anything* more," he answered inscrutably.

I read on and on, and he interrupted me only twice — once in the philosophy course to point out politely that what I constantly referred to as "Hobbe's Octopus" ought to be "Hobbe's Leviathan," and once in the questions in English Literature, to explain that somebody or other's "*Apologia Pro Vita Sua*" was not — as I had translated it — "an apology for living in a sewer." (I could have killed Berrisford for that — and it sounded so plausible, too; for any one who lived in a sewer would naturally apologize.) He let me proceed, and after a time I couldn't even bring myself to stop and contest the decisions as I had done at first; for I dreaded the way he had of making my most serious remarks sound rather childish. So I rattled on, faster and faster, until I found myself mumbling in a low tone, without pronouncing half the words; and then I suddenly stopped and put the blue-book on the table and stared across the room at the wall. He didn't express any surprise, which, on the whole, was very decent of him, and after a minute or two of silence, during which he gathered up the evidence and put it back in his desk, we began to talk football and our chances of winning the big game. He said some nice things about Duggie, and hoped the rumor that he was overtrained wasn't true. I told him that I lived in the same house with

Duggie and knew him very well, and feared it was true. He seemed glad that I knew Duggie. I stayed for about fifteen minutes so as not to seem abrupt or angry at the way my visit had turned out, and then left. We didn't refer to the exams again, so I don't see exactly how I can ever right the wrong they have done me. If my adviser were a different kind of man, I could have managed it, I think.

1901

Critical thinking points: After you've read

1) Can you discover from this dialogue any of the reasons the student may have failed his exams? What are some of them?
2) The narrator says, "I told all I knew." "Yes," his advisor says. "Your instructors were convinced of that." Why do you think the advisor treated the student in the way he did? What does the advisor wish to accomplish?
3) Do you believe the student actually learned anything from this encounter? Why or why not? What might the student have learned?

Some possibilities for writing

1) Have you ever found yourself in a situation similar to this one? Write the scene.
2) Imagine you were going to film this scene. Write it as if it were a film script. Now update the scene to the present day. What might change about the characters and their dialogue?
3) Failing is one thing, but coming to terms with your failure is even more difficult. Write about a time when it was hard for you to face your failure.
4) Interview your advisor about what he or she feels to be the advisor's role. How much does your advisor feel he or she can and/or should do for advisees? How much are students expected to do for themselves?
5) Research and write a report on the various kinds of formal and informal advising available to students at your school.

Hunters and Gatherers

Jennifer Hale

"

Not knowing what to expect for college, I was poorly prepared. I have not brought with me the special tools required for a successful transition to college life.

"

Critical thinking points: As you read

1) What kind of student is the author? What specifically from the journal do you base your opinion on?

2) Each college student brings his or her unique perspective to college. What is the author's perspective? What is yours?

3) Consider how the author "learned" her course work as she wrote in her journal. Have you ever used this technique of applying course work to your personal life?

Due to the fact that I am currently a history major I have the extreme pleasure of learning the same thing in three classes. In Anthropology, US History and World History all my professors are talking about pre-historical societies and hunting/gathering groups as a foundation for the classes. This is highly beneficial for a person who selectively attends class such as I. I can take notes for one class and still do well in the others. However lackadaisical this approach may seem I have still learned a great deal. In studying hunting and gathering societies I have found parallels to my own life.

In a hunting and gathering society the food-getting strategies involve the collection of "naturally" occurring plants and animals. In this type of community there are little economic practices. Except for the occasional bartering there is no currency exchange. Primitive societies like this one are also extremely superstitious, having natural gods that provide for people and are also feared by the clan.

"Hunters and Gatherers" is an excerpt from a journal Jennifer Hale (b. 1977) kept for an Introduction to College Learning Strategies course.

Maybe the connection is not clear to you, so I will give examples.

> ***In hunting/gathering societies the food getting strategies involve
> the collection of naturally occurring plants and animals.***

Not knowing what to expect for college, I was poorly prepared. I have not brought with me the special tools required for a successful transition to college life. These "tools" would be things like tape, nail-polish remover, highlighter, and, of course, sleeping pills. Fortunately I live in a very fertile and lush place where these things are easily attainable. However, like primitive societies, I must make offerings to the God that provides these needed "tools," namely my roommate Karen. I try to use naturally occurring products when Karen is out of the room so not to anger her but sometimes a complimentary can of Coke helps to keep the peace. Another item that I find I can't live without is cereal. Luckily for me Karen thinks all food goes bad a week after it is bought (an idea I introduced into her puny skull) so she often throws out perfectly good food. At this point I do "creative hunting/gathering" by removing the good trash (cereal) and throw the bad trash down the trash shoot. This way I am not stealing the food only recycling it. I also get points for taking out the garbage.

> ***In this type of community there are little economic practices.
> Except for the occasional bartering there is no currency exchange.***

Besides prison, maybe college life is the most cash free environment alive today. However true this may be, there is still a free exchange of goods. Since money is used for tobacco, alcohol, and weed, other ways of obtaining goods must be developed. After all, necessity is the mother of invention. The use of CDs from a neighbor might involve the use of one of your good sweaters. Term papers can be bought for carpeting, and let's not underplay the value of sexual favors.

> ***Primitive societies also are extremely superstitious,
> having natural gods that both provide for the clan and are feared by it.***

I can't stress the importance of abusing your roommate enough. Hey, the way I see it, this college thing is an egalitarian society, and we all should share. Or at least that's what I tell myself as I am eating out of the trash. However wonderful this might seem there are prices to pay. Like tuition.

1996

Critical thinking points: After you've read

1) *In what other ways might first-year students become "hunters and gatherers"? How else might they be described?*
2) *In addition to concrete tools the author mentions, what kinds of personal skills are needed to make the transition to college life? Does this student possess any of those?*

3) *Read or reread Andrew Hicks' "My First Week at Mizzou." How is Hale similar to Hicks? How is she different?*

4) *Does Hale's approach of "learning" her coursework as she wrote in her journal work in some courses better than others? Why?*

Some possibilities for writing

1) *Build on Hale's list of the tools necessary for college life. Make it your own personal list, however far-fetched.*

2) *Hale says, "Not knowing what to expect for college, I was poorly prepared." Write briefly about one way you have already realized you were the most poorly prepared for college. What steps should you be prepared to take to rectify this situation?*

3) *Use specific course work from one of your classes and find parallels to your personal or social life in the way the author of "Hunters and Gatherers" does. Some possibilities might include concepts you've learned in your courses in psychology, sociology, economics, or any other social science field.*

4) *Hale and her roommate have what might be called a "symbiotic relationship"; that is, as the dictionary defines it, "A close, prolonged association between two or more different organisms of different species that may, but does not necessarily, benefit each member." Write, either as fiction or nonfiction, about two other roommates who seem to have such a relationship.*

Waiting for Daylight

Linda Mannheim

——————————— 66 ———————————

I felt Dale's hand come near me, and I ignored it at first, because I knew what was happening should not have been happening, so I ignored it, but then his hand was very close to my chest, and, automatically, my hand shot up to stop his.

——————————— 99 ———————————

Critical thinking points: As you read

1) Speculate, as you read, on some implications of the title. What situations cause a person to be "waiting for daylight"?

2) Mary Vega chose Stockton College because of the lifestyle that was promoted in its catalogue: students who were clean, happy, loved, and, most of all, rich. What does this say about Mary?

3) What kind of an image, if any, did you have of your school before you came to it? Did the material you received from the school or comments you heard from other people contribute to that image?

It's true I remember noon in Stockton as blinding — waking up groggy and hurting, pushing the covers aside and lifting the shade the only time sun shone there in winter time. The walk to McCusker's was all a blur. I always charged along the January sidewalks angry and fast, taking the wind against me personally. The snow was gray from the soot of car exhaust. The ice melted and reformed in slick, sharp puddles I accidentally walked into, soaking my sneakers with painfully cold runoff. Then, in McCusker's, I welcomed the steamy windows and the smell of bacon fat. The other regulars nodded to me. Jimmy Sloane, the landlord and coke dealer who had gone to Stockton College and never left town, holding court at one of the booths and regarding everyone else with the knowledge of a man who owned the town; Avery Todd, damp-haired and looking over her paper at the man damp-haired across

Linda Mannheim (b. 1962) has a B.A. in English from New England College and an M.F.A. in Creative Writing from the University of Massachusetts, Amherst. One of her goals as a student was to take classes in as many different countries as possible. Her writing has appeared in *Gettysburg Review*, *Alfred Hitchcock Mystery Magazine*, *Sojourner*, and *Bridges*.

from her too, a different boy every time; and Louis Scott, who, like me, was just a little too strange to fit in at the college and took his coffee alone — they were all there.

I had chosen Stockton College based on the pictures in its catalogue — happy, slightly hippy looking students smiling before a torch-red background of New England leaves, leaning back against stone walls as they read, walking with friends across the town's covered bridge and then sitting ruddy-faced in the school's snackbar sipping cocoa after, I assumed, the earlier walk across the bridge. They looked clean and happy and loved, and, most of all, rich, and I'd wanted to be one of them.

Stockton College had chosen me based on my ability to con, or so I believed. They could not have chosen me based on my high school grades, because I had dropped out of high school, and, instead, after spending two years on the road and taking my GED, presented them with an essay outlining the best Laundromats to sleep in between Albany and Cape Cod. "Brilliant," said Dale Curran, the school's academic dean, when I showed up for my campus interview. He'd asked me if I'd read any Jack Kerouac. I lied and said I had. He told me the school could come up with some scholarship money to make up the difference between my basic grant and student loan, should I decide to go there. Tuition at Stockton College cost more than anyone I knew made in a year. I looked around at the campus, the verdant, lush lawns then preening in the August air. I walked through the solid, stone dormitories, certain they would be warm and easy in winter. Students at Stockton College were all given private rooms — not sharing anything except cocaine in the bathroom between classes. I said I would be happy to attend Stockton College in the fall.

Very quickly I discovered that Stockton College needed me as much as I needed it. Stockton was where rich kids got sent when they fucked up too much to go anywhere else. At Stockton's tiny classes, I was one of the few students who showed up for lectures, and one of the fewer who spoke during seminars and wrote papers. I quickly began to draw more attention to myself than felt healthy, and, as a result, I needed to go to the pub at night in order to fit in, downing shots of tequila until everything but me and Avery Todd faded.

Avery was startlingly beautiful, tall and dark-haired, with eyes so devastatingly deep, no one could stare at them for too long — it was that dangerous. Avery wore heels to accentuate her height and red lipstick that made her large, laughing mouth seem positively elastic. "Wouldn't wish someone here sober," she would say, after looking around the damp basement bar and before knocking back a V and T, what she'd taken to calling vodka and tonics.

"Damn straight," I'd agree, downing another shot.

"Next time my daddy says it's Stockton or Siberia," she continued, "I'll take Siberia."

Avery was from an oil rich Texas family who hadn't acted kindly when she'd taken to the Houston streets trying life under an assumed name to keep them back. She'd slipped into the arms of a lover who she spoke of constantly, but had never seen again after a nasty bust, during which the cops found her and her lover Michael with lines of liquid sky all cut to go. Michael, older than Avery, was somewhere doing time while Avery was let go after an in-patient detox stint and signed up at school. The judge said it was okay after Avery's father had slipped him five thousand dollars. Avery's parents stuck her in Stockton with no spare cash, fearing she'd spend it on drugs, and, as a result, Avery became a bar fly hustler extraordinaire. "Querida, querida, querida," she'd say, sidling up to some shy preppy boy who wriggled beneath her touch. "You getting something? Get me something too. I don't have any money. My father doesn't love me."

"Jesus," I said to Avery. "What're you complaining about? He bought you a frigging judge."

"This girl doesn't understand anything," Avery explained to that evening's boy, as she gestured towards me. "Just right out of New York City's gutters, isn't that right, hon?"

It was one of those stupid things that Avery only said when she was very drunk, so I figured the best thing to do was walk away. I walked right into Dale Curran, the academic dean at the college, who said to me, "Hey, it's Mary Vega!"

"Hello," I said.

I was not at all surprised to see him there. We were in the only bar in town.

"Mary, your professors are saying great things about you."

"They are?" I asked. Unlike Avery, I did sometimes like the town's smallness — that everyone, having to live together, crossed the lines that would normally be between someone like Dale and me.

Dale sat near the door like a father wanting to ask where each of his children was going, his prematurely gray hair hanging in damp bangs against his forehead, a man from the 1960s who wore his suit and his age awkward, like he wanted to tear them both off. He had a trick eye that never focused like the other one, and as I watched his face now, I wondered whether one eye was glass.

"It's cold out there," he said, motioning to the door with his head.

I smiled and shrugged.

"Whyn't you have a seat?"

I stared at the empty seat next to Dale. If I sat there, he would feel compelled to buy my drinks. Avery, remarkably, could manage to hustle drinks for both of us. "Buy a drink for my friend too," she would whisper, tracing her long, red nails against the broadcloth backed buttons of a man's shirt. And it almost always worked, as if she was buying for me by proxy, but now I was on my own. I sat.

"What can I get you?" Dale asked.

"Tequila sunrise," I said, surprised to find my voice was a whisper.

"Well, well," Dale laughed. "Mary Vega. I remember when I could drink tequila all night. Who says that youth is wasted on the young?"

I smiled and lifted my drink when the bar tender brought it, touching my glass to Dale's as he brought his to mine, downing half of it in a gulp and wishing the sweetness lasted longer than the bitterness.

"Aren't you going to take your coat off?" he asked.

"I'm cold," I answered, unable to get my voice loud again.

"Ah yes," Dale answered. "Those damned New Hampshire winters. You can't get them out of your blood."

I nodded.

"Something wrong?" he asked.

"No," I answered. "Nothing's wrong."

"Just the winter blues then," he said reassuringly. "I get them too."

I tried to smile, looked behind me, back where Avery was dancing with the awkward preppy boy, moving all over him like she was god and wind and the boy was just a lamp-post. Avery never dressed like she was cold, came down to the bar dressed in a tight black T-shirt and light cotton skirt, leaving trails of patchouli to take over the stale beer air.

"Mary," he said. "I've been wanting to talk to you because I admire your sense of poetry, and there's so little to admire this time of year, and so little poetry in this town. I used to write too, you know."

"You did?" I asked.

"Now look at me. I'm just an administrator in a shit town college."

It was funny to hear Dale use the word "shit," as if someone else had lent it to him, but he didn't own it. I was drunk enough so I even laughed a little. Dale looked disturbed, and I immediately felt a little bit bad, as if all I could do that night was hurt people, not hard, but with the impact of a ballpoint pen accidentally jabbed.

"This isn't the greatest place," I said quickly.

"How do you like it?" he asked.

"Me?" I asked. "It's all right."

He sneered.

"It's not bad," I fished.

"Not bad," he repeated. "Not bad for who?"

"Me, I guess," I whispered again.

"No," he answered. "It can't be good for you either. Look at what it's doing to you. When you came here, you were all yourself. Now you're turning into one of them."

"What do you mean?" I asked, slightly hurt.

"You were loud and meaningful," he said. Then hunting for something in the pocket of his sports jacket, and coming up with a packet of cigarettes, he continued, "You had style, charisma."

The word charisma didn't work for him either. He said it like a man speaking a foreign language from a phrase book.

"And that great accent."

"Accent?" I asked.

He laughed out the side of his mouth. "People with accents never know they have accents."

He switched the subject to William Carlos Williams, and Williams' love of immigrants. I was hungry to talk poetry. "Where are your people from?" he slipped in.

"New York," I answered.

He raised one eyebrow, the one over the eye that moved.

"My father's Cuban," I said at last, giving him the answer he wanted.

"Do you speak Spanish?" he asked me.

"No," I told him.

The he veered again back to poetry. And we talked poetry during the rest of the night that came, the boys who played la crosse on the lawns leaving in a group, the girls who skied walking along in disappointment to a midnight clear without promise of snow, and finally Avery giggling as the boy in the broadcloth shirt followed. "Goodnight," she whispered, to both Dale and me, and as she went, I recognized that moment was my last hope, like a life preserver being pulled in so that only the gray of sea stretched in icy peaked waves.

The lights flickered for the final warning on last call.

"Can I give you a ride home?" Dale asked.

"Yes," I said, when I heard Avery's steps end at the top of the flight of stairs.

We walked out into the dark parking lot, lit occasionally by cars pulling out. He fished in his pockets and came up with an empty packet of cigarettes.

"Do you mind?" he asked, showing me the empty packet. "I have a carton in my office. Can we stop there first?"

"Of course," I said.

He led me to a beat up Volkswagen, laughed as I was about to get in. "Just kidding," he said, then unlocked the door of the new BMW parked next to it.

We drove down the vacant streets to the administration building, the smell of cigarettes and leather seats thick in the air. "Come in," he said, when we arrived. "I want to show you something."

The administration building at night was frightening, enormous and gothic, and Dale did not turn the lights on. We felt our way to his office with hands against the wall, squinting in the dim shadows lit by the single street-light from the main street. When we arrived in his office and he flicked the switch, the light was blinding, and I stood for a minute letting my eyes adjust. Avery was in the warm cave of her room with the boy, showing him what she called her womb room, the tapestries softening the hard walls. She'd slip her shirt off giggling, undo the skirt, fall with him on the feather eiderdown her mother had ordered for her from Germany. She'd light the candles she wasn't supposed to have in her room, put on an old Billie Holliday album, humming like Lady Day. Avery, one big fire hazard.

My eyes focused on the skull Dale kept on a shelf. He took it down, showed it to me, his pale, awkward hands more awkward with drunkenness. He said something about a romantic poet thrown out of college for drinking from a skull — I don't remember. Then the room began to move slightly, like an image in a slide projector the projectionist has not found the right height for, slipping then stopping, again and again.

"Sit," said Dale. "You look dizzy."

I sat in the leather seat across from the couch far from his desk. He placed the skull back on the shelf.

"They were all cut off from the others," he said. "Byron for being a madman and H.D. for being a lesbian."

I nodded as if I knew what he was talking about.

"Are you a lesbian?" he asked.

I stared at him.

"Avery," he threw in. "You're in love with her, aren't you?"

And if anyone, if anyone else at all would have said that to me then, I might have said yes, it's true. But instead, Dale Curran asked, like a threat, so I told him, "We're friends."

"Of course," he told me.

He went to the desk, pulled a carton of cigarettes from a drawer, took a packet out, tapped the packet against the desk, opened it. He lit one with a lighter he pulled from his pocket, then sat on the couch across from me. "This is as good a time as any," he said, "to let you know that there's one dean's scholarship to give out for next year, and I want to see to it that you're the one who has it."

"Thank you," I whispered.

"I know you can't keep coming here without it."

He looked at his cigarette for a moment, as if it would provide him with the next thing he needed to know.

"Mary," he said, continuing the transfixion with what burned. "Tell me how you feel about this college."

"I like it," I told him quickly.

"Tell me how you feel about me."

I looked outside, wishing it was light already, wishing it was high noon, wishing I was walking into McCusker's hung over and wanting coffee, and seeing everyone I knew — Jimmy Sloane rubbing his nose, Louis Scott lonely, and, most of all, Avery Todd rubbing her red-nailed fingertips against the moisture on the window, drawing a space that she could look out, so she would see the world through condensation. And while I was thinking this, I felt Dale's hand come near me, and I ignored it at first, because I knew what was happening should not have been happening, so I ignored it, but then his hand was very close to my chest, and, automatically, my hand shot up to stop his.

He shook my hand off.

"Carol Lynley," he said, "was a movie star who used to play street kids who thought they knew everything, but she looked so innocent, nothing could touch her. Nothing can touch you, Mary."

He reached for my chest again, and again, I tried to stop him, and again, he shook me off, harder this time. Then he had his hand down the front of my shirt and he said to me — He said, "You really don't get it, do you?"

1992

Critical thinking points: After you've read

1) *What details in the story help you have a better understanding of what the title might mean?*
2) *Why does Mary feel that she's "just a little too strange to fit in at the college"? What makes her "strange" or different from the other students?*
3) *What other characters in the pieces collected here may have felt out of place at a school like Stockton?*
4) *In what ways are Mary's and Dale's reactions to one another propelled by what they think the other is like?*
5) *When Mary and Dale leave the bar together he leads her to a beat-up Volkswagen and laughs as she is about to get in. Mannheim writes, "'Just kidding,' he said, then unlocked the door of the new BMW parked next to it." Why do you think Dale does this to Mary? Does it say anything about the type of person he is?*
6) *What is Dale looking for in Mary? Is it just sex? What do Mary and Dale have in common?*
7) *What might Dale mean when he says to Mary at the end of the story, "You really don't get it, do you?" Does she really not "get it"?*

Some possibilities for writing

1) *Write the scene the next day. How does Mary react to her episode with Dale? Does she tell Avery about it?*
2) *Have you ever felt out of place on campus? What led to your feeling that way? Describe the scene.*
3) *Dale repeats to Mary the old cliché, "Who says that youth is wasted on the young?" Do you think "youth" is wasted on the "young"? Why or why not?*
4) *Read or reread Jennifer Sheridan's "Carmen" and/or Cristina Salat's "50% Chance of Lightning." Compare Mary and Avery's relationship to that of Kate and Carmen in "Carmen" or to that of Robin and Malia in "50% Chance of Lightning."*
5) *Gather the kinds of materials — brochures, catalogues, handouts, and so on — that your school sends out to prospective first-year students and write an analysis of the material as "advertising." What kinds of images and information does your school try to communicate to prospective students? From your experience, how accurate is that information?*
6) *What are your school's policies on sexual harassment? Does Dale's interaction with Mary qualify as such? Why or why not? Write a brief report for your class on what students can/should do if they feel they have been sexually harassed.*

Grading Your Professors

Jacob Neusner

❝

Since professors stand at the center of the student's encounter with college learning, students ought to ask what marks a good professor, what indicates a bad one.

❞

Critical thinking points: As you read

1) Which statements in this essay do you strongly agree or disagree with? Which inspire you or make you angry?

2) While reading through this essay, recall teachers, classes, and/or experiences that illustrate what Neusner is talking about. What details in the essay remind you of those?

3) What makes a "scholar"? Are there specific qualifications for a person to become a scholar?

Since professors stand at the center of the student's encounter with college learning, students ought to ask what marks a good professor, what indicates a bad one. The one who sets high standards and persists in demanding that students try to meet them provides the right experiences. The professor who gives praise cheaply or who pretends to a relationship that does not and cannot exist teaches the wrong lessons. True, the demanding and critical teacher does not trade in the currency students possess, which is their power to praise or reject teachers. The demanding professor knows that students will stumble. But the ones who pick themselves up and try again — whether in politics or music or art or sports — have learned a lesson that will save them for a lifetime: A single failure is not the measure of any person, and success comes hard. A banal truth, but a truth all the same.

The only teacher who taught me something beyond information, who gave me something to guide my life, was the only teacher who read my work carefully and criticized it in detail. To that point everyone had given me *A's*. After that I learned to

Jewish scholar and author Jacob Neusner (b. 1932) has written nearly two hundred books on Judaism including several multivolume works; textbooks for children and college students; and books for the general reader. His impressive level of productivity inspired Roy Bongartz, in *Publishers Weekly*, to liken Neusner to "the inexhaustible pillar of salt that filled the waters of the seven seas in ancient legend." Neusner is currently retired in Florida.

criticize myself and not to believe the *A's*. The teacher who read my writing and corrected not so much the phrasing as the mode of thought — line by line, paragraph by paragraph, beginning to end — and who composed paragraphs as models for what I should be saying is the sole true teacher I ever had. But I did not need more than one, and neither do you.

I do not mean to suggest that for each one of us there is one perfect teacher who changes our lives and is the only teacher we need. We must learn from many teachers as we grow up and grow old; and we must learn to recognize the good ones. The impressive teacher of one's youth may want to continue to dominate — as teachers do — and may not want to let go. The great teacher is the one who wants to become obsolete in the life of the student. The good teacher is the one who teaches lessons and moves on, celebrating the student's growth. The Talmud relates the story of a disciple in an academy on high. The question is asked, "What happened in heaven that day?" The answer: "God clapped hands in joy saying, 'My children have vanquished me, my children have vanquished me.'" That is a model for the teacher — to enjoy losing an argument to a student, to recognize his or her contribution, to let the student surpass the teacher.

In the encounter with the teacher who takes you seriously, you learn to take yourself seriously. In the eyes of the one who sees what you can accomplish, you gain a vision of yourself as more than you thought you were. The ideal professor is the one who inspires to dream of what you can be, to try for more than you ever have accomplished before. Everyone who succeeds in life can point to such a teacher, whether in the classroom or on the sports field. It may be a parent, a coach, employer, grade school or high school or art or music teacher. It is always the one who cared enough to criticize, and stayed around to praise.

But what about college professors? To define an ideal for their work, let me offer guidelines on how to treat professors the way we treat students: to give grades.

Professors grade students' work. The conscientious ones spend time reading and thinking about student papers, inscribing their comments and even discussing with students the strengths and weaknesses of their work. But no professor spends as much time on grading students' work as students spend on grading their professors as teachers and as people. For from the beginning of a course ("Shall I register?") through the middle ("It's boring . . . shall I stick it out?") to the very end ("This was a waste of time."), the students invest time and intellectual energy in deciding what they think, both about how the subject is studied and about the person who presents it. Since effective teaching requires capturing the students' imagination, and since sharp edges and colorful ways excite imagination, the professor who is a "character" is apt, whether liked or disliked, to make a profound impression and perhaps also to leave a mark on the students' minds. The drab professors, not gossiped about and not remembered except for what they taught, may find that even what they taught is forgotten. People in advertising and public relations, politics and merchandising, know that. A generation raised on television expects to be manipulated and entertained.

Yet the emphasis on striking characteristics is irrelevant. Many students have no more sophistication in evaluating professors than they do in evaluating deodorants. This should not be surprising, since they approach them both in the same manner. The one who is "new, different, improved," whether a professor or a bar of soap, wins attention. In this context people have no way of determining good from bad. I once asked an airline pilot, "What is the difference between a good landing and a bad one?" He replied, "A good landing is any landing you can pick yourself up and walk away from." To this pilot, the landing is judged solely by its ultimate goal — safely delivering the plane's passengers. Can we tell when a teacher has safely delivered the student for the next stage of the journey? Can we define the differences between a good teacher and a bad one?

Students have their own definitions of *good* and *bad*, and professors generally have a notion of the meaning of students' grades. Let us consider how students evaluate their teachers, examining in turn the *A*, *B*, and *C* professors. We will begin at the bottom of one scale and work our way up. Let us at the same time consider what kind of student seeks which grade.

Grade C Professors

The first type is the *C* professor. This is the professor who registers minimum expectations and adheres to the warm-body theory of grading. If a warm body fills a seat regularly and exhibits vital signs, such as breathing at regular intervals, occasionally reading, and turning in some legible writing on paper, then cosmic justice demands, and the professor must supply, the grade of *C* or *Satisfactory*. The effort needed to achieve *F* or *No Credit* is considerably greater. One must do no reading, attend few class sessions, and appear to the world to be something very like a corpse.

The professor who, by the present criteria, earns a *C* respects the students' rights and gives them their money's worth. He or she sells them a used car, so to speak, that they at least can drive off the lot. At the very least the professor does the following:

1. Attends all class sessions, reaches class on time, and ends class at the scheduled hour.
2. Prepares a syllabus for the course and either follows it or revises it, so that students always know what topic is under (even totally confused) discussion.
3. Announces and observes scheduled office hours, so that students have access to the professor without groveling or special pleading, heroic efforts at bird-dogging, or mounting week-long treasure hunts.
4. Makes certain that books assigned for a course are on reserve in the library and sees to it that the bookstore has ample time in which to order enough copies of the textbooks and ancillary reading for a course.
5. Comes to class with a clear educational plan, a well-prepared presentation, a concrete and specific intellectual agenda.
6. Reads examinations with the care invested in them (certainly no more, but also no less) and supplies intelligible grades and at least minimal comments; or keeps

office hours for the discussion of the substance of the examination (but not the grade); and supplies course performance reports — all these as duty, not acts of grace.

These things constitute student rights. No student has to thank a professor for doing what he or she is paid to do, and these six items, at a minimum, are the prerequisites for professional behavior. They are matters of form, to be sure, but the grade *C* is deemed by (some) students to be a matter of good form alone; the warm-body theory of this grade applies to professors and students alike.

"Tell me my duty and I shall do it" are the words of the minimally prepared. Just as students of mediocre quality want to know the requirements and assume that if they meet them, they have fulfilled their whole obligation to the subject, so mediocre professors do what they are supposed to do. The subject is in hand; there are no problems. The *C* professor need not be entirely bored with the subject, but he or she is not apt to be deeply engaged by it.

Grade *C* professors may be entertaining, warm, and loving. Indeed, many of them must succeed on the basis of personality, because all they have to offer is the studied technology of attractive personalities. They may achieve huge followings among the students, keep students at the edge of their seats with jokes and banter, badger students to retain their interest, but in the end what they have sold, conveyed, or imparted to the students' minds is themselves, not their mode of thinking or analyzing. Why? Because *C* professors do not think much; they rely on the analysis of others.

Above all, the grade *C* professor has made no effort to take over and reshape the subject. This person is satisfied with the mere repetition, accurate and competent repetition to be sure, of what others have discovered and declared to be true. If this sort of professor sparks any vitality and interest in students, then he or she will remind students of their better high school teachers, the people who, at the very least, knew what they were talking about and wanted the students to know. At the end of a course, students should ask themselves, *Have I learned facts, or have I grasped how the subject works, its inner dynamic, its logic and structure?* If at the end students should be grateful — at least they have learned that much — but award the professor a polite *C*. For the professor has done little more than necessary.

Grade B Professors

A course constitutes a large and detailed statement on the nature of a small part of a larger subject, a practical judgment upon a particular field of study and how it is to be organized and interpreted. The grade of *B* is accorded to the student who has mastered the basic and fundamental modes of thought about, and facts contained within, the subject of a course.

The grade *B* professor is one who can present coherently the larger theory and logic of the subject, who will do more than is required to convey his or her ideas to the students and who will sincerely hope he or she is inspiring the minds of the students. *B* professors, as they continue to grow as scholars, are not very different from *A* professors; they might be described as teachers striving to become *A* professors. But they are definitely very different from *C* professors. Let us, then, move on to consider *A* professors, keeping in mind that *B* professors will probably become *A* professors.

Grade A Professors

Grade *A* professors are the scholar-teachers, a university's prized treasures among a faculty full of intangible riches. America has many faculties of excellence, groups of men and women who with exceptional intelligence take over a subject and make it their own, reshape it and hand it on, wholly changed but essentially unimpaired in tradition, to another generation.

The grade of *A* goes to student work that attends in some interesting way and with utmost seriousness to the center and whole of the subject of the course. Notice, I did not say that an *A* goes to the student who says something new and original. That is too much to hope, especially in studying a subject that for hundreds or thousands of years has appeared to the best minds as an intricate and difficult problem.

The grade *A* professors may have odd ideas about their subjects, but they are asking old-new questions, seeking fresh insight, trying to enter into the way in which the subject works, to uncover its logic and inner structure. What makes an effective high school teacher is confidence, even glibness. What makes an effective university teacher is doubt and dismay. The scholarly mind is marked by self-criticism and thirsty search; it is guided by an awareness of its own limitations and those of knowledge. The scholar-teacher, of whatever subject or discipline, teaches one thing: Knowledge is not sure but uncertain, scholarship is search, and to teach is to impart the lessons of doubt. What is taught is what we do not know.

On whom do you bestow a grade *A*? It is given to the professor who, stumbling and falling, yet again rising up and walking on, seeks both knowledge and the meaning of knowledge. It is to the one who always asks, *Why am I telling you these things? Why should you know them?* It is to the professor who demands ultimate seriousness for his or her subject because the subject must be known, who not only teaches but professes, stands for, represents, the thing taught. The grade *A* professor lives for the subject, needs to tell you about it, wants to share it. The Nobel Prize scientist who so loved biology that she gave her life to it even without encouragement and recognition for half a century of work, the literary critic who thinks getting inside a poem is entering Paradise, the historian who assumes the human issues of the thirteenth century live today — these exemplify the ones who are ultimately serious about a subject.

One who has made this commitment to a field of scholarship can be readily identified. This is the one full of concern, the one who commits upon the facts the act of advocacy, who deems compelling what others find merely interesting. The scholar-teacher is such because he or she conveys the self-evident, the obvious fact that facts bear meaning, constituting a whole that transcends the sum of the parts. True, to the world this sense of ultimate engagement with what is merely interesting or useful information marks the professor as demented, as are all those who march to a differ-ent drummer. What I mean to say is simple. Anybody who cares so much about what to the rest of the world is so little must be a bit daft. Why should such things matter so much — why, above all, things of the mind or the soul or the heart, things of nature and mathematics, things of structure and weight and stress, things of technol-ogy and science, society and mind? Professors often remember lonely childhoods (for my part, I don't). As adults, too, professors have to spend long hours by them-selves in their offices, reading books, or in their laboratories or at their computers, or just thinking all by themselves. That is not ordinary and commonplace behavior. This is what it means to march to a different drummer. A student earns an A when he or she has mastered the larger theory of the course, entered into its logic and mean-ing, discovered a different way of seeing. Like a professor, the student who through accurate facts and careful, critical thought seeks meaning, the core and center of the subject, earns the grade *A*.

Yet matters cannot be left here. I do not mean to promote advocacy for its own sake. Students have rights too, and one of these is the right to be left alone, to grow and mature in their own distinctive ways. They have the right to seek their way, just as we professors find ours. The imperial intellect, the one that cannot allow autonomy, is a missionary, not a teacher. Many compare the imperial teacher with the *A* profes-sor, but if you look closely at their different ways of teaching, you will see that this is an error. The teacher leads, says, "Follow me," without looking backward. The mis-sionary pushes, imposes self upon another autonomous self. This is the opposite of teaching, and bears no relevance to learning or to scholarship. The teacher persuades; the missionary preaches. The teacher argues; the missionary shouts others to silence. The teacher wants the student to discover; the missionary decides what the student must discover. The teacher enters class with fear and trembling, not knowing where the discussion will lead. The missionary knows at the start of a class exactly what the students must cover by the end of the class.

Grade *A* professors teach, never indoctrinate. They educate rather than train. There is a fine line to be drawn, an invisible boundary, between great teaching and self-aggrandizing indoctrination.

Knowledge and even understanding do not bring salvation and therefore do not have to be, and should not be, forced upon another. And this brings me back to the earlier emphasis upon scholarship as the recognition of ignorance, the awareness not of what we know but of how we know and of what we do not know. The true scholar, who also is the true teacher, is drawn by self-criticism, compelled by doubting, skep-tical curiosity, knows the limits of knowing. He or she cannot be confused with the imperial, the arrogant, and the proselytizing. By definition, we stand for humility before the unknown.

A good professor wants to answer the question, *Why am I telling you these things?* A good student wants to answer the question, *Why am I taking these courses? What do I hope to get out of them? Why are they important to me?* I have not put before you any unattainable ideals in these questions. Some of us realize them every day, and nearly all of us realize them on some days. Just as students' transcripts rarely present only *A's* or *No Credits*, so professors rarely succeed all of the time. No one bears the indelible grade of *A*.

1984

Critical thinking points: After you've read

1) What does Neusner mean when he says, "The professor who gives praise cheaply or who pretends to a relationship that does not and cannot exist teaches the wrong lessons"? What are some of those lessons?

2) Do you agree with Neusner that the "true scholar" is also the "true teacher"? Why or why not?

3) What does Neusner mean when he says, "The only teacher who taught me something beyond information . . ."? What kinds of things can teachers teach that are 'beyond' information, and how might they teach those things?

4) In his criteria for the C professor, Neusner establishes six minimum standards for what he calls "Students' rights." Evaluate this list by considering how important to students each item on the list is. Would you add or subtract any? Why?

Some possibilities for writing

1) Compare and contrast the best and worst teacher and/or class you've had since starting college.

2) Many students spend nearly as much time devising ways to "con" or "suck up" to a professor as impressing one. Write an essay that compares and contrasts "sucking up" to "impressing" a teacher.

3) The lowest "grade" Neusner gives is the C professor. What is a professor who fails? Write at least a page that illustrates what constitutes a "failing" professor.

4) Neusner seems to distinguish between a "Teacher" and a "Professor/Scholar." Write at least a page in which you compare and contrast these two terms.

5) Given the generally low pay and social status, why would anyone want to teach at the college level or any other level? Write an analysis of what might cause or inspire someone to become a teacher.

Theme for English B

Langston Hughes

"

It's not easy to know what is true for you or me

"

Critical thinking points: As you read

1) What do you imagine were the teacher's goals in making such an assignment? How successfully did the student fulfill them?

2) The narrator's specific audience is his instructor. What other audience might Hughes have had in mind?

3) In what way is this poem a reflection of its time? What details or word choices are relevant to the time?

4) What kinds of students might enroll in "English B"?

The instructor said,

> *Go home and write*
> *a page tonight.*
> *And let that page come out of you —*
> *Then, it will be true.*

I wonder if it's that simple?
I am twenty-two, colored, born in Winston-Salem.
I went to school there, then Durham, then here
to this college on the hill above Harlem.
I am the only colored student in my class.
The steps from the hill lead down into Harlem,
through a park, then I cross St. Nicholas,
Eighth Avenue, Seventh, and I come to the Y,

Langston Hughes (1902–1967) is known for the use of jazz and black folk rhythms in his poetry. He was born in Joplin, Missouri, and educated at Lincoln University in Pennsylvania. In the 1920s he was a prominent figure during the Harlem Renaissance and was referred to as the Poet Laureate of Harlem.

the Harlem Branch Y, where I take the elevator
up to my room, sit down, and write this page:

It's not easy to know what is true for you or me
at twenty-two, my age. But I guess I'm what
I feel and see and hear, Harlem, I hear you:
hear you, hear me — we two — you, me, talk on this page.
(I hear New York, too.) Me, who?

Well, I like to eat, sleep, drink, and be in love.
I like to work, read, learn and understand life.
I like a pipe for a Christmas present,
or records — Bessie, bop, or Bach.
I guess being colored doesn't make me not like
the same things other folks like who are other races.
So will my page be colored that I write?
Being me, it will not be white.
But it will be
a part of you, instructor.
You are white —
yet a part of me, as I am a part of you.
That's American.
Sometimes perhaps you don't want to be a part of me.
Nor do I often want to be a part of you.
But we are, that's true!
As I learn from you,
I guess you learn from me —
although you're older — and white —
and somewhat more free.

This is my page for English B.

1924

Critical thinking points: After you've read

1) *Why isn't it easy, as Hughes says, to write "a page that comes out of you,"
   especially one that is "true"?*
2) *Hughes says, "I like to eat, sleep, drink, and be in love." Why does he begin with
   general items? Why might Hughes include detailed directions to his home?*
3) *Hughes says, "So will my page be colored that I write? / Being me, it will not
   be white. / But it will be / a part of you, instructor." What do you think he
   means? How is his page a "part" of the instructor?*

4) *Why might the words "white" and "Harlem" recur throughout the poem? What other words appear more than once? Speculate why they do.*

Some possibilities for writing

1) *Hughes wrote his theme as a poem. Rewrite his poem as prose and add longer scenes built on the details in the poem.*
2) *Write one page that describes your identity. Keep in mind you have limited space, so be specific and selective about what you include. How, like Hughes, are you made up of what you "feel and see and hear"?*
3) *Write about a time when a teacher did, should have, or could have learned from you.*
4) *Locate some of the following poems by Hughes, which can be found in either his selected or collected poems: "Graduation," "Genius Child," "Daybreak in Alabama," "College Formal: Renaissance Casino," and "To Be Somebody." Using these poems, write briefly on what you think Hughes' views on learning might be.*
5) *Research the Harlem Renaissance. Why is Langston Hughes recognized as a prominent figure?*

College Students Speak about ADD

Erik and Chris

"

A positive self-image, environmental factors, and mental and physical fitness are the primary issues to be concerned with during college, particularly if you have ADD.

"

Critical thinking points: As you read

1) Who is the specific audience the authors may have had in mind? Who is a secondary audience?

2) What are some stereotypes of people with ADD? Does this essay help dispel some of those stereotypes? Why or why not?

3) In what way is this an "advice" piece? Keep track of the advice that Erik and Chris offer.

4) What problems or situations do you share with Erik and/or Chris, even if you do not have ADD?

Erik

At Georgetown University, I am surrounded by an extremely competitive, conservative, motivated, intelligent, and often annoying and disconcerting student body. As an example, let's look at how this affected me. First of all, it contributed to a sense of intellectual insecurity. Many of the students like to boast of their achievement. I soon learned that I was far from being the most intelligent person around. Not that I was the smartest guy in high school, but I was much closer to the top there. Also, the work was much harder than I had been prepared for in high school. Although this is often the case at college, it was particularly exaggerated at Georgetown. Because my grades were not as high as I had hoped, this contributed to my insecurities.

About this time, I was diagnosed as having Attention Deficit Disorder (ADD), but was not taking Ritalin. My decline continued through the first semester of my

Erik and Chris wrote their essays when they were college students. Their essays originally appeared in *ADD and the College Student*, edited by Patricia O. Quinn. Washington, D.C.: Magination Press, 1994.

sophomore year. At that time, I was reevaluated, and decided to begin taking Ritalin upon the recommendation of a physician.

The change was obvious. Almost immediately, my productivity increased nearly tenfold. My social life, which never had posed any problems, remained much the same. Social interactions seem to be an issue for many individuals with ADD, but were not a problem for me.

Looking back, there were a number of other factors contributing to my difficulties. Researchers often state that a stable, structured environment, in conjunction with Ritalin, is the most effective treatment of ADD and Attention Deficit with Hyperactive Disorder (ADHD). Nothing could be more true. Students must realize that when they leave home for college, they are also leaving behind the structure and balance that have made treatment most effective. Regular hours are often disrupted by academic strains and the tendency of college students to maintain odd hours. This often entails late nights and early classes. Diet and exercise are also compromised in the transition to college life.

While these conditions influence everybody, they especially affect students with ADD. The more sedentary types will notice a dramatic change in overall mental sharpness, and will also feel better with only minimal daily exercise. I do 25 to 50 sit-ups daily, take vitamins, and make a conscious effort to eat a balanced diet. Occasionally I'll swim or lift weights, but not very regularly. The difference is really quite surprising. Try it.

This is a logical point at which to address a related health issue. Ironically, a nation that tells its young to "just say no" to psychotic drugs has become inured to prescribing them. Ritalin (the trade name for methylphenidate hydrochloride) is an amphetamine-type drug, a stimulant. The federal Drug Enforcement Administration (DEA) has classified Ritalin as a Schedule II controlled substance, the most potent category of drugs that can be prescribed. Gene Haisliq, Deputy Assistant Administrator of the DEA Office of Diversion Control, said in an interview, "Its potency ranks right up there with cocaine." Furthermore, Ritalin use has increased enormously in the past few years. In 1988, the number of prescriptions of Ritalin filled and refilled was 14 percent higher than for the five years before. One per cent is a normal growth rate for most prescriptions.* Because of growing demand, caused by research indicating that its effects are the same for children, adolescents, and adults, a view that remained in question for many years, the DEA has raised its production ceiling. This has opened debate as to the relationship between the use of psychostimulants on young people and the increased probability of drug abuse later in life. The long-term research clearly indicates that there is no documented increase in drug abuse in later life if psychostimulants are taken during childhood or adolescence. Other studies have raised the concern about drug abuse in later life, particularly considering the evidence that a familial tendency toward alcoholism is seen in families with hyperactive children.

---

* "Fourth R is Elementary: Reading, 'Riting, 'Rithmetic — and Ritalin." Fred Boyles and Scot McCarthy. Los Angeles *Herald-Examiner*. April 5, 1988.

The warning label on your prescription should be heeded. Stimulants should not be used with alcohol or other drugs. In college, drugs are far more prevalent than in high school. In addition to interactions with Ritalin (especially with cocaine; the combination of the two stimulants can easily cause respiratory failure and it increases the probability of an overdose), drugs also pose a number of other problems. First, drugs will upset the balance you have achieved. Second, they will work to destroy your motivation and health. Third, the implications of addiction, outside the obvious physical ones, are very serious — expulsion from school, jail, or death. They pose a big risk to your chances for the future success that you as individuals with ADD or ADHD have worked harder than most to attain. Stay away.

Finally, as stated earlier, a positive self-image, environmental factors, and mental and physical fitness are the primary issues to be concerned with during college, particularly if you have ADD. In a certain sense, college is a Zen experience. Great strides can be made. One must be ever watching the mind and body. It's very personal. Become conscious of who you are, where you're going, how you're growing, and what you're doing. The idea is mental freedom and transformation of the familiar. Stay busy, in phase, and in love. Carpe diem.

Chris

I tried to keep it as secret as I could that I had ADD, but when everyone else has to turn in their test paper and I'm still working, and they come back an hour later and I'm still there, it looks very suspicious. My friends would say, "Oh, if I had extra time, too, sure, I'd be able to do this." It was hard for me to convince them that I would rather be in their shoes, I'd much rather not have ADD and not need help than have ADD and need help. Because even if you have unlimited time on a test, after a while your brain just starts to go. If you have been sitting down and working on a test for three hours, believe me, the last thing you want to do is check your problems over and check everything a second time. You just want to get out of there. There were many times I would be taking a test and I knew I needed to spend more time to do well, but I just needed to get outside. I needed a breath of fresh air.

As a student with ADD, I encountered academic problems. These included memorization of facts, problem solving, and reading comprehension. To aid in memorization of facts, I'd use different cue terms and poems and acronyms. I was careful to study definitions both ways because they could be presented either way on the test. I did not just use mental images, but knew the facts.

Logic and problem solving were not difficult for me. I think I could figure things out better than most people. It just took me a lot more time to do it. I needed to concentrate, and to keep down the mental fatigue as well.

Reading comprehension was much more of a problem. I would miss key terms or read over them in a paragraph. A paragraph could be in a completely different tense or totally different gender and I wouldn't even realize it. I would miss one word and need to keep going back and reading the passage over again and again. I'd read it and it didn't make any sense. This was because I had missed the one word. You have to be really careful when you're reading, or at least I did, so you don't miss anything.

Besides reading comprehension, reading anything was really a chore just because of the amount of time it took. It takes me about five minutes to read a page in a novel. It can take me up to 15 minutes to read one page in a textbook. This is just an enormous amount of time — time I didn't have.

Here are the methods I came up with to help. If you're reading a novel, first read the Cliff notes or some summary (I'm not saying you should just read the Cliff notes). You read the Cliff notes first so you have a basic idea of what is going on. Then if you miss a key word or key term, it doesn't throw you off. It is also important to discuss your reading with a friend afterward. You may be looking at it from one perspective and he may be coming at it from another; if you share those perspectives, you'll gain a much better picture of the whole concept. It's very rare that you're going to miss something entirely and he's going to miss it, too.

The same is true when reading textbooks. It's really helpful when there's a chapter summary before the chapter. It's also important always to read the bold print. If you read through all the bold print, all the highlighted information and outlines, then you'll understand what is going on. In addition, read any questions in the back of the book or chapter first, then read just to answer these questions. This will give you a good idea of the basic points. You can then skim through and you will have all the facts that you're going to need.

And above all else, in everything you do, whenever you have a problem, talk to your teacher or professor. They enjoy teaching and like to talk to the students. Many college students feel intimidated about going to their professors' offices or going to dinner or lunch with them. They really want you to learn, and they can help you a lot. If you talk to your professors, you're going to do so much better. I wish more college students realized that.

1994

Critical thinking points: After you've read

1) Which of Erik's and Chris's suggestions for reading and studying might apply to all students, not just those with ADD? Why?

2) Have you ever experienced the "intellectual insecurity" Erik talks about? In what circumstances? How did you overcome it or get past it?

3) Read or reread the excerpt from Davina Ruth Begaye Two Bears' "I Walk in Beauty." How does Erik's experience compare to Two Bears' experience?

4) Chris writes about his friends doubting he really had a disability. Why might "hidden" disabilities sometimes be more difficult to explain than "obvious" disabilities?

5) Do you believe that if you talk to your professors, as Chris says, you're going to do so much better in college? Why or why not?

Some possibilities for writing

1) Choose some piece of advice that either Erik or Chris offers and write about how you apply the advice to your own life.

2) Attention Deficit Disorder is being diagnosed in school children at alarming rates. Research some potential causes of ADD, and prepare a report to your class, or research some alternative treatments for ADD.

3) Interview a college student with ADD or another learning disability about the difficulties he or she encountered at the university.

4) Research some of the "social interactions" that Erik refers to that may be an issue for some individuals with ADD.

5) As a student, you know that revisions always make a paper better. How would you rewrite either Erik's or Chris's paper to improve it? What kinds of research would you do?

Outside In:
The Life of a Commuter Student

Patti See

———————————————— 66 ————————————————

**I didn't know as a freshman that there are many ways
to experience college and mine was just one of them.
I didn't know that there were other students in my classes
who weren't having the "traditional" college experience.**

———————————————— 99 ————————————————

Critical thinking points: As you read

1) *What is a first-generation college student?*
2) *What is the significance of the title? In what ways is See "outside in"?*
3) *What are some general characteristics of "commuters"? What do you think of
    when you hear "commuter"?*
4) *What are some of the things that might "define" your generation of college
    students?*
5) *Does your experience of the first days, weeks, or months of college compare to
    the narrator's? Why or why not?*

It was long ago and far away, the way many of us think of our undergraduate
years. I started college in the mid-'80s, a time when women my age defined themselves with big hair and a closet-full of stone-washed denim. There were few causes
for college students then, just Just Say No, and abortion if you were into that sort of
thing. I pined for a cause, for a purpose, for a normal life as a college student. I was
a commuter, living a community away from the university with roommates who
spent winters in Florida and took their teeth out at night.

I didn't know as a freshman that there are many ways to experience college and
mine was just one of them. I didn't know that there were other students in my classes

Patti See (b. 1968) is a Student Services Coordinator at the University of Wisconsin–Eau
Claire. Her poetry, fiction, and essays have been published in *The Evansville Review*, *The
Southeast Review*, *The Mother Is Me*, *Savoy*, *Women's Studies Quarterly*, and other magazines
and anthologies.

who weren't having the "traditional" college experience. I only focused on the fact that I wasn't living in a dorm with a stranger, trying out different men like shoes, joining a sorority or student organization, experimenting with lifestyles.

I was embarrassed that my parents didn't pay for me to go to college away from home. They gave me a place to live, a car with insurance, every meal, everything that allowed me to commute the twenty minutes to school. At eighteen I didn't realize that putting myself through college, managing work and books, might be an experience in self-reliance. As the youngest of eight children, four of whom had gone to the university closest to home, I accepted that commuting was just what my family did. Like other teenagers, I thought my family was abnormal.

Though I was the last of their children to go to college, my parents still had no idea what it was about. They saw college as extended high school, what people did these days, go to classes for another four years, get another diploma, get a job that pays more than factory work. My father spent elementary school taught by Polish nuns in a one-room school house. He graduated from high school without quite learning how to spell. My mother left school in eighth grade to work in the canning factory. The highlight of her academic achievement was being crowned Spelling Bee Champion of St. Killian's Grade School, 1942.

My father was a railroad man who worked his way up from switchman to yard master over forty years. My mother's career was built around children and rosary beads. She was never without either of them for almost forty years and had no way nor need to retire from either. I didn't consider the humble beginnings of my peers, didn't know then that half of the university population was made up of first-generation college students like me. I only focused on my own history. I didn't see myself as progress.

At new student orientation, the summer before my first semester, I watched the other first-years wander around campus with their parents, touring buildings, reading the course catalogue over lunch. I didn't even consider telling my parents about orientation. I recognized even then I was in it alone for the long haul. One morning when I was suffering from something as banal as menstrual cramps or a hangover, my mother said into my pale face at breakfast, "If you feel sick at school, just go to the office and tell them you need to come home. You can do that, can't you?"

I didn't bother to explain there was no office, no one to tell, that the campus spans for miles. I nodded an "okay."

When I walked into my first class of 250 students, more bodies than my entire high school and its faculty combined, I had no point of reference. It was straight out of *The Paper Chase*, I thought then, without the sophistication. That was the first time in my life I was truly anonymous, a number, and I liked being in a flood of strangers. I graduated from a Catholic high school where everyone knew everyone else, and I was tired of it.

I learned early on that college freshmen don't talk to one another in class, and I had no way outside of class to get to know any of them. My first semester, the closest

I came to forming any sort of relationship with another person on campus was with janitors and professors. We swapped a familiar nod and hello in the hallways and nothing more. My first year of college evolved around my courses and working as a supermarket cashier and a nightclub waitress. I didn't give much thought to changing my situation, or even, in retrospect, outwardly disliking it. It was just what I did. I often felt so involved in the lecture and class discussions (though I didn't actually open my mouth in class till my sophomore year) that I felt as if I was going one on one with the professor.

Around midterm, my Psych. professor wrote in the margin of a paper he returned, "Interesting insights. I'd like to talk about this sometime." My first reaction was, "Well — hadn't we?" Sure, 249 other students were in the class, but I knew he was talking to me. I just took his comments a step further. Leaving class, walking to my car, all the time I drove down Highway 53, he was there in the passenger seat, conversing with me as I wrote my paper in my mind. Students who live in the dorms or even in off-campus housing in clusters of men and women don't have the opportunity to bring their professors home with them. Why would they? They've got clubs to join, games to attend, dorms to decorate, parties to go to. Poor things. That mentality sustained me throughout my undergraduate years. I relied solely on what went on in the classroom. I thought that was all there was to college: rigid professors who lectured to blank faces. I didn't have a blank face, and after taking my professors home with me, I no longer saw them as rigid.

Intellectually, I thrived. Socially, I didn't. I hung onto the three friends from high school who were still in the area. One was a commuter like me, engaged to a mechanic and simply looking for a piece of paper that allowed her to teach. She didn't seem to care that she had no connections, since she had already begun her real life by picking out china and flatware. Sometimes we had lunch together and talked about old friends who'd gone away to school. Once we went together to the bookstore to rent our textbooks, but it felt all wrong. Too high school for me. I had already adapted to the life of a loner on campus.

Another high school friend bounced from menial job to menial job and had enough money to celebrate with me at the end of the week. We spent weekends in honky-tonk bars, under-aged but dressed much older, and talked about the people we worked with, men and women twice our age, putting in their time at jobs they hated. We promised that wouldn't happen to us.

Another friend was a mother at nineteen, a woman who once wrote poetry like me. I loaned her my American Literature text books and visited her when her boyfriend was gone. We smoked cigarettes and watched movies when the baby was asleep, and sometimes I coaxed her into talking about what she read.

My life as a student was a balancing act between my old life as a "townie" and my new life as a "college girl," perfected by the twelve-mile difference between my childhood home and the university. I didn't get the do-over I always imagined students were given when they went away to school. I didn't get to reinvent myself, no longer a jock, a class clown, a stoner. I was just invisible. Looking back, I know that becoming nobody was the seed of my reinvention of myself. Time and distance help me recognize that without my experience I wouldn't be writing this now. But then, I was merely an outsider in both worlds. Friends and family teased me for staying home on a Saturday night reading and becoming a Beatnik. I was anonymous to other first-year students in my courses because, I thought then, I didn't live in a dorm. The saddest part of my college career, I see now, was that there were no late night talks about Neitzche or Anne Sexton or hot men in my gym class. Anything. Nothing. I had no one to tell what I was learning, no shared knowledge, so I made a game of sharing with myself on the way to and from school. I learned a lot in my twenty-minute commute.

I wouldn't have continued in school, would have quit to work in the plastics factory, the allure of a 401(K), if not for my passion for knowledge and desire to be somebody. I didn't know at eighteen who that somebody might be, but I had an inclination I'd find it in books, not a time card.

I started out as a journalism major because it was easy to explain to my parents. They understood what journalists do. My siblings chose "working" professions: nursing, dietetics, accounting, engineering. I was the only freak hooked on knowledge for learning's sake, not a job. Early in my sophomore year I declared English, though even months before I graduated my mother told relatives, "She's going to be a journalist." I never tried to explain what a liberal-arts degree meant. Even the phrase in my mother's mouth made me self-conscious. "English major," she said, like some people say in-surance with the emphasis on the "in." It's like the way she still says someone "knows computer," something foreign and odd, too much for her mouth in one breath. I couldn't explain that I was a writer in training, taking in the world and its details until I was ready to write it. It's something I just knew, like having blue eyes. Even in high school after I bought a pair of sea-green Incredible Hulk–eyed contacts, I was still blue underneath, still a writer. It's something inside, like serendipity that works only if you know what you're looking for or where you've been.

That meant as a freshman I discovered Walt Whitman and e.e. cummings and Kate Chopin and still talked like a townie, a walking Ole-and-Leena joke who knew proper grammar. I could diagram a sentence and write a persuasive paper to save my soul, but I was still factory-worker potential. It's what I feared as a college freshman, and even after I graduated, finding myself someday dull at the machine. That fear made me drag myself out of bed every morning at 7 a.m., eat Wheaties, and drive to school. Mornings were for classes, afternoons and evenings for work. Late nights and weekend days were for homework. It wasn't ideal, but it was productive. I was never dull but sometimes led a dull life.

Throughout my four years, I had contact with other commuters, mostly former high school classmates. Though we had similar stories, tied to the area by families and not enough money for the dorms or off-campus housing, I believed my experience was somehow different. I avoided them and their offers to car pool. These were people I'd known for thirteen years, and they were beyond interesting to me then. We knew who wet her pants in second grade and who threw up at the senior class New Year's Eve party and who made out with whom on the sixty yard line after the Homecoming game. These commuters represented where I came from and wanted desperately to forget, details imbedded in my hometown DNA that I thought, at eighteen, I needed to lose in order to make room for more important details.

Though I eventually had many acquaintances, I made only one friend throughout my college career, a woman who commuted her first year when she lived with her dying grandfather. We met in a five-hour-a-week French class after she transferred from a school in her hometown. The first year I knew her, she lived in an apartment with twelve other women. I often imagined myself in her place: what all of us might talk about as we made dinner or came home from the bars. Then I met some of her roommates and discovered business majors don't have intriguing late-night discussions or even intriguing discussions in daylight. I don't recall how we got to be more than passing acquaintances or the circumstances that led me to bring her home, only twenty minutes but a lifestyle away from the college town.

"You have afghans," she said when she walked through my living room. She immediately sat in my mother's chair. What she meant was, *You live in a real home, with canned goods bursting from cupboards, no one screaming drunk upstairs at 2 a.m.*

"You have a lot of trophies," she said in my bedroom. Commuters often have no reason to pack their past lives away. I told her stories about before I was anonymous. She slept over when it was too late to drive home and we drank too much wine and ordered pizza at midnight, and I almost felt like a real college student.

Sometimes we'd get tipsy during some campus bar happy hour, and I'd tell her, "You're my only friend, man." So pathetically honest that she still teases me about it.

The first time she said, "You're so smart and nice, how can that be?" She didn't have many friends herself, and it comforted me as someone who always felt on the outside of campus life.

"Commuter," I answered, and she understood.

Later as a graduate student I continued to commute, but by then it was no longer something to be embarrassed about. It was even exotic to the other 23-year-olds too old to be slumming in student housing, while I was driving home to my rented house "in the suburbs." I was still on the outside, but I had good reason to be. I went home to see my husband and put my two-year-old to bed after class. My peers went to the bar, but some of them traveled in the front seat with me as I imagined our conversations about the literature we discussed in class.

When I was given the graduate student of the year award, my mother hinted about coming to the awards banquet. It would have been the first time either of my parents was on a college campus for something besides a commencement ceremony. Selfish or appropriate, I filled my table with professors who had influenced my life or at least my degree program.

I still commute the same route to and from school, though now I'm an instructor. When I landed my first job I considered moving nearer to campus, but — odd as it sounds — I knew I'd miss the time in the car. Even now, as I write this, the bulk of it I compose in my mind as I drive home from school, a conversation with a professor or peer or old friend, who has traveled with me a long time now.

1998

Critical thinking points: After you've read

1) *How are parental expectations or pressures addressed in this essay? How does the narrator cope with what seems to be expected of her from her parents? From her friends?*
2) *See says, "I didn't get the do-over I always imagined students were given when they went away to school." What might she mean? Does everyone automatically receive a "do-over"? Why or why not?*
3) *Why does the narrator feel isolated on campus, especially her first semester? Does she "choose" to be isolated? If so, in what ways?*
4) *Do you think the narrator has a positive relationship with her parents? Why or why not? What details in the essay support your answer? Can a parent–child relationship be "healthy" without being supportive? Why or why not?*
5) *What "causes" are available for college students today? How does this compare to the mid-1980s?*

Some possibilities for writing

1) *Recall a time when you were embarrassed by your family or something in your family history.*
2) *Interview a freshman commuter. Then interview an upper-class commuter. How do their experiences compare? How is the freshman making connections? How did the upper-class student make connections?*
3) *See discusses the difference between her education and her parents' education. What are some differences between your education and that of your parents? What are some similarities?*
4) *Schools often have programs for commuters that help them get more involved in campus social activities. Contact your Dean of Students Office or Residence Life Office to find out what kinds of programs for commuters are available on your campus. Write a report to deliver to your class.*
5) *Why do many schools require students to live in the dorms, at least their freshman year? Does your university have any such requirement? Argue for or against mandatory student housing in an opinion piece for your school newspaper.*

Homeward Bond

Daisy Nguyen

66

This is a new reality, one I did not expect to face
when I came 'home-home.' Still, I call this place home because
my family treats me as one of them when I am there.
They share their world with me, even when they are sometimes
harsh realities. It is something I am not exposed to
behind the safe confines of the university.

99

Critical thinking points: As you read

1) The author uses two "home clichés" : Home is where the heart is *and* A house is not a home without love. *What are some other sayings or clichés about home?*

2) Think of your own definition of "home." What are some details that you associate with "home"?

3) In what ways do the author's home life and university life differ? Make a list.

For as long as I can recall, perhaps since the day I moved to college, I have had trouble defining the word "home." It is one of those vague terms that lead people to create metaphors or clichés of their own to define. You've heard it all before: "Home is where the heart is," or "A house is not a home without love."

Webster Dictionary defines it as the region in which something is familiar or native. A friend of mine, when he chooses to visit his family on weekends, always says "I'm going home-home for the weekend." The place he stays at college is simply called "home."

Almost every weekend now, since I have returned to Northern California from a one-year hiatus in France, I go "home-home." After a week of study at school, I go back to visit my family and hang out with friends in San Francisco — basically

Daisy Nguyen (b. 1976) is a graduate from the University of California at Davis, majoring in Sociology and French. She was born in Di Linh, Vietnam, in 1976. She has contributed many personal essays and travel writings for the on-line magazine Blast@explode.com. Her essay "Homeward Bond" was written and appeared on Blast in March 1998. She is currently pursuing a career in print journalism.

doing a lot of catching up. Indeed, many things have changed since I've been away and I'm often struck by the oddities that should be familiar to me.

One Saturday, for example, I went over to my cousin May's house to help put together some cards. She rolled to the door, opened it and greeted me. "Daisy! Hurry up and come in here. I've been waiting all week to show you these cards!"

I am now getting used to seeing her look up at me when she opens the door. It didn't use to be that way. May and I used to ride our bikes around Golden Gate Park on Sundays when we were little girls, and as teeny boppers we sashayed through downtown's hippest streets in our best skirts.

Now she stays home more often and she is putting together a small business: selling homemade greeting cards. They include beautiful photos that her father has taken throughout his extensive travels around Asia and North America. We sat in the kitchen pasting photos onto countless cards, while gossiping about family affairs. May also told me her future plans and outlook on life, now that she is in a wheelchair.

This is a new reality, one I did not expect to face when I came "home-home." Still, I call this place home because my family treats me as one of them when I am there. They share their world with me, even when they are sometimes harsh realities. It is something I am not exposed to behind the safe confines of the university.

At home-home, they don't demand me to analyze every problem nor do they demand brilliant response to every question. At home-home, mom just asks me how I have spent my week and how I like her soup. At home-home, I just sit around and listen to the radio with May, recounting stories of our adventures in life and love.

Sometimes, May's mom passes by, in her loud voice, and asks "Is the show on yet?"

"It's time! It's time! Jelly Spring-uh is on! Come and see!"

"Jelly Spring-uh?" I asked myself. "How can she like that awful show?" Here is a woman who has lived in the United States for almost 20 years, who does not understand much English, yet she enjoys the Jerry Springer show. Guess I can't comprehend it all, not everything is familiar to me at home-home.

Andric, the son of my oldest cousin, is the most observant little two-year-old I have ever seen. When May and I sat by the radio chatting, he ran around the kitchen chasing a beach ball and giggling to himself. Occasionally, he came to us and looked inquisitively, wondering what we were doing. When he wanted an apple, he would lift his tiny hand and make a fist, then put it to his cheek, making a sign for "apple." May gave him the apple and lifted him up to her lap. Celine Dion's hit from the "Titanic" soundtrack, "My Heart Will Go On," played on the radio, once again.

"I love this song!" May squealed. We listened to the haunting melodies and May hugged Andric. "I love music," she sighed. "I don't think I can live without it in my life, and when I think about how Andric can't hear music, it makes me love him so much more."

I looked into his smiling eyes and understood even more the reason the whole family adores him, and will do everything to protect him. His big round eyes, with long feathery eyelashes, are so bright you can clearly see life happening inside of him. It was a moment so heartbreaking and so inexplicable, even I couldn't describe it in words.

Now on Sundays, many members of my family go to the Buddhist temple to meditate and pray. There's a nice temple on Van Ness Avenue that my grandma and aunts frequent, so does May and Andric. One rainy morning, I hopped into my aunt's van and tagged along with her and my grandma to the temple.

On the way, grandma told me her worries for everyone in the family and asked about my life. We were driving up Van Ness, a very congested street even on Sunday mornings, when the van stopped at a red light. We waited a moment and my grandma saw a homeless man in crutches standing at the island, asking for money. She quickly grabbed a dollar from her purse and told my aunt, at the drivers' seat, to give the money to him. I looked at the light about to change, the huge distance between the van and the island, and the helpless man who couldn't reach to grab the dollar bill. "No, no, Grandma!" I panicked. "You can't do that! He can't reach for it and we must go."

The light turned green long ago, and cars behind us were honking incessantly. My aunt also panicked and she tossed the bill out the window, hoping he'd catch it. The van sped off. I turned around, and saw through the back window the dollar bill flying away, disappearing in the sea of cars.

To my grandma's dismay, all she could say was "Ay-yah, in America it is even hard to give bums some money when you want to." I knew right then her remark couldn't have been more profound nor appropriate.

When we arrived at the temple, my grandma's face brightened as she saw the crowd sitting there peacefully, chanting ancient songs. Most of all, her daughters, grandchildren and great grandchild, Andric, were there too.

We sat down, I crossed my legs and positioned myself for the upcoming meditation exercise. One of the monks came by, gave me a book and turned to the page where I followed the songs. Of course, I hardly understood the characters on the page, and mimicked to my grandma's singing instead.

After a while, the singing stopped and we sat in a long moment of silence. I was told that during meditation, you're supposed to not think about anything at all. How radical of an idea! It was so strange to me, but I didn't mind. While everyone else were attempting to put this theory into practice, I was happy to listen to the rain drops on the roof and think about how wonderful it was to sit in a room with my family in complete silence.

1998

Critical thinking points: After you've read

1) *The author says when she returns from college on weekends, "I call this place home because my family treats me as one of them when I am there." Is that true of you? Why or why not?*
2) *In what ways is a university life, as the author calls it, "a safe confine"? In what ways is going home often a "safe confine"?*

3) *How might the grandmother's empathy for the homeless man contribute to the story?*

4) *Consider the following statement: "Knowledge without compassion is dangerous." How is this statement reflected in the story?*

5) *What might Nguyen mean when she says, "I'm often struck by the oddities that should be familiar to me"? What are some of these?*

Some possibilities for writing

1) *Recall a trip home from college when you felt most welcomed and at ease with your family. Write the scene.*

2) *Recall a trip home from college when you felt like an outsider among your family members. Write that scene.*

3) *Even if you feel college has not changed you, imagine ways in which it might. Write a scene that shows rather than tells some of those changes.*

4) *Read Alice Walker's "A Sudden Trip Home in the Spring" (found in her book* You Can't Keep a Good Woman Down *or the anthology* First Sightings: Contemporary Stories of American Youth). *How are the two main characters different? How are they the same? Which experience of "going home" from college is most like yours? Why?*

an excerpt from

I Walk in Beauty

by Davina Ruth Begaye Two Bears

---------- 66 ----------

On this day I sat next to my professor, and as usual was lost. The words, ideas, arguments, and opinions whirled around me like a tornado in which I was mercilessly tossed.

---------- 99 ----------

Critical thinking points: As you read

1) Human nature says that we sometimes stake our self-esteem on one failure. How and why do you think Two Bears does that?

2) What makes an Ivy League school? What might make them better than any other school?

3) What kind of insecurities does the author have during her first year of college?

During "Freshmen Week" incoming students get a head start on Dorm life at Dartmouth and take placement tests

It was during this time that our Undergraduate Advisor (UGA) group held its first meeting. I had just finished moving into Woodward, an all-female dorm. The UGA group was designed to help freshwomen/men during their first year at college. Most of the women in my dorm belonged to my group.

We decided to meet outside, and shuffled onto the front lawn, scattered with bright red and yellow leaves. As we sat in a circle, I promptly began to freeze my ass off on the damp grass. The sun was out, but it was a chilly fall day.

Our UGA, a sophomore, smiled sweetly and began to explain a name game to us. As I looked at all the unfamiliar faces, I felt afraid, intimidated, alone, and different. I was, of course, the only Navajo or Native American person in our group. A pang of home sickness stole into my heart. Our UGA finished her instructions and we began.

The rules were to put an adjective in front of our name that described us and

---

Davina Ruth Begaye Two Bears, a proud member of the Dinè Nation, graduated from Dartmouth in 1990 with a degree in anthropology.

began with the first letter of our name. The object of the game was to introduce ourselves in a way that would help us to remember everyone's name. "Musical Melody" said a proud African American woman. A friendly voice chirped, "Amiable Amy," and everyone smiled in agreement. I couldn't think of an adjective to describe me that began with D. I racked my brain for an adjective, anything! But it was useless. "Oh, why do I have to be here? I don't belong here with all these confident women. Why can't I do this simple thing?" I remember thinking. My palms were sweating, my nose was running, and my teeth began to chatter. I looked at all their faces, so fresh, so clean and confident. It was finally my turn. I still couldn't think of an adjective. In agony, I uttered "Dumb Davina." "Nooo!" they all protested. Amiable Amy interjected, "Why not Divine Davina?" I shot her a smile of gratitude, but I was horrified and embarrassed. How could I have said that and been serious? Talk about low self-esteem.

My first term at Dartmouth went well academically. I received an A, a B, and a C. But I was lonely, even though I was friends with several women in my UGA group. It was hard for me to relate to them, because I felt they did not know who I was as a Native American, and where I was coming from. They also didn't understand my insecurities. How could they, when they believed so strongly in themselves?

I look back at my first year at Dartmouth, and realize that I made it hard on myself. I took it all too seriously, but how could I have known then what I know now? It took me years to be able to think of myself in a positive light. My mother always told me, "You are no better than anybody else. Nobody is better than you." Unfortunately, at Dartmouth her gentle words were lost in my self pity.

Going home for Christmas almost convinced me to stay home. I was so happy with my family, but I didn't want to think of myself as a quitter, nor did I want anyone else to think of me that way. I came back to an even more depressing winter term. My chemistry course overwhelmed me and I flunked it.

Chemistry was torture, and I could not keep up no matter how hard I tried. A subject that I aced in high school and actually liked did me in that term, and made me feel like a loser. What went wrong? It was just too much information too fast. I was depressed, and my heart was not really in the subject. Finally, I accepted my predicament. I'm not science material, and that's that.

Why did I do so horribly? My note taking skills were my downfall. They were poor at best. The crux of my problem was trying to distinguish the important facts that I needed to write down from the useless verbiage quickly. By the time I got to writing things down, I'd already have forgotten what the professor had just said. In this way, valuable information slipped through my fingers. Not only were my note taking skills poor, but so was my ability to participate in class discussion. At Dartmouth, one was expected to follow everything that was being said, think fast, take notes, ask questions, and finally deliver eloquent opinions, answers, and arguments. It was beyond my limited experience and self-confidence to do so. "Say something!" I screamed mentally, but it was useless. Fear paralyzed me in class. Outside of class I'd talk, but not in class amid the stares of my peers. My freshman English professor and I would have conversations in her office lasting two or three hours, but in her class, when faced with all my peers, I became mute. Once Michael Dorris, my Native American studies professor, asked me outside of class why I did not speak up in his freshman seminar on American Indian policy. I was tongue-tied. Incredibly, I felt that if I spoke up in class, I would be perceived as stupid. It did not help matters that the discussions there utterly lost me most of the time during my first couple of years at Dartmouth.

On one occasion I did speak up in an education course, "Educational Issues in Contemporary Society." It was a tough course with tons of reading. Participating in the weekly seminar was a significant part of the grade. I never talked to anyone in the class. But the professor was always nice to me, saying "Hi" whenever we ran into each other. That day was just like all the other days of the past few weeks. Seated around the oblong table were about fifteen students, the professor and a teaching assistant. The professor did not lead the discussions; he was there as a participant just like us students, and we determined the content of the seminar. I came in, sat down, and my classmates began to express themselves, taking turns at center stage. I looked from one student to another and wondered how they made it look so easy, wishing that I could, too.

On this day I sat next to my professor, and as usual was lost. The words, ideas, arguments, and opinions whirled around me like a tornado in which I was mercilessly tossed. Too many unfamiliar words, analogies, and thoughts were being expressed for my brain to comprehend, edit, sort, pile, delete, save, etc. But this was nothing new — all of my classes at Dartmouth were confusing to me and extremely difficult.

Out of the blue, as I sat there lost in thought, my professor turned his kind face toward me and asked "Davina, why don't you ever say anything?" His question was totally unexpected, but not malicious. Rather, it was asked in a respectful tone that invited an answer. Everyone stared me down; they wanted to know, too. I was caught off guard, but thought to myself: this is my chance to explain why I am the way I am. I began hesitantly, frightened out of my wits, but determined to let these people know who I was and where I was coming from.

"Well, I have a hard time here at Dartmouth. I went to school in Arizona. That's where I am from. I went to school in Tuba City, Flagstaff, Bird Springs, and Winslow, Arizona. So I've gone to school both on and off the Navajo reservation. The schools on the reservation aren't that good. But in Flagstaff, I used to be a good student. Bird Springs, which is my home community, is where I learned about Navajo culture in sixth and seventh grade. I got behind though, because the school didn't have up-to-date books. I mean we were using books from the 1950s. I really liked it though, because I learned how to sing and dance in Navajo and they taught us how to read and write the Navajo language. I learned the correct way to introduce myself in Navajo, so even though I got behind and had to catch up in the eighth grade, it was the best time of my life, and I learned a lot about my language and traditions. Then when I went to eighth grade and high school in Winslow, I had to stay in the Bureau of Indian Affairs dorm away from my family, because the bus didn't come out that far. So the dorm was for all the Navajo and Hopi students who lived too far away on the reservation. Winslow was a good school, but I don't think I was prepared for an Ivy League school like Dartmouth. I mean it's so hard being here so far away from home. I used to be in the top ten percent of my class — now I'm at the bottom of the barrel! Do you know how that makes me feel?"

I couldn't help myself and I began to sob. My words were rushing out like they had been bottled up inside for too long.

"It's awful. I feel like I can't do anything here and that the students are so much smarter than me. It seems like everyone knows so much more than me. All of you, it's so easy for you to sit there and talk. It's hard for me to do that. I envy you. I feel like I'm always lost. I hardly ever understand what you guys are talking about. It's that bad. My note taking skills aren't that good either and it causes me a lot of problems in class, makes me get behind. I mean we never had to take notes like this at Winslow. And it's hard for me to participate in class discussion. I mean at Winslow we had to, but not like this. My teacher would put a check by our name after we asked one question. We didn't sit around a table and talk like we do in here. We didn't have to really get into a subject. We didn't even have to write essays. I only wrote one term paper in my junior and senior year. My English teacher would always tell us how much writing we'd have to do in college, but he never made us write! I'm barely hanging on, but here I sit and that's why I don't participate in class discussion."

I finished my tirade. It was quiet. Nobody said a word. Then my professor leaned over and jokingly admitted, "Don't feel too bad, Davina, I don't understand what they're talking about half the time either." We all smiled, and it was as if a great weight had been lifted off my shoulders. I'm so glad he prompted me to speak that day, and his comment helped me to put it all in perspective. Not everything a Dartmouth student says is profound. It was in this class that I received a citation, which distinguishes a student's work. My professor wrote, "Courage is a sadly lacking quality in the educational world we've created. Davina dared to take steps on behalf of her own growth (and ultimately for her fellows) in an area where she could reasonably expect to be tripped by an insensitive and dominating culture. It was a privilege to accompany her." For Education 20, I received a grade of D with an academic citation, simultaneously one of the worst and best grade reports a student can receive. "Only I would receive such an absurd grade," I said to myself in exasperation, but I was proud despite the D. After that day in class, my self-confidence went up a notch. In my junior and senior years at Dartmouth I began to participate in class little by little. By the time I hit graduate school, you couldn't shut me up.

1997

Critical thinking points: After you've read

1) *Two Bears says she was determined to let her classmates know "who I was and where I was coming from." Why do you think her "explosion" in class happens when it does?*
2) *When Two Bears failed chemistry she says, "I felt like a loser." Has this ever happened to you? How is your experience the same or different from the author's?*
3) *Two Bears says, "Not everything a Dartmouth student says is profound." What might she mean? Why is realizing this important to her progression as a student?*
4) *How do you feel about "talking in class," answering a teacher's question? Why is this easy for some people and harder for others?*

Some possibilities for writing

1) *Interview at least five first-year students about some of their fears in the classroom.*
2) *What do you think are the best predictors of success at college? Does high school class rank really mean as much as experts say? Why or why not?*
3) *Research the effects of low self-esteem and the effects of overly high self-esteem on how well students learn.*
4) *Two Bears' professor says, "Courage is a sadly lacking quality in the educational world we've created." What do you think he means?*

an excerpt from

The Freshman Year Thrill Ride

Missy Loney and Julie Feist

---- 66 ----

Just because the class is called calculus
does not mean you get to use your calculator.

---- 99 ----

Critical thinking points: As you read

1) As you read, consider how this list might be a reflection of the two authors and their personalities or how this list might apply to many college students in general? What items in the list support your ideas?

2) Do you believe peers give you the most pertinent advice? Why or why not?

3) Were you offered advice from parents, teachers, siblings, and friends before you came to college? What pieces of advice were helpful? What pieces were outdated, silly, or unnecessary to you?

1. Your family become your friends, and your friends become your family.
2. If you don't wear your contacts in the shower, you don't notice the moldy walls as much.
3. If you wear a T-shirt under everything, you only have to wash once a month, or whenever you spill.
4. A bag of chips and a can of salsa can last a whole month.
5. Christmas lights are good year round.
6. When you go to bed at 4 a.m. and get up at 6 a.m., it's not worthwhile to get into PJ's or slide under the covers.
7. Some teachers really do care, others really don't.
8. The average college student has more appliances than plug-ins in her dorm room.
9. If you study at the bookstore, you don't need to buy any books.
10. Even when they're wrong, college teachers are always right.

Missy Loney and Julie Feist were first-year students when they published their list in the St. Paul *Pioneer Press*.

11. The word adviser is misleading.
12. It's possible to oversleep for the 4:45 p.m. Sunday Mass.
13. To study is not the reason most people come to college.
14. You never realize the value of a couch until you don't have one.
15. You can live for an entire month on 75 cents.
16. Homesickness visits at the most peculiar times.
17. It no longer matters what the job is, as long as it pays money.
18. Life isn't fair, but you always get what you deserve.
19. In a group of 100 people, you can still be alone.
20. There are some things that Mom and Dad shouldn't know.
21. It's important to fully screen a guy before you go out with him. Blind dates are dangerous.
22. When around friends, sandbagging is a social activity.
23. Fire drills at 3 a.m. let the whole world know where everyone is sleeping.
24. If you thought you knew your roommate first semester, wait until second semester.
25. When the power is out for 12 hours, the freezer will defrost onto the carpet.
26. You never truly value your car until you don't have one.
27. Quarters are the world. They mean the difference between wearing your underwear inside out for the third time or just the first.
28. E-mail makes the world go round. It's a college student's lifeline.
29. Saying you're not going to drink and not drinking are two separate subjects.
30. Pizza, pizza, pizza. A staple diet.
31. Pizza is only delivered until 2 a.m.
32. Sleep doesn't have to always happen between 10 p.m. and 6 a.m.
33. Brushing your roommate's teeth is an exciting activity at 4 a.m.
34. Some relationships are strengthened by distance while others disappear.
35. If the sign says free food, it must be a worthwhile activity.
36. You don't get any credits for watching football.
37. All books must be removed from the shelves at least once a semester. To sell them back.
38. Getting snail mail makes the whole week wonderful.
39. Packages are even better.
40. Dorm rooms are not good places to study.
41. Just because the class is called calculus does not mean you get to use your calculator.
42. Half a bottle of perfume is a good substitute for a shower.
43. Don't talk to a "Days of Our Lives" addict between noon and 1 p.m.
44. College can change you 100 times and then mold you back into the person you were when you first came.

1997

Critical thinking points: After you've read

1) *What do you learn about the authors from their list? Write down personality traits about the young women.*
2) *Which items on the list strike you as particularly important to learn your first year at college? Why?*
3) *Which items on the list are ones that you need to learn on your own and not from experienced college students? Why?*
4) *Is it easier to accept advice from your peers than from your parents? Why or why not?*

Some possibilities for writing

1) *Create a list called "The Things I Learned in High School."*
2) *Create your own list of things you've learned your first week or month or semester at college.*
3) *Choose one item from this list and write a paragraph or two that illustrates it.*
4) *Compare this list to other advice pieces collected here. Which do you think is the most valuable to college students? Why?*
5) *What are some "college issues" this list does not address? Make a list of your own ideas. Next, seek out students who have been on campus longer than you have been. Ask them for advice.*

"Who Shall I Be?"
The Allure of a Fresh Start

Jennifer Crichton

"

The student is a soul in transit, coming from one place en route to someplace else.

"

Critical thinking points: As you read

1) Is a "fresh start" at college alluring to everyone? Why or why not?

2) Do you believe people, especially college freshmen, choose who they will become? Why or why not?

3) In what ways is a student a "soul in transit," as Crichton says? In what ways can college offer students the chance to "re-make" themselves? To "re-make" their lives? Do you believe it will happen to you? Why or why not?

The student is a soul in transit, coming from one place en route to someplace else. Moving is the American way, after all. Our guiding principle is the fresh start, our foundation the big move, and nothing seduces like the promise of a clean slate.

"Do you realize how many people saw me throw up at Bob Stonehill's party in tenth grade? A lot of people," says my friend Anne. "How many forgot about it? Maybe two or three. Do you know how much I wanted to go someplace where nobody knew I threw up all over Bob Stonehill's living room in tenth grade? Very much. This may not seem like much of a justification for going away to college, but it was for me." Going away to college gives us a chance to rinse off part of our past, to shake off our burdensome reputations.

We've already survived the crises of being known, allowing how American high schools are as notoriously well-organized as totalitarian regimes, complete with secret police, punishment without trial, and banishment. High school society loves a label, cruelly infatuated with pinning down every species of student. Hilary is a klutz, Julie is a slut, and Michele a gossiping bitch who eats like a pig.

No wonder so many of us can't wait to be free of our old identities and climb

Jennifer Crichton is the author of *Delivery: A Nurse-Midwife's Story* (1986) and *Family Reunion* (1998).

inside a new skin in college. Even flattering reputations can be as confining as a pair of too-tight shoes. But identity is tricky stuff, constructed with mirrors. How you see yourself is a composite reflection of how you appear to friends, family, and lovers. In college, the fact that familiar mirrors aren't throwing back a familiar picture is both liberating and disorienting (maybe that's why so many colleges have freshman "orientation week").

"I guess you could call it an identity crisis," Andrea, a junior now, says of her freshman year. "It was the first time nobody knew who I was. I wasn't even anybody's daughter any more. I had always been the best and brightest — what was I going to do now, walk around the dorm with a sign around my neck saying 'Former High School Valedictorian'?"

For most of my college years, I was in hot pursuit of an identity crisis, especially after a Comparative Literature major informed me that the Chinese definition of "crisis" was "dangerous opportunity," with the emphasis on opportunity. On college applications, where there were blanks for your nickname, I carefully wrote "Rusty," although none of my friends (despite the fact that I have red hair) had ever, even for a whimsical moment, considered calling me that. I was the high-strung, sensitive, acne-blemished, antiauthoritarian, would-be writer. If I went through a day without some bizarre mood swing, people asked me what was wrong. I didn't even have the leeway to be the cheerful, smiling sort of girl I thought I might have it in me to be. My reputation seemed etched in stone, and I was pretty damn sick of it. As I pictured her, Rusty was the blithe spirit who would laugh everything off, shrug at perils as various as freshman mixers, bad grades, and cafeterias jammed with aloof strangers, and in general pass through a room with all the vitality and appeal of a cool gust of wind.

But when I arrived at college, Rusty had vaporized. She was simply not in the station wagon that drove me up to campus. Much of college had to do with filling in the blanks, but changing myself would not be so easy, so predictable, so clichéd.

My parents, acting as anxious overseers on the hot, humid day I took my new self to college, seemed bound by a demonic ESP to sabotage my scarcely budding new identity. After a summer planning how I would metamorphose into the great American ideal, the normal teenage girl, I heard my mother tell my roommate, "I think you'll like Jenny — she's quite the oddball." Luckily, my roommate was saturated with all kinds of information the first day of college had flung at her, and the last thing she was paying attention to were the off-the-cuff remarks this oddball's mother was making. My unmarked reputation kept its sheen as it waited for me to cautiously build it up according to plan. My parents left without any further blunders, except to brush my bangs from my eyes ("You'll get a headache, Sweetheart") and foist on what had been a blissfully bare dormitory room an excruciatingly ugly lamp from home. As soon as the station wagon became a distant mote of dust on the highway, I pulled my bangs back over my eyes in my New Wave fashion of choice, tossed the ugly lamp in the nearest trash can, and did what I came to college to do. Anonymous, alone, without even a name, I would start over and become the kind of person I was meant to be: like myself, but better, with all failures, rejections, and sexual indiscretions relegated to a history I hoped none of my new acquaintances would ever hear of.

Why was it, I wondered, when *any* change seemed possible that year, had it been so impossible in high school? For one thing people know us well enough to see when we're attempting a change, and change can look embarrassingly like a public admission of weakness. Our secret desires, and the fact that we're not entirely pleased with ourselves, are on display. To change in public under the scrutiny of the most hypercritical witnesses in the world — other high school students — is to risk failure ("Look how cool she's trying to be, the jerk!") or succeeding but betraying friends in the process ("I don't understand her any more," they say, hurt and angry) or feeling so much like a fraud that you're forced to back down. And while we live at home, parental expectations, from the lovingly hopeful to the intolerably ambitious, apply the pressure of an invisible but very effective mold.

Jacki dressed in nothing but baggy Levi's and flannel shirts for what seemed to be the endless duration of high school, even though she came to a sort of truce with her developing woman's body in eleventh grade and wasn't averse any longer to looking pretty. Looking good in college was a fantasy she savored because in high school, "I didn't want to make the attempt in public and the fail," she explains now, looking pulled-together and chic. "I thought everyone would think I was trying to look good but I only managed to look weird. And I didn't want a certain group of girls who were very image-conscious to think they'd won some kind of victory either, that I was changing to please them.

"So I waited for college, and wore nice, new clothes right off the bat so nobody would know me any other way. I had set my expectation too high, though — I sort of thought that I'd be transformed into a kind of *femme fatale* or something. When I wasn't measuring up to what I'd imagined, I almost ditched the whole thing until I realized that at least I wasn't sabotaging myself any more. When I ran into a friend from high school, even though I had gotten used to the nice way I looked, I was scared that she could see right through my disguise. That's how I felt for a long time: a slobby girl just pretending to be pulled together."

At first, any change can feel uncomfortably like a pretense, an affectation. Dana had been a punked-out druggy in high school, so worried about being considered a grind that she didn't use a fraction of her considerable vocabulary when she was around her anti-intellectual friends. She promised herself to get serious academically in college, but the first night she spent studying in the science library, she recalls, "I half-expected the other kids to look twice at me, as if my fish-out-of-water feeling was showing. Of course, it wasn't. But it was schizophrenic at first, as if I were an impostor only playing at being smart. But when you do something long enough, that thing becomes *you*. It's not playing anymore. It's what you are."

Wanting to change yourself finds its source in two wellsprings: self-hatred and self-affirmation. Self-affirmation takes what already exists in your personality (even if slightly stunted or twisted) and encourages its growth. Where self-affirmation is expansive, self-hatred is reductive, negating one's own personality while appropriating qualities external to it and applying them like thick pancake makeup.

Joan's thing was to hang out with rich kids with what can only be described as a vengeance. She dressed in Ralph Lauren, forayed to town for $75 haircuts, and complained about the tackiness of mutual friends. But after a late night of studying, Joan allowed her self-control to slip long enough to tell me of her upbringing. Her mother was a cocktail waitress and Joan had never even found out her father's name. She and her mother had trucked about from one Western trailer park to another, and Joan always went to school dogged by her wrong-side-of-the-tracks background. That Joan had come through her hardscrabble life with such strong intellectual achievement seemed a lot more credible — not to mention interesting — than the effortless achievements of many of our more privileged classmates. Joan didn't think so, and, I suppose in fear I'd blow her cover (I never did), she cut me dead after her moment's indulgence in self-revelation. Joan was rootless and anxious, alienated not only from her background but, by extension, from herself, and paid a heavy psychic price. This wasn't change: this was lies. She scared me. But we learn a lot about friends from the kinds of masks they choose to wear.

After all, role-playing to some degree is the prerogative of youth. A woman of romance, rigorous academic, trendy New Waver, intense politico, unsentimental jock, by turn — we have the chance to experiment as we decide the kind of person we want to become. And a stereotypical role, adopted temporarily, can offer refuge from the swirl of confusing choices available to us, by confining us to the limits of a type. Returning to my old self after playing a role, I find I'm slightly different, a little bit more than what I was. To contradict one's self is to transcend it.

As occasional fugitives from our families, we all sometimes do what Joan did. Sometimes you need a radical change in order to form an identity independent of your family, even if that change is a weird but transient reaction. My friend Lisa came from a family of feminists and academics. When she returned home from school for Thanksgiving, dressed as a "ditsy dame" straight out of a beach-blanket-bingo movie, she asked me, "How do you think I look? I've been planning this since tenth grade. Isn't it great?" Well, er, yes, it was great — not because she looked like a Barbie doll incarnate but because nobody would ever automatically connect her life with that of her parents again.

Another friend, Dan, went from a Southern military academy to a Quaker college in the North to execute his scheme of becoming a serious intellectual. The transformation went awry after a few months, partly because his own self was too likably irrepressible. It wouldn't lie down and play dead. "I kept running into myself like a serpent chasing its tail," as he puts it. But his openness to change resulted in a peculiar amalgamation of cultures whose charm lies in his realizing that, while he's of his background, he's not identical to it. Most of our personalities and bodies are just as stubbornly averse to being extinguished, even if the fantasy of a symbolic suicide and a renaissance from the ashes takes its obsessive tool on our thoughts now and again. But a blank slate isn't the same as a blank self, and the point of the blank slate that college provides is not to erase the past, but to sketch out a new history with a revisionist's perspective and an optimist's acts.

And what of my changes? Well, when I was friendly and happy in college, nobody gaped as though I had sprouted a tail. I learned to laugh things off as Rusty might have done, and there was one particular counterman at the corner luncheonette who called me Red, which was the closest I came to being known as Rusty.

What became of Rusty? Senior year, I stared at an announcement stating the dates that banks would recruiting on campus, and Rusty materialized for the first time since freshman year. Rusty was a Yuppie now, and I pictured her dressed in a navy-blue suit, looking uneasily like Mary Cunningham, setting her sights on Citibank. I was still the high-strung, oversensitive, would-be writer (I'm happy to report my skin did clear up), but a little better, who left the corporate world to be Rusty. For myself, I have the slate of the rest of my life to write on.

1984

Critical thinking points: After you've read

1) Crichton recalls the following high school labels, "Hilary is a klutz, Julie is a slut, and Michele a gossiping bitch who eats like a pig." What labels or details did you want to leave behind when you came to college? Do you feel you have left "labels" behind? Why or why not?

2) How can even flattering reputations become as "confining as a pair of too-tight shoes"?

3) What might Crichton mean when she says, "Wanting to change yourself finds its source in two wellsprings: self-hatred and self-affirmation"? Which is more motivating? Why?

4) Crichton says, "We learn a lot about friends from the kinds of masks they choose to wear." In what ways do people "choose" to wear "masks"? Do you know anyone who does this? Do you sometimes wear "masks"? In what types of situations?

Some possibilities for writing

1) Crichton creates a new persona in "Rusty." Create a new persona for yourself and write a scene that shows, not tells, what this character is like by what the character does and/or how it's done.

2) How have you changed since you've been at college? Have you noticed yourself acting, eating, socializing, or dressing differently than you did in high school? If you don't see any noticeable changes yet, speculate about why you might or might not change dramatically.

3) Crichton says her friend Dan realized that "while he's of his background, he's not identical to it." Do you feel as though you are "identical" to your background or ideology? Why or why not? What part of your background have you held onto? Why? What part or parts of your background have transformed with your personality? Why?

4) *Read or reread Patti See's essay "Outside In: The Life of a Commuter Student." In what way is See's search for identity or reinvention of herself like Crichton's? How are their "re-makes" different? How do their experiences contribute to these similarities and differences?*

Further Suggestions for Writing — "School Daze"

1) *One of the most important "study skills" to develop as a college student is time management. Create a weekly schedule for your semester. Write a "lesson plan" for yourself, including how you will manage deadlines, test preparation, work, and social time.*

2) *Browse through this semester's schedule of classes and make a list of courses you would love to take regardless of any requirements you may have for your major or minor. Write a paragraph for each one, explaining why you would like to take that course.*

3) *One of the objectives of a university education is that it challenges your beliefs, perhaps even changes your mind. Briefly explain one thing that you are sure you will never change your mind about and why you think so. Then choose something you might be likely to reconsider, or already have begun to at this point in your life. Again, be sure to include why.*

4) *Education, or what it means to be educated, signifies different things to different people. Choose two or three people from your life – parents, teachers, siblings, friends – to whom education means something quite different and examine some of these differences.*

5) *Evaluate your high school's ability to prepare a student for college.*

6) *Visit your campus Career Center and investigate the resources they have for exploring careers. Take at least two of their evaluations and decide if the outcome describes you and/or the careers you'd like to have.*

7) *Argue for or against working a part-time job as a first-year student.*

8) *Write about your own personal attitude toward alcohol and/or drugs and how you came to that position.*

9) *What connection does goal setting have to success at college? Interview two upperclass students about their opinions on setting short- and long-term goals.*

10) *Write a paper titled "How to Fail a Course."*

11) *Write a paper titled "How to Make and Keep Friends at College."*

12) *Write a paper titled "How to Protect Yourself at College."*

13) *Write a paper titled "How to Cope with Homesickness When You Go Away to College."*

14) *Write a paper titled "How to Succeed as a Student Athlete."*

15) *Write a paper titled "How to Avoid Wasting Time at College."*

16) *Write a paper titled "A History of the Greek System on American Campuses."*

17) *Argue for or against Co-ed Dorms.*

18) *Research the number of alcohol-related deaths on college campuses each year. Come up with some potential solutions to this problem.*

19) *Argue for or against a "no alcohol rule" in college dorms, fraternities, and sororities.*

20) *Do you believe binge drinking (five or more drinks in one sitting) is an epidemic on your campus? Contact your campus counseling services for any research they have conducted on your campus concerning binge drinking and its effects. Evaluate your school's program for alcohol awareness.*

21) *Argue for or against Alcohol Advertising on Campus.*

22) *Argue for or against Affirmative Action Policies on College Campuses.*

23) *Suggest specific ways that students can fight prejudice and bigotry on campus. What resources should be provided? How should the issue be presented to students to ensure a positive outcome?*

24) *Choose a problem with your campus environment that you think would be relatively easy and inexpensive to solve and propose a solution.*

25) *Argue that students with learning disabilities should or should not receive accommodations at college, such as note takers, scribes, extended test time, or tutoring support.*

26) *Compare and contrast college when a student is living on campus to college when a student is living at home.*

27) *Contact your Admissions Office or Dean of Students Office to find out the number of students involved in collegiate athletics on your campus. Do athletes on your campus have to meet the same admissions requirements as other students? What type of support services are available to student athletes? How do these services compare to those offered to the general student population?*

28) *Choose one of your responses to "Some possibilities for writing" in this section and do further research on some aspect of the topic you addressed in your narrative. Write about how and why this new information would have improved your previous effort.*

Selected Films — "School Daze"

The Addiction (1995, USA). Heroine Kathleen (Lili Taylor) is a Ph.D. candidate in philosophy at NYU, lost in her ivory-tower world. This world dissolves after an attack by a vampire (Annabella Sciorra). Now instead of pondering the phenomenon of bloodshed, Kathleen finds herself subsumed within it. An ambitious exploration of the metaphor of the undead and the very human love of pain and violence. Horror/Drama. 90 min. R

Back to School (1986, USA). Fiftyish millionaire Rodney Dangerfield goes to college to help his son become a big man on campus. Comedy. 96 min. PG-13

Bonzo Goes to College (1952, USA). A smart, spunky chimpanzee stars on the varsity football team. Comedy. 80 min.

Campus Man (1987, USA). Two college buddies, an entrepreneur and a studly athlete, team up to create a beefcake calendar. Comedy. 94 min. PG

Circle of Friends (1995, Ireland-USA). Three friends from a strict Catholic small town face old inhibitions and new freedoms when they go away to college in Dublin. Adapted from the Maeve Binchy novel. Romantic drama. 96 min. PG-13

Class of '44 (1973, USA). College sequel to sentimental coming-of-age classic *Summer of '42*. Drama. 95 min. PG

College (1927, USA). Brilliant silent film comedian Buster Keaton tries out for every sports team on campus. Comedy. 65 min.

College Humor (1933, USA). Classic crooner Bing Crosby stars as a singing professor. Musical comedy. 80 min.

Drive, He Said (1972, USA). Jack Nicholson directed this oddly told tale of coming-of-age angst and alienation. Scene stealer Bruce Dern plays the maniacal college basketball coach. Sports/Drama. 90 min. R

Fraternity Row (1977, USA). Fraternity hazing at an elite Eastern college in the mid-1950s. USC students formed the bulk of the cast and crew. Drama. 101 min. PG

French Postcards (1979, USA). American college juniors abroad in France. Reunites the writing team behind *American Graffiti* (minus George Lucas). Drama/Comedy. 92 min. PG

Frosh (1993, USA). Filmmakers spent a year living in a multicultural, co-ed dormitory at Stanford University. The film highlights such key issues as maintaining ethnic identity on a predominantly white campus, Eurocentric versus multicultural curricula, and minority student retention. It documents students' difficult search for personal identity within an increasingly diverse student population. Documentary. 98 min. N/R

Good Will Hunting (1997, USA). Yale dropout Matt Damon and his costar Ben Affleck won an Oscar for Best Original Screenplay for their story of four working-class friends in South Boston, one of whom is a genius. When an M I T math professor "discovers" Will Hunting, he insists that he stop wasting his talents and sends him to psychologist/teacher Robin Williams to motivate him. Drama. 126 min. R

Greetings (1968, USA). In this Vietnam War farce (an early effort by thrill-meister

Brian De Palma) Robert De Niro helps a buddy try to flunk his physical and escape the military draft. Comedy. 88 min. R

The Heart of Dixie (1989, USA). Three white southern college women find their lives and politics shifting as they confront the civil rights movement in the late '50s. Drama. 96 min. PG

Higher Learning (1995, USA). Political correctness and race issues haunt several students, whose lives intersect briefly and tragically on the campus mall. Drama. 127 min. R

Horse Feathers (1932, USA). In this classic Marx Brothers farce, Groucho heads Huxley College, whose football team is in no shape for the big game. Musical comedy. 67 min.

House Party 2: The Pajama Jam (1991, USA). Rap duo Kid 'n' Play raise their past-due college tuition with a house party "jammie jam jam." All-star cast includes Queen Latifah and Martin Lawrence. Comedy. 94 min. R

Kent State (1981, USA). Emmy-winning made-for-TV movie about the 1970 tragedy at Kent State University, in which National Guardsmen shot and killed four college protesters. Political drama. 120 min.

Life Begins in College (1937, USA). The comedy/singing team The Ritz Brothers (Harry, Al, and Jimmy) help a college win the big game. This film catapulted the trio to stardom. Sports/Comedy. 94 min.

Mr. Belvedere Goes to College (1949, USA). Part of a series of films (*Sitting Pretty*, *Mr. Belvedere Rings the Bell*) in which a self-important genius gets into various situations to prove one or another of his theories. Comedy. 83 min.

National Lampoon's Animal House (1978, USA). Set pre-Vietnam in the early '60s. What to do when a cabal of snobbish Greek societies and school administrators imperils your slushy frat house? Road trip, of course. Comedy. 109 min. R

P.C.U. (1994, USA). A freshman falls in with dorm mates who organize offensive activities. A social satire of political correctness. Comedy. 81 min. PG-13

The Program (1993, USA). A college football team's cultish dedication to championship play drives some players nearly over the edge. Sports/Drama. 114 min. R

Real Genius (1985, USA). The treacherous head of an elite California technology institute scouts a team of the nation's best physics students to achieve his own morally bankrupt agenda. Comedy. 104 min. PG

Revenge of the Nerds (1984, USA). A ragtag team of nerds, geeks, losers, and freaks starts its own fraternity in rebellion against the Greek elites. Comedy. 90 min. R

The Revolutionary (1970, USA). A college student gets caught up in the role of political revolutionary, until he's dangerously in over his head. Drama. 100 min. PG

Roommate (1984, USA). Set in the '50s, the film finds a straight-laced valedictorian and a political rebel sharing room and board. A PBS presentation based on John Updike's story "Christian Roommates." Comedy/Drama. 96 min.

School Daze (1988, USA). Homecoming weekend on a southern campus highlights how some blacks deny or affirm their racial identity. Directed by Spike Lee. Musical comedy. 114 min. R

School Ties (1992, USA). A handsome young Jewish prep school athlete hides his religion to survive anti-Semitism in the '50s. Drama. 107 min. PG-13

Seniors: Four Years in Retrospect (1997, USA). The filmmakers of *Frosh* (*see page 130*) returned to Stanford three years later to see how college life had changed five of these students. Combining extensive footage shot during senior year with prophetic clips and "outakes" from *Frosh*, the two directors have produced an altogether new film focusing on the different trajectories students from diverse backgrounds take to a fulfilling and successful college experience. Documentary. 56 min. N/R

Soul Man (1986, USA). A white student masquerades as a black for the sake of a minority scholarship — until he's overcome by guilt after meeting the single black mother who was second in line for the money, and after learning lessons on race from his hectoring black professor (James Earl Jones). Comedy. 101 min. PG-13

Undergrads (1985, USA). Estranged from his son, feisty Art Carney decides to get to know his grandson better by attending college with him. Made for TV by Disney. Comedy. 102 min. N/R

With Honors (1994, USA). After he finds a student's honors thesis, a street bum (Joe Pesci) holds it for ransom. Comedy/Drama. 103 min. PG-13

For Critical Thinking Points on these films, see Appendix (p. 335).

Chapter Three

Student Affairs:
Friends and Lovers

Much of the education at college often takes place outside of the classroom as students learn to live in groups, to view and treat one another as adults.

This chapter will explore —

- The sensuality of young love
- The ritual pairing off that occurs in student dorms
- The difficult choices involved in relationships
- The physical and emotional perils of being sexually active
- The friendships that will last a lifetime or at least a semester

Raspberries

Jennifer Fandel

"
I hang on to the bush, / ready to fall heavy / full and red.
"

Critical thinking points: As you read

1) Speculate about the poet's age. What makes you think that?

2) What are some of the sexual images in the poem? List them as you read.

3) What is the difference between a simile and a metaphor? How are both at work in the poem? List examples from the poem of each of them.

My love is heavy
as raspberries.
Silent as the fall
and red, turning
scarlet as an old heart
heavily thumping,
slow in beat, thinking.

My love is silent
as the waiting.
If only the sun and rain
could be enough.
I hang on to the bush,
ready to fall heavy
full and red.
Cupping his palm
he curves to me,
falling apart
at his touch.

1993

Jennifer Fandel (b. 1973) is currently enrolled in the graduate program at Mankato State University.

Critical thinking points: After you've read

1) Why might the poet compare her love for another to raspberries?

2) Who are some characters from TV or movies who might compare their love to raspberries? Why do you choose those characters?

3) Read or reread John David Rose's "Revision." What are some similarities to Fandel's poem? What are some differences?

Some possibilities for writing

1) The poet writes, "My love is heavy as raspberries." Write three more similes using this prompt: "My love is heavy as _____." The poet writes, "My love is silent as the waiting." Write three more similes using this prompt: "My love is silent as _____." Substitute five other adjectives other than "silent" or "heavy" and write three similes for each. Now write something that uses as many of your images as possible.

2) Make several of the following abstractions come to life by rendering them in concrete, specific details and/or images of varying length: racism, injustice, ambition, growing old, salvation, poverty, growing up, wealth, evil. Make up some of your own.

3) Write a dialogue between the author of this poem and John David Rose, author of "Revision." How do you think they would get along as friends? How do you think they would get along as lovers?

First Love

R. A. Sasaki

"

There was an unspoken law of evolution which dictated that in the gradual march toward Americanization, one did not deliberately regress by associating with F. O. B.s. Jo's mother, who was second generation, had endured much criticism from her peers for 'throwing away a college education' and marrying Jo's father, who had graduated from high school in Japan. Even Jo's father, while certainly not an advocate of this law, assumed that most people felt this way. George, therefore, was a shock.

"

Critical thinking points: As you read

1) Watch for images of cages in the story. How might a "cage" be important to the plot of the story?

2) Watch for references to dramas in the story. How might this be important to the plot of the story?

3) George is considered an "FOB" (fresh off the boat) because he was not born in America. What are some other stereotypes or "anti"-stereotypes of characters used in the story?

4) The story is set in the late 1960s. What are some clues to the era?

It was William Chin who started the rumor. He had been crossing California Street on a Saturday afternoon in December when he was almost struck down by two people on a Suzuki motorcycle. As if it weren't enough to feel the brush of death on the sleeve of his blue parka, a split second before the demon passed, he had looked

R. A. Sasaki (b. 1952) is a third-generation Japanese American, born and raised in San Francisco. She attended the University of Kent in Canterbury, England; received a B.A. from the University of California at Berkeley; and received an M.A. in creative writing from San Francisco State University. In 1983, she won the American Japanese National Literary Award for her short story "The Loom." Her fiction has been published in *Short Story Review*, *Pushcart Prize XVII*, *Story*, and other journals and anthologies. "First Love" is one of nine stories in her collection *The Loom*, published in 1991.

up and caught sight of two faces he never would have expected to see on the same motorcycle — one of which he wouldn't have expected to see on a motorcycle at all. No one would have imagined these two faces exchanging words, or thought of them in the same thought even; yet there they were, together not only in physical space, but in their expressions of fiendish abandon as they whizzed by him. He was so shaken, first by his nearness to death, then by seeing an F. O. B. hood like Hideyuki "George" Sakamoto in the company of a nice girl like Joanne Terasaki, that it was a full five minutes before he realized, still standing in amazement on the corner of California and Fourth, that Joanne had been driving.

When William Chin's story got around, there was a general sense of outrage among the senior class of Andrew Jackson High — the boys, because an upstart newcomer like George Sakamoto had done what they were too shy to do (that is, he had gotten Joanne to like him), and the girls, because George Sakamoto was definitely cool and Joanne Terasaki, as Marsha Aquino objected with utter contempt, "doesn't even like to dance." Joanne's friends remained loyal and insisted that Jo would come to her senses by graduation. George's motorcycle cronies were less generous. "Dude's fuckin' crazy," was their cryptic consensus. Opinions differed as to which of the two lovers had completely lost their minds; however, it was unanimously held that the pairing was unsuitable.

And indeed, the two were from different worlds.

Hideyuki Sakamoto ("George" was his American name) was Japanese, a conviction that eight years, or half his life, in the States had failed to shake. He had transferred into Jackson High's senior class that year from wherever it was the F. O. B.s (immigrants fresh off the boat) transferred from; and though perhaps in his case the "fresh" no longer applied, the fact that he had come off the boat at one time or another was unmistakable. It lingered — rather persisted — in his speech, which was ungrammatical and heavily accented, and punctuated by a mixture of exclamations commonly used on Kyushu Island and in the Fillmore District.

An F. O. B. at Jackson High could follow one of two routes: he could be quietly good at science or mathematics, or he could be a juvenile delinquent. Both options condemned him to invisibility. George hated math. His sympathies tended much more toward the latter option; however, he was not satisfied to be relegated to that category either. One thing was certain, and that was that George wanted no part of invisibility. As soon as his part-time job at Nakamura Hardware in Japantown afforded him the opportunity, he went out and acquired a second-hand Suzuki chopper (most hoods dreamed of owning a Harley, but George was Japanese and proud of it). He acquired threads which, when worn on his tall, wiry frame, had the effect — whether from admiration, derision, or sheer astonishment — of turning all heads, male and female alike. He had, in a short span of time, established a reputation as a "swinger." So when William Chin's story got around about George Sakamoto letting Joanne Terasaki drive his bike, the unanimous reaction among the girls who thought of themselves as swingers was voiced by Marsha Aquino: "God dog, what a waste."

Joanne Terasaki, or "Jo," as she preferred to be called, was, in popular opinion, a "brain." Although her parents were living in Japantown when she was born, soon afterwards her grandparents had died and the family moved out to "the Avenues." Jo was a product of the middle-class, ethnically mixed Richmond District. She had an air of breeding that came from three generations of city living, one college-educated parent, and a simple belief in the illusion so carefully nurtured by her parents' generation, who had been through the war, that she was absolutely Mainstream. No one, however, would have thought of her in conjunction with the word "swing," unless it was the playground variety. Indeed, there was a childlike quality about her, a kind of functional stupidity that was surprising in a girl so intelligent in other respects. She moved slowly, as if her mind were always elsewhere, a habit that boys found mysterious and alluring at first, then exasperating. Teachers found it exasperating as well, even slightly insulting, as she earned *A*'s in their classes almost as an afterthought. Her attention was like a dim but powerful beacon, slowly sweeping out to sea for — what? Occasionally it would light briefly on the world at hand, and Jo would be quick, sharp, formidable. Then it would turn out to faraway places again. Perhaps she was unable to reconcile the world around her, the world of Jackson High, with the fictional worlds where her love of reading took her. In her mind, she was Scarlett O'Hara, Lizzy Bennet, Ari Ben Canaan. Who would not be disoriented to find oneself at one moment fleeing the Yankees through a burning Atlanta, and the next moment struggling across the finish line in girls' P. E.? Tart repartee with Mr. Darcy was far more satisfying than the tongue-tied and painful exchanges with boys that occurred in real life. Rebuffed boys thought Jo a snob, a heartless bitch. The world of Andrew Jackson High was beneath her, that was it — a passing annoyance to be endured until she went out into the wider world and entered her true element. It must be on this wider world, this future glory, that her vision was so inexorably fixed.

Or perhaps it was fixed on a point just across San Francisco Bay, on the imposing campanile of the Berkeley campus of the University of California. She had always known she would go there, ever since, as a child, she had often gone to her mother's dresser and surreptitiously opened the top drawer to take out the fuzzy little golden bear bearing the inscription in blue letters, "CAL." It was one of the few "heirlooms" that her mother had salvaged from the wartime relocation. She had taken it with her to internment camp in the Utah desert, an ineffectual but treasured symbol of a shattered life. The government could take away her rights, her father's business, her home, but they could never take away the fact that she was U. C. Berkeley, Class of '39. Jo would have that, too. People often said of Jo that she was a girl who was going places; and they didn't mean on the back (or front) of George Sakamoto's bike.

Only love or drama could bring together two people cast in such disparate roles. When auditions began for the play that was traditionally put on by the senior class before graduation, Jo, tired of being typecast as a brain, tried out for the part most alien to her image — that of the brazen hussy who flings herself at the hero in vain. For a brief moment she stood before her fellow classmates and sang her way out of the cramped cage that their imaginations had fashioned for her. The moment was indeed brief. Marsha Aquino got the part.

"You have to admit, Jo," said William Chin apologetically, "Marsha's a natural." And Jo agreed, somewhat maliciously, that Marsha was.

George, for his part, went for the lead. It was unheard of for a hood (and an F. O. B., at that) to aspire to the stage, much less the leading part. So thoroughly did George's aspect contradict conventional expectations of what a male lead would be, that the effect was quite comic. His good-natured lack of inhibition so charmed his audience that they almost overlooked the fact that his lines had been unintelligible. At the last moment, a voice of reason prevailed, and George was relegated to a nonspeaking part as one of six princes in a dream ballet, choreographed by Jo's friend Ava.

And so the two worlds converged.

"Grace," Ava was saying. "And — flair." She was putting the dream princes and princesses through their paces. "This is a ballet."

The dancers shuffled about self-consciously. After hours of work the princes and princesses, trained exclusively in soul, were managing to approximate a cross between a square dance and a track-and-field event.

"You've got to put more energy into it, or something," Jo, who was a princess, observed critically as a sheepish William Chin and Ed Bakowsky leaped halfheartedly across the floor.

"Like this, man!" George yelled suddenly, covering the stage in three athletic leaps. He landed crookedly on one knee, arms flung wide, whooping in exhilaration. There was an embarrassed silence.

"Yeah," Jo said. "Like that."

"Who is that?" she asked Ava after the rehearsal.

"I don't know," Ava said, "but what a body."

"That's George Sakamoto," said Marsha Aquino, who knew about everyone. "He's bad."

Jo, unfamiliar with the current slang, took her literally.

"Well, he seems all right to me. If it wasn't for him, our dream ballet would look more like 'The Funeral March.' Is he new?"

"He transferred from St. Francis," Marsha said. "That's where all the F. O. B.s go."

Jo had always had a vague awareness of Japanese people as being unattractively shy and rather hideously proper. Nothing could have been further from this image than George. Jo and her friends, most of whom were of Asian descent, were stunned by him, as a group of domesticated elephants born and bred in a zoo might have been upon meeting their wild African counterpart for the first time. George was a revelation to Jo, who, on the subject of ethnic identity, had always numbered among the ranks of the sublimely oblivious.

George, meanwhile, was already laying his strategy. He was not called "*Sukebe Sakamoto*" by his friends for nothing.

"This chick is the door-hanger type," he told his friend Doug. "You gotta move real slow."

"Yeah," Doug said. "Too slow for you."

"You watch, sucker."

He called her one weekend and invited her and Ava to go bowling with him and Doug. Jo was struck dumb on the telephone.

"Ha-ro, is Jo there?"

"This is Jo."

"Hey, man. This is George."

"Who?"

"George, man. Sakamoto."

"Oh." Then she added shyly, "Hi."

The idea of bowling was revolting, but Jo could bowl for love.

She told her mother that she had a date. Her mother mentally filed through her list of acquaintances for a Sakamoto.

"Is that the Sakamoto that owns the cleaner on Fillmore?"

"I don't think so," Jo said.

"Well, if Ava's going, I guess it's all right."

When George came to pick her up, Jo introduced him to her father, who was sitting in the living room watching television.

"Ha-ro," George said, cutting a neat bow to her startled father.

"Was that guy Japanese?" her father asked later when she returned.

"Yeah," Jo said, chuckling.

There was an unspoken law of evolution which dictated that in the gradual march toward Americanization, one did not deliberately regress by associating with F. O. B.s. Jo's mother, who was second generation, had endured much criticism from her peers for "throwing away a college education" and marrying Jo's father, who had graduated from high school in Japan. Even Jo's father, while certainly not an advocate of this law, assumed that most people felt this way. George, therefore, was a shock.

On their second date, Jo and George went to see Peter O'Toole in a musical. From then on, they decided to dispense with the formalities, a decision owing only in part to the fact that the musical had been wretched. The main reason was that they were in love.

They would drive out to the beach, or to the San Bruno hills, and sit for hours, talking. In the protective shell of George's mother's car they found a world where they were not limited by labels. They could be complex, vulnerable. He told her about his boyhood in Kyushu, about the sounds that a Japanese house makes in the night. He had been afraid of ghosts. His mother had always told him ghost stories. She would make her eyes go round and utter strange sounds: "Ka-ra . . . ko-ro . . . ka-ra . . . ko-ro . . ." — the sound made by the wooden sandals of an approaching ghost. Japanese ghosts were different from American ghosts, he said. They didn't have feet.

"If they don't have feet," Jo asked curiously, "how could they wear sandals?"

George was dumbfounded. The contradiction had never occurred to him.

They went for motorcycle rides along the roads that wound through the Presidio, at the edge of cliffs overlooking the Golden Gate. Then, chilled by the brisk winter fog, they would stop at his house in Japantown for a cup of green tea.

He lived in an old Victorian flat on the border between Japantown and the Fillmore, with his mother and grandmother and cat. His mother worked, so it was his grandmother who came from the kitchen to greet them. (But this was later. At first, George made sure that no one would be home when they went. He wanted to keep Jo a secret until he was sure of her.)

The Victorian kitchen, the green tea, all reminded Jo of her grandparents' place, which had stood just a few blocks away from George's house before it was torn down. Jo had a vague memory of her grandmother cooking fish in the kitchen. She couldn't remember her grandfather at all. The war had broken his spirit, taken his business, forced him to do day-work in white people's homes, and he had died when Jo was two. After that, Jo's family moved out of Japantown, and she had not thought about the past until George's house reminded her. It was so unexpected that the swinger, the hood, the F. O. B. George Sakamoto should awaken such memories.

But they eventually had to leave the protective spaces that sheltered their love. Then the still George of the parked car and Victorian kitchen, the "real" George, Jo wanted to believe, evolved, became the flamboyant George, in constant motion, driven to maintain an illusion that would elude the cages of other people's limited imaginations.

He took her to dances Jo had never known existed. Jo had been only to school dances, where everyone stood around too embarrassed to dance. The dances that George took her to were dark, crowded. Almost everyone was Asian. Jo knew no one. Where did all these people come from? They were the invisible ones at school, the F. O. B.s. They *dressed* (unlike Jo and her crowd, who tended toward corduroy jeans). And they danced.

George was in his element here. In his skintight striped slacks flared at the calf, black crepe shirt open to the naval, billowing sleeves and satiny white silk scarf, he shimmered like a mirage in the strobe lights that cut the darkness. Then, chameleonlike, he would appear in jeans and a white T-shirt, stocking the shelves of Nakamura Hardware. At school, George shunned the striped shirts and windbreaker jackets that his peers donned like a uniform. He wore turtleneck sweaters under corduroy blazers, starched shirts in deep colors with cuff links. When he rode his bike, he was again transformed, a wild knight in black leather.

"The dudes I ride with," George confided to Jo in the car, "see me working in the store, and they say, 'Hey, what is this, man? You square a-sup'm?' Then the guys in the store, they can't believe I hang out with those suckers on bikes. 'Hey George,' they say, 'you one crazy son-of-a-bitch.' In school, man, these straight suckers can't believe it when I do good on a test. I mean, I ain't no hot shit at English, but I ain't no dumb sucker neither. 'Hey George,' they say, 'you tryin' to get into college a-sup'm?' 'Hey, why not, man?' I say. They can't take it if you just a little bit different, you know? All them dudes is like that — 'cept you."

Jo was touched, and tried to be the woman of George's dreams. It was a formidable endeavor. Nancy Sinatra was the woman of George's dreams. For Christmas Jo got a pair of knee-high black boots. She wore her corduroy jeans tighter in the crotch.

"Hey, George," Doug said. "How's it goin' with Slow Jo?"

"None of your fuckin' business, man," George snapped.

"Oh-oh. Looks bad."

On New Year's Eve Jo discovered French kissing and thought it was "weird." She got used to it, though.

"You tell that guy," her father thundered, "that if he's gonna bring that motorcycle, he doesn't have to come around her anymore!"

"Jesus Christ!" Jo wailed, stomping out of the room. "I can't wait to get out of here!"

Then they graduated, and Jo moved to Berkeley in the spring.

The scene changed from the narrow corridors of Andrew Jackson High to the wide steps and manicured lawns of the university. George was attending a junior college in the city. He came over on weekends.

"Like good ice cream," he said. "I want to put you in the freezer so you don't melt."

"What are you talking about?"

They were sitting outside Jo's dormitory in George's car. Jo's roommate was a blonde from Colusa who had screamed the first time George walked into the room with Jo. ("Hey, what's with that chick?" George had later complained.)

"I want to save you," George said.

"From what?" Jo asked.

He tried another analogy. "It's like this guy got this fancy shirt, see? He wants to wear it when he goes out, man. He don't want to wear it every day, get it dirty. He wears an old T-shirt when he works under the car — get grease on it, no problem. It don't matter. You're like a good shirt, man."

"So who's the old T-shirt?" Jo asked, suddenly catching on.

"Hey, nobody, man. Nobody special. You're special. I want to save you."

"I don't see it that way," Jo said. "When you love someone, you want to be with them and you don't mind the grease."

"Hey, outasight, man."

So he brought her to his room.

George's room was next to the kitchen. It was actually the dining room converted into a young man's bedroom. It had the tall, narrow Victorian doors and windows, and a sliding door to the living room, which was blocked by bookshelves and a stereo. The glass-doored china cabinet, which should have housed Imari bowls, held tapes of soul music, motorcycle chains, Japanese comic books, and Brut. In Jo's grandparents' house there had been a black shrine honoring dead ancestors in the corner of the dining room. The same corner in George's room was decorated by a life-sized poster of a voluptuous young woman wearing skintight leather pants and an equally skintight (but bulging) leather jacket, unzipped to the waist.

George's mother and grandmother were delighted by Jo. In their eyes she was a "nice Japanese girl," something they never thought they would see, at least in conjunction with George. George had had a string of girlfriends before Jo, which had dashed their hopes. Jo was beyond their wildest expectations. It didn't seem to matter that this "nice Japanese girl" didn't understand any Japanese; George's grandmother spoke to her anyway, and gave her the benefit of the doubt when she smiled blankly and looked to George for a translation. They were so enthusiastic that George was embarrassed, and tried to sneak Jo in and out to spare her their effusions.

They would go to his room and turn up the stereo and make love to the lush, throbbing beat of soul. At first Jo was mortified, conscious of what her parents would say, knowing that "good girls" were supposed to "wait." But in the darkness of George's room, all of that seemed very far away.

So her first experiences of love were in a darkened room filled with the ghosts of missing Japanese heirlooms; in the spaces between the soul numbers with which they tried to dispel those ghostlike shadows, sounds filtered in from the neighboring kitchen: samurai music from the Japanese program on television, the ancient voice of his grandmother calling to the cat, the eternal shuffle of slippers across the kitchen floor. When his mother was home and began to worry about what they were doing in his room, he installed a lock, and when she began pounding on the door, insisting that it was getting late and that George really should take Jo home, George would call out gruffly, "Or-righ! Or-righ!"

But there was that other world, Jo's weekday world, a world of classical buildings, bookstores, coffee shops, and tear gas (for the United States had bombed Cambodia).

Jo flitted like a ghost between the two worlds so tenuously linked by a thin span of steel suspended over San Francisco Bay. She wanted to be still, and at home, but where? On quiet weekday mornings, reading in an empty courtyard with the stillness, the early morning sun, the language of Dickens, she felt her world full of promise and dreams. Then the sun rose high, people came out, and Jo and her world disappeared in a cloak of invisibility, like a ghost.

"Her English is so good," Ava's roommate remarked to Ava. "Where did she learn it?"

"From my parents," Jo said. "In school, from friends. Pretty much the same way most San Franciscans learn it, I guess."

Ava's roommate was from the East Coast, and had never had a conversation with an "Oriental" before.

"She just doesn't know any better," Ava apologized later.

"Well where has that chick been all her life?" Jo fumed.

Then she would long for George, and he would come on the weekend to take her away. Locked together on George's bike, hurtling back and forth between two worlds, they found a place where they could be still and at peace.

George tried to be the man of her dreams. They went on hikes now instead of soul dances. He would appear in jeans and a work shirt, and he usually had an armload of books. He was learning to type, and took great pains over his essays for Remedial English.

But they began to feel the strain. It began to bother George that Jo made twenty-five cents an hour more at her part-time job in the student dining room than he did at the hardware store. He had been working longer. He needed the money. Jo, on the other hand, never seemed to buy anything. Just books. Although her parents could afford to send her to college, her high-school record had won her a scholarship for the first year. She lived in a dream world. She had it so easy.

He asked to borrow fifty dollars, he had to fix his car, and she lent it to him immediately. But he resented it, resented his need, resented her for having the money, for parting with it so easily. Everything, so easily. And he tortured her.

"Hey, is something wrong, man?" George asked suddenly, accusing, over the phone.

"Wrong?" Jo was surprised. "What do you mean?"

"You sound funny."

"What do you mean, funny?"

"You sound real cold, man," George said. His voice was flat, dull.

"There's nothing wrong!" Jo protested, putting extra emphasis in her voice to convince him, then hating herself for doing so. "I'm fine."

"You sound real far away," George went on, listlessly.

"Hey, is something bothering you?"

"No," George said. "You just sound funny to me. Real cold, like you don't care." He wanted her to be sympathetic, remorseful.

And at first she was — repentant, almost hysterical. Then she became impatient. Finally, she lapsed into indifference.

"I have the day off tomorrow," George said over the phone. "Can I come?"

Jo hesitated.

"I have to go to classes," she warned.

"That's okay," he said. "I'll come with you."

There was another long pause. "Well . . . we'll see," she said.

As soon as she saw him the next day, her fears were confirmed. He had gone all out. He wore a silky purple shirt open halfway to his navel, and skintight slacks that left nothing to the imagination. There was something pathetic and vulnerable about the line of his leg so thoroughly revealed by them. As they approached the campus, George pulled out a pair of dark shades and put them on.

He was like a character walking into the wrong play. He glowed defiantly among the faded jeans and work shirts of the Berkeley campus.

Jo's first class was Renaissance Literature.

"If you want to do something else," she said, "I can meet you after class."

"That's okay, man," George said happily. "I want to see what they teaching you."

"It's gonna be real boring," she said.

"That's okay," he said. "I have my psych book."

"If you're going to study," Jo said carefully, "maybe you should go to the library."

"Hey," George said, "you tryin' to get rid of me?"

"No," Jo lied.

"Then let's go."

They entered the room. It was a seminar of about ten people, sitting in a circle.

They joined the circle, but after a few minutes of discussion about *Lycidas*, George opened his psychology textbook and began to read.

Jo was mortified. The woman sitting on the other side of George was looking curiously, out of the corner of her eye, at the diagram of the human brain in George's book.

"Would you care to read the next stanza aloud?" the lecturer asked suddenly. "You — the gentleman with the dark glasses."

There was a horrible moment as all eyes turned to George, bent over his psychology textbook. He squirmed and sank down into his seat, as if trying to become invisible.

"I think he's just visiting," the woman next to George volunteered. "I'll read."

Afterwards, Jo was brutal. Why had he come to the class if he was going to be so rude? Why hadn't he sat off in the corner, if he was going to study? Or better yet, gone to the library as she had suggested? Didn't he know how inappropriate his behavior was? Didn't he care if they thought that Japanese people were boors? Didn't he know? Didn't he care?

No, he didn't know. He was oblivious. It was the source of his confidence, and that was what she had loved him for.

And so the curtain fell on their little drama, after a predictable denouement — agreeing that they would date others, then a tearful good-bye one dark night in his car, parked outside her apartment. Jo had always thought it somewhat disturbing when characters who had been left dead on the set in the last act, commanding considerable emotion by their demise, should suddenly spring to life not a minute later, smiling and bowing, and looking as unaffected by tragedy as it is possible to look. She therefore hoped she would not run into George, who would most certainly be smiling and bowing and oblivious to tragedy. She needn't have worried. Their paths had never been likely to cross.

Jo was making plans to study in New York when she heard through the grapevine that George was planning a trip to Europe. He went that summer, and when he returned, he brought her parents a gift. Jo's parents, who had had enough complaints about George when Jo was seeing him, were touched, and when Christmas came around Jo's mother, in true Japanese fashion, prepared a gift for George to return his kindness. Jo, of course, was expected to deliver it.

She had had no contact with him since they had broken up. His family was still living in Japantown, but the old Victorian was going to be torn down for urban renewal, and they were planning to move out to the Avenues, the Richmond District where Jo's parents lived.

As Jo's dad drove her to George's house, Jo hoped he wouldn't be home, hoped she could just leave the gift with his mother. She was thankful that she was with her father, who had a habit of gunning the engine as he sat waiting in the car for deliveries to be made, and was therefore the ideal person with whom to make a quick getaway.

George's grandmother opened the door. When she saw who it was, her face changed and she cried out with pleasure. Jo was completely unprepared for the look of happiness and hope on her face.

"Jo-chan!" George's grandmother cried; then, half-turning, she called out Jo's name twice more, as if summoning the household to her arrival.

Jo was stunned.

"This is for George," she said, thrusting the gift at George's grandmother, almost throwing it at her in her haste. "Merry Christmas."

She turned and fled down those stairs for the last time, away from the doomed Victorian and the old Japanese woman who stood in the doorway still, calling her name.

1991

Critical thinking points: After you've read

1) *Why do you think "first love" often ends tragically? Do you believe it has to? Why or why not?*
2) *What are some characteristics of "first love" as it is portrayed in contemporary film or fiction? Are these characteristics apparent in this story? Why or why not?*
3) *When did you know Jo and George were doomed or drifting apart? What details in the story led to this?*
4) *What kind of "pecking order" or hierarchy exists among Japanese Americans in the story? Why might non–Japanese Americans, especially Caucasians, misunderstand this hierarchy?*
5) *Throughout the story there are references to World War II, Japanese internment camps, and the Vietnam War. Why are these important to the plot?*

Some possibilities for writing

1) *List some outdated terms that appear in the story. Now update those terms using contemporary phrases that have close to the same meaning. What are some of the positive and/or negative associations with these terms?*
2) *First year students often leave a boyfriend or girlfriend behind when they come to college. Interview a classmate who is dealing with a long-distance relationship. How does that couple cope with the separation?*
3) *Recall other "first love" stories (perhaps the most famous is* Romeo and Juliet*) or films. Write an essay comparing Jo and George's experience to that of another fictional couple or a couple you know.*
4) *Contact your Admissions Office or Dean of Students Office to find out the number of Asian-American students on your campus. Are there any student groups specifically for Asian Americans? What type of support do they offer?*

Revision

John David Rose

"

> ## I wish I could compare a rose to you
> ## Without repeating what's been said before

"

Critical thinking points: As you read

1) The form of this poem is a "sonnet." Even if you don't know what that means, can you guess some of the elements of that form simply from reading this poem?

2) What is a cliché? How is the notion of cliché at work in this poem?

3) Why might a poet use the image of a rose in a love poem?

I wish I could compare a rose to you
Without repeating what's been said before
By Shakespeare or Burns. The master poets do
It best. I should refrain from saying more.
But when the sunrays through the windows fall
Upon a crystal vase, diffuses light
Everywhere, I feel a quiet call
To write about the beauty in my sight:

The space between the petals is the pause
Between your breaths at night when you're asleep.
I love the color of the rose because
It's like the color of your breasts, a deep
Pink. I see the rose and think of new
Contrivances to equate its allure to you.

1993

John David Rose (b. 1971) wrote this poem while a graduate student.

Critical thinking points: After you've read

1) *Research the sonnet form. Does this poem fit the form of a traditional sonnet? Why or why not?*
2) *Rose says, "The master poets do /It best. I should refrain from saying more." Why do you think love poems, stories, and songs continue to be written?*
3) *Read or reread Jennifer Fandel's "Raspberries" in which she compares love to raspberries, a unique image, while this poet compares love or his lover to a rose, a common image in poetry. Does Rose's poem work even with the cliché of love as a rose? In what ways does this poem step outside of clichés?*
4) *What makes this a poem? Would this work as a short story or an essay? Why or why not?*
5) *What are all the reasons you can think of that the poem is called "Revision"?*

Some possibilities for writing

1) *Choose a sonnet by William Shakespeare (numbers 18, 29, 73, 116, or 130 are good candidates) and rewrite it in poetry or prose attempting to update it in terms of vocabulary and imagery.*
2) *Rewrite this poem as a dialogue between two people. Use lines from the poem as one of the person's conversation, and create a response from another person. First, write the scene as two people in love.*
3) *Same as above, but this time write the scene as one person in love and one not so interested. Next, write the scene for two people who have just met. Remember, one half of the dialogue (the lines in the poem) will not change.*
4) *Find and read the following poems by famous English Poets: "O Rose, Thou Art Sick!" by William Blake, "A Song: When June Is Past, the Fading Rose" by Thomas Carew, and "A Red Red Rose" by Robert Burns. After reading these poems, write briefly on how knowing these poems has changed or deepened your appreciation of "Revision."*

Carmen

Jennifer Sheridan

I thought I might throw up after all the booze,
and Aaron winking at me, so I dug another vanilla wafer
out of the box and drank some tap water out of my cupped palm.
Carmen lay face down on her bed, trying to light a cigarette.

Critical thinking points: As you read

1) Why do you think the story is called "Carmen"?
2) Do you know people who are as disconnected from their academic lives as Carmen and Kate? Why are they disenchanted and disengaged characters?
3) Romantic ideas surrounding lost virginity for young people are promoted in movies, TV, and books. How are these romantic ideas reflected in the story?
4) Consider the "reality" of Carmen's and Kate's individual sexual experiences. How does this contrast to the romantic ideas they both have?

My best friend Carmen leaned against the sink and arched her back. She blew smoke at the ceiling and it curled back down the face of the mirror behind her. She was telling me the story of her virginity in that slow, sultry way she had. She'd just finished the orgasm part. We were cutting all our Monday afternoon classes and sharing a cigarette in her dorm bathroom.

It had happened over Thanksgiving break the previous week, in Greece with an older cousin who spoke no English. Late, nearly dawn. Parted French doors. An ocean.

I draped my arms over the still warm hand dryer. Carmen's tan was a deep berry color that rolled out of the sleeves of her T-shirt.

"Afterwards he paced around the room," she whispered. I pictured a leopard crisscrossing by the open window. Outside the sky would glow lavender. A breeze. The sound of water. The smell of salt and sky and beach.

"What did it feel like?"

"Watching him pace?"

Jennifer Sheridan has a Master of Fine Arts degree in fiction from Columbia College in Chicago.

"Yeah." I pictured myself in her place, lying on starched white sheets as my first lover, foreign and chiseled, paced like a wild animal.

"It was awesome," she said. "It was my favorite part." Passing the cigarette, she gave me a smile no one else for miles ever saw. She knew the pacing part would be my favorite too.

"God, Carmen, leave it to you to have the perfect first time," I said.

"Let's get drunk," she suggested. I nodded, dropping the half-smoked cigarette into the sink. It landed in a fierce sizzle.

By five-thirty the pint of Jack Daniel's was finished and the dinner migration began. When Aaron Klinger sauntered by Carmen's doorway he winked at me. Aaron Klinger who'd phone me late at night. *What was I doing? Nothing much.* I'd follow the scent of stale cigarettes into his bed. But it was a secret.

I thought I might throw up after all the booze, and Aaron winking at me, so I dug another vanilla wafer out of the box and drank some tap water out of my cupped palm. Carmen lay face down on her bed, trying to light a cigarette.

At six-fifteen her date appeared, standing at the door for God knows how long before I noticed him. Byron. He had black pubic curly hair on his face and head, and bugged-out eyes. His hands fluttered over his chest, landing at his sides.

Carmen insisted I come to an ancient Warren Beatty film that I'd seen twice to make sure I really hated, but what the hell, Carmen wanted me to go.

During the movie I watched her face flicker in the light coming off the screen. Occasionally I saw Byron glaring at me from the other side. I thought about Aaron, how we smoked in silence sometimes, afterward, staring at the ceiling, not touching.

"Kate," he once said. "You know Scott, the football player?"

"Yeah?"

"Well, every day he goes to this one girl's room and they do it." He leaned on one elbow and tapped his cigarette into the ashtray lying between us. I pulled the sheet up to my chin. "She makes him a cheese omelet, and that's it." Aaron rested his chin on my sheet covered chest. His greasy hair fell onto the back of my hand as I stroked the nape of his neck.

"That's great, Aaron," I said.

In the science auditorium a ten-foot Warren Beatty leaned into an open refrigerator against a half-naked Goldie Hawn.

"Juicy bootie," Carmen growled. I laughed, but I felt a hundred years old. I just wanted to go home. Maybe the phone in my hallway would be ringing. Maybe my brother would call from Yale.

"Hey, Sis, how's that Anthro class?" He'd never called me from Yale. He didn't know what classes I had.

Outside the air smelled of frost. Carmen sang a Christmas carol. Byron jammed his hands into his pockets, his eyes on Carmen, twirling in and out of sight on perfect ballet points.

"My mother is such a bitch," she said. "I hate her guts." I thought about flannel sheets against my naked skin.

"She's just drunk," I mumbled to Byron.

"Kiss me," Carmen screamed, grabbing him. She knew how bad he wanted her. I thought it was cruel, the way she treated guys. But maybe I was wrong to feel bad. Byron didn't give a shit about her either. He wanted what he wanted; we all did. At the time I gave everyone a million times more credit than they deserved.

Byron puckered his skinny chapped lips. I could see them quiver in the moonlight. Carmen wouldn't be happy about this in the morning, if she remembered it at all.

"Carmen . . ." I started. Carmen was in my face like a guard dog.

"Mind you're own fucking business," she screamed.

"Yeah," said Byron. His hand gripped her arm. Carmen turned to him with a low laugh. I tried again. This time she whipped around and slapped me hard across the face. We all heard the sound. While I stroked the stinging place on my cheek his arm wrapped around her back, sliding down over her ass. She squeaked a little as he kissed her. Carmen pulled away, almost falling over backwards. Byron licked his lips and steadied her with his spindly hands.

"Good night to you," she slurred. She'd forgotten his name. Carmen disappeared into the darkness. When I found her she was throwing up in the bushes. I half-dragged her to her room.

Carmen pulled her limp dress over her head and fell naked onto the bed. She laughed at me, standing by the sink holding an empty vanilla wafer box. I could see her shape in the dim light from the hall.

"I do love you, Katie," she mumbled, rolling toward the wall. I hung her dress on the closet doorknob and stood very still on her carpet. She whimpered slightly, a sharp stab, then nothing.

I took the two steps to the side of the bed. She rolled onto her back, cradling her long arm behind her head.

"My mom," she said.

"I know," I whispered. I pulled the damp hair out of her eyes and smoothed it down along her pillow. She smelled terrible, of vomit and whiskey. She sobbed again. Her eyelids fluttered. I ran my hand over her forehead. She leaned into my fingers, cool against her hot skin. I kissed her cheek and pressed my face against hers.

Suddenly Carmen came to life. She wrapped her sweaty, strong arms around my neck and pulled my face to hers by my hair. I clamped my jaw shut, stifling a scream. Adrenaline shot through me so fast my fingers shot out straight. The next thing I knew her mouth was on mine, her lips grinding against me, her tongue forcing my teeth apart. Carmen, my best friend. Her mouth felt swollen and hot, but her tongue was cooler. It glided finally past my stubborn teeth, into my mouth. Only after she had fallen back onto the bed, eyes shut, breathing even and deep did I feel the sensation of our tongues together, like warm snakes in a twisting, sinewy pile.

When I stood up my legs wobbled. Carmen's naked chest rose and fell, half under the sheet. I staggered through the door and up the stuffy hall. One long, florescent light bulb flickered purple as I passed under it.

In the morning Carmen called me on the phone.

"God, Katie," she laughed. "I feel like hell."

I was angry, not because she'd slapped me but just because of everything. She wore me out. I'd watched her dance and flirt and held her head while she barfed. Carmen wasn't meant for quiet, Midwestern evenings. Her green-tinted skin and wild ways, her elegance made me hate myself.

She admitted sheepishly that she'd been pretty drunk the night before. No, she didn't remember the movie, or spilling her Raisinets, licking melted chocolate from her fingers.

"Do you remember kissing Byron?" I asked.

"I didn't."

"Do you remember slapping me?"

"Katie, I never did!"

"Yeah, you sure did."

I thought about Carmen putting badly typed love letters signed with Aaron's name in my mailbox, Carmen calling at two a.m. to talk about Ingmar Bergman, Carmen saying I looked like a Gypsy princess in the sweater I was sure people thought was weird.

"Katie, did I? Tell me I didn't."

"You didn't."

"I did, didn't I?"

"Yeah, you did."

"I'm sorry, Katie," she said. "Do you forgive me?"

I forgave Carmen. I met her for lunch. She looked the same. Standing at the bottom of the stairs leading up to the dining hall her hands did not shake. She reached for me, a fake worried look on her face.

"Help me up the stairs, daughter," she said in an old lady voice. "I feel like shit." She leaned against me as we climbed the stairs, mumbling how much coffee she would need, twenty-nine cups, black.

We blew off all our classes that day. We smoked and laughed and bought a bottle of gin. Coming out of the liquor store Carmen said she'd call her evil, stingy father for more money.

"If I'm lucky my mom will answer the phone. She always throws in an extra fifty," she said.

Sitting in the grass outside the library Carmen apologized again and shook her head, smiling into her lap. I watched her bring her cigarette to her lips. I watched her close her eyes. I listened to the ache behind her laugh that only I ever heard. I told her a thousand times to forget the whole thing. I promised to forget it myself. I really had no choice in the matter.

1996

Critical thinking points: After you've read

1) Do you believe Carmen's story about losing her virginity? Why or why not?

2) Kate and Carmen take turns being the mother and the daughter. Find examples of this role switching in the text. Why do you think that is?

3) Why does Kate seem to worship Carmen? What is Carmen's attitude toward Kate? What details in the story support this?

4) What do you think makes the scene in which Carmen kisses a Kate a pivotal one in the plot?

5) How would the story be different if the two lead characters were male?

Some possibilities for writing

1) Write about friends, family members, or acquaintances who remind you in some way of Kate or Carmen.

2) Compare and contrast Carmen's and Kate's attitude(s) toward sex.

3) Universities are notorious for promoting a lifestyle that accepts promiscuity and many sexual partners. What are your views of college life and its reputation for creating sexually active students? What do you think are some of the causes of this? What might be some of the results?

4) Why does Kate say in the last line of the story, "I promised to forget it myself. I really had no choice in the matter." Does Carmen have a "choice in the matter"? Why or why not?

5) Many young men and women take pride in preserving their virginity until marriage. Write a dialogue between two men or two women in which one of them explains to the other why virginity is valued. Now write a scene between a man and a woman based on the same premise.

What It's Really Like

Frank Smoot

"
---

you think it's too bad you'll never know each other,

"

Critical thinking points: As you read

1) *What do you make of the title? Does this poem portray "what it's really like"?*
   Why or why not?
2) *What kind of people are the characters in this poem? List some adjectives that*
   describe them.
3) *Keep track of all the things that the narrator can and cannot know in this*
   poem.

It would be comforting to know something
about her that would annoy you: she laughs
like a hyena or likes a kind of music that you hate.
But the truth is that she's nice and so are you,

and as you drive away from the small light
of the restaurant on the highway in another state
you think it's too bad you'll never know each other,
and you look at yourself in the rearview mirror,

your face lighted dimly by the dashboard,
and smile because she smiled at you.
You kick it out a little, thumbs tapping
to the sweet song on the radio, to which,

you have no way of knowing,
she's dancing as she closes up.

1995

In addition to poems and short stories, Frank Smoot (b. 1961) has published some two hundred articles, including editorials, essays, features, interviews, and critiques of art, dance, film, literature, and music. He is currently at work on a biography of 1940s film star Carole Landis.

Critical thinking points: After you've read

1) Why is this brief moment significant enough to write about? Is it important to anyone but the characters? Why or why not?

2) Life is usually made up of a series of regulated and predictable moments that happen again and again. How does this poem portray that even within such dull moments adventure waits, hides, and perhaps even stalks?

3) Why do you think the United States' system of dating and marriage is based on romantic love? How is this sentiment promoted? How does this compare with other countries or other times in American history?

4) Should the speaker of the poem have "said something" to the woman? Why or why not?

Some possibilities for writing

1) Write the next scene for one or both of the characters in the poem. Where do they go after this scene? Who do they talk to? What do they do?

2) Write what might be called a "pre-nuptial agreement" in which you list the obligations and/or expectations for a husband and wife. You can base your list on couples you know whose relationship works, couples whose relationship disintegrated, or couples whose relationship you think is failing.

3) Visit some gathering place for college students — a student lounge, a commons area, or a cafeteria — and write a "history" for some of the couples you see around you but do not know anything about.

Virginity

Jane Barnes Casey

"

Eleanor has a problem she considers 'old fashioned and obsolete.' 'How is it possible that she, a college girl in 1970, assumed sex must lead to marriage?'

"

Critical thinking points: As you read

1) The story is set in 1970. What are some clues to this time period? What are some themes or details in the story that still pertain to college students today?

2) Watch for stereotypes of male and female college students. Make a list. Are these stereotypes simply about men and women in general or men and women who attend college?

3) Why is loss of virginity associated with loss of innocence?

The first phone call she got at college was from her parents. They asked her about her room, her roommate, her teachers, and her courses. What they were really asking, Eleanor knew, was if she was aware of how much they had sacrificed so she could go to college. In the conversation going on beneath the spoken one, Eleanor could hear them saying, "We have always lived on the fringe. We have always lived on the fringe of beauty, money, position, and style. We gave our lives fighting for that place on the edge so you could live in the interior. We gave our lives so you would have a better life than we did."

They had taught her to listen with her soul, and now as she absorbed her parents' tacit reminder, her being took on the shape of their words. When she hung up, she felt like ticker tape. She knew that in matters of ambition and taste she had only to consult the cardinal rules imprinted on the inside of her chest. (1) The only way for a

Jane Barnes Casey (b. 1942) is the author of two novels, *I, Krupskaya* (Houghton Mifflin, 1974) and *Double Lives* (Doubleday, 1981). Her short stories and essays have appeared in such magazines as *Shenandoah, MLLE, Denver Quarterly Review,* and *The Virginia Quarterly Review.* She has been a writer on several award-winning documentaries, including "Richard Avedon: Darkness and Light" (for American Masters) and "The Choice, '96" (for Frontline).

woman to rise is through marriage. (2) The fastest way for her to rise the furthest is for her to marry a rich and socially prominent man — socially acceptable if worse comes to worse.

When she met Mitchell Kent at Yale, Eleanor recognized him as the man her parents wanted her to marry. He was rich and he was also upper-class. His family had houses in Long Island and in New York City, owned a highly prized Impressionist painting (as well as two Picassos), were descendants of a famous abolitionist, and had reputations for their own selflessness as public servants.

It came as a happy surprise when Eleanor also discovered she liked him for other reasons beside those which qualified him as her groom. First of all, she liked him for his indifference to her. He took her out, but remained aloof, leaving her room to imagine what his character and feelings really were. Mitchell remained a mystery of her own making until, towards spring, he began calling her late at night, after he'd returned from the library. He was warmer on the phone, described what he was studying and talked about his thesis. She was braver on the phone, flirted with him and asked him questions about the girls he'd known. One night he started to describe his sister, and then went on to tell the story of his life. By the time he'd finished they were drawn violently together by his show of vulnerability, but though they knew they were in love, neither of them said it. They were too shy to confirm in person what had happened on the phone, and made no plans to see each other. The next night he called again, and once more they discussed and probed the story of his life. They were like primitives rubbing a talisman, evoking the mysterious ruling spirit of their universe — like primitives they could not resist the urge to test their power, to see if they could wake the fearful spirit.

Mitchell called every night that week, and they talked for hours about themselves, their motives, and the themes they felt their lives embodied. Gradually, their communications by phone grew so ritualized they felt lonely and separate each time they spoke, and finally Mitchell said he was hanging up and driving down to see her.

Eleanor went to wait for him outside the college gate, and while she waited she had never been so happy. The suspense had a sensual, soothing effect on her mind's constant impulse to picture what was happening to her. Her confidence in the outcome, her sure sense that she and Mitchell would get married, quieted her parents' qualms, qualms which like alarm clocks going off made her sit up suddenly, rubbing her eyes and wondering where her life had gone. Now, filled with expectations and released from worry, she felt she was floating, as light and gay as air.

When Mitchell arrived, he showed no sign of sharing her emotions. She was ready to interpret anything he did or said as meaningful, but then nothing he did seemed meaningful enough. Clenching her arm above the elbow, Mitchell drew her down a dark street of haywire suburban mansions, describing in minute and tedious detail how careful he had been not to wake his roommate when he left. Mitchell recalled how he crawled around the dark bedroom, groping to find his socks, and how, once he'd found them, his roommate switched the light on, laughing because

he'd never been asleep. The word "bedroom" made Eleanor stiffen with embarrassment and terror, but she relaxed immediately, went limp with disappointment when
she realized Mitchell had said it in all innocence.

They crossed a bridge and found an entrance to the vast back yard of an estate.
Mitchell led her into the garden and then steered her to a grove of pine trees. They sat
on the needles, breathing the fragrant, heartbreaking spring air and making feverish
small talk. Towards dawn, beneath the grey ceiling of sky, Mitchell pitched himself
unhappily into her lap, stroking her and murmuring, "Please, let me make love to
you. You're so beautiful and I love you."

His sudden coming to the point bruised Eleanor's romantic sense, confusing her
still more about his feelings. She could not understand his timing, could not interpret
him with any confidence; and without his word for his affection, she didn't know
what it would mean if she complied and slept with him. "What does it mean?" she
whispered.

"I don't know," he said, leaning his hot cheek against her arm. Then he added in
an unnatural voice, "It means us."

But the ambiguities multiplied until Eleanor, given time to think, had no idea of
who the two of them were or why they were sitting there. The situation began to
seem so complex she felt their bodies were pathetic oversimplifications. He hadn't
mentioned marriage, and so she didn't know if sleeping with him would be a step to
or from the altar. She did not know how else to think of making love except in
relation to marriage, and now, when she tried to consider it by itself, she did not
know where to start or how to assign meaning. What did desire have to do with the
question of God's existence? How did it fit into her freshman history course? Would
sleeping with Mitchell affect him in the same way it would affect her? Did the time
of day have an influence on the inclination to fall in love? If so, was it important?
Was desire both natural and sinful? Who said it was sinful and why? Categories
clashed in her mind and she could not keep things straight. Questions swirled about
her until she thought she'd faint. She was surprised and relieved to hear Mitchell say,
"I'm sorry. I couldn't stand to hurt you. Please don't be angry."

She was incredibly grateful to him for not making her decide, and, for a long
time, they were closest in the moments when he forgave her for not sleeping with
him. Whenever he pressed her, sides of the question filled her mind, and she moved
among them as sensuously as a fish feeding on sea ferns. As long as the problem
remained in question form — should she? shouldn't she? and why? — Eleanor felt
complete. If, from worry or impatience, a decision began to crystallize, she panicked, and felt she was shattering. The closest she could come to acting was by not
sleeping with him and that way keeping open the possibility of one day doing so.

She spent hours with Mitchell discussing calmly and gravely why she was afraid
to sleep with him.

"I know," she said. "I know it's irrational and illogical of me to think this way,
but basically I do. I'm afraid my parents will be mad."

"But why?"

"I don't know. They never said I shouldn't sleep with the person I loved. Obviously, they'd never find out anyway if I did."

"It's just an excuse, a defense you don't even know you're using," Mitchell said. "You feel that if you sleep with me you'll relinquish your innocence and therefore your childhood. You don't want as yet to be thought of as responsible, so you say your parents will be mad; but really you're saying you don't want to."

"I'm sure that's right," she said. "I'm sure of it."

He smiled and tried to embrace her. She pulled back. "What's wrong?" he asked.

"My parents will be mad," she said apologetically.

They approached her problem like a crossword puzzle, testing solutions and different points of view and listing all the synonyms they knew to see if they could find the key to Eleanor by finding which nuance fit her best. But no label ever fit; at least no label set her free, and she knew no label they devised together would describe her. No label could because she was too embarrassed by the truth to say all she knew about her difficulty. She felt her problem was old-fashioned, obsolete, and that she shouldn't be affected by it. How was it possible that she, a college girl in 1970, assumed sex must lead to marriage?

Her parents had been adamant about the groom and marriage, but they'd never laid down sexual taboos. To attract the kind of quality they wanted for her, they insisted that she be perfect in appearances. They were sticklers in matters of the clothes she wore, the things she said, the friends she picked, but they'd never specifically forbidden her to sleep with men. By herself and by association, Eleanor arrived at the principle of purity. She deduced her morals from their rules for her appearance; and through no virtue of her parents, her morals were as firm and fast as gold. In fact, her morals were her gold: all she had to prove that she was the well-groomed virgin she seemed to be.

For as long as Mitchell did not mention marriage, she would not sleep with him, was literally unable to because her virtue was all she had, and spend it she would not unless by doing so she bought a new and better way of life. Her pride would not let her mention marriage first, and the merchant in her would not let her go for less; but though this was the simple truth about her, Eleanor could not bring herself to say so. Instead, she went on discussing her reluctance in terms of Passive and Active, Historical Forces, Theories of Id and Ego. In time, she and Mitchell ceased talking about their frustrated physical relationship, though that frustration poisoned all their other efforts to stay happy.

They continued to see each other long into her sophomore year at college. Eleanor felt she didn't have the right to end it because she was the one who'd ruined it. Her guilt was of the sort which felt relieved only by persisting in the crime, prolonging her punishment by constantly anticipating it. Mitchell stayed because Eleanor was the first girl he'd ever been in love with, and so he felt for her twice the responsibility he felt for women anyway. They both hoped and secretly believed that the original promise would return and that then they'd consummate their relations. But the early promise did not return, and they felt less and less inclined to sleep together, increasingly aware that doing so would be a further blasphemy of the innocence they'd already lost.

The next summer Mitchell went to Europe to study the Italian Masters. This seemed like a natural time to bring everything to an end, though neither of them wrote the final words. After a month of not hearing from him, Eleanor began to worry. When Mitchell was present, analyzing their difficulties and her character, she felt secure because she always knew how near or far he was from the truth. That was, she always felt that she was constantly reminding herself of the truth and so never fooling herself about her honesty. She believed that if he ever hit upon the truth, she'd admit to it even though it was unflattering. Because she planned to be open with him, Eleanor had the feeling that she was, in general, frank with him.

In his absence, she lost her sure grip on his opinion of her. She began to imagine all the possible things he could think about her: that she was a coward or frigid or stupid or just so hysterically selfish she could not stand to share herself with anyone. Eleanor pictured him in the future, talking to a friend and saying, "Do you know who I was first in love with? Do you realize it was Eleanor Davies? Can you believe that? It is really funny how bad people's taste is when it comes to first girlfriends."

She was so upset by the picture of him laughing at her in the future that she decided she would write the simple truth to him. She hoped this would elicit his honest opinion of her which, no matter how ugly, would at least follow from his knowledge that she was a serious person.

> Dear Mitchell,
>
> A lot has come clear to me this summer, and while it stands still I want to tell you what I see, most of all to show you no malice on my part drove us to distraction. One memory tugs violently. Staying at the beach house with the great four-poster bed. I woke on Sunday morning in that room hurricane-struck by our quarrel. Clothes flung everywhere. My green dress was sprawling on the bureau, my stockings were draped across the chair like rag-doll legs. Sweaters, shirts, pants were spattered everywhere. I realized slowly that it looked like a scene of the most marvelous abandon, a prelude to an 18th century romp. But for us the fight was all — and it was all my fault.
>
> What, until now, was not absolutely clear was why it was my fault. But I was programmed by my parents to believe certain things about them, to believe they were especially good to give things up for me, and that I, in turn, must be especially good to justify their sacrifice. I thought the better life they meant for me demanded utter purity. I thought they meant by being very good, I'd marry very well, but they meant simply: marry well or else.

She went on, describing her assumptions about marriage and what she believed her parents thought of it and her. She apologized in every other line, ending by wishing him luck and saying that she hoped they would be friends in the future.

Dear Eleanor,

he replied,

Well, you sure picked the right guy for a groom. I'm pretty well fixed for cash and culture and heritage — and if you'd caught me, you'd have had a catch. Sorry I didn't know about your impending marriage to me, maybe if I had things would have been different. At least, I might have taken advantage of you and gotten some pleasure out of it all.

Mitchell's letter horrified her. The difference in their views of what had happened made Eleanor uncomfortable at the very root of her energies. She had never meant him to feel so humiliated, and she wondered if he might really have the right to be so bitter. Until their disagreement was at least partially reconciled, she knew she would not feel at home in her own skin.

If she hadn't been what she thought, how did she know what to become? With Mitchell's dissent afoot in the world she might encounter disbelief at any corner, might go into rooms where people thought she was a plain materialist because Mitchell had given them their first impression of her.

In the fall, she contrived through friends to see Mitchell again. She found out when he was going to be at Yale alone over the weekend, and drove to New Haven with another couple. After the game, while her friends went to a cocktail party, Eleanor "dropped by" Mitchell's room. She found him there, and the sight of him made her feel so petty, she blurted out the truth: "I was terribly upset by your letter and had to see you. I couldn't stand to have you think of me that way."

"I'm sorry I ever wrote it," he said. "I was terribly excited to find a letter from you and then it turned out to be a complicated 'Dear John,' so I wrote the one I sent you in a fury and mailed it before I calmed down."

They began to talk of common friends, of their vacations and their plans. Through the windows streamed warm autumn sun, enriching the carpet's green and putting a hazy veil of dust between them. She felt she could say anything and did, and as she did they were drawn closer, in a finer mesh, a deeper intimacy than any they had known. They drifted onto the sofa, entwined and lingering in slow, hot kisses. When they finally made love, it was with the freshness of spontaneous desire; yet they brought to this, their original experience, all the pain they'd ever inflicted on each other.

Later, Mitchell said nothing had ended between them, that they'd arrived at last at the real beginning. Eleanor agreed, but only because agreement was her way, at that moment, of being grateful. No experience had ever touched her so profoundly or surprised her so much. She was amazed by her feelings; she felt freed, not fallen. By sleeping with Mitchell, she discovered her virtue was not locked up in her virginity.

Now that her parents' spell was broken, Eleanor felt buoyant, billowing, released to a state where she was all things at once. Nothing need be excluded from her, and no one thing need sum her up. By living with Mitchell on weekends, she fulfilled an aspect of herself, but the rest of her sought other, equally characteristic outlets. Wasn't she a collection of qualities, a group of combinations, each requiring a separate way of life? During the week she went out with different people, but never told Mitchell. She saw no reason why the discrete parts of her life should be in touch with one another — their coherence and unity lay in being aspects of her life.

She began to have an affair with David Bryant, a graduate student at Columbia, and never mentioned Mitchell to him or him to Mitchell. Her feelings for Mitchell did not exclude her feelings for David; her affection for Mitchell's qualities did preclude her having equal affection for David's quite different qualities. She could be considerate and kind to both without feeling contradictory or treacherous. She knew that if she had time, and if she met someone she liked, she could have an affair with a third person simultaneously.

Mitchell was graduating in June, and a job awaited him at the Modern Museum of Art. He suggested to Eleanor that it was a good time for them to get married, and Eleanor, seeing this was sensible, accepted his proposal. Marriage was the natural outcome of their kind of relationship, and refusing to marry him would be killing some living part of herself. She thought of marriage as a step in only one of her progressions so the engagement did not stop her from seeing David, though she still did not tell him that she was going to be married in July. Sometimes Mitchell demanded to see her on a day when she planned to meet David, and Eleanor felt that Mitchell's request was his way of robbing David of her feelings. She resented Mitchell when he made her pay him attention at the expense of her other, her various selves, and yet she could not resent him entirely, for she enjoyed many gains on account of her engagement.

For one thing, her father and mother were fulfilled by the match. Mr. and Mrs. Davies went around smiling and patting Eleanor and crooning over Mitchell. Their ambitions satisfied, the Davies softened, and though they were still subject to outbursts about how much they'd done for her, they were mainly awed by the size of their daughter's catch, and gave her most of the credit for catching him.

Two weeks after the wedding invitations were mailed, the presents began to arrive, and Mrs. Davies displayed them in the small living room, treating each with all the delight and respect she felt for the marriage itself. In the evenings, when her husband was home from work and her daughter was getting ready to go out, Mrs. Davies liked to discuss the merits of the china pattern Eleanor had picked. Her husband would join in, praising workmanship in the carved wooden things, hailing taste in the lamps and glasses. The Davies knew the presents lit the way to another life for Eleanor, but by learning her reaction to the silver, glass, and china, they hoped they'd get an education in what she'd be like later.

Eleanor felt removed from her parents, far enough away to want to make them happy. Though she did not know her real feelings for the presents, to please her parents she devised ways to make it possible for her to say she liked having them. She pretended that she was a child come upon the presents her parents were going to give her for Christmas. By imagining she was a little girl, Eleanor swelled her pleasure voluptuously, filling herself with a gratifying, succulent sense of being an adored only child, the sort of spoiled only child she hadn't been herself. When she was alone with the presents, she fed on this fantasy until it finally soured and she found, as she drifted from antique silver spoons to jars for coddled eggs, that she was gripped by a sickening guilt. These were the tools, she realized, with which to fashion her escape. This was the equipment for the life that was better than her parents'. She dreaded the thought of them visiting her in the future house. It made her miserable to picture them — apologetic and uncomfortable in the very world they'd chosen for her.

It was a world peopled by the unfamiliar names printed on the calling cards before the presents. More than half the people were as strange to her as they were to her parents. The difference was, these strangers were her future friends or relatives or neighbors; but to her parents they were wedding guests, and barely that, because, publicly, the wedding was more the wedding of the Seth Kents' eldest son.

When she saw how the crystal and porcelain stood between her and her parents, she wanted to cross back to where they stood. She had no idea what was in store for her. She tried to memorize the names and test herself by putting together a pile of calling cards, shuffling them and then trying to match the right name with the right present. Instead of making her feel more intimately connected to the presents, knowing the names of people she'd never met made her feel as though she were calling roll in a graveyard. She said the names aloud to give them life, but they rang on her tongue with a terrible hollow emptiness. This made her feel all the more the weight of her new possessions, pressing down on her existence, edging her out to make room for the bride. Eleanor saw how she was being pinned down, rendered finite, understood, girdled and imprisoned in a single definition: bride, the blushing bride, the big, fat, and wide.

She was surprised by an intense desire to go off with a stranger. In an instant, she'd pictured herself picking up a sailor in a bar. In another instant, she's envisioned a rendezvous with a bus driver. She was embarrassed by her thoughts, but intrigued by them. She was only afraid they were pushing her towards an hysteria from which she would never return. Did she really want to go off with a stranger? Was it possible to talk to anyone? Was communion something unusual? Was every serious relationship forced to become marital? Or was marriage special to certain relationships?

There was no way she could answer the questions occurring to her because she did not know where she began, did not know her own premise; and seeing this, realizing she'd dug up her character's sole cornerstone when she overturned her parents' law. Eleanor felt herself drowning in fluency, in the liquid essence of herself. For a moment her ego was stilled, and her will swooned, freed from its dry striving, not by love, but by her admission of chance. She saw how points of Mitchell's character were tangent to points of her own, how their tangencies were constantly changing so that his generosity sometimes bordered her own generosity and sometimes bordered her greed. Any combination could occur. His bitterness might be aligned with her fear. His shyness could lie by her curiosity or his courage coincide with her love of antiques. They were like mattresses at sea, bumping and touching with no final arrangement, aimlessly drifting together and apart, buffeted by mood and tossed about by egotism. These were the terms of every human encounter, and marriage was the official recording of one. Knowing this, she also knew she could marry as easily as not, and all that held her to her promise was the honor of her word. At that time, in that situation, her honor was tangent to Mitchell's request, and that tangency would carry them over the crest to whatever lay beyond.

1970

Critical thinking points: After you've read

1) *Summarize Eleanor's response to virginity. What does virginity symbolize in this story? What does virginity symbolize in American culture?*
2) *Do you think Eleanor and Mitchell will get married? Why or why not?*
3) *As Eleanor and Mitchell discuss whether or not they should make love the first time, they analyze what holds her back and never discuss nor act out passion. Is this a believable scenario for these characters? Why or why not?*
4) *In what way might social class have affected Eleanor's choices at college? What pressure does she feel from her parents that seems to be rooted in class structure?*
5) *Casey writes of Eleanor, "If she hadn't been what she thought, how did she know what to become?" What might she mean? How is this a reflection of what you already know about Eleanor before she sends Mitchell the letter?*

Some possibilities for writing

1) *Eleanor gets what she originally wished for when Mitchell proposes to her. In what ways has she changed over the course of the story? Why doesn't her original wish, to marry, seem as fulfilling after her transformation?*
2) *In the middle of her letter to Mitchell, Casey has Eleanor stop writing and says, "She went on, describing her assumptions about marriage and what she believed her parents thought of it and her. She apologized in every other line, ending by wishing him luck and saying that she hoped they would be friends in the future." Write that missing part of the letter.*
3) *In some ways, Eleanor is more sophisticated than the young women we've seen in other pieces collected here. Choose one other female character in this collection who is grappling with her sexuality and write a scene in which Eleanor offers the other woman advice. Some appropriate characters might be Carmen or Kate from "Carmen," Alma from "Irreversible Seasons," or Robin from "50% Chance of Lightning."*
4) *Interview at least six men and women about their attitudes toward a woman who is still a virgin in college and their attitudes toward a man who is. Speculate why you found the answers that you did.*

5) *Make a list of contemporary movies or TV programs that have depicted young people losing their virginity. How is loss of virginity portrayed in popular culture such as novels, films, and TV programs? Why do you think it is portrayed the way it is?*

Irreversible Seasons

Anita Santiago

> **66**
>
> Professor Alcazar stepped into the classroom, the crisp scent of pipe smoke on his wool coat. He looked thick and feral, like a bull hunched over by too many New York winters. He tapped his pipe gently on the edge of the desk. The gesture made Alma think of a blind man with a cane. She noticed he wore a wedding ring.
>
> **99**

Critical thinking points: As you read

1) *Look for allusions to seasons throughout the story. What might the author mean by "Irreversible Seasons"?*
2) *Watch for images of doom and death as you read. Make a list of them. How do these images prepare you for the end of the story?*
3) *Look for foreshadowing in the story that sets up the impending doom for Alma and Carlos. When did you know they were doomed lovers?*
4) *What impresses Alma about Professor Alcazar? Make a list of his qualities that she finds attractive.*

    The classroom smelled like ripe bananas, an odor offensive to Alma so early in the morning. This was her first day of college, and she felt a strange combination of excitement and sleepiness. Students shuffled at their desks, adjusting themselves to the hard wooden seats. The sun came in at an angle, journeying millions of miles to land at the floor near Alma's feet. Cumulus clouds were twisting themselves into a knot high in the sky. She was distracted, longing for someone to love her.

    Professor Alcazar stepped into the classroom, the crisp scent of pipe smoke on his wool coat. He looked thick and feral, like a bull hunched over by too many New

Anita Santiago was raised in a Standard Oil camp in the jungles of Venezuela. She went to school in New York, first at Adelphi University where she received a B.A. in anthropology, and then at State University of New York at Stony Brook where she obtained an M.A. in Spanish language and literature. She has published her work in literary journals and anthologies, and most recently her work appeared in a collection of short stories by women from California entitled *Palm Readings*.

York winters. He tapped his pipe gently on the edge of the desk. The gesture made Alma think of a blind man with a cane. She noticed he wore a wedding ring.

As the Professor wrote on the blackboard, Alma traced his flowery handwriting with her finger, moving it imperceptibly on the desk. She followed the way the loops on the *S's* turned inward in a heavy curve like a woman's hips. He stopped to add scrifs to his letters, making the *T's* overhang like protective arms and the *M's* flatten out as if they were wearing shoes. He wrote about the songs of whales off an island in the Caribbean, about sunsets in wheat fields, when tiny particles fly in the golden rays just before another day is lost.

When class was over, Alma looked around to see if the other students were as moved as she was, but they just picked up their books and walked out placidly. She had just seen a man point to an ordinary object and, like an alchemist, make it shine. Three weeks later Professor Alcazar followed her out of class.

"Coffee?" he asked, sucking on his pipe. It took a moment to realize he was inviting her to the cafeteria. She was confused and not sure whether she had the option to say no.

"I walked all the way up from Chile, through rivers without bridges, through barren flats, through kilometers of humanity," he said over his cup of black coffee, as if the thought weighed on him. She imagined him packing his hopes into beaten suitcases which he carried the whole length of the continent through colonial cities with broken light bulbs and dirty towns with hungry dogs. She saw him arriving in California, contemplating his first American sunset in an artichoke field, his suitcases at his side. Alma stared into her cup and pictured him and his wife waking up to the flat silver light of the winter sun.

"It was a Friday night, the night I became a citizen. The judge who swore us in, forty of us in all, smelled of whiskey." Professor Alcazar told her these things as if he were in a confessional.

"I haven't seen my father in fifteen years," he said. "He may be dead." His father was an Arab who owned a hacienda in Chile. "My last memory of him was hearing him call for the servant girls to bring more wine. There was a full moon on the night I walked out, with just the clothes I was wearing." His mother had died, years before, of grief or madness, he did not know which.

"Look at these," he said, handing Alma letters addressed to him from Cortazar, Llosa, Marquez. She touched them delicately, wondering about the famous hands that had touched them. "Dear Carlos," she read, "I thank the angels for men like you who cherish our savage words carved out in stone." She looked at Professor Alcazar. He looked pleased, puffing on his pipe, watching her. He explained he was editing a series on Latin American authors, the first of its kind.

Alma ran into him several more times during the following weeks. She sat outside, propped against her books in the quadrangle of grass and trees near the building where his class was held. She had never met anyone who spoke to famous authors and received letters from them. She daydreamed about what his wife looked like, what she said when he got home.

"Ah, the jaguar soaks up the last feeble rays of sun. How will she survive the winter?" Professor Alcazar said, smiling. She was startled by the comment. She sat up quickly, wondering if he could tell she had been thinking about him. He seemed awkward outside, at odds with the fresh air and trees.

"I think I'll survive. I have a coat," she said. She stood up, brushing the grass off her jeans, for something to do.

"Well, winters here make you want to cry. So enjoy what's left of the sun," he said.

"You make it sound like doomsday, Professor," she said. He laughed.

"Call me Carlos," he said. There was an easy familiarity on his part. But she could never call him Carlos. She was only seventeen and he was old enough to be her father. She suddenly felt shy, as if she had been thinking dirty thoughts.

"I have to go on an errand. Want to come?" he asked. It was a strange invitation. She was bored and not in the mood to study.

"My journal arrives after Christmas. It's like waiting for a baby. And on a more practical level, it will also help me get tenure, I hope." He smiled. She had the fleeting sensation that he should not be confiding his professional strategies to her, but she was honored. She had always felt smarter than her masculine peers, who tediously explored their manhood in rough talk and beer.

They drove to a jewelry store, and she waited in the car, looking around inside it, curious about the details of his life. There were books in the backseat. When Carlos came out, he showed her a gold ring inlaid with the profile of a man carved out of tiger's eye.

"This was my father's lucky ring," he said. He handed it to her. It felt old, as if many people had previously worn it.

"I had it adjusted for you," he said.

"Oh, no," she exclaimed, extending it back to him, "I can't accept this."

"I won't take it back," he said. "It was meant for you." He started the car.

"Fine. Then I'll just borrow it for a while," she said, slipping the ring on her finger. It felt hot and she had the sensation that she was burning down a house with it.

"Do you like Chinese food?" he asked. They both acted as if what had just happened was perfectly reasonable, and that now it was okay for a professor and his student to have dinner together. Maybe it would be acceptable if they discussed semantics or linguistic theories. And besides, she really did want something hot and spicy after months of bland cafeteria food. They sat at a table near the window with a large red lamp that hung like a harvest moon over them.

"Your face is like sculpture," Carlos said. "The slope of your lips, the way your eyelashes reach down towards your cheeks. You could have been a model for a Renaissance master." Alma blushed.

"There were none in Caracas last time I was there," she said. The waiter had just brought the tea and left them again when Carlos stared at her across the wide expanse of white tablecloth.

"Alma, I love you." It almost sounded like a complaint. She felt a wave of apprehension and excitement sweep down on her. She fought off the discomfort by pretending that the table between them was a wide savanna of snow, and she was a Mongol riding away on a horse, through a sparse forest made of salt and pepper shakers, soy sauce bottles. The horse's hooves kicked up snow and she could hear it huffing with exertion. I'm getting away, she thought. But Carlos reached over and took her hand, bringing her back to the Chinese restaurant, to the table, to him.

Alma propped her chin on her hand, suddenly fired, and said, "I'm sorry."

"I'm sorry too. But I know enough not to fight love when it finally comes for me," said Carlos.

"You make it sound like death," Alma said. He shook his head sadly. "I didn't think this could happen to me," he said. "I had planned my life. Found a wonderful woman. I thought I could love her, given time. But it's been ten years and there is no passion. The magic is either there or it isn't. You can't force it or will it into being."

And when magic happens, it's not right, thought Alma. She was shot through with sadness. Professor Alcazar was so much older and married. They didn't have a chance. And yet she felt that turning him away was like throwing a diamond into the sea. Maybe this was the only time she would ever be loved. *How do I know he's not the love of my life?* she thought. On the way home, the green light from the dashboard lit up his face. A pawn shop, with dented plates and old silverware and outdated cameras, the dregs of someone else's life, looked desolate. They drove past a dusty bridal shop, with faded dresses in the window.

"Everything reminds me of you," he said. "I dream about you. I think of you when I wake up, every second of the day." He parked outside her door. They sat in silence, contemplating the quietness of the street. The neighborhood had an orderly quality to it, as if in the houses there were only families at peace, families started by men and women who had no problems, who were the same age, who were legal. She was envious. Then suddenly his mouth was on hers and she was engulfed by a sensation of urgency. It's madness, she thought, but she couldn't stop. He kissed her until she lost all sense of time and geography.

The following day, Alma was astounded by the blue fluorescence of a bird's feather on the sidewalk, the crisp taste of an apple, the clarity of a note struck on a piano. She avoided him at the university. She was embarrassed by the heated kiss. There was no one she could turn to. She thought of his wife, and felt a sorry kinship with her. She was ashamed to have become the catalyst of a betrayal. It bothered Alma that she had willingly become his accomplice, plotting to be at the right place, staying just a bit later after each class, trying to make it seem casual. Maybe she could still pretend it was an intellectual friendship. No one else had to know that she looked at the way his hands cupped his pipe and imagined them cupping her breasts. Several days passed and she did not see him.

It was a cold black Orion night when she heard a tap on her window. He was standing in the chilled air, breathing fog, like a drowning man surfacing at her window. She felt a sense of horror when she realized his bags were packed and loaded onto the top of his station wagon.

"I'm leaving her," he said. His eyes shone with victory and despair. Alma stared at him, overwhelmed by the irreversibility of this action. She thought of his wife, dissolving his absence in her mouth like a communion wafer. Life was moving forward too quickly.

"Are you crazy?" she whispered through the window.

"Yes," he said. "I can't live without you. Come here to me." She hesitated, and then went outside into the frosty air. He took her to an apartment, empty except for a kitchen table and a bed. In the kitchen, they danced to a slow Latin American song about heartbreak, their feet shuffling loudly on the white linoleum floor. Alma had the sensation that they were breaking all the rules. That they would be prosecuted. That it would mean life or death. But it didn't matter because it was love. He held her tightly, he kissed the top of her head. Then he stopped dancing and leading her by the hand, took her into the bedroom.

The moonlight was blue and intrusive, bouncing off the snow and illuminating them through the curtainless window. He lay down next to her, the full length of his body pressed against hers. He ran his hand through her long dark hair and in the shadows she saw a waterfall in Africa. His hand glided over her stomach, spreading warmth. She felt the bulk of his body on her and she was in space, looking at the green and blue earth from above. The earth they inhabited was silent, primitive, as it must have been before humans. We are round and complete, she thought, holding onto each other as the planet spins. Red rivers of thought ran underground. I am selfish. This is suicide. This is love. This is the end of the world.

Everything they did was cloaked in guilt. They felt like outlaws or refugees, meeting in distant parking lots, entering movie theaters separately to find each other in the dark. They spent late afternoons together in cafeterias that smelled of grease and Pine Sol, where they pretended to care about the lukewarm cups of coffee in their hands, while the feeble Long Island sun sank in the city smog. She was captivated by his stories: his sinking ships and sharks, his prayers and coffee beans. She was enchanted by the way he traveled through literature, stopping to admire paragraphs polished like stone, putting his arm around characters he loved.

Then at night, they went to stores. He was good at pretending that they were just a couple out shopping. Carlos let her choose the curtains, the chairs, the plates. She wanted bright colors: the reds of the butterflies that lived in Amazon trees, the blues and purples of oceans full of turtles.

Winter was streaked a dirty pink, and the days were short and muted. Carlos filed for divorce. He sat at the edge of the bed, on the white cauliflower bedspread. His eyes were red. Alma held his hand, and it felt as if she were holding the word betrayal for him.

"There is always pain in everything," he said.

"Go back," she said. He shook his head.

"There's no going back. It's not that. It's the pain of a newborn breathing oxygen for the first time," he said. "You give me life."

Alma was scared. She wanted to go home for Christmas, back to the warm blue light of Venezuela. She wanted to see if she could think of him in the hot green fields of Caracas, when the orchids released their fragrance into the humid evening air. Carlos drove her to the airport. There were tufts of snow on the ground, and in the distance, stacks of desolate brick buildings stood condemned to death.

In Venezuela, the balmy air rolled down from the folds of the mountain every afternoon. Alma dreamed of gigantic giraffes who craned their necks into the windows of her seven-story apartment, and large black birds that blocked out the sun.

Francisco, her high school boyfriend, picked her up at dawn in his jeep. He brought her a gardenia for her hair. He was young and healthy, a Viking with a copper-streaked beard. He had somehow acquired more manliness in the few months she had been gone. She was tired of the burden, the responsibility of love.

"Kiss me," she commanded. Francisco braked suddenly in the middle of the road. He lunged at her, kissing her nose, her lips and pulling at her bathing suit top. She screamed in laughter, batting him off, as startled iguanas darted back and forth in the bushes near the side of the road.

Francisco flew them to an island. The plane was like a sheet of paper, shivering at each cloudy draft. They headed out into nothingness. Then the island, a green fleck embedded in the water. There was no airport, only a sandy strip cutting across the island.

The water was melted aquamarine. They took their bags and walked up the beach. The sand was white and soft as sifted flour. As the day wore on, the water got warmer, and they took their bathing suits off, reveling in their nakedness like children. Francisco held her as she floated, running his hands up and down her back. Then he bent over and kissed her, a long salty kiss, pulling her closer. Their bodies slipped against each other in a delicious, muscled, soft and hard way. There were no promises, only a sense of abandon, and she was grateful.

They flew back that evening. The lights of the city appeared along the coast like a citrine necklace. Alma thought about Carlos. She pictured him sitting at his kitchen table in New York, with a sink full of rust and dirty dishes, reading a book, surrounded by silence. He was waiting for her. She regretted her fickleness, her indecision, her confusion.

The next day, she went to a woman who could tell the future. There was something severe about her, something thin and Caribbean. She gave Alma a cigar to hold, showing her how to wrap her fingers around it, in order to instill it with her essence. After a while, the woman took the cigar from Alma and lit it, staring at the ashes, making clicking sounds with her mouth while she turned the cigar around.

"You come from a white country. A land full of snow." Alma nodded. She felt a cold draft in the air, though the day was sunny. The woman closed her eyes and Alma sensed she could see Carlos in his house.

"There's a man there. He's much older than you," she said. "And he loves you more than his own life." The woman opened her eyes. "There is fire," she said, staring at Alma. "You are playing with love." Alma felt the weight of the accusation and remained silent. The woman gave her the name of someone to see in New York.

When she returned, Carlos met her at the airport. She saw his dark curly hair in the crowd and for an instant thought of taking another exit, getting in a taxi, escaping. Then he saw her and came over and picked up her suitcases. He did not kiss her in public. He wrapped her in his pipe-scented coat, even though she had her own coat, and they stepped outside into the winter. She was again surrounded by gray pigeons and steel.

In the car, Carlos did not say much. His coat felt oppressive, like a heavy hand claiming her again, as they joined the stream of slow-moving cars.

"So how's the journal?" said Alma. She wondered if he could tell she had been unfaithful. She felt loathing for her inability to control herself.

"It's extraordinary. I have a copy in the back seat for you."

They stopped at a traffic light. There was some heaviness between them as he lit his pipe.

"What's the matter?" asked Alma.

He paused. "I didn't get tenure."

"But why not?" she said.

"Apparently the dean has heard rumors about you and me. But it's really professional envy. All my colleagues voted against me," he said. Alma sat in silence. She felt guilty, as if she had caused the problems in his life. If only he knew that she had been thinking of leaving him, of returning to Venezuela. If only he knew she had been disloyal.

"I've heard about a man who can help you. His name is Don Raimundo," said Alma. "Why don't we go see him?" Carlos gave a short, bitter snort.

"Nobody can help me," he said.

"Please?" said Alma. She told him about the woman in Caracas. She convinced him to try, one time only. Carlos drove faster than usual, clanking over bolted metal bridges. Don Raimundo's apartment was filled with plastic statuettes of saints, crosses, palm leaves, rosaries, and candles.

"There are white nuns flying around your head," Don Raimundo said to Alma, "and they don't like my cigar." He crushed it in an ashtray. "They can get pretty nasty," he added with a smile. Alma smiled and thought, this man must be a Santero. Immediately Don Raimundo turned to look at her, slightly offended.

"No, you're wrong," he said. "I'm not a Santero." Alma felt as if he had stepped right into the red cave of her head, helping himself to her thoughts. She tried not to fight it.

"My job on earth is to bring guidance to troubled souls." At least he believes in miracles, she thought spontaneously.

"What can I do about my tenure?" Carlos asked.

"Accept what life has in store." Carlos began to object, but Don Raimundo raised his hand. In her mind Alma screamed, *How can I know if I love him?*

"Stop analyzing. The answer will come some day soon."

"I'm not sure," said Alma, knowing he would understand. Outside, the city flowed into the smoggy orange sunset, the slanted light in the room was rusty. Alma looked at Carlos. It felt like a dream.

Don Raimundo frowned. He took Carlos' hand in his and said, "Trouble will come soon. And there is nothing you can do about it. Here, let me cleanse you both of bad spirits." Alma felt foolish standing in the middle of the living room, as Don Raimundo blew candle smoke on a leafy twig. Then he blew the air around Alma's head and shoulders. She began to relax. The air in the room was pure, blue oxygen. She closed her eyes and thought she felt the thin wisp of a nun's wing glance against her hair.

The following week, they went back to Don Raimundo. He said that the spirits of four African horsemen were causing chaos in Carlos' life, and it was important to signal that they were not welcome. He told Carlos to place glasses of water with knives crossed over the top in each room in his home. He was to walk down the hallways of the university, particularly near the offices of those colleagues who had voted against his tenure, and saturate the air with the smoke of his pipe. He was to pray and have faith. Don Raimundo lit candles for him.

One night, Carlos fell asleep on the couch. He heard his ancestors speaking languages that he could suddenly understand. He woke up at dawn pronouncing Arabic words he had not spoken since childhood.

"Alma," he exclaimed, "I know the word for father! I know the word for house!" He had seen angels in his dreams.

"The spirits are here! I can see things," he laughed, reckless with new powers. After that, he looked into bodies and saw what was hurting, which bone was weak, which heart needed care.

"Please don't drink any more," he told a colleague. "I am seeing black silhouettes."

And every day Carlos went to Don Raimundo. Alma stopped going. On those nights, she sometimes felt Carlos' presence near her, when she was alone reading. The house would creak and moan with winter sounds, the snow-filled winds spitting cold on her windows, and she missed being in his arms, missed the way he was before Don Raimundo.

"Faith," the old man repeated to Carlos. "I see you teaching somewhere upstate, in a big University."

"Will Alma be there with me?" asked Carlos. But Don Raimundo could not answer. So Carlos went on interviews, taking his books and journals with him. But he was sidetracked by his vision.

"I have a special power," he told stunned interviewers. He was innocent, almost childlike. Out of politeness, the interviewers would murmur what he took for admiration.

"In fact, you will soon see major changes," he continued. "Your mother will come live with you," he said to a smallish dark-haired woman. "And you will have another son, your third," he said to a man with glasses.

"How did you know I have two sons?" the man asked. Carlos smiled. He never heard from them again.

"Stop it," said Alma. "You're scaring people. They think you're crazy."

But Carlos didn't care. His complex linguistic and analytic theories had evaporated, and in their place was an absolute credence in the invisible. It was his goal to harness the mischievous spirits Don Raimundo saw around him. They were responsible for his difficulties. Following Don Raimundo's mandate, he made himself a gold tunic with a large red cross on the back. Alma hated it. It made her fear the meanings behind everything he brought home: medals of saints, candles with prayers printed on them that burned all night, masks made of shells. There were too many instructions from Don Raimundo.

"Please stop seeing Don Raimundo for a while," she pleaded.

"He's the one who stood by me," said Carlos. "All those so-called friends, whom I helped publish, don't even talk to me any more." He reached for her hand. "Don't worry. Something will come up," he said.

But nothing seemed to make a difference. Alma was becoming restless. She longed for fun, for the firm flesh and smooth skin of boys her own age.

"Marry me," said Carlos. But Alma would just smile. She lay in bed hearing him snore and thought that she had no business trying to be the life companion of someone from another generation. She feared her hunger for other men, and pictured herself still young but beginning to gray, pushing a wheelchair. Carlos sensed a change in her, and became suspicious.

One evening, Carlos saw her at the library with another student, a boy who sometimes studied with her. He stormed up to them and said to Alma, "May I have my ring back, please?" The boy stared at him, and then at her, wondering what was going on. Alma was stunned. If word got out about this, it would not help his cause. There was a tense silence. She was not wearing his ring. Carlos looked at her with intensity and then walked away, leaning into the astringent wind. Alma shrugged, fighting a burning sensation in her eyes as she said laughingly to the boy, "He's nuts." Instantly she regretted it, feeling disloyal, but also as if she had just inadvertently spoken an undeniable truth. That night Alma did not go to his home. He called and called until she picked up. He pleaded with her to come back, saying he had been foolish and had reacted out of love.

"I'm not sure I love you." said Alma.

"You do," he said. "This was meant to be."

"You shouldn't have left your wife, even for love, even for me," she told him.

"I'll always look after her. But I can't sacrifice my soul," he said. "You're the one I love." She stayed away for several days. But then a longing started in the pit of her stomach, as she thought about the endless hours they had spent talking, creating their own striated worlds. The longing grew, filling her like a vine, until she felt that leaves would come out of her mouth, like green tongues of backed up words. So she went back. He was solicitous, taking her out at night, buying her trinkets, unable to hide his joy.

But soon the burden of his love was again too much and she ran from him, telling him she was visiting relatives. Instead, she would lose herself in the anonymous city with young men. He followed her to the train station, hiding behind oak trees. In her absence she was sure he opened her class notebooks, looking for betrayal. He reached into her purses and stole letters from Venezuela. Carlos and Alma fell into an unspoken agreement, a conspiracy of silence, a condition she imposed in return for staying with him. He didn't ask, she didn't answer.

One Saturday, Carlos and Alma were reading on the bed. Alma touched his shoulder, feeling genuine affection for him. Carlos took the book out of her hand, and kissed her gently on the lips. She tasted the tobacco, the yellowness of it, the decay. Then he rolled over onto her, and above his shoulder she felt presences, as if Santa Barbara had stopped her white horse mid-air, and with her ruby-tipped staff in hand, was watching them. Alma looked to the side. San Isidro, with his white beard overflowing, was sitting in the armchair, softly shaking his head. Carlos kissed Alma's neck, as Santa Rita, the saint of impossible miracles, stood in another corner of the room. Even love can't conquer these illusions he wants to follow, she thought. Alma heard the wind chime, made of white translucent shells, clink softly. She knew instantly that something precious was gone forever.

That evening, Alma saw Carlos kneeling in the living room, wearing his gold tunic as he prayed at an altar he had constructed.

"Carlos, I've asked you to stop seeing Don Raimundo."

Carlos said nothing. He continued to kneel. The sound of a bus pulling away from the curb outside seemed to punctuate the silence.

"Well, then I think we should not see each other for a while," said Alma, digging her nails into the palm of her hand. She wasn't sure about anything any more. Carlos turned and stared at her.

"But I love you," he said. The way he said it made her feel ungrateful.

"I think it's best," she said.

"I need you," he said. He touched his heart.

"I've made up my mind," she said softly. The image of this moment burned into her mind: Carlos wearing his tunic with the big cross, kneeling in the middle of the living room on the green rug, his hand on his heart. Just outside was the sound of traffic, of people going home to dinner.

Alma went back to the small house she had shared with another student. Several months passed. She avoided the quadrangle of grass at the university, the library, the cafeteria. Every now and then, she thought she saw him out of the corner of her eye, but she was wrong. She was almost surprised that he didn't make more of an effort to find her. She missed the afternoons together, the dinners, the discussions. She wondered what was happening with Don Raimundo. She wondered if his wife knew she had left him. She felt relieved that she was no longer standing in their way, in case their relationship could somehow be fixed.

One night Carlos ran outside his home holding a gun, threatening to put a bullet through his brain. A neighbor called the police, and they came and surrounded him, talking to him for hours. Alma did not know about it for several days, until she saw an article in the newspaper. She could not believe what she was reading, and had to read it several times. "University professor in asylum after suicide attempt." *How did he get a gun? Was this another command from the spirits?* she wondered.

Alma went to see Carlos at the hospital. The windows were covered with green wire. He was in his room, looking small and wasted. He smiled happily when he saw her.

"You cut your hair," he said. She sat down on a chair, just far enough to be out of reach. Carlos ran his hand across the white bed.

"I like it here. They bring me my food and the doctors want to hear about my visions." Alma nodded.

"What do you tell them?" she asked.

"That I can see my dead father now. Soon I will get a job. You will come back to me." He smiled. "I can wait." Alma looked out the window. A car moved slowly down the street. There were red buildings surrounding an island of sand, an empty playground. She looked at Carlos and saw that his eyes looked as if he were a hundred years old. *Was he always like this*, she thought, *and I just didn't notice? Or had love aged them both?*

"The doctors ask me questions all the time. They know I understand the meaning of life."

Alma said, "Carlos, they don't believe you. They are just trying to find out what is wrong with you."

"No," he said. "Some of us see more than others, glimmers of truth in the universe." *Why*, she wondered, *why did you want to kill yourself because of me?*

"There is only one man on earth who knows the meaning of life, and he has written it down in an obscure book," he said. "I'll share it with you."

"Tell me," she said, still curious as to what he would say.

"First, tell me that you love me," he said. Alma lowered her head. She regretted getting into this, she knew it would lead nowhere.

"Wait," he said, looking at the space above her head. "You used to have an aunt named Ursula. I see her, right now," he smiled. "She's old, frail. She wears her hair in a bun. She is now your guardian angel." She could almost believe him.

"It's getting late," she said, "I have to go now." Alma got up to leave. Carlos stood up, too. He reached for her hand and kissed it.

"You smell like lilacs, my lady. Remember the ones that grew by our window?" he said. She looked at him, wondering if she was about to throw her life away.

"I will die for you," he said.

Alma turned to leave. Maybe this was it, this had been her experience with love. Maybe she would never know love again. She walked away from him, his touch still warm on her hand. She walked down the empty halls of the hospital, to the exit.

Once outside, her vision became blurred by tears from the sensation of abandoning him to a place with caged windows, and her thoughts of what could have been. In the distance, a small gust of wind was lifting the sand off the playground, creating a whirlwind. She stopped and watched the rapid movement of the spinning funnel. For a moment she could see the silhouette of Santa Isabel, the saint of forbidden love, her golden hair and her robes fluttering in the wind, and she heard the sweet music of a single clarinet. But it was only a car horn in the distance, and the soft, shimmering sand settling down after its sudden flight.

1994

Critical thinking points: After you've read

1) *What may lead a young college freshman to fall in love with his or her professor?*
2) *Events in the story move quickly. Is it believable that Carlos professes his love for Alma when he does?*
3) *Why might Carlos be the sort of person to get caught up in the visions of Don Raimundo? What leads to this? Is it believable to you as a reader?*
4) *Does Alma truly love Carlos? What details in the story lead you to your conclusion?*
5) *What are the differences between Alma's life at home and her life at school?*
6) *What makes this a love story? Is it like other love stories you've seen or read? Why or why not?*

Some possibilities for writing

1) *Recall a time when you were entranced by a teacher. Write about the qualities you found attractive and why you respected or liked that teacher.*
2) *We only see Carlos through Alma's point of view. Without adding anything to the story, write a more objective description of Carlos.*
3) *Alma wonders if love aged both her and Carlos. How does love "age" people? Write about an experience in which love aged you or someone you know.*
4) *Both Carlos and Alma are, in their own ways, looking for the "right" person. Create your Mr./Ms. Right. Allow yourself no abstractions, such as handsome, intelligent, or sensitive. Do not simply describe, but use concrete details. Concentrate, without ever saying why, on what it is about the person that "fits the bill."*
5) *The same as above, except it should be from the point of view of someone who hates Mr./Ms. Right, but your purpose is the same.*
6) *Research your university's policy on faculty and staff dating students. Do you agree with it? Why or why not? Would Alma's relationship with Professor Alcazar be considered "ethical" at your campus? Why or why not?*

No More Kissing — AIDS Everywhere

Michael Blumenthal

"

"You must remember," he said, "that every time you make love
you tamper with fate."

"

Critical thinking points: As you read

1) *What are some sexual images in the poem? List them as you read.*
2) *Traditionally, images of love are linked with images of death in love poems.*
   What are some images of love paired with death in this poem?
3) *What are "etymological roots"? What does it mean for a metaphor to be*
   "literalized"?

He says it to the young couple
passionately kissing on the street
and, when he does, the four of us just stand there,
laughing, on this cold wintry day in Cambridge,
nineteen hundred and eighty-eight,
as if there could be no such danger
to a kiss, as if the metaphors of love and dying
had not been literalized.

Pausing a block later, my cheeks kissed
by the cold, my lips cracking
in the January air, I think back
to what a man once told me, long before

Michael Blumenthal (b. 1949) is the author of five volumes of poems, most recently *The Wages of Goodness* (Univ. of Missouri Press, 1992) as well as the novel *Weinstock Among the Dying* (Zoland Books, 1993), which was awarded *Hadassah Magazine*'s Harold U. Ribelow Prize for Fiction. He has just published a collection of his essays, *When History Enters The House: Essays From Central Europe* and completed a new manuscript of poems, entitled *Dusty Angel*, which includes the poem reprinted here. He currently lives and writes in Austin, Texas.

risk had so clinical a name,
so precise a passage. *"You must remember,"*
he said, *"that every time you make love*
you tamper with fate."

Now, the early wisdoms grow clear:
the serpents slither into the year,
the elegies are writing themselves
on desires' sheets, passion and suffering
are fusing their etymological roots
into a single trunk. *Yet why should they not embrace,*
these beautiful two? They are, after all, part
of the oldest story in the world — before God,
before microbes, before the sea had licked
the earth and the air clean with its long tongue.

1989

Critical thinking points: After you've read

1) *How is this poem a reflection of the time in which it was written?*
2) *People were just becoming aware of AIDS in the late 1980s. Would someone be likely to call out "No More Kissing — AIDS Everywhere" as a joke today? Why or why not?*
3) *What might be some of the things suggested by the "oldest story in the world" that the poet refers to?*
4) *In what ways have the "metaphors of love and dying" been "literalized"?*
5) *What is the kiss a metaphor of? What details in the poem lead you to that conclusion?*

Some possibilities for writing

1) *Do you believe "that every time you make love you tamper with fate"? In what ways is this statement true? What aspects of fate are tampered with? Write a one-page response supporting or negating this statement.*
2) *Write a response from the point of view of the kissing young couple. What might they say to the man who yells out his warning to them? To the advice given in the second stanza? To the poet at the end of the poem?*
3) *Look at this poem after reading or rereading Jennifer Fandel's "Raspberries," John David Rose's "Revision," and Frank Smoot's "Moon June Spoon." Each in its own way is a "love" poem or a poem about "love." Write a paper that explores the various perspectives of love present in these four poems.*
4) *Research and write a paper about the changes, if any, in sexual behavior*

among college students pre- and post-AIDS. What surprises you about your findings? What does not surprise you? Why?

The Blue-Light System
from The Morning After:
Sex, Fear, and Feminism on Campus

Katie Roiphe

66

In this era of Just Say No and No Means No, we don't have many words for embracing experience. Now instead of liberation and libido, the emphasis is on trauma and disease. Now the idea of random encounters, of joyful, loveless SEX, raises eyebrows. The possibility of adventure is clouded by the specter of illness. It's a difficult backdrop for conducting one's youth.

99

Critical thinking points: As you read

1) *What kind of precautions were you told about at new student orientation on your campus? Do you feel that orientation prepared you for a safe life on campus? Why or why not?*
2) *In this essay, what kinds of "warnings" concerning sex are aimed specifically at male college students? How do these compare to the warnings aimed at female college students?*
3) *Roiphe builds her essay on "oppositions," seemingly self-contractory ideas. List some as you read.*

With its magnolia trees, its gray Gothic buildings, Princeton's pastoral campus looks like it hasn't changed much over the last century. But when the sun goes down, it's clear that the last five years have altered the face of the campus. There are still freshmen wandering around late at night, but there are also blue lights up all over campus in case someone pulls you into the darkness. The blue lights above security

---

Her book *The Morning After: Sex, Fear, and Feminism on Campus* catapulted Katie Roiphe (b. 1968) into a media spotlight. Its pronouncements on issues of violence against women, victimization, and contemporary feminist thinking demonstrated that the scholar clearly had some strong opinions in these areas and was critical of the direction that she felt the struggle for women's rights had taken during the 1980s. This selection is from that book.

phones, part of what is often called the blue-light system, were erected on many campuses in the eighties. Since the phones aren't actually used much for emergencies, their primary function seems to be to reassure the lone wanderer. Having started with fifteen lights and added some each year, Princeton now has around seventy. The blue lights mark a new and systematic sense of danger. People may have always been scared walking around campuses late at night, but now, bathed in blue light, they are officially scared.

As freshmen in the late eighties and early nineties, we arrived at college amid a flurry of warnings: "Since you cannot tell who has the potential for rape by simply looking, be on your guard with every man." "Do not put yourself in vulnerable situations." "Condoms are not perfect and they do not provide 'safe sex.'" "To eliminate risk, abstain from sex or avoid sexual intimacy beyond fantasy, massage and mutual masturbation." "Over fifty percent of all female college students experience some form of sexual victimization or sexual harassment." "No birth control is one hundred percent effective except the word 'No!'" "Are you hearing LOVE when your boyfriend is saying SEX?" "One in four college women has experienced rape or attempted rape since age fourteen."

As we are settling into our new surroundings, there are fliers and counselors and videotapes telling us how not to get AIDS and how not to get raped, where not to wander and what signals not to send. By the end of freshman week, we know exactly what not to do. Once we make it through the workshops and pamphlets on date rape, safe SEX, and sexual harassment, no matter how bold and adolescent, how rebellious and reckless, we are left with an impression of imminent danger. And then there are the whistles. Female freshmen arriving at Wesleyan and other campuses are given whistles to protect them against rape and assault. For the past couple of years at Princeton, there has been someone outside the building during registration offering these whistles to female students on their way out.

Several years ago, parents and prospective students on tours of the Wesleyan campus saw more of college life than they expected. As they were touring the campus, looking at the library and the classrooms, the students playing Frisbee on the grass and the freshman dorms, the cheerful patter of the tour guide was interrupted by the impassioned words of a feminist student. She delivered a three-minute speech about the danger of rape, warning parents and prospective students to take the university's response to the rape crisis into consideration when applying to college. She urged them to ask the administration questions about security and blue lights. The rape crisis is not just at Wesleyan but everywhere, she told them.

That spring she and another student involved in this dramatic effort at what would have once been called consciousness-raising disrupted many tours, raising the ire of the administration. Parents and prospective students were shaken. Needless to say, the admissions office was not happy to have the issue of date rape thrust at students on the brink of their decision about colleges. Parents, already worried about sending their children to a strange place, had another source of concern to add to their list. But the guerrilla feminists were effective in their purpose: they successfully planted the fear of rape in the minds of prospective students before they even reached the Wesleyan campus.

Word of mouth, then, comes from older students as well as university staff. The barrage of warnings is not just the product of a bureaucratic mechanism churning out pieces of paper. The warnings are not just official university policy filtering down to us from above. There are faces and stories behind these warnings. They have taken hold of student attention. Students run women's centers and hot lines, workshops and peer-counseling groups. They write plays and design videos and posters about rape. Campus literary magazines and political journals are filled with stories and poems about sexual danger. Most visibly, most dramatically, students organize and march against rape. I remember myself, a bewildered freshman, watching candle-lit faces weave snakelike through campus. Angry voices were chanting "Two, four, six, eight, no more date rape," and the marchers carried signs saying "Take Back the Night." I remember an older student from my high school, whom I'd always respected, always thought particularly glamorous, marching, her face flushed with emotion, and I wondered what it was about. Before the chants condensed into meaning, when they were still sounds instead of words, I wondered whom they wanted the night back from and what they wanted it back for. The confusion was not just mine. The vague poetic symbols of the campus movement against rape speak of a more general fear. As the marchers passed, I wandered back to my dorm through the still-unfamiliar campus, the darkness suddenly charged with a nameless threat.

•

In this era of Just Say No and No Means No, we don't have many words for embracing experience. Now instead of liberation and libido, the emphasis is on trauma and disease. Now the idea of random encounters, of joyful, loveless SEX, raises eyebrows. The possibility of adventure is clouded by the specter of illness. It's a difficult backdrop for conducting one's youth.

What further complicates sexual existence is that the sexual revolution hasn't been entirely erased by a new ethos of sexual conservatism. Free love hasn't been entirely eclipsed by safe SEX. Sexual climates do not rove across our experience like cold fronts on a weather map. Instead, they linger and accumulate. Today's culture of caution coexists with yesterday's devil-may-care. Encouraged, discouraged, condemned, condoned, youthful sexual activity is met with powerful and conflicting responses. Everywhere we look there are signs of sexual puritanism, but there are also signs of sexual abandon. Adding to the mixed messages are signs of sexual danger.

On the subway, next to a condom ad in Spanish, there is an ad for perfume showing a naked man carrying a naked woman over his shoulder. On an average day we are flooded with images of erotic promise: the topless couple in a Calvin Klein underwear ad; a poster of an ecstatic Madonna with her stomach bare, her jeans unbuttoned, her book, SEX, on the cover of *Newsweek*; the pornographic section of our video store; the XXX movie houses in certain neighborhoods; men with long hair, chests bare, arms around each other, in an advertisement for Banana Republic, and the list goes on. We may not always notice these images, but like buildings and trees, they are part of our landscape.

This is a culture that pulls both ways. Pat Buchanan rails about the importance of sexual morality, and Banana Republic uses SEX to sell clothes. We've been hearing Reagan and then Bush drone on about family values for as long as we can remember, but we haven't lost the myth of the casual encounter. Pressures clash. Our ears were filled simultaneously with Nancy Reagan's Just Say No and George Michael's late-'80s hit song "I Want Your SEX." An image from deep childhood perfectly captures today's conflicted sexual climate: *Dr. Dolittle*'s two-headed creature, the pushmi-pullyu.

There's no doubt that some people are running around thinking only about pleasure and whom they're going to go home with after a party. But that is not the whole story. Many are more concerned with getting ahead and getting a nice car than getting drunk and getting laid. The pressure to do well and make money in an age of diminishing economic expectations looms larger than it did for those who went to college in the '60s and '70s.

Finding yourself pales in comparison to supporting yourself. These days desire is often tailored by a pre-professional pragmatism, and many undergraduates, although not necessarily the ones I knew, are keeping their lives, sexually and otherwise, in relative order.

Yes, they are arguing about whether to teach abstinence in New York City's public schools, and yes, there are more pressures to stay faithful and stay at home, but we still haven't lost the idea of the sexual revolution. We still hear stories from older brothers, sisters, cousins, and aunts about sleeping around and not caring, and feeling free and pretending to feel free.

I remember, when I was young, hearing my older sister tell my mother that she was the last person on earth who was faithful to her husband. I turned to look at my mother, imagining her as a dinosaur, the kind they keep at the Museum of Natural History. Everyone else, my sister told me, was into free love and all that. I remember exactly where we were sitting when we had that conversation. I remember the color of the couch. And I remember the visions of having dozens of husbands, like a bouquet of flowers, running through my mind.

The sexual revolutionaries, then, have made their impression, and we are still impressed. Warnings about sexual harassment and sexual disease compete with wanton images of sexual freedom. Even though attitudes toward sexual experimentation have changed, many people still think of it as a necessary stage. We are still intrigued and pressured and exhausted by the sexual revolution. Although we may have developed an almost blase attitude toward the absolute ideals of libertinism, they still exert a strong presence in the way we think and the choices we make.

People tell me that SEX should be as free as it was not so long ago, that we shouldn't have to use discretion and condoms. We may have been thinking about AIDS for about as long as we've been thinking about SEX, but many of us still expect to experiment. While there is a strong cultural belief that sexual adventure is a minefield of rape and disease, there is also a lingering refrain: this is not the way it's supposed to be.

The shift from free love to safe SEX is itself part of our experience. Our sexual climate, then, incorporates the movement from one set of sexual mores to another. The presence of the past complicates our decisions. Messages mix, and our imaginations catch hold of one, then the other, dragging our bodies this way and that. I remember the parties, dark rooms, beer, cigarettes, dancing shadows dressed in mostly black. In the corner a vodka punch, with a cherry taste. Girls were dancing with girls, some because they were interested in each other, others because they were trying to catch the attention of the boy across the room. That spring, girls had started taking their shirts off at parties. I remember the bras, black lace, white lace, pink lace. There was a drama in dancing in bras, in crushing taboos beneath our feet. For most people, boys were in the background those nights. They were not the point. Dancing without shirts was intended as a bold statement about the triumph of the female body, an eye-catching, spirit-lifting display of sexual availability. As music surged, as bodies pressed against each other, it was a show of sexuality, freedom, and power, a charade of earlier, wilder days. We definitely had something to prove, and beneath all the bacchanalian urgency, there was something calculating, something self-conscious, something designed to impress. But what was there to prove in the dark room surrounded by people who had eaten breakfast, lunch, and dinner together every day for years? The point, I think, was to exhibit a power, as well as a freedom we didn't quite have. In the dark, without shirts, it was ourselves we were trying to impress. It was, above all, a dance of control, and the rhythm was frustration.

That same spring, most of the shirtless dancers would shout about date rape until they were hoarse at Take Back the Night. To many observers the conjunction of these two activities seemed contradictory, even hypocritical. But dancing without shirts and marching at Take Back the Night are, strange as it seems, part of the same parade. The different drums of sexual desirability, strength and vulnerability, frustration and fear, are all part of the group exhibitionism: the same show of power, and the same dance of control.

•

Liquor and parties still hold their allure for the freshman, but it's an allure full of complications and second thoughts. Hormones run high at this age, but they mix uneasily with worry. Maybe the freshman hasn't had much experience with boys. Maybe her parents were strict about curfews. In jeans, lipstick, and a tight black shirt, maybe she's finally at a real party with upperclassmen.

This is a generic story. Our freshman gets a beer, and a handsome boy from one of her classes, she doesn't remember which, comes up and flirts with her. She smiles at him, and in that instant she tries to calculate the risks. She tries to remember which girl she saw him with last week. she looks at his torn jeans, he looks bisexual, he looks like he might be one of those sullen-youth types who have spent a summer in the East Village injecting heroin. People are dancing to the pounding music, "However do you want me. However do you need me." The music makes it hard to hear each other, and he suggests they go up to his room to talk.

She hesitates. Flashes of the play she just saw about date rape run through her head. His invitation evokes the black-and-white print of the manual warning her about AIDS. Someone she knows has just caught herpes. All around her people are dancing. Her drink is beginning to blur the edges of her vision. Maybe she goes with him, maybe she doesn't, but either way the situation is complicated. Pleasure is charged with danger, safety with regret.

For both male and female college students, the usual drive toward sexual experience collides with the powerful drive against it. No matter how you choose to behave when it comes down to it at midnight on a Saturday, the conflicting pressures and contemporary taboos are with you in one way or another.

These pressures and taboos leave their traces all over campuses, in conversations and classrooms, in meetings and on bathroom walls. In the women's bathroom in the basement of the Princeton library, someone has scribbled "Sex is death," and in another bathroom someone has written "Sex is rape." These extreme and dramatic aphorisms spring from a fierce suspicion of sex. For most seventeen-year-olds college opens up a whole realm of sexual possibility, and some of the attention lavished on the darker, violent side of sex comes from a deep ambivalence about what that freedom actually entails.

In another Princeton bathroom, someone has written "There is no such thing as safe sex," and underneath it someone has added in bold letters, "Isolation is the best protection." Another person asks the communal wall, "Are you scared walking around late at night?" Several scribblers have answered yes.

At Wesleyan, the bathroom walls are filled with written conversations about rape and sexual harassment. Some people have named names, and there are comments back and forth. At Carleton College, in the bathroom on the third floor of the library, there is a list of alleged date rapists, popularly referred to as the "castration list."[†] Brown has a similar list. These lists are intended to allow victims to voice their experience in a safe, anonymous space. They enable victims to accuse without confrontation and consequences. Several campuses have erected "Walls of Shame" with a similar, though more public purpose, and at Columbia, students have posted the names of alleged date rapists on pieces of paper all over campus.

From cynical truisms about sex to written exchanges about date rape, on these campus walls expressions of sexuality are mingled with fear. The message is about danger and safety, about the perceived conflict between sex and well-being. Students have lost their faith in the simplicity of the sexual encounter, in the do-what-you-want-and-don't-worry-about-it mentality. The proverbial locker room is cluttered with a whole new set of sexual anxieties. These graffiti writers aren't worried about enough freedom anymore; they are worried about too much danger.

1993

[†]*Chronicle of Higher Education*, 15 May 1991.

Critical thinking points: After you've read

1) *Why might the author capitalize SEX throughout her essay? What effect does this have on the reader? On the essay?*
2) *Do you believe "castration lists" and "walls of shame" are appropriate methods for warning women of potential rapists? Why or why not? What are the possible effects of public warnings such as these?*
3) *Weselyan is an all-women university. Why might parents and students have been shocked or at least uneasy about the feminist student who interrupted the pre-college tour to offer warnings about rape?*
4) *Roiphe says, "Now instead of liberation and libido, the emphasis is on trauma and disease." What might she mean? How is this a sign of the times? How might various characters in this book support or negate Roiphe's statement?*
5) *Roiphe started college during the Reagan/Bush administration. How might the American public's perception of sexuality have changed since then, considering the sex scandals associated with former President Bill Clinton?*
6) *Roiphe says, "We still hear stories from older brothers, sisters, cousins, and aunts about sleeping around and not caring, and feeling free and pretending to feel free." What might she mean? How might Eleanor Davies, the main character in Jane Barnes Casey's "Virginity," react to this statement? How might Carmen and Kate in Jennifer Sheridan's "Carmen" react to it?*

Some possibilities for writing

1) *Imagine that Roiphe is visiting your campus as part of a lecture series. Write down five questions you'd like to ask her.*
2) *This essay neglects the choices that male college students must make concerning sex. Write a letter to Roiphe from the male point of view describing what she has overlooked in her essay.*
3) *Evaluate your school's program and policies concerning rape education, prevention, and intervention.*
4) *For an entire day, record the sexual images you see around campus. Watch for images on signs, posters, billboards, books, TV prgrams, or other private or public places. Did you notice these images without conciously looking for them? Why or why not? Write a composite of the kinds of images you found and the purpose of the image, such as attempting to sell a product or promote a lifestyle.*
5) *Roiphe says, "The rape crisis is not just at Wesleyan but everywhere. . . ." Is there or has there been such a "crisis" at your school? Why or why not?*

Dancing

Paul Durica

"

You see them standing outside lighted windows, reciting poems or strumming guitars. And their paramours always let them in. Because they're interesting, despite all the pretensions. They're sensitive. Like women. They're different than the frat boys and the jocks and the math whizzes. And they have a respect, a reverence for beauty, even if it's completely whacked-out.

"

Critical thinking points: As you read

1) *Speculate on the implications of the title. How many "dance" references appear in the story? Make a list.*
2) *Speculate why Durica gave Perry the last name he did. Is Perry "vain"? Why or why not?*
3) *Many students come to college with an idea about what certain types of students are like, such as football players, fraternity or sorority members, theater majors, writers, etc. What is Amber's "idea" of herself? What is her "idea" of Perry? What is Perry's "idea" of Amber?*

Until this day I have pursued virtue with rigor. I have labored long hours to relieve my fellow men. I have worked and worked the talent You allowed me. *You know how hard I've worked!* Solely that in the end, in the practice of the art which alone makes the world comprehensible to me, I might hear Your Voice! And now I do hear it — and it says only one name.

— *Saliere*, Amadeus

Don't take it all so seriously.

— *Kurt Vonnegut, Jr.*

Perry and I met in front of the student union or on the steps of the library, also in the English department, the chapel, the campus coffee house, or on the benches by

---

Paul Durica (b. 1978) wrote this story while a student at Dennison University in Granville, Ohio.

the entrance, at the entrance with its biblical propaganda carved in concrete, and at times in the laundry room of the "quiet" dorm, even at the faculty graveyard. That was last Halloween. Every time he would bring twenty or more pages for me to read. And I'd perhaps bring five. And we'd sit there discussing poetics.

The first time we met was after Perry read a poem in creative writing class. After he told our peers what point of view was, to the delight of Dr. Mills, Bill Faulkner Jr. "Splendid, Mr. Yvain," dripped off his tongue in a Mississippi drawl. Most of the students sneered at Perry's answer. Didn't the little fuck know this was a gut course? Stupid freshman, who does he think he is? Ginsberg? Whitman? Perry didn't look like a beatnik, a bard for the campus in his black Vans and Catholic boy cut — strict sanctions on hair below the collar and sideburns past the ear lobes. His chin bore wiry flecks of orange, the grotesque birth of a goatee. But he was the only one of interest in the class, which was the only one of interest for me this semester. And he was the only one of interest in this place. He was the one. Most of the time, I wrote in my notebook and ignored classroom proceedings. But when Perry read I listened. He read a poem about girls at his high school entitled "why i hate barbie blond bitches a lot," which made our peers sneer some more. After that, I had to meet him.

"Your lines really groove," I told him in the hall.

"Thank you." He looked at my eyes. "So do your sunglasses."

"Thanks." I smiled. "What do you think of class?"

"I like it. Feedback's useful." He tugged the straps of his backpack and smiled but not at me.

"I meant — what do you think of our classmates?"

"I don't."

"Really?"

"I don't think about them." His smile vanished. He was serious. Very serious about this writing thing. "What do you write?"

"Poetry. But I've been bitten by the drama bug lately."

"I'm just a poet. I'd like to see some of your work."

I handed him ten poems from my folder — amber rae mcdonough, always in lower case, typed at the bottom of each. When I wrote those poems my sophomore year of high school, I was one pretentious bitch. But Sean loved them all. "They're only rough drafts," I told him.

An hour later, as I was leaving Issues in Feminism, Perry and I collided in the hall. He stuffed the ten sheets into my hand, poems scarred for life with jigsaw lines of red-inked criticism. "I loved them," he cried. "There's so much I wanted to say. I couldn't fit it all on the paper. Maybe we can get together and discuss them."

"If I get to see more of yours."

"Of course." He produced a black folder with at least fifty typed sheets of paper between three rings and three silver tabs. Damn serious about this writing thing. He withdrew a pen and planner from his Jansport and waited for me to say when and where.

Sean still called every day from Georgetown. I didn't want to think what his phone bill would be. But it was his money. Every day he strung together a litany of his sorrows and heart breaks until I confessed my love for him. And then he started with a chain of "You're my love, my inspiration," "You're the giver of purpose in my life," "My one and my all," and other, probably rehearsed, lines of sentiment. After that, believing me as basted as a holiday ham, he assaulted me with pleas to transfer, to join him, and when I ignored his pleas, he insulted me — "You never really loved me. You know nothing about loyalty. You're a spoiled child." I cried, he cried, and then he apologized hastily, re-affirmed his eternal passion, and told me what they served for lunch that afternoon. The whole ritual lasted some forty minutes, and after it, I was ready for a whole pack of L&Ms. And with my blood to nicotine ratio properly established, I sank into the bean bag in my room and flipped to a yellow page in my notebook, half-painted in inky scrawl — "Indigo Bride: A Play in Three Acts." I wrote through dinner.

"I really like the repetition," I said of the poem in my lap as we sat on the brick ledge in front of the student union. Me with a lighted cigarette and crossed legs. Perry with his Vans kicking the salmon-colored side. The poem was entitled "man conquers women." It was about this abusive high school relationship. It was set on a bus. And the girl's ambivalence — her fear of the boy and her longing for his love — was nicely underscored with the repetition of "bites her thumb." That's all she did throughout the poem — bite her thumb. She never said anything. Not when the bastard swore at her. Not when he wrote he loved her, he couldn't live without her, in papers he crumpled into balls and tossed in her lap, because she decided to sit a seat apart. She just bit her thumb.

"Anything else?" he asked. "It's not like most of my work."

"Did any of this really happen?" I took a quick hit.

"All of it. That's how Fontaine treated his girlfriend. They'd fight, but be back together the next day. He was a total prick."

"No doubt."

"It's not like most of my work. I have a more refined vision of women."

"I'd have kneed the bastard in the balls."

He smiled and said it wasn't a real possibility. He said he went to a Catholic high school where his only friend was a girl who smoked L&Ms. "Smoked them like a fiend," he said. I told him I went to school here, in this town of four churches and a hardware store, that my mother was a tenured professor of anthropology who enjoyed observing my cultural development, accompanied by significant tuition cuts. "Ever the fac brat," I told him. I talked about friends who fled to Carleton, Oberlin, Antioch, and Brown; the hometown hubby who left for Georgetown. "That's my life." I took another hit. "Corn and cows, dear."

"What did you say?" He turned to me, clutching the poems tightly in his hands.

"Corn and cows. You know, central Ohio living."

"You called me 'dear.' My one friend always called me 'dear.' The one who smoked the L&Ms. It just rolled off her tongue."

"Rod Serling, where are you?" I laughed and lit a fresh cigarette, placing it between the index and middle of my left hand. I could tell he was watching how I held it. "Just who is this friend? Any other similarities?"

"Just a friend."

"Only a friend?"

"She used to read my poetry."

"Let me guess. She was a bohemian goddess." I smiled and flicked ash at passing students. "I've seen lots of people on this campus over the years. I know who hangs with who. She's not like her." I waved my cigarette at a girl walking past us. She wore khaki shorts and a swimming jacket. Her legs were tan, smooth, thick, and endless. They moved with confidence, strength, and beauty.

"Sarah? She's not like her."

"You know that girl?"

"Sure. Sarah works at the Cafe Grind. But she's something of an athlete. My friend was bohemian, I guess. She was rather tall and very thin. With long auburn hair. Long and stringy and coarse like horse's hair. But it was beautiful. I'd play with it as I read her my poems. I'd read my poems and twist those long strands of hair in my hands."

"How sweet." I patted his shoulder. "What else?"

"She had green eyes. And very pale skin. She always wore one-piece dresses and combat boots. She smelled like vanilla and tobacco."

"Did she write?"

"No. But she read everything."

I smiled and returned to the poems in my lap.

dancing

By the old telephone pole
on which the rusted bus sign hung,
I used to wait for a ride
that was a long time in coming.

Along with me there always stood
a girl about my age;
we never exchanged a single word
as we waited there together.

Never simply standing put,
she would click her heels
on the pavement, and mouth
words of silent songs.

The girl would sway
from side to side

as passing drivers
turned their eyes
from the road
to her shifting form
always dancing
to that song
in her head.

Rain, snow, hail
and wind never
chased away her
rhythm.
I would stand
in the cold
and swear
about gloves
and a hat
or a forgotten
umbrella,
and she would laugh
as the rain weighted
her jacket and the hail
stuck in her hair.

I would always wait
in quiet with my
hands dug deep
in my pockets,
one finger upon the fare,
looking down the
endless road,
straining my
eyes watching
for the distant
bus.

Time passed
hellishly slow,
all the while
the girl danced
and swayed past
the long winter
days.

God, sometimes
I too could
hear that song
    — perry yvain

Drama was new to me. That must have been why I embraced it. It was time for a change. Throughout high school, I just wrote sappy poetry, the type easily published in the literary magazine. I covered all the big topics — suicide, depression, alcohol, and love. Mostly love. My love for Sean. I wrote about drives in the country with Sean. I wrote about making love under the bridge in the park and sneaking into frat parties, getting drunk and throwing up in his car. Or going to the Cafe Grind and sharing our words, like I now did with Perry. I wrote about Sean. He wrote about me. And now I was writing about us again, locked in my room, listening to my mother in her room dictate a lecture into her microcassette tape recorder: "In the Annang culture of Nigeria, obese women are considered the ideal of beauty and refinement, women of substance, in direct opposition to the Western female ideal . . ." My character's boyfriend wanted her to go with him to college. She wanted to go. She wanted to get out of her life. "Upon reaching adolescence, female members of the Annang are placed in specially designed huts, fattening rooms . . ." But she didn't want to go with him. She didn't want to go because he wanted her to. The choice must be hers. He loved her. "They are as much symbols of class as the environment where the ideal could be achieved. By maintaining the female in a fattening hut, an Annang family demonstrates its wealth and its ability to mold . . ." But he wasn't really in love with her. There was more to her than he knew. I couldn't ignore the inherent conflict in the situation — her desire to flee versus her desire not to flee on account of him. "As the female's weight increased, so did her value in the marriage market . . ." My grades suffered — except in creative writing. I worked on the play every day. Perry kept giving me poetry. I'd read it every evening at the athletic complex.

public bathhouse

Amid bars of roll-on deodorant
pH balanced, of course,
and crimson speckled cotton,
she watches her.

watches her emerge
from sheets of steam,
Aphrodite
enveloped in the
coarse ivory
of an issued towel,

one foot upon milky bench
the other on the moist floor.

watches her massage
red calves,
aroused by sport,
shaved and sleek
to breasts
ripe with heat
rounded by creation

watches her back bend
wet, black hair
slipping past her shoulders
as she wipes away beads of azure
clutching peach fuzz
about the navel
where the scent of
soap and lavender
hangs heavy
she turns from her
quickly to button
her blouse
          — perry yvain

How does he see me, I thought. I'm not like the girl in this poem. My hair is short and blonde. Shorter than his. Over-alls and sandals aren't as stylish, as chic, as one-piece dresses and combat boots. He didn't seem to see me. He smiled at me sometimes. That's about all. There's nothing behind the smile. It's more like he's smiling to himself, not at me. He smiled when I said something good about his poetry. He said, "Yes, yes," and smiled when I noticed some contrived complexity, a carefully phrased line. And he snapped or sulked when I offered words of criticism, rubbed the toe of his Vans into whatever surface we're standing on. I should be happy he doesn't look.

"So are you going to submit?" Perry asked, cue stick in hand. We were in the lounge of his dorm. I ran the rack back and forth across the velvet surface, balls banging and rolling against the wooden frame.

"To *Exile*? I'll break, dear." I took the cue stick from him. "No. All I've got is old high school stuff. I haven't written anything new."

"Isn't that good enough? What about 'Down with the Sigma Chi's'?"

"Maybe." I pressed my belly against the end of the table, and slid the stick between the index and middle of my right hand, aiming for the yellow one, one eye open. "Did you and your friend play pool?"

"All the time."

"Was she good?"

"I usually beat her. She didn't care. Pool was beneath her." The crack of collid-
ing spheres, then their scattering across the velvet field. The six dropping in the right
corner pocket, on the rack side. "What do you think I should submit?" he asked.

"I don't know. 'dancing' and 'public bathhouse.'"

"Those two?"

"I liked them. Did you make the changes I suggested?"

"I'm not one for revision."

"What do you mean? Five in the side."

"I don't like to revise. The way the words flow the first time. It's the best time."

"Really? Seven in the corner. I revise all the time. You can always make something better, dear."

"But you can never recapture the feeling which inspired it. The first draft is the
most pure."

"I suppose. One in the corner."

"I know." He smiled as I handed him the stick. I had seen Perry before. I had seen
him come and go over the years. There's always a Perry here — a looking-starved kid
with dark eyes, uncombed hair, and a bundle of papers squeezed into his thin hands,
papers thicker than any muscle. There's always a Perry walking swiftly across the quad,
wide strides, with his head raised high, and his eyes vacant, tripping on breaks in the
concrete, stubbing his toe on a sudden rise. I had seen him while smoking outside the
student union. I had seen him in the Cafe Grind. There's always one. And that's the
thing. At a place like this, there was only one at a time. Which I guess is a good thing,
because two of them would have led to a double homicide. "I don't like to revise" —
what a dope! But he's smart. They're smart, the ones I saw passing through here over the
years. Talking about Kant or Sartre with wild, florid gestures and arcane words — soph-
ists of the college circuit — as they walk between classes, followed by a horde of sorority girls, who don't understand and desperately need an *A*.

You see them standing outside lighted windows, reciting poems or strumming
guitars. And their paramours always let them in. Because they're interesting, despite
all the pretensions. They're sensitive. Like women. They're different than the frat
boys and the jocks and the math whizzes. And they have a respect, a reverence for
beauty, even if it's completely whacked-out.

"Shit." The eleven limped into the corner pocket. "That's not what I called," he
said. "Can I go still?"

"Sure."

"You're whipping my ass."

"And you're going to change that, right?"

"Damn straight." He leaned into the table, the stick thick and awkward between
his fingers. He looked worried.

"Shit," he said softly. The end of the cue sliced the green velvet, propelling the cue
ball into the right corner pocket. "I must be out of practice. I'm usually not this bad."

"Sure." I sank the three and the two in one shot. "You're probably not used to playing someone this good." Sean was like Perry in a lot of ways. He was a poet but drank too much Heineken to maintain the body type. I was his inspiration. Fuck that. He could be horrifically male. I hit the cue across the table, nicking the edge of the one, sending it in a soft roll into the corner pocket. "I played every day during the summer."

"Every day?"

"There was nothing else to do. Wait till your senior year, then you'll know what I'm talking about. Four in the side pocket."

"You're very good." He slipped his hands into the pockets of his jeans and leaned against the dull brass edge of the table. "So you're not going to submit this semester?"

"I'm considering it." I leaned across the table. This would be a difficult shot. There was no fucking bridge in sight. "Your friend, is she the girl in 'dancing'?"

"Someone like her. Nice shot."

"Why didn't you talk to her?"

"What?"

"Why didn't you or your persona or whatever talk to the girl? She's standing right there. You missed connecting."

"It's not about connecting," he said, very pissy. "It's about two different worlds. His world of anticipation. Her world of the moment." He knocked in the ten and the thirteen. "I'm not calling. Is that OK?"

"What about 'public bathhouse?' You have to admit that's about connecting. About missed connections."

"You're closer there. I'm deliberately ambiguous with that one. Is it love or envy the watcher feels? I want the reader to decide." So-long fifteen.

"Christ, you're heavy in that one."

"Shit." He scratched on the twelve. He looked at me. "What do you mean?"

"Look at your description — 'red calves, aroused by athleticism,' 'breasts ripe with heat.' You succeeded in making your Aphrodite."

"I wanted to give the poem a classical feel."

"I never saw a girl like that in high school. Athletes are more muscle, less breasts. You've been reading too much *Seventeen*. Eight in the corner again."

"Tamara was. Tamara was just like that."

"Who?" I missed the shot.

"My friend. She's just like that. She wasn't an athlete. But that's how she looked." He dropped the twelve. "Eight in the side."

"No," I corrected him. "That's how you saw her."

"Shit," he said softly, as the eight rolled towards the side pocket, not the one he called. "I can't believe it," he said, tapping the floor with the stick, as the ball fell into the plastic net.

"Good game." I smiled and lit a triumphant cigarette, right there in the lounge. This was fun. Especially if, as Vonnegut said, you don't take it too seriously. I liked poetry. I used to write it. But it's only poetry. Only high school poetry masked as college poetry.

"You really think I should submit those two?"

"Those are the two I would pick."

"You're not going to submit anything?"

"Do they take unfinished plays?"

He said he didn't think so. He said he thought they only took poetry and fiction. Then I would wait for spring. But I didn't tell him that.

Sean stopped calling after I read him the second act. He cried. He couldn't handle the content. "Karo," my mother said into her recorder, "is the name of the psychological disorder particular to Chinese males — shrinking penis syndrome." He understood why the girl wouldn't join the guy; but he didn't like the reason. "Are you sure?" he asked, his voice thick with sorrow. "I love you. I thought you loved me. Doesn't that prove something? You're my one and my all. I'm lost here without you. And you decide on this through writing a fucking play?" I told him I liked the play. I told him I was always like this. He just never bothered to notice as he sat at the Cafe Grind, composing odes to my everlasting radiance. "The fear that the phallus is slowly shrinking and disappearing usually occurs in males who have experienced emotional or physical humiliation of some sort . . ." He stammered, he protested, "I'm not good enough for you. That's it. You've found someone else." Yes and no I told him. "I'm going crazy. I need to see you again, to hold you in my arms. Then you'll see how right I am." I told him the play would be produced in the spring. I had shown it to a theatre professor, who loved what I had written so far and who saw it as perfect black box material. "Guess this means you won't be coming to Georgetown." He hung up. "In males who have been severely beaten . . ." I blocked-out mom's voice, packed my notebook in my bag, and headed out to the athletic complex.

Exile arrived in the dining halls and the student union in late November, right before winter break. Both of Perry's poems appeared in the issue, "dancing" being the first poem in the book, right after the epigraph and a photo of a woman's naked torso — her arms wrapped around her large breasts. He read the poems in class. Without the revisions. Our peers clapped. They actually seemed to understand. Bill Jr. drooled, "Splendid. Truly superlative verse, Mr. Yvain." I smiled and kept writing in my notebook. He read the poems at the Cafe Grind on open mike night, to clicking fingers and raised mocha lattes. I waited for spring.

"I'm going to write a sonnet sequence over break," he said on the last day of class. "I'll show it to you when I get back."

"Sure. I'm still working on the play."

"You should be writing poetry. We'd make a better team that way."

"You stick with the poetry. Critiquing is fine by me."

"We'll get together again next semester."

"Sure."

"I have to thank you for suggesting I submit those two poems. Your judgment was perfect. I'll never doubt you."

"They're your poems."

"Yes, but you were the first person here to appreciate them. I've dedicated them to you." He smiled.

"Thanks." I longed for my cigarette break.

"The winter formal is sometime next month." He leaned over my desk, Colgate heavy on his breath. "I was thinking of going. Usually I don't go to dances — I didn't even go to prom — but I thought maybe . . ."

"I'm not one for dances. I don't dance."

"But I was thinking you and . . ."

"Sean and I went to prom. We stayed for thirty minutes, then went out to his car for the vodka in the trunk."

"You drink?"

"When I was with Sean. We were young, silly poets."

"I don't drink." He paused and smiled at me, looking straight into my eyes.

"I'd never be caught dead at a Student Activities event."

"Oh." He drew back and gathered up his papers. "I'll see you when I return. Write on."

"Bye." I dug in my purse for my pack; I'd fucking light up right there. Then Bill Jr. said he wanted to see me. In his office.

"I really like your work," Bill Jr. said smoothly, no Mississippi drawl, with palms pressed together, fingers against the curve of his tanned chin, and polished loafers up on his desk. A framed portrait of Pound hung on the wall behind him. His own poetry books were stacked on the desk, the spines facing visitors. "Not that you say much in class," he continued. "But what you put on paper more than makes up for any verbal silence. Your words resound! reverberate! resonate! They speak!"

I sat in a wooden chair with a thin leather cushion, which was not nearly as comfortable as the padded leather, swiveling variety in which he rested his tweed-embossed body. I sat in silence and stiff-backed, with my legs crossed, and wondered if he meant it. Or if my mom had set this up as a bit of encouragement after seeing my midterm grades.

"However, Amber," he said, breathing deeply, with grave concern, "I see nothing of yours in *Exile*. This disappoints me. A young lady of your talent should take advantage of every opportunity for her work to be showcased. Perhaps you feel *Exile* is below you. However, I assure you, it is a fine publication. The student body should be able to appreciate your writing the way I do. I am, of course, saying this under the assumption that you did not submit any of your work to *Exile*. After all, they never could have rejected it."

I told him I didn't submit anything. I told him I was working on a play.

"The play's the thing," he said with a chuckle, "But the poetry will receive attention. Now promise me that you'll submit your work next semester. There is no shame in submitting. You should also know of the writing contest next semester. Cash prizes of substantial value are awarded to the winners. You should strongly consider entering. No, you should enter. In fact, if you don't, I will take your work from this semester and enter it myself."

I told him I would. I told him I would submit to *Exile* despite its silly photographs and enter the contest. He smiled, skimmed his lower lip with the tip of his tongue. His eyes twinkled. Really. I told him my play would be produced in the spring. He would have to see it. And I left him with his palms pressed together and his feet on the polished top of the desk.

An envelope from Georgetown arrived three days before Christmas. It contained a gray Hoyas post-it note and a thimble-size pile of ash: "Season's Greetings. Thanks for the card." I returned it to the sender after adding all the ash a notebook of poetry could produce. Our notebook of poetry — the poetry I wrote for him. One day after New Year's I went to the theatre professor's home with the second act. He leapt about his den, acting out scenes and tossing out names of potential cast members, as I sank into an afghan-draped sofa, sipping hot chocolate from a mug decorated with a lank of ham dressed in a doublet and holding a skull.

When Perry returned from winter break, he did not have a sonnet sequence. He had more of the same poetry. Much like the two in the magazine. He showed them all to me the first time we met, which was in the Cafe Grind on a Tuesday night when I should have been studying for a Sexual Inequality quiz — *How has the emergence of the Twiggy body type thwarted attempts to realistically portray physical womanhood in the American media?* and so forth. But feminist criticism of Perry's poems interested me more.

this bird has flown

BOOMBA! BOOMBA!
sweet, jumpy girl,
up, down like Tigger
on a trampoline,
mattress contracts
springs shriek.

BOOMBA!
I rest my head
against the wall,
watch you
on my bed,
listen to the Beatles play.

Rubber Soul shakes the room
with ethereal sitar rhythms.

outside beneath a street lamp
moths perform a liturgical dance

for their electric god,
so alluring they race from the dark
to its sides,
encircling,
never touching.

BOING!
up you go
tossing back
spooky chick hair,
seen in parks
shading the poems
of Emily D.

tumbles over your face,
misfit Cousin Itt.

long legs
denim clad,
wide cuffs that cover Damascus sandals
stomp on the metal frame.

trip and slip,
you're in my lap,
I feel your
sweaty skin.

I try to hold on,
but you're up again,
in a second.

— perry yvain

"Back to the old themes," I said of his poem before me, taking a thick sip of a cafe latte, white froth slipping down the brown sides of the mug. "Besides ripping off the Beatles, you're back to connection."

"I admit it this time." He was buttering his bagel and looking at the girl behind the counter — a pale, wispy thing dressed all in black with hair dyed black and seven rings in each ear. "One man's sad realization that true beauty, true perfection is transient. One can grasp it, if at all, for only a second."

"And then it's up and bouncing again." I laughed. "You and your girls, Perry." He looked at her. There was nothing to her. I'd seen her or girls like her in here countless times. Now the other girl behind the counter, Sarah, was a real gem. Sarah with short golden-brown hair and dark brown eyes. High and freckled cheek bones.

She wore blue jeans, a sweatshirt, and sneakers. Her breasts were medium and firm, her legs toned from hours of swimming. There was something there.

Or was I acting like Perry? Sarah could pass for the girl in "public bathhouse." But her breasts were hardly "ripe with heat/rounded by creation" and the "scent of soap and lavender" didn't hang heavily about her. She wasn't perfect beauty. I'd seen her slip on the ice before Ellison Hall. I'd seen her wear a brace in the fall and puke in the bathroom of Carver Hall after partying too hard with her sisters. But there was something there. Something Perry didn't know, because he kept his distance. I corrected that. Something the frat guys didn't know, stumbling down the halls with their pants at their ankles. She was strong. She was her own woman. Or so I thought from watching her.

"Do you like it?" His eyes stayed with the wispy one as she made a mocha latte and licked the excess cream from the top.

"Yeah. But lose the lines 'watch you/on my bed.' Get rid of the 'the' before 'poems' and put 'by' instead of 'of.' It flows better that way."

"Should I submit this one to *Exile*?"

"Why not."

"Do you think other people will like it?" His look stayed with the girl. I admit I was looking at Sarah.

"I'm up for another latte," I said.

"I'll go with you."

As he placed his order with the Goth goddess, I talked to Sarah. "Monica just broke up with her boyfriend," she said of her co-worker, pouring steamed milk into my mug. "She's in another one of her 'life is nothing but dead orchids' phases. But she'll come out of it in a month. And they'll be together again. If your friend wants to hook-up, he's out of luck."

"She's a real Shirley Manson."

"Evan's a real Trent Reznor. That's $1.75."

I handed her the money. "I hate it when bad things happen to subculturally hip people."

She laughed, and I tossed some extra change into the tip tray.

"There's something else I want to show you," he said, after we returned to our booth, digging in his blue Jansport for what I expected to be another page from the black folder; but he produced a small envelope which smelled the way fragrance companies claim a summer morning does. "I got it in my box yesterday."

I opened the envelope and removed a page of purple, unlined stationary with a paragraph of writing in a small, precise, female's hand:

Dearest Perry,

Your poems in Exile filled me with joy and wonder. They were truly, truly wonderful. I also enjoyed talking to you at lunch. We should do it again soon. You are obviously a very intelligent, witty, and charming man.

Adieu,

rebecca harris wade

"Who's Rebecca Harris Wade?" I asked.

"An amazing girl I met at lunch."

"I gathered as much." I placed the letter back in the envelope and handed it to him.

"What do you think?" he asked turning it over in his hands.

"She obviously thinks you're Adonis. Her affection is as thick as her perfume."

"She's amazing. Completely. Short red hair and green eyes. Really tall and thin. You've had to have seen her in the dining hall before. She demands attention. Like at lunch, she wore these lime green bell-bottoms, a velour top, and white, vinyl boots."

"Retro-chick."

"I guess. She's intelligent. She quoted Adrienne Rich and Anne Sexton."

"And you're hooking-up."

"I'll see her at lunch again."

"Go to her room. Look her up and go to her."

"She barely knows me."

"She obviously likes you. Connect. Hook-up. That's how things are here. She could be another Tamara."

He stirred his mocha with his finger. "Tamara and I never hooked-up."

"Why is that?"

"She didn't want that type of relationship."

"Well, now you have a chance for it. She wants you. You don't have to pine for her. Here people just take what they want. I've seen countless hook-ups like this. That's how it works in college. No more lonely nights writing poetry. Just jump in her bed."

"Did you just jump into Sean's bed?"

"Yes. But that was high school. For most people, relationships were different there. And I'd be the first to admit that Sean wasn't perfect beauty. Not like Rebecca seems to be."

"What if you're wrong about her?"

"Trust me. If she rejects you, choose someone else. Like the girl behind the counter. But she likes you. You're 'intelligent, witty, and charming.' Don't fail to grasp perfect beauty."

"I think I will. She's beautiful. She's intelligent. She likes me."

"And your poetry."

"Yes, my poetry." He smiled, drank his mocha slowly, and didn't look at the girl behind the counter for the rest of the evening.

We didn't meet the next week. We didn't meet the week after that. I didn't mind. I was revising the end of the second act. The boyfriend dies in a freak accident, while setting fire to past correspondences. The third act has the girl go off to California and hook-up with an Olympic swimmer. One Wednesday evening Perry called and asked if we could meet at the Cafe Grind, the only real place to meet in the ankle-high snow and slush of February.

"How are things with Ms. Rebecca Harris Wade?" I held the latte up to my lips with both hands. "Taking her to the formal?"

"Read this." He thrust a piece of notebook paper in my face, leaned back in the booth and smiled.

imagine

Imagine
allen ginsberg poetry
fills the room,
ballerina body
on top of you
the light reflects
long, thin strips
of blonde in her
otherwise red head

and you realize you forgot the condoms.
      — perry yvain

"Condoms, Perry? I knew you'd end up in her bed."

"You were right. Very right."

"Is Ms. Wade the little sexual tigress?"

"Now, Amber," he smiled. "Some poetry goes unwritten. I have a funny story about the condoms. She uses her Big Red card to buy them from the vending machines. It's her parents' money on the card. Her parents are buying our contraceptives." He laughed.

"I'm sure they advocate safe sex and birth control."

"She's so amazing. I'm so happy. Much happier than I was first semester. You should see her room. She has a single. Which makes things easier. She has all these paintings on her walls. Original paintings. Even a full-length self-portrait."

"A renaissance woman."

"She writes poetry too. She's rather good. I'm encouraging her to submit to *Exile*. Which reminds me, have you seen the posters for the writing contest?"

"They're posted all over campus."

"Are you going to enter it?"

"I don't have a choice. Dr. Mills said he'd enter my work from last semester if I didn't enter something myself."

"He said that? To you? Personally?"

"In his office."

"In his office," he repeated softly. He took a sip of his mocha and returned to talking about Rebecca Harris Wade, leaving me only five minutes to chat with Sarah before closing. Only enough time to ask her if she'd had any acting experience. He didn't have anymore poetry.

"Nothing. I have nothing," he said when we met in the hall a few days before the contest deadline. "No ideas. The words don't flow. No inspiration." He tore at his hair, tugged his goatee.

"What about Rebecca Harris Wade?" I asked.

"She's my bane! We're always together. She insists on it. We're always fighting. Like George and Martha. She's always saying I'm not doing this right, or that right. Or she's saying that I'm not noticing something about her. She insists that we spend time together and work it out. But how am I supposed to write? I can't write with her demanding every second of my attention. And then when I am alone, no ideas. Not a single one. I just sit at my Mac looking at the blank screen. Yesterday I typed 'the white bull' a hundred times. It was all I could do. I'm going crazy."

"Writer's block, Perry. Something we all go through. You'll escape it. Tell me more about Rebecca Harris Wade."

"Last summer I wrote a poem a day. I would take long walks by myself, and I always came up with something. The deadline's in three days. I have nothing."

"Submit your work from last semester."

"But it's not good enough. It's just not good enough . . . You're the poet. Mills himself said so. In his office." He paced back and forth in front of the secretary's office, clawing his goatee. "He never told me anything like that. He must be right."

"I never should have told you that."

"No, you should have. Because I knew. I always knew how that's what he thought. Why should I even bother entering? You're the poet. But if you're the poet, then what does that make me?"

I didn't answer. I wanted to tell him Vonnegut's motto. But I couldn't. He clutched the handle of his plastic mug tightly, so that his hands grew red then white. His eyes were bloodshot; thick shadows circled them. Lines of sweat trailed down his forehead. And it was only the second week of March.

I won the contest. First place with its one hundred and fifty dollar prize. A junior from my creative writing class came in second. Two sophomores tied for third. Perry didn't place. I saw him in the elevator — right after a sign announcing the names of the winners had been posted there and in several other places around campus — and he offered solemn congratulations with lowered head and drooped shoulders. He said he wasn't going to submit "this bird has flown" to *Exile*; he needed to revise it. He said, "Rebecca and I are breaking up. It's mutual." Later, when I rode the elevator back down after class, I saw scrawled in black ink on the poster, next to Amber Rae McDonough First Place, the completion of a simple sentence — "IS A DYKE." Well, I thought, frowning, that's a revelation.

Weeks went by without a word from Perry. I didn't even see him in our old haunts. I heard through Sarah that the break up between him and Rebecca had been rather nasty. She was seen making out with another guy at a party the night after they split. But Perry had a new crush — a girl he had met in the English department. They hooked-up at the Cafe Grind and talked until three in the morning, after the place had closed. She told me they agreed to remain friends for the time being. And then the phantom poet re-appeared on the gray slate before the student union as I sat smoking an L&M on the well-worn brick ledge. He smiled. He said I looked beautiful. Then he said, "I'm sorry about what happened a while back. I was under a lot of stress because of Rebecca. I don't want you to think that beating you in that contest was more important than our friendship. You're a great writer. I really mean it. I knew it from the first line of yours I read. We shouldn't be competing against one another. We should be working together. You've helped me a lot with my writing. And I only hope I've helped you a little bit too."

"You made the semester interesting." I smiled. "I like your writing too, Perry. I mean it. I always have. But you need to learn to revise."

He grinned and let his bag fall off his shoulder.

"Then I guess that means we can meet regularly again." He removed the black folder from his Jansport and handed me twenty sheets of paper. "I've been back at the old Mac. Some new things. Some old. I re-worked 'this bird.' I think it's ready for *Exile*. But see what you think." He took my hand in his.

I shook for us. "Sure," I said.

I didn't tell him sets were going up the next week.

1997

Critical thinking points: After you've read

1) The story is written in the first-person, female point-of-view, yet the author is male. Is the point of view believable? Why or why not?
2) Why do writers revise their work? Why do you think Perry originally refuses to revise his poetry? What does this say about Perry?
3) How do Amber's mother's recorded lectures reflect what is happening in the story?
4) Why do you think Amber and Sean break up? What details in the story lead you to that conclusion?
5) How does Amber evolve throughout her freshman year? What are some causes? What are the effects of this evolution on her life?

Some possibilities for writing

1) Write a critique of one of Perry's poems. Now imagine you are giving him your critique. How might that change what you say or how you say it?
2) What will become of "amber rae mcdonough, poet"? Write a scene that depicts what you believe might be her future.
3) Perry compares Amber to a girl he knew in high school. Many people make

friends in new situations by associating them with old friends. Recall a time when you did this or when someone did this to you.

4) *Write a scene in which Amber meets Carmen and Kate from Jennifer Sheridan's "Carmen." Add Perry to the scene. Which woman does he choose for a girlfriend? Why? Which woman does he choose for a platonic friend? Why?*

The Good Student Apologizes to His Professor and to the Girl in Room 303

Ron Watson

"

It was only as they say / A phase I was going through with a girl my age / Who chose to sit with me / And tune you out each afternoon.

"

Critical thinking points: As you read

1) There are many vague recollections in the poem. Why might that be so? List some of them.

2) What qualities make a "good" student? Is the narrator a "good" student? Make note of what details in the poem lead you to believe what you do.

3) What might lead any student to write an apology to his teacher? Is this a sincere apology? Make note of what details in the poem lead you to believe this.

This is to apologize
For not learning my maps in World Civ I and II
Which you took personally
Being an uncommon teacher loving what you do,
But it had nothing to do with you.
It was only as they say
A phase I was going through with a girl my age
Who chose to sit with me
And tune you out each afternoon.
We failed your tests together, those maps
With blanks where the names of countries go,
Although she knew enough to list the continents
And I had no choice but to be creative.
I have forgotten her name
But not the coldness her leaving left me with.

Ron Watson's poems have appeared in such journals as *Kansas Quarterly* and *South Dakota Review*. He is a teacher for the Gifted and Talented Program in Madisonville, Kentucky.

I failed you by inattention
And her by indecision
In the murky chambers of the heart.

To repent
I have scratched the state of Alabama
On a table in Roy's Bar, and sketched a road
From Tuscaloosa where she lived
Back to Birmingham.
And on the bathroom wall
I have added to the thighs
Of a local Picasso's naked lady
The continents of Africa and South America
And shaded the ocean blue between her legs.

1988

Critical thinking points: After you've read

1) *Do you believe the teacher took his student's failure "personally"? Why or why not? What might have led the student to believe his teacher took it personally?*
2) *How is this poem an apology to "the girl in Room 303"? Do you believe the narrator is sincerely apologizing to the girl? Why or why not? What else might he be trying to accomplish?*
3) *What might Watson mean when he says, "I failed you by inattention / And her by indecision"?*
4) *Why might the poem end the way it does? Is that an appropriate image? Why or why not?*
5) *In what ways is this a "love" poem?*

Some possibilities for writing

1) *Write "A Day in the Life Of . . ." (similar to the poem by Greg Adams from this anthology) for this student, based on what you know of him from the poem. Use concrete details, most of which you'll have to make up.*
2) *Have you ever felt bad for a teacher because you did poorly on a paper or test or even the entire course? Write about your experience. Explore why you felt the way you did.*
3) *Recall a time when you were influenced by your peers in the classroom. Did you have a positive or negative experience? Explore why the experience was positive or negative.*
4) *Rewrite the last five lines of the poem in at least three different ways.*

Further Suggestions for Writing — "Student Affairs"

1) As the poet says, "The course of true love never runs smooth." Though this is true of all people "in love," there are some pressures particular to college students involved in romantic relationships. Write about some of those pressures.

2) Many students when they come to college leave behind or are otherwise separated from a "significant other." What are some of the advantages and disadvantages of being in such a situation?

3) What is the story of the "greatest" love you know? Why have you made the choice you have? Feel free to choose from your or others' experiences, as well as literature, film, or popular culture in general.

4) Discuss what you believe to be the association between love and sex within a relationship. How and when do they seem to be exclusive and/or interrelated, and what is the nature of that interrelationship? Are there differences between the male and female symbolic or realistic estimation of sex and/or love? If so, what do these differences imply?

5) What kinds of influences do you think your religious and/or family upbringing have had on your attitudes about sex and sexuality and/or love, marriage, and divorce?

6) Describe an incident or pattern of gender discrimination that you have noticed since you arrived at college.

7) Organize a discussion between a group of male and female friends, in which the subject is "College Men are from Mars; College Women are from Venus." Write a report of the "findings" of your discussion to present to your class.

8) Compare and contrast some aspect of sexual behavior, love, romance, or dating between college men and college women.

9) Find a few recent issues of two different magazines, one of which is directed primarily at women, the other at men. Compare and contrast the way that attitudes about gender are revealed in these two publications. In what way are gender stereotypes reinforced and/or challenged?

10) Do you believe men and women communicate differently? If so, discuss what you feel to be some of these differences. Is it possible for a man and a woman to be "just friends?" Why do you think the way you do about this subject?

11) Research some of the metaphors men use for women at your school and some women use for men. Compare and contrast them in an investigation of how the sexes view each other. What kinds of insights does this lead you to?

12) Argue for or against Co-ed Dorms.

13) Many of the pieces in this book depict males in unflattering terms. Do you think "male bashing" is acceptable on college campuses? Why or why not?

14) *Evaluate your school's policy on student-to-student and faculty/staff-to-student sexual harassment.*

15) *What are some of the benefits of abstaining from sex until marriage?*

16) *Music played a major part of the sexual revolution of the sixties and seventies. Research songs of the era and especially look for songs that promoted sexual freedom for young people, either openly or covertly. Some songs masked their underlying sexual messages ("Everybody come together right now" or "Come together, right now, over me.") with messages of peaceful unity. Record some of the specific lyrics of songs you've found. What are some popular songs in recent years that promote sexuality? Record some of the specific song lyrics.*

17) *Interview some older people about which three or four songs they feel were the most popular love songs of their respective generations. Get and listen to those songs. Now choose three or four songs from your own generation. What changes, if any, do these songs display in regards to attitudes toward love, sex, sexuality, and/or gender roles? What kinds of causes or conclusions can you draw from your findings?*

18) *Evaluate your school's support services for gay and lesbian students,*

19) *Choose one of your responses to "Some possibilities for writing" in this section and do further research on some aspect of the topic you addressed in your narrative. Write about how and why this new information would have improved your previous effort.*

Selected Films — "Student Affairs"

Double Happiness (1994, USA). A young Chinese-American woman has a romance with an Anglo college student against the wishes of her very traditional father. Comedy/Drama. 87 min. PG-13

First Love (1977, USA). An idealistic college student finds that neither his classmates nor his girlfriend takes sex as seriously as he does. Based on Harold Brodkey's story "Sentimental Education." Romantic drama. 92 min. R

The First Time (1982, USA). A movie-loving college freshman has no luck with women despite counsel from his psych prof, who uses his dilemma as research. Comedy. 90 min. R

Foreign Student (1994, USA). A French foreign exchange student falls for a professor's housekeeper, but she being black and this being 1954, their affair stirs up trouble at the conservative Virginia college. Adapted from the best-selling memoir of French filmmaker Phillipe Labro. Romantic drama. 96 min. R

The French Lesson (1986, Great Britain). A young English woman goes to Paris for a romantic education. Romantic comedy. 90 min. PG

Happy Together (1989, USA). A would-be playwright discovers that through a mix-up his new college roommate is a flashy actress. Romantic comedy. 102 min. PG-13

How I Got Into College (1989, USA). A second-rate student scratches his way into college to pursue his dream girl. Comedy. 89 min. PG-13

Les Cousins (1959, France). Within the milieu of Parisian student life, a decadent city boy and his pure country cousin vie for the affections of the same young woman. Drama. 112 min.

A Little Stiff (1991, USA). A gen-X UCLA film student pines hopelessly for his classmate. Written by and starring Caveh Zahedi. Romantic comedy. 85 min. N/R

Maurice (1987, Great Britain). Two male students feel they have to repress their mutual attraction, given the stifling sexual mores at Cambridge in the Edwardian era. Based on E.M. Forster's novel of the same name. Drama. 140 min. R

Mother Is a Freshman (1949, USA). A beautiful mother and daughter, both attending the same college, both fall for the same handsome lad. Comedy. 81 min.

The Sterile Cuckoo (1969, USA). Liza Minnelli plays an aggressive college student pursuing a shy freshman boy. Comedy/Drama. 107 min. PG

Student Prince in Old Heidelberg (1927, USA). A young prince leaves his sheltered life to attend the university, where he falls for a beautiful commoner. A silent-film adaptation of Sigmund Romburg's operetta, directed by master Ernst Lubitsch. Romance. 105 min. N/R

The Sure Thing (1985, USA). Spatting college students thrown together on a trip cross-country find love on the way. Romantic comedy. 94 min. PG-13

When He's Not a Stranger (1989, USA). Intensely portrayed date-rape story. Made for TV. Drama. 100 min. N/R

For Critical Thinking Points on these films, see Appendix (p. 335).

Chapter Four

Teacher, Teacher:
Will This Be on the Test?

A teacher can effect an eternity or simply make a class period feel like one. The selections here present teachers in the roles of disciplinarian, mentor, instructor, scholar, and friend, but most of all, as people with many of the same downfalls, inadequacies, and fears as their students.

This chapter will explore —

- Your own influences in the classroom
- A better understanding of the university system
- The inspiration, however misguided, of teachers on students' lives
- Lessons about life that students and teachers give one another

Teachers: A Primer

Ron Wallace

"

She had a policy: A tattletale / or liar had to face the wall,
a tail pinned to his sorry ass, / and wear the laughter of the class.

"

Critical thinking points: As you read

1) What is a "primer"?
2) What grades does Wallace cover in the poem? As you read, speculate about the grade-level for each teacher and what subject he or she teaches.
3) Why do you think the poet chooses the names he does for the teachers he describes?
4) Each teacher is described in the sonnet form. Each piece is made up of fourteen lines, but what are the differences in rhyme scheme from teacher to teacher?

MRS. GOLDWASSER
  Shimmered like butterscotch; the sun
  had nothing on her. She bangled
  when she walked. No one
  did not love her. She shone,
  she glowed, she lit up any room,
  her every gesture jewelry.
  And O, when she called us all by name
  how we all performed!

  Her string of little beads,
  her pearls, her rough-cut

Ron Wallace (b. 1945) is the author of many books of poetry and criticism — including *Time's Fancy*, *The Makings of Happiness*, and *God Be with the Clown: Humor in American Poetry* — and editor of *Vital Signs: Contemporary American Poetry from the University Presses*. He is director of creative writing at the University of Wisconsin–Madison, and poetry editor for the University of Wisconsin Press. He is married and has two daughters, and divides his time between Madison and a forty-acre farm in Bear Valley, Wisconsin.

gemstones, diamonds, we hung
about her neck. And when
the future pressed her flat,
the world unclasped, and tarnished.

MRS. SANDS

Always dressed in tan. Her voice
abrasive as her name. What choice
did a second grader have? You got
what you got. Her room was hot
but she wore wool and heavy sweat
and worked our childhoods, short and sweet.
You didn't sass her or the school or
she'd rap your knuckles with a ruler.

She had a policy: A tattletale
or liar had to face the wall,
a tail pinned to his sorry ass,
and wear the laughter of the class.
So, to this day, my knuckles bent,
I tell the truth (but tell it slant).

MRS. ORTON

The perennial substitute, like some
obnoxious weed, a European interloper
in our native prairie, her instructions
full of nettles, her gestures parsnip
and burdock. Every day at 3:00 p.m.
we'd dig her out of our small lives,
and every morning she'd pop back.
We prayed she'd get the sack.

And to that end we taunted her —
tacks on her chair, a set-back clock —
as, weeping, she plodded through the week
turning, and turning the other cheek.
And every time we thought that we'd
eradicated her, she'd gone to seed.

MISS WILLINGHAM

A Southern Belle, she read *Huck Finn*
aloud to us, dropping her chin
to get the accent right. And me,

for some odd reason, she
singled out to learn the books
of the Bible and recite them back
to her in my high voice
I tried to measure lower. *Nice*

boys go to Sunday school, she said,
and made me promise, when I was grown,
to glorify our heavenly Lord
and take His teaching for my own.
And when she finished that dull story,
she lit out for the territory.

MR. AXT

The basketball coach. Short, tough.
Three days growth on his sharp chin.
Liked to see us all play rough,
and beat up on the stupid, thin,
weak kids who couldn't take it.
He wore white T-shirts, shoes, and slacks,
and taught us all to fake it
if we somehow naturally lacked
the mean competitive spirit.
Once a week he'd have us
bend over and spread our cheeks
for him and old Doc Moffett
who liked to slap us on the butt
and watch as we took leaks.

MRS. REPLOGLE

Her name forbidding, reptilian,
her reputation like a snake
around my expectations.
But then she played *Swan Lake*
and Ferde Grofe's *Grand Canyon Suite*,
a Bach chorale, a Beethoven quartet,
and when we were all back on the street
even the traffic kept a beat.

One day she had us close our eyes
and listen to a symphony
and write whatever image rose
in our small imagination's dark.

And what I saw was poetry,
each note a bird, a flower, a spark.

MR. GLUSENKAMP

His gray face was a trapezoid, his voice
droned on like an ellipse.
He hated students and their noise
and loved the full eclipse
of their faces at the end of the day.
No one could have been squarer,
and nothing could have been plainer
than his geometry.

He didn't go for newfangled
stuff — new math, the open classroom.
And yet he taught us angles
and how lines intersect and bloom,
and how infinity was no escape,
and how to give abstractions shape.

MR. WATTS

Sat cross-legged on his desk,
a pretzel of a man, and grinned
as if chemistry were some cosmic joke
and he'd been dealt a hand
of wild cards, all aces.
He drew for us a "ferrous" wheel
and showed when formic acid reverses
HCOOH becomes HOOCH, a peal
of laughter ringing from his nose.
He gave us Avogadro's number
and in his stained lab clothes
formulas for blowing the world asunder
or splitting genes. God knows
why he died shouting "No!" in thunder.

MISS GOFF

When Zack Pulanski brought the plastic vomit
and slid it slickly to the vinyl floor
and raised his hand, and her tired eyes fell on it
with horror, the heartless classroom lost in laughter
as the custodian slyly tossed his saw dust on it
and pushed it, grinning, through the door,

she reached into her ancient corner closet
and found some Emily Dickinson mimeos there
which she passed out. And then, herself
passed out on the cold circumference of her desk.
And everybody went their merry ways
but me, who chancing on one unexpected phrase
after another, sat transfixed until dusk.
Me and Miss Goff, the top of our heads taken off.

1989

Critical thinking points: After you've read

*1) When do you think the poem is set? What details in the poem support your
theory? How is the time of the poem important?*
*2) What lessons does Wallace learn from each teacher? Make a list. How do they
reflect his becoming a poet? Do you think they helped make him a poet, or does
his being a poet now simply make these lessons more memorable in retrospect?*
*3) What painful or disheartening memories of school are reflected in the poem?
What fond memories? Why might the poet include both?*
4) What stereotypes of teachers are apparent in the poem?
*5) Do you expect your relationship with your college teachers to be similar or
different from earlier experiences with teachers? In what ways?*

Some possibilities for writing

*1) Choose one of the teachers and a write a letter to the poet from the teacher's
point of view.*
*2) Recall a teacher who stands out in your memory because of his or her
personality, mannerisms, and so on. Write a one-page description of that
teacher using specific details.*
*3) Choose another teacher from a work in this collection and compare him or her
to one of Wallace's teachers.*
*4) Interview your current teachers and ask them who were the greatest or most
important teachers they had. After a number of interviews, write an essay on
what makes a successful teacher.*
*5) Choose a teacher you did not understand or appreciate during the time you
were in that teacher's class but learned to appreciate later. What happened to
change your mind?*

Take This Fish and Look at It

Samuel H. Scudder

> I was piqued; I was mortified. Still more of that wretched fish! But now I set myself to my task with a will, and discovered one new thing after another, until I saw how just the Professor's criticism had been. The afternoon passed quickly; and when, towards its close, the Professor inquired: 'Do you see it yet?'

Critical thinking points: As you read

1) *Consider why observation skills are necessary for students to grow and learn. In what academic situations are these skills most critical? How do you rate yourself as an observer?*
2) *Consider the type of student Scudder was before his episode with the fish. How might he have changed as a student? As a scientist? As a person?*
3) *What are some clues to the era in which the essay is set?*

It was more than fifteen years ago that I entered the laboratory of Professor Agassiz, and told him I had enrolled my name in the Scientific School as a student of natural history. He asked me a few questions about my object in coming, my antecedents generally, the mode in which I afterwards proposed to use the knowledge I might acquire, and, finally, whether I wished to study any special branch. To the latter I replied that, while I wished to be well grounded in all departments of zoology, I proposed to devote myself specially to insects.

"When do you wish to begin?" he asked. "Now," I replied.

This seemed to please him, and with an energetic "Very well," he reached from a shelf a huge jar of specimens in yellow alcohol. "Take this fish," he said, "and look at it; we call it a haemulon; by and by I will ask what you have seen."

With that he left me, but in a moment returned with explicit instructions as to the care of the object entrusted to me.

"No man is fit to be a naturalist," said he, "who does not know how to take care of specimens."

Samuel H. Scudder (1837–1911) was a famous entomologist who was schooled at Harvard University.

I was to keep the fish before me in a tin tray, and occasionally moisten the surface with alcohol from the jar, always taking care to replace the stopper tightly. Those were not the days of ground-glass stoppers and elegantly shaped exhibition jars; all the old students will recall the huge neck-less glass bottles with their leaky, wax-besmeared corks, half eaten by insects, and begrimed with cellar dust. Entomology was a cleaner science than ichthyology, but the example of the Professor, who had unhesitatingly plunged to the bottom of the jar to produce the fish, was infectious; and though this alcohol had a "very ancient and fishlike smell," I really dared not show any aversion within these sacred precincts, and treated the alcohol as though it were pure water. Still I was conscious of a passing feeling of disappointment, for gazing at a fish did not commend itself to an ardent entomologist. My friends at home, too, were annoyed when they discovered that no amount of eau-de-Cologne would drown the perfume which haunted me like a shadow.

In ten minutes I had seen all that could be seen in that fish, and started in search of the Professor — who had, however, left the Museum; and when I returned, after lingering over some of the odd animals stored in the upper apartment, my specimen was dry all over. I dashed the fluid over the fish as if to resuscitate the beast from a fainting fit, and looked with anxiety for a return of the normal sloppy appearance. This little excitement over, nothing was to be done but to return to a steadfast gaze at my mute companion. Half an hour passed — an hour — another hour; the fish began to look loathsome. I turned it over and around; looked it in the face ghastly; from behind, beneath, above, sideways, at a three-quarters' view — just as ghastly. I was in despair; at an early hour I concluded that lunch was necessary; so, with infinite relief, the fish was carefully replaced in the jar, and for an hour I was free.

On my return, I learned that Professor Agassiz had been at the Museum, but had gone, and would not return for several hours. My fellow students were too busy to be disturbed by continued conversation. Slowly I drew forth that hideous fish, and with a feeling of desperation again looked at it. I might not use a magnifying-glass; instruments of all kinds were interdicted. My two hands, my two eyes, and the fish: it seemed a most limited field. I pushed my finger down its throat to feel how sharp the teeth were. I began to count the scales in the different rows, until I was convinced that was nonsense. At last a happy thought struck me — I would draw the fish; and now with surprise I began to discover new features in the creature. Just then the Professor returned.

"That is right," said he; "a pencil is one of the best of eyes. I am glad to notice, too, that you keep your specimen wet, and your bottle corked."

With these encouraging words, he added: "Well, what is it like?"

He listened attentively to my brief rehearsal of the structure of parts whose names were still unknown to me: the fringed gill-arches and movable operculum, the pores of the head, fleshy lips and lidless eyes; the lateral line, the spinous fins and forked tail; the compressed and arched body. When I finished, he waited as if expecting more, and then, with an air of disappointment: "You have not looked very carefully; why," he continued more earnestly, "you haven't even seen one of the most con-

spicuous features of the animal, which is plainly before your eyes as the fish itself —
look again, look again!" and he left me to my misery.

I was piqued; I was mortified. Still more of that wretched fish! But now I set
myself to my task with a will, and discovered one new thing after another, until I saw
how just the Professor's criticism had been. The afternoon passed quickly; and when,
towards its close, the Professor inquired: "Do you see it yet?"

"No," I replied, "I am certain I do not, but I see how little I saw before."

"That is next best," said he, earnestly, "but I won't hear you now; put away your
fish and go home; perhaps you will be ready with a better answer in the morning. I
will examine you before you look at the fish."

This was disconcerting. Not only must I think of my fish all night, studying,
without the object before me, what this unknown but most visible feature might be;
but also, without reviewing my discoveries, I must give an exact account of them the
next day. I had a bad memory; so I walked home by Charles River in a distracted
state, with my two perplexities.

The cordial greeting from the Professor the next morning was reassuring; here
was a man who seemed to be quite as anxious as I that I should see for myself what
he saw.

"Do you perhaps mean," I asked, "that the fish has symmetrical sides with paired
organs?"

His thoroughly pleased "Of course! Of course!" repaid the wakeful hours of the
previous night. After he had discoursed most happily and enthusiastically — as he
always did — upon the importance of this point, I ventured to ask what I should do
next.

"Oh, look at your fish!" he said, and left me again to my own devices. In a little
more than an hour he returned, and heard my new catalogue.

"That is good, that is good!" he repeated; "but that is not all; go on"; and so for
three long days he placed that fish before my eyes, forbidding me to look at anything
else, or to use any artificial aid. "Look, look, look," was his repeated injunction.

This was the best entomological lesson I ever had — a lesson whose influence
has extended to the details of every subsequent study; a legacy the Professor had left
to me, as he has left it to so many others, of inestimable value, which we could not
buy, with which we cannot part.

A year afterward, some of us were amusing ourselves with chalking outlandish
beasts on the Museum blackboard. We drew prancing starfishes; frogs in mortal combat; hydra-headed worms; stately crawfishes, standing on their tails, bearing aloft
umbrellas; and grotesque fishes with gaping mouths and staring eyes. The Professor
came in shortly after, and was as amused as any at our experiments. He looked at the
fishes.

"Haemulons, every one of them," he said; "Mr. _____ drew them."

True; and to this day, if I attempt a fish, I can draw nothing but haemulons.

The fourth day, a second fish of the same group was placed beside the first, and
I was bidden to point out the resemblances and differences between the two; another

and another followed, until the entire family lay before me, and a whole legion of jars covered the table and surrounding shelves; the odor had become a pleasant perfume; and even now, the sight of an old, six-inch, worm-eaten cork brings fragrant memories.

The whole group of haemulons was thus brought in review; and, whether engaged upon the dissection of the internal organs, the preparation and examination of the bony framework, or the description of the various parts, Agassiz's training in the method of observing facts and their orderly arrangement was ever accompanied by the urgent exhortation not to be content with them.

"Facts are stupid things," he would say, "until brought into connection with some general law."

At the end of eight months, it was almost with reluctance that I left these friends and turned to insects; but what I had gained by this outside experience has been of greater value than years of later investigation in my favorite groups.

1874

Critical thinking points: After you've read

1) *Professor Agassiz says, "A pencil is one of the best of eyes." What does he mean? How and why might this be true?*
2) *Scudder says, "I see how little I saw before." Professor Agassiz answers, "That is next best." What does the professor mean? In what ways is this realization a step toward the lesson Scudder learns?*
3) *What makes this a humorous story? Would it be as effective without the humor? Why or why not?*
4) *Artists, scientists, and writers use observation skills in similar and different ways. List them. What are some other occupations in which observation is an especially important skill?*

Some possibilities for writing

1) *Recall a teacher who taught you a lesson you didn't expect to learn. What led to your acquiring that lesson? Write an essay describing your experience.*
2) *Bruce Taylor's poem "The Lesson" is made up of three lines:*

> Pay attention.
> This is everything.
> Pay attention.

Discuss how Scudder's essay reflects this poem.
3) *Observation is a skill that is used constantly in social and academic situations.*

What are some experiences you've had in which your observation skills were absolutely integral to your success? Choose one experience and describe it.

4) *Recall a personal experience that turned out poorly because your observation skills failed you. Write about the situation, and speculate how it could have turned out differently if you would have been more observant.*

When I Heard the Learn'd Astronomer

Walt Whitman

66

When I sitting heard the astronomer where he lectured with much applause in the lecture room,
How soon unaccountable I became tired and sick,

99

Critical thinking points: As you read

1) Exactly what is an "astronomer"? What kinds of people might be attracted to or successful in such a field?

2) Walt Whitman is famous for his sounds. As you read, write down phrases that strike you as particularly wonderful or odd arrangements of words. What makes these phrases "poetic"?

3) What makes the astronomer "learn'd"? In what ways is he or is he not "learn'd"?

When I heard the learn'd astronomer,
When the proofs, the figures, were ranged in columns before me,
When I was shown the charts and diagrams, to add, divide,
    and measure them,
When I sitting heard the astronomer where he lectured with
    much applause in the lecture room,
How soon unaccountable I became tired and sick,
Till rising and gliding out I wander'd off by myself,
In the mystical moist night-air, and from time to time,
Look'd up in perfect silence at the stars.

1892

In 1855, Walt Whitman (1819–1892) published the first of many editions of *Leaves of Grass*, a volume of poetry undisputably ranked among the greatest in American literature. Today, Whitman's poetry has been translated into every major language. It is widely recognized as a formative influence on the work of such American writers as Hart Crane, William Carlos Williams, Wallace Stevens, and Allen Ginsberg.

Critical thinking points: After you've read

1) Read or reread Antler's "Raising My Hand." What common themes do the poems share?
2) What kinds of statements might the poet be making about formal education? What in the poem leads you to your opinions?
3) The "learn'd astronomer" speaks about stars, while the poet is silenced by them. What might this say about their different areas of expertise: science and language?
4) Who do you think has a better appreciation for astronomy, the learn'd astronomer or the poet? Why?
5) The poet Jack Gilbert wrote, "We must unlearn the constellations to see the stars." How is his statement a reflection of Whitman's poem?

Some possibilities for writing

1) Why might the speaker of this poem at the very end look up "in perfect silence at the stars"? Explore at least two different reasons.
2) Find Walt Whitman's Song of Myself and read Section 6, the one beginning "A child said, What is the grass?" The speaker of that poem, the poet, seems to be the "teacher" in that situation. How does reading this poem change your reading of "When I Heard the Learn'd Astronomer," if at all?
3) Write a scene in which Antler, the author of "Raising My Hand," or Calvin Jefferson in "Open Admission" by Shirley Lauro meets Walt Whitman. What do they talk about? How is each conversation a reflection of what you know about this author or character?
4) Recall a time in your life when you read or talked about something rather than experiencing it for yourself. What circumstances led you to reading or talking about it? What held you back from or urged you on to experiencing it?
5) Read or reread Samuel H. Scudder's "Take This Fish and Look at It," and write an essay comparing it to Whitman's poem. What theories of education and knowledge do the two pieces share? How are they different?

Mayday

William Crawford Woods

———————————— 66 ————————————

You could be a good writer, Jill, but you must stop staking everything on deceit.

———————————— 99 ————————————

Critical thinking points: As you read

1) What kind of person do you think the professor is? What kind of person do you think Jill is? What details in the story support these characteristics?

2) As you read the student's assignments in this story, make note of some characteristics they seem to have in common. What are some of the recurring themes and images in Jill's stories?

3) What effect does the form of the story — notes, assignments, stories within the story — have on your reading of it? How might the story be different if it had been written in a more traditional way?

This handout is for the benefit of those who slept through the first — and final — lecture. It is full of rules, and one reminder: if you think this course can teach you how to write, get out while you can still get your money back. Flannery O'Connor, of whom some of you may have heard, was once asked whether she thought writing classes ruin young writers, and she replied: they don't ruin enough of them.

Books required for the course include any decent dictionary of your choosing (I look on the unabridged *O.E.D.* with favor); Pound's *ABC of Reading*; and *Fiction &*

William Crawford Woods (b. 1944) was born in Philadelphia and educated at George Washington University (B.A., philosophy) and Johns Hopkins (M.A., writing seminars). He served in the Army as a broadcast journalist at Far East Network, Tokyo, before joining the staff of the *Washington Post* as a pop culture critic in 1969. He is the author of a novel, *The Killing Zone*, and of journalism and short fiction that has appeared in such national journals as *Esquire*, *Harper's*, and *New American Review*. A fellow of the National Endowment for the Arts and a one-time Hollywood screenwriter, Woods has since 1976 been a member of the language and literature faculty at Longwood College in Virginia. "Mayday" appeared in the *Atlantic Monthly* in 1974.

the Figures of Life by William Gass. You need not produce these to prove that you have them. Your submissions will do that.

Manuscripts must be put in the IN box in my office by Wednesday if you expect to have them returned at Monday's meeting. Please do not give me any poems. Those go to Professor Tarn. If they go to me, they go into my fireplace. I hate poems because I hate poets who are always tugging at your sleeve in the halls.

Manuscripts must be typewritten and double-spaced. I prefer pica but do not refuse elite. Electric but do not reject manual. Type must be clean and crisp. The ribbon must be black. Handwritten manuscripts will be returned unread.

The paper must be good-quality bond of at least 25 percent rag content. I do not accept onion skin or toilet tissue. There must be one-and-a-half-inch margins on all sides, and pages two to the finish must carry the name of the author and title of the story in the upper left-hand corner, and the page number in the upper right. Page one is the title page. There should be no cover sheet and no pretty plastic binders; a butterfly clip is sufficient.

In the upper left-hand corner of page one will be my name, the course title, and the date of submission. You will center the title of the story half-way down the page, in caps, with your name below. And begin the story a well-proportioned space below that.

Miss Fuller,

We are into the fourth week of the semester, and I have yet to have the pleasure of seeing any of your work. There is no minimum weekly requirement, but there is a minimum requirement for the course, and unless you buckle down you'll find yourself with fifty pages of prose to put out between Christmas and New Year's. Your comments in seminar on the work of others have been so astute I am eager to see some of your own.

```
                         SUMMIT
                           by
                       Jill Fuller


     In a huge meeting hall around a vast oval table, the lead-
ers of the world were gathered. There were mighty regents of
great nations, businessmen of wealth and power, military lead-
ers who could arrange the deaths of fifty thousand human beings
with as much style and expedition in the flesh as on the sand
tables of their war colleges. Economists whose theories put in
practice had been the structure of the real world since the
Industrial Revolution. Sociologists who had studied man's farms
and cities and so knew man. Historians who saw the future of
the race in history they knew. Philosophers who knew the real
history of the race but wouldn't tell. Priests who knew the
Church and so, to be sure, knew God. A number of poets, newspa-
```

permen, others. There were even a few educational administrators who knew what color to paint walls of a classroom to make it restfully conducive to the learning experience.

Their knowledge, surely, must have gone into the making of this room: the walls were a soft pastel, unmarked by fixtures, undisturbed by paintings; the table was of a plastic that looked and felt like wood; the thousand graceful chairs were wood coated with plastic that looked and felt like leather. The lighting fell evenly from the ceiling, so clear and soft that it surely must have been the way the sun would shine were it but able to.

The men -- now all seated at their places -- wore on their faces the uniform of a shining hope, as well they might, for these men were gathered in this room to bring a final, lasting peace to earth. From the best of the past, they would forge a perfect future, in which the business of the planet might proceed uninhibited by danger.

The conference began. Men spoke, were heard and heeded, ideas exchanged. Leaders advanced the goals of their nations: changed, compromised, accepted. The social scientists stood by as midwife to the world in labor, ready to deliver the newborn State. The philosophers balanced their system, the historians postulated new dialectics. The priests promised the aid of God.

It was awe-inspiring, incredible, more than a meeting of giants. Man was at last taking the measure of his possibilities. And then, in the middle of it all, the great doors at the north end of the room swung open. There was a pause, and one leader looked around expectantly, but no one seemed to be there. Then he, and several of the men nearest, and eventually every man in the room, saw the animals. The animals were small furry things about eight inches tall and rather round. Only their beady little eyes could be found in their furry faces, but they had a friendly, disinterested air. There were about thirty of the little animals. They came in single file, very purposefully and with some deliberated speed, into the room up the legs of the great table, down its center, off onto the floor again, and out the south door, which closed after them.

Miss Fuller,

   The tale has charm, but the promptness of its appearance forces me to wonder whether it wasn't squeezed out to meet some deadline you fancied my note to you imposed. Please relax a little. This one about the absurdity of human ambitions is a little too close to that moralizing vignette about the folly of same you submitted with your application to join this class: the allegory about the dinosaurs in the foothills of the ice age. Here, as there, you fall into certain cutenesses — "and so, to be sure, knew God," "beady little eyes" — that leave the reader unclear as to whether you're writing a children's story, and writing down to the children, or an allegory for big folk that leaves too much for them to think about with too little chance of profit at the end of their reasoning.

Beyond that, I have to confess I can't muster much empathy for anthropomorphism as a device or the short-short-story as a vehicle. Please stop writing about bunnies or whatever they are.

Jill,

No, I don't give letter grades for works of fiction.

THE GLASS OF FASHION
by
Jill Fuller

The senior class was having its picture taken. It filed onto the football field and stood patiently before the bleachers, waiting to be told what to do. The teachers milled round its edge in benign confusion, watching the photographer set up his equipment. After a time, one teacher said, "All those whose names begin with A to M file into the top rows of the bleachers. Hurry up now, so we can get this done as quickly as possible." A large number of students moved forward obediently and began to scramble onto the stand; the rest stood quietly and waited to be told what to do.

Someone nodded to the teacher in charge, and he said, "All those with names beginning with N to Z fill in the rest of the bleachers now. Let's keep in line there, shall we?" The rest of the class surged forward. In five or ten minutes more, they were all seated.

A few minutes after that, the senior class spoke in perfect unison, not loudly, but in a distinct conversational tone. No one within earshot could believe the words had been spoken. They did not seem to be directed toward anyone in particular.

The teachers could not believe their ears. Each one thought guiltily that he was the victim of some sick hallucination. Each smiled wanly at the senior class on the bleachers. As if so calm a class could . . . as if anybody could . . . there were girls in the class, at that! "This will only be another minute," said the photographer uncertainly, "if you'll just bear with me."

The senior class waited several moments politely, as though

to assure the speaker their remark was not addressed to him. Then, with one clear voice, they said it again. The sound of those several hundred throats made a terrific quiet noise.

The teachers looked at each other. They had all heard it, and there was none who could not read that on his fellows' faces. To his eternal credit, the teacher in charge reacted to the incident in the entire class the way he would have reacted to it in a single student. He stood before them and roared, "This entire class is suspended for three days, and a mention of this unforgivable incident will be entered in each of your records. You will be silent for the rest of the period. Now let's get this done as quickly as possible . . . before the bell . . . ." He ended gamely. Fortunately, he was thinking of nothing more than how "shocked" he was. The class waited a long time, then opened its mouth and spoke again, in a voice quite devoid of challenge or even of much life.

The cameraman said loudly, "Say cheese."

"Fuck you," said the senior class.

"STOP IT!" howled the teachers.

"Wait a moment," said the head teacher. He addressed the bleachers in a nervous tone. "All right, file down. Back to your classrooms, all of you. Let's go. Now."

"They aren't moving," said another teacher, "and I . . . don't think they're going to."

Three hours later, the senior class still had not moved.

A large crowd gathered. The principal called the fire department, and the firemen came down with their high-pressure hoses. "If you don't come down out of those bleachers by the time I count three, I'm going to have to turn those hoses on you. I'd better see a rush before I stop counting. One."

The hoses were turned on and the thick white streams of water cut into the stands. In a minute the class had been forced from the stands onto the ground in a huge thrashing pile. The hoses were not turned off for three minutes. When they were, the receding water revealed the senior class crushed against the visiting team dugout wall. "All right," said a teacher calmly, "we'll settle this matter later. Get up and get back to your classrooms."

By nightfall, a battery of searchlights described the area where the class lay huddled in the middle of the field. One hundred uniformed policemen walked onto the field at nine o'clock with nightsticks. "Are you going to do as you're told?" they asked. The policemen walked among the students and clubbed them. Since organization was difficult, one of the students got clubbed over six hundred times. However, he lived and is now the father of five. When all the students had been clubbed into unconsciousness, the policemen roared, "What do you say now?" No voice answered them.

With no little trouble, the senior class was loaded onto trucks and driven away. An armed guard rode on each truck.

Jill,

This is rather more like it. In limning the presence, even predominance, of the absurd in institutionalized ambition, you are getting closer to finding out what you want to write about, and getting rid of those furries and fuzzies and overblown serpents in the process. You are also showing willingness to develop a story more fully, though you are still — for my taste — only a little out of the league of the shaggy-dog syndrome. If a novel is an invasion and a short story a raid, then your stuff is little more than a sniper's bullet. And it's still low and left. But I won't harp. You're coming along.

Again, you stay in the camp of the cute. "There were girls in the class, at that!" At what? So what? Tighten up. And, "however, he lived . . ." turns a death march into a diatribe. Learn by going where you have to go.

Next time out. I'd like to see you do a little more with character.

Keep up the good work.

MK303PUM

NAPLES, ITALY, MAY 18 (UPI) — A NAPLES MEDIUM AND A DOCTOR FRIEND TODAY APPEALED THEIR CONVICTIONS FOR RAPING A SIXTEEN-YEAR-OLD GIRL WHO SAID SHE THOUGHT "THE SPIRIT OF THE ARCHANGEL GABRIEL" WANTED TO HAVE A CHILD BY HER.

LUIGI MAURO, 59, A CABINET-MAKER AND PART-TIME SPIRITUAL-IST, AND DR. FULLER DI PASQUALE WERE APPEALING THEIR CONVICTION ABSENTIA. THEIR LAWYERS SAID MAURO, SENTENCED TO TEN YEARS IN PRISON LAST YEAR, AND DI PASQUALE, SENTENCED TO NINE YEARS, WOULD COME OUT OF HIDING BEFORE THE APPEALS TRIAL REACHES A VERDICT.

THE CASE STEMS FROM A SERIES OF SEANCES MAURO CONDUCTED FOR 11 MONTHS IN 1961 AT WHICH DI PASQUALE AND LUANA PONTICELLO, THEN A TEENAGER, WERE PRESENT.

MISS PONTICELLO TESTIFIED IN THE EARLIER TRIAL THAT MAURO AND DI PASQUALE CONVINCED HER IN THE COURSE OF THE SEANCES THAT THE "SPIRIT OF THE ARCHANGEL GABRIEL" HAD CHOSEN HER TO BEAR HIM A CHILD AND SHE FINALLY SUBMITTED TO INTERCOURSE IN ONE SESSION.

PROSECUTORS SAID MAURO WAS THE FATHER OF THE BABY BOY MISS PONTICELLO EVENTUALLY BORE.

THE APPEALS JUDGES HEARD MISS PONTICELLO'S TESTIMONY TODAY
BEHIND CLOSED DOORS. THE TRIAL WAS THEN RECESSED UNTIL JUNE 1.
MK303PUM

Miss Fuller,
   Before I waste any time on this, are you really trying to pass it off as a story?

Jill,
   Ah, I see. An *objet trouvé*. Well, I have my suspicions of that little gambit in art and in poetry, two places where it seems to have found a happy home as a refuge for the talent-free, the temporarily blocked, or simply those fortunate in the matter of tripping over something. But as a new direction for prose fiction, I have my doubts. Maybe Burroughs has done something lasting with his scissors, but I'm not persuaded you're ready to emulate him yet with rip-and-read.
   However: I'll play along for the hell of it, but you must help. This is one case where I have no qualms about asking a forbidden question: what's your story "about"?

Jill,
   Oh, hell, never mind.

Jill,
   Was that a story or a letter? It's sometimes hard to tell with you — ah — experimental writers. No, I hadn't meant to dismiss your first piece altogether (though why you dig that up at this point I'm not sure). It got you into the class, didn't it? You should be beyond needing pats for your promise, but if it will help you face the next blank sheet, you may go back over that story and extract the following like teeth and place them later like dentures:
   1. dim silver trunk of a petrified tree
   2. bellies up
   3. cyst of style
   4. all the while the cathedral of organs within his endless body struck ancient chords of liquid rumble, while his breath hung above his mouth like a rotting cloud.
   Though how you're going to find a use for 1 and 4 is beyond me.

                              TASTE
                               by
                           Jill Fuller

   Once there was an old man who feared all living things he
could not see that were not him. His dishwashing gloves he kept
in a pan of liquid surgical soap. He laced his windows with
caulking compound to fend off unconditioned air. Outdoors, he

wore a gauze mask like a Japanese on a Tokyo subway. His bathroom fixtures glistened and his waxed floors shone.

His mind was good and dirty, though. He had a taste for pornography. He felt relaxed and comfortable about it because he never disguised it as anything else. He had no taste for the transfigured product that is masked as sociological banter: books of case histories bearing some such banner as FOR SERIOUS STUDENTS OF THE PSYCHO-SEXUAL MENTALITY stamped on the front. Books about buggery for the edification of clergymen and the police.

No, he liked it straight in plain brown wrappers: there was a cyst of style within him that made it as hard for him to approach a drugstore clerk with a newsstand product as it had been for him to buy rubbers over the counter when he was a kid. He liked to come home from a soft day at the office to find a new load of Danish specialties waiting for him on the floor inside the door, bellies up for his privacy. Usually he had himself to hand before he reached the bedroom, his member looking like the dim silver trunk of a petrified tree on the afternoon light.

One day there was a mail strike. It went on and on. The old man was reduced to going through his substantial collection over and over, which pleased him no more than it pleases a brainless virile lad to return to old conquests when there are new there for the asking. Finally he had to go to the drugstore and buy its watery simpering fare because anything seemed better than going on in the expensive, spiritless, wasteful, shameful way he had been. But he felt so awkward about it that he stopped off at a dimestore first and bought a Halloween mask to hide behind while making his purchase.

At home he went through his new acquisitions with distaste. He really disliked the flirtatious aura of the drugstore pornography. He was also irritated by the fact that the best parts of one book sank into Latin, which he was perfectly able to read, but he found it hard to keep up an interest through the whiffs of the clinic the language wet the page with.

A week before the mail strike ended, he took sick. As a dog. He lay on his bed full of parasites who were digging tunnels in his organs. The day the mail strike ended, he lay on his deathbed. All the while the cathedral of organs within his endless body struck ancient chords of liquid rumble, while his breath hung above his mouth like a rotting cloud.

Dear Jill,

Either you're in pursuit of a parable of the force of institutionalized absurdity in a dramatic stress relationship, or you're playing games in a coy effort to disarm a bad story. I suspect the latter, but why should I have to suspect at all? Level with me. That's what I'm here for. I'm a writer playing reader, working as both at the same time. That's the paradox your momma's paying money for you to dwell briefly in the midst of.

As always, the MS leaves me with some problems. I don't see how you can expect to write convincingly about dying old germy jackoff's, and the Shakespearean echoes seem contrived at best, even though your purposes may be far from realistic; fantasy must be firmly rooted to the world if it's not to be mistaken for foolishness. I'm not giving you the old write-what-you-know saw, though there's no better rule to engrave on your tabletop. But if you haven't been on a deathbed, you take chances — at this point — writing of who has.

Longer stories. Stop being so formal. Lean out a little.

PARKER AT HOME
by
Jill Fuller

That spring Parker got a new job and they were able to move to a new house. Home. Parker, Mrs., Jonathan aged nine, Susan aged six, Fluffy the kitty, Rover the doggy, Chipper the goddamn cute blue budgie-bird leaking feathers and gravel all over the floor of his cage.

The job kept Parker away from home every other month, which would have been hard on them except that the loss was recompensed by money and more than rewarded by the fact that Parker, when he was home, seemed to be a new man, almost literally new — fresh-faced and shining, wise, patient, always free to play with the kids or his wife, throw sticks for the dog. Before, full-time, he had been much like other husbands and daddies, an on-again off-again fellow, alternately ready with a kiss or a curse.

But now he was really something. Although he was underfoot all day long during the month he was off the road, they never tired of his company. He would play catch with Jonathan hour after hour, read Susan books of Beatrix Potter with such animation that she used to fall off his knee in a surplus of giggles, uncork wine for a candlelight dinner before an evening of well-schooled loving. Play with the dog. Incredible. There was never a harsh word or unkind anything.

Then one day, owing to some confusion, Parker left home at the end of May to begin his month-long absence and reappeared the very next day, June 1. His mood was of the blackest. In a sullen storm, he prowled the house like a drunk or a madman, seeming not to recognize his wife and children or his pets, ignoring their pleas for explanation. He fed Chipper to Fluffy and Fluffy to Rover. He flogged Jonathan for playing with his tie-tac, held Susie's head underwater while the child was in her bath until her curls were mixed with bubbles, and did things to his wife in bed that made her call her doctor in the morning.

When Parker awoke the next day, he wore a look that said he was himself again. Glanced around at his horrified wife and terrified children. Clapped one hand to his head. "My God," he muttered, "I forgot what house I was living in this month."

Jill,

I'm not trying to tell you how to run your business, but, I ask you to stretch out and you tighten up. I ask you to ban the wildlife, and you give me a story full of pets. Another suggestion: try to make your prose rougher. Clean out the formal rhythms, like "uncork wine for a candlelight dinner," the neat balances — "a drunk or a madman" — in sum, the whole kit of poetic prose, fine writing.

I thought I knew what you were getting after for a while, but I'm not so sure any longer. You could be a good writer, Jill, but you must stop staking everything on deceit.

Jill,

It isn't a question of actually hating and loathing and abhorring poetry and poets. I have a few favorites that would startle you. It is true that student poets make my skin crawl; maybe I expect them to spring from Minerva's brow or at least have their birthpangs elsewhere. And I do try to render rancid poetic language out of the narratives you all traffic in.

As you point out, my own pollution is the tendency toward alliteration. When I'm writing fiction, I weed that out, but I can't take time when the prose is for another purpose.

I'd like to ask you a favor. The next time you have a story ready for me, don't turn it in. Let it cool a few days, then look at it again. It will either have gone bad like milk or stale like bread, or it will be even better than you thought it was. Or it will need a few repairs and another rest and then you can test it again. Following this method, you will pretty reliably end up with either something to junk without regrets or submit without hesitation.

This advice is sound, though I impose is now for selfish reasons: yesterday Sam Cassio, who has kept his counsel for eleven weeks, delivered me a 750,000-word novel.

VEDI NAPOLI E POI MORI
by
Jill Fuller

Once there was a man distinguished by the fear of death.
Clearly we are all as subject to the fear as to the fact, but
rarely is it all-pervasive. If it is, we characteristically
lose our "ability to function," as I believe F. Scott
Fitzgerald, the novelist, put it; though again it may have been
Shakespeare in some such play of Hamlet. That is to say we go
mad. The man of whom I will tell you did not go mad. He did not
cease to function. Indeed, he functioned rather well.

He was a man of some accomplishment. He read a good deal
and was politically well-informed; golfed; drank and smoked
moderately; he well, it is all so unsatisfactory somehow, I do
not see his picture shaping before me in these lines. A healthy
man, healthy. But he was terribly afraid of dying.

I cannot insist too strongly on the . . . private nature of
that fear. It pushed him to neither of the two usual extremes.
He did not, on the one hand, immerse himself in automobile
racing or alligator wrestling, but nor did he, on the other,
remain perpetually in bed.

His naturalness was not an affectation. The man who so
deeply feared death did not permit that fear to intrude upon
the proper conduct of his life. It might be thought, then, that
he had made a thoroughly satisfactory adjustment.

So great a fear, however, must have some way of manifesting
itself. Perhaps a more subtle observer could have noticed a
hint in the cast of an eye, the movement of a hand. But I have
had to content myself with more immediate evidence: his library, for example, filled with hundreds of volumes on the
topic which so fascinated him.

He was a methodical man with a keen analytical mind. He
read thanatopsical literature voraciously in an orderly fashion. There was no approach he did not cover thoroughly over the
years: religious, philosophical, psychological, historical,
medical. Moreover, as time and leisure permitted, he sought
instruction in languages and technical matters, opening his
inquiries at continually increasing depth so that where he was
originally obliged to take Will Durant's word as to what Plato
might have to say on death, he was later to hear from Jowett or
Cornford, and finally, however haltingly, from Plato himself.
Where he had once been obliged to satisfy himself with simpli-

fied guides, massive medical tomes of the most detailed nature were at last open to him.

My other evidence -- my best, perhaps -- comes to me from the lips of the man himself. As he confessed it -- no, expressed would be the better word -- his fear took a special and terrible form. He feared that in death he would cease to exist in a very curious way, that he would have consciousness of his non-existence.

Of course, there are a host of classic arguments which bear on this not uncommon view, serving to either comfort or dismiss it. In any case, to so qualify it as to render it either painless or worthless. That none of them had relevance for him, existential impact was his phrase, should demonstrate sufficiently how inexactly the verbal formulation shows what he felt. Nor have I the power to depict the terror that would seize him when he spoke of it, the only time his fear ever became visible.

In any case, such moments were of little consequences, if much account. He conducted his life, as I have said, in social fullness, in family happiness, in contemplation and study that grew ever broader, deeper, and more profound. It might be thought that his obsession would be strictly limiting; but it gradually drew in so vast a spread of relevant concerns that his life and his library -- with the literature of death at its core -- became a paragon. His nature, always agreeable, became a revelation. I liked to sit with him, late in the evenings, after his family were in bed, and listen to him talk.

Jill,

Rather nice. What *did* Plato say? Philosophy is the study of death. Yes, it's not bad. Sits on the mind like a skull in a medieval study. It's becoming increasingly clear that you're a poet, not a writer, particularly when you've airbrushed the fat away, as here. There's something in your work that makes me begin to feel forgiving toward your faults.

If you want to submit this one to *Vendetta*, I'll gladly push it for you. The last issue was dominated by English majors, and it's time the writing shop made a decent showing.

Not sure about all the name-dropping.

Jill,

Let's see something else. Nothing in my IN box now but Southern Gothic and stream of unconsciousness.

THE INTERPRETATION OF DREAMS
by
Jill Fuller

One day Parker went into town and bought a Sony tape recorder, a very large and expensive model that could be fitted
with arms to hold ten-inch reels. He got the arms and the reels
and eight hours' worth of mylar tape and set the whole thing up
in his bedroom with an omnidirectional microphone on the night
table beside his bed.

He got into bed and read for a while, then started the
recorder and switched off the light and settled down to sleep.
Lulled by the whirr of the reels, charmed by the idea that the
machine was recording the noise it was making, he at last
drifted off.

By morning, the tape had run through. Parker awoke to the
sound of it slapping through the recording heads. He went into
the kitchen and infused a quart of tea, took it back to his
room and settled into bed again to listen to the tape.

The hours went by. For the first hour there was nothing
distinguishable save for fifteen or twenty seconds that might
have been snoring. Then, well, into the second hour, there was
snoring, as rhythmic and pompous as an actor's. It gave way to
an occasional groan. Then some thrashing noises. Then a horrible sound that he realized suddenly was the grinding of his
teeth. Then more patches of snores and quiet. Finally the words
came, and Parker grew nervously alert. They were muttered and
distressed. He heard one -- "No" -- distinctly, but had to stop
the tape and play back again and again to catch others. He
jotted them down on a legal tablet.

Get out.

Infection.

Where is the (garbled).

Furniture.

Release (or relief).

Help me.

That one was repeated, rose to a shout. There was no need
to use the playback any longer.

Help me.

HELP ME.

HELP ME.

Jill,

I can't tell you how much better I like this story than any of your others. It's spare instead of merely short, simply written, and highly charged. In a small space, the reader senses the complexity of this man.

The story is like a gloss on an epigram of Nietzsche I'm very fond of: "Have you ever looked at your friend's face when he was sleeping? Weren't you terrified?" Indeed I was. Well done.

(If I may make a small suggestion, there is an international code for distress, from the French *m'aidez*, which might make an even better title. Though yours works fine for me.)

Jill,

We are close to the end of the semester. I don't think you should permit yourself any more of these long absences.

Steve,

This a real horror. As chairman of the department, you should be advised of something I missed until I reread all of her stories after what happened yesterday. I thought each one was "about" schizophrenia but I realize now they were merely by a schizophrenic. How's that for a trick ending? I feel sick, but I'm a writer, not a doctor. (I suppose if I were a doctor I wouldn't drop Freudian categories that are probably discredited by now.)

I know you're a personal friend of her parents, but if you go see them, I don't think you should mention this. And I think maybe, at the very least, they ought to get their money back.

        M'aidez.
        M'aidez.
        M'aidez.

1974

Critical thinking points: After you've read

1) In what ways do Jill's stories seem to respond to the professor's criticism? Why do you think she responds the way she does?

2) Does the professor misread Jill's stories? What details in the story support your theory?

3) What do you think is the professor's attitude toward his students? What evidence in the story supports your opinion of the professor? Is it surprising that he misses Jill's cry for help? Why or why not?

4) What do you think of the professor's letter to the chair of his department? Does he feel any remorse over his student's death? What in his letter supports your opinion?

Some possibilities for writing

1) *You can often tell as much about people by the way they write as what they write about. Write an essay that compares and contrasts Jill and the professor based on their respective writings.*
2) *Imagine near the end of the story, Jill and her professor meet face-to-face. Write that scene.*
3) *A "suicide" often seems an easy way out of a story. Write an alternative ending.*
4) *Rewrite the professor's instructions for this class as if he were a completely different personality type.*
5) *Imagine that the story "Mayday" was turned in to the professor. Write his critique of the story.*

No Immediate Danger

Mary McLaughlin Slëchta

"

At the center of attention, I reposed like Play-Doh, forming and unforming itself at the pleasure and whim of the committee.

"

Critical thinking points: As you read

1) There is a stark contrast between the narrator's neighborhood and the college where she interviews. What are some details in the story that show this?

2) The narrator is always running behind schedule and comments about her dilemma of always being late. What does this say about her lifestyle and her personality?

3) The narrator is an outsider in many scenes in this story. What are some of them? What leads to her feeling this way in each of the scenes?

4) What pressure to succeed does the narrator feel? What creates that pressure?

On my fourth run through the kitchen, I remembered I'd made up my face but forgotten mascara, so I went to do that and the bacon burned. Fifty cents worth of smoking burnt pork and Hank screamed like it cost a week's paycheck. His week's paycheck. His empty stomach. "Don't even bother frying eggs if there's no bacon!"

"And did you finish feeding the baby?" he shouted as he slammed open windows. "I said, has the baby had her breakfast?"

When I rushed back to the kitchen, the baby was banging a spoon into a pool of cereal on the tray of the high chair. Her brown face and hair, like the nearest wall, were speckled with white flakes of oatmeal. She'd somehow broken the suction cup hold on her bowl and toppled it onto the floor. I quickly scraped the bacon pan into the trash and covered the steaming mess with newspaper. With a few quick sweeps of damp paper towels, I cleaned everything else: baby, spoon, chair, wall, and floor. Then I popped open a jar of pears and tried to coax the spoon from her hand. On top

Mary McLaughlin Slëchta (b. 1956) is a fiction writer and poet whose work has appeared in many journals and anthologies, including *New to North America* (1997) and *Identity Lessons: Learning American Style* (November 1998). She lives in Syracuse, New York with her husband and two sons.

of the rude cleaning she'd received, this indignity was too much. She opened her mouth wide and howled.

"The smoke could have killed her!" Hank screeched from the outer limits of the apartment, still slamming open windows and doors. "Or were you planning a grease fire?"

I searched the utensil drawer and drain and then faced the sink where two days of breakfast, lunch, and dinner had crusted into a tottering mountain. There wasn't a spoon, clean or dirty, in sight and no dish detergent anyways. I'd known this. I'd known, been to the store more than once, and forgotten each time. There remained no choice but to wrestle the spoon from the baby's hand. She wailed even louder.

"See! See!" Hank shouted from the threshold. "You take care of your face and the baby goes hungry. Not to mention I gotta get up early to no breakfast and a stinking house that looks like a pigsty. What happens when you get a job?"

I spooned the runny pear into the baby's screaming mouth and caught it as it ran straight down her chin. Eat, eat, eat, stupid baby, I thought, and immediately promised to be kinder. It wasn't baby's fault. It wasn't Hank's either, though I'd like to think so. It's just that there's always too much to do. Like that morning, for instance. I had a 10:00 interview at a state college twenty miles out of Syracuse, and it was going to be tight.

Since morning, I'd given the apartment, baby included, what my mother would call "a lick and a promise." Only a Friday night never passes without her keeping those promises, mopping the kitchen floor at midnight if it comes to that. In the middle of the night, my promises hang before me like an unbalanced ledger. Specks of cereal on the wall would remain as reminders of one more unfinished job. A week later, I'd find traces of cereal matted in the coarse tangles of my daughter's hair. If I got to the dishes at all today, I'd have to use laundry detergent and rinse extra long.

Hank thrust the checkbook in my face. "You forgot to write in another check," he said with disgust.

"I wrote it down somewhere," I lied. "I'll put it in later."

"Later, later," he said. "Always later with you."

I'd coaxed the baby to take half of the pears before panic pushed against the bottom of my stomach. It felt dangerously late and traffic might be heavy. I wasn't exactly sure where I was going, where I'd park, and how far I'd have to walk or run.

"What's for her lunch, I'd like to know," Hank asked, breaking into my thoughts. I handed him the spoon.

To keep the peace, I bit my tongue at his nasty face twisted into a red knot and quietly relished small instruments of revenge: the baby bawling as I rummaged for keys; the phone ringing on my way out the door; Hank hollering "Mom!"

"Milk's in the freezer," I shouted over my shoulder. "Sweet potato, something else."

"You're gonna be late!" he screamed back accusingly, possibly shattering his mother's eardrum.

In my haste, I nearly tripped over the boy from upstairs curled pitifully on the front porch like a lost puppy. When I asked about school, he sank deeper inside his jacket and stared longingly at another boy in the street toting a boom box on his shoulder. The heavy bass and drive of the rapper clamped my chest like two tight fists pulling forward. But when the boy nodded towards us, I managed to smile and raise my arm hello. These boys needed to be in school or at least at home. I backed out the driveway and turned in a direction opposite from the teen hangout corner. I meant to avoid any more eyes of those whose mothers and grandmothers I knew. Knowing I was a teacher, they expected more of me, some way of helping that they couldn't articulate and which I didn't want to bear.

With the late registration sticker on the car, I was careful not to speed within the city limits. Once on the highway, I made up time by keeping the needle quivering above sixty-five.

Now, plan for the interview, I ordered myself. In the same instant, I snapped on the radio for the time without realizing Hank had left the tape in play. The song that blasted through the speakers was one of our favorites back in college. A real funky dance beat like you don't hear anymore. My shoulders and head remembered how to swing to the beat. Hank and I were starting over again on the dance floor of the Student Union. No marriage, no baby — so little money that money wasn't a concern.

Eight years earlier, I'd waited in the car with the volume high like this, swinging my shoulders, fixing my hair, touching up my lipstick. Things I hadn't done with such ardor ever before in life — or since. Hank was my first boyfriend, and at twenty years old I was primping like a high school girl. Beyond the rearview mirror I watched Hank striding back from the supermarket, a bag of wine coolers under one arm. I could still count the number of times we'd kissed, and I was anticipating another within the next minute when I happened to turn my head towards the car beside ours. A bear of man with mean little eyes raised his white fist with the thumb down.

"Let's get out of here," I told Hank when he dropped into the driver's seat and reached for that kiss.

I never got used to people staring at us like we'd offended them personally. Neither did Hank, I think. Having a child didn't legitimize our relationship either. People actually asked if it really was my baby. Eventually we found set patterns to follow that made isolation not only bearable but also indiscernible to the larger world. We found a word for our life together: "private." Dancing stopped. Holding his white hand against my brown one. We became simply ourselves, growing older and encased in a glass bubble with a baby. Safe enough, but never knowing when someone might turn a microscope on our very existence: *So how did you two meet? What did your parents think?* On the highway, the morning of the interview, I turned the music up like the boy in the street had done and sang louder.

I must have lost all sense of time and place because I was suddenly seeing signs for the exit in ten miles. Switching to the radio, I discovered I had ten minutes to be only five minutes late for a job interview — provided I was lucky with parking. Here it was again. Always when it counts the most, I'm running late. Drive and sheer luck usually cut the lateness to around five minutes. My twenty-four-hour-and-five-minute day. I imagine as time passes and old age and mental weariness take their toll, the time will increase proportionally. Ten minutes, twenty, thirty, forty — until I don't show up anywhere at all.

At this point in route, I passed a string of cars behind a semi when a girl in a bright red Trans Am raced behind me flashing her brights. As I slipped back into the right to the horn of the semi, she zoomed past like somebody leaving the scene of a crime. Almost immediately, I zigzagged around a blue sedan with a businessman yapping into a cell phone. For just an instant, my mouth wide open in song, our eyes met, and he gave me a disagreeable sneer. I set aside any possible meaning behind his features, snapped off the radio, and began to formulate my interview speech on setting up peer-group activities, very much in vogue in those days for Freshman Comp. Suddenly I noticed blue lights flashing in the rearview mirror. In the tension of the moment, my breasts stung with milk.

I instantly eased my pressure on the gas and moved back to the right lane, but there seemed to be no question. In a moment I would be sitting by the side of the road waiting for someone in a tall hat to finish writing a ticket. After a while, he would strut over and, barely looking at me, ask how fast I thought I was going. I would lie, of course. But then there would be other unpleasantries: the expired registration, previous points on my license. I prayed for divine intervention, promising that here- after I would accept my destiny to arrive everywhere late and to do so without the pain of struggle. I must admit, I also began to see the fortuity of actually being stopped. Surely my interview could empathize with an all too human predicament.

Instead, nothing happened — to me, at least. In the mirror, I watched the blue sedan with the disagreeable businessman pull over, and my heart sank along with my adrenaline level. Someone else would be late somewhere for a legitimate reason. Sometime later this morning, a portly white man in a dark suit would stride into a meeting delayed for his convenience. Chances were he was right now phoning ahead while he waited for the opportunity to dispute the ticket. Afterwards he would hitch his pants up around his crotch and complain about the inequities of law enforcement. Not that anyone needed to know why he was late, but because it made a good story: how some black bitch passed him going seventy-five in a friggin heap of junk and he'd gotten screwed.

When I turned up thirteen minutes late to the English department office, the secretary glanced at the wall clock and let me pretend not to squirm while she fin- ished a phone conversation, distinctly personal in tone. Her upturned nose seemed to turn up a little higher at the sight of my face, shiny with sweat from running, and encircled by a frizzy halo of hair.

"They've been waiting for you," she whispered ominously as she finally ush- ered me into a conference.

"They?" I wondered with panic. Before I could bolt, eight very annoyed white faces stared up at me from a long narrow table. I apologized immediately, and some of the greying heads nodded politely. White people are never late, I thought, acknowledging their lukewarm greeting with a redemptive air of humility. I calculated they'd been early and would meanly count that fact against me. I'd have to work harder to convince them of my abilities as a teacher.

I made a conscious effort not to let this inauspicious beginning injure my demeanor. I'd hung along the periphery of academic circles long enough to recognize that many who are prompt to a fault work far below 100-percent capability. Perhaps it's the prospect of free coffee and Danish that pulls them from the stagnant compartments of the university. Several of my interviewers were even now using the scattered copies of my resume as makeshift coasters and plates. What other small perqs might they enjoy as members of an ad hoc hiring committee for adjuncts? Did they have a favorite pub in this provincial New York town where the locals, terrified of any threat to employment, pretended to be a soundless backdrop to their posturing eccentricities?

They went around the table with introductions and then around again with questions: B.A., M.A., thesis work, work experience, philosophy, method, approach. . . . The majority of questions I'd accurately predicted and actually planned for, although when and how I couldn't say. Maybe the night the baby kept me on the edge between sleep and wake with a racking, croupy cough. At any rate, now that I'd arrived and the issue of lateness had been handled with some finesse and the questions found to be manageable, I let my stiff back appreciate the cushions and began to critique the surroundings.

I found the formality of the setting particularly galling. Eight interrogators, coffee, Danish, and a pitcher of water for a low-paying, part-time, temporary position seemed superfluous, to say the least. The low pay compounded by a restrictive medical plan for the one-semester post — assuming I got it, which I figured I had a pretty good shot at doing since scuttlebug had it the school was under legal pressure to hire more minorities and women — didn't warrant such extravagance. Was each candidate scrutinized so closely, I wondered, or did I appear to be a radical upstart in her last good jacket? One of that vast encroaching horde of minorities predicted to outnumber whites in the twenty-first century? There had been plenty of flags in my resume to sound off alarms.

As four or five of the interrogators forgot me and pursued a gentlemanly disagreement over the work of a well-known professor I'd used as a reference, I silently made prophesy. There would be no office space where I could meet my students during the required office hours. Two chairs in a corridor would have to do. The faculty would quickly come to know my name. Many of those not in attendance already did. At no point, however, would I have occasion to learn most of theirs. Some would be friendly at first, to a fault; some later; others never. Yet each would maintain a courteous air of detachment, much as they kept towards certain segments of their "diverse student body." I would be the subject of a story around the dinner table, part of an anecdote told at the next meeting of the hiring committee and the reason, if things did not go well with my "tenure," to resist hiring another minority. ("It never seems to work out!") I might perhaps be invited by marginal faculty members — the strident feminist at my right or the downstate transplant at my left whose every vowel made the others wince — to join them at that favorite pub. But having once stopped for lunch in a town like this one and been heckled by the locals back to my car, I had no intention of pushing my luck. I would truthfully say that my little girl needed me home. In fact, judging from one professor's surreptitious glances at my nursing mother's chest, I might enter the canon as a dusky paramour or the foil in a book about white angst. In my hoop earrings and fringed scarf, I could symbolize sensuous free expression in contrast to the cold analytical world of dust and doom around the table. At the center of attention, I reposed like Play-Doh, forming and unforming itself at the pleasure and whim of the committee.

The chairwoman at the head of the table called her chickens back to the yard. I hadn't understood this seat of control until she rapped firmly for attention and cleared her throat. She'd been in hiding among the others, and perhaps watching me watch them. The plain, matronly mask of indifference fell away and a fierce military expression took its place. The true guardian of the word, she meant to question me rigorously now, herself, and the others must be quiet and listen to a real expert. Each breath rattled in my gut before it came out my chest and throat and mouth a harmonic line of Standard English. Each word hung in the air as long as it took my interrogator to examine it top to bottom, inside to out. Sentence diagrams danced in the air above my head. You know this language, I reminded myself at intervals. But if you do too perfect a job, they'll doubt that you're a native speaker.

It was during my responses to the chairwoman, in fact, that I first became distracted by a barely perceptible but definitely rank odor. It was totally inconsistent with the paleness of the people, the walls, and the few impressionist paintings. I waited for the predictable allergy sufferer, frontline sufferer of sick building syndrome, to insist upon opening a window.

"We had a black adjunct a few years ago," the chairwoman told me later in her sunny office. "Things didn't work out," she added with a sad smile. "Are you sure you don't remember Professor W— at Amherst?"

Without a copy of my resume in hand, I was having great difficulty recalling names and places. I'd been accepted by a mysterious vote of approval around the table and now had secured the measly comp sections that would keep food on the table, Hank off my back, and my car on the road; yet, I was unable to satisfy the chairwoman's desire for small talk. My efforts to steer the conversation towards a more general topic proved futile. Already she was well into another story about the "very articulate Professor W—," whom I assumed to be black.

Despite the tediousness of her chatter, or because of it, relief began to flood my entire body. A feeling of tenderness fluttered through my breasts and sent milk gushing into the pads of my bra. Over the course of a morning, this place had become comfortable. Here were a job and people, at least on the surface, who asked manageable questions and told anecdotes as they pleased. For whatever reason or reasons, they'd mutually decided to allow me some small entry into their private club. The fierce Germanic features of the chairwoman had taken on a cast of gentle Irish, and I forgave her her cultural insensitivity. The pale, well-manicured hand that reached across the desk and set a silver figurine swinging in perpetual motion would neither strike me nor point me towards the door. I was in no immediate danger.

When she stepped out a moment to check my paperwork with the secretary, I quickly straightened a trouser sock that had twisted like a child's in my shoe and gulped a cup of tepid coffee. As I grew sleepy watching the figurine swing back and forth between its narrow bars, only one nagging factor was left to concern me. The odd odor I'd detected in the meeting room was even more apparent in the office. It was a rancid smell much like city children carry on them when they come indoors after heavy play. Clinging to their clothes and hair like nubby lint, it's an unwholesome mixture of exhaust fumes, sweat, fear, and greasy food. I wondered how such an odor had penetrated these walls and why the school hadn't removed it.

I found my answer waiting at home. A hungry daughter nestled at my breasts. I burrowed my nose into it. Burnt bacon.

1997

Critical thinking points: After you've read

1) Why do you think the narrator gets the job? Did you expect her to? Why or why not?

2) Why does she believe she gets the job? Do you agree with her? Why or why not?

3) After she finds out she has the job, the narrator says, "I was in no immediate danger." What impending or future danger is implied by her statement?

4) The narrator says to herself during the interview, "You know this language. . . . But if you do too perfect a job, they'll doubt that you're a native speaker." What might she mean?

5) The narrator carries the smell of burnt bacon with her to the interview. What details from the story portray how she "carries" other pieces of her neighborhood and/or past with her to the interview? What parts of her past does she leave behind in order to "properly" interview for the position?

6) Hank appears to be a verbally abusive, condescending husband. Speculate what led to this in the narrator's relationship with him. Why do you think she stays with Hank?

Some possibilities for writing

1) Consciously or not, we all carry with us characteristics we have acquired from families, friends, neighborhoods, towns, or even larger geographic regions. Describe a time when your past or the place from which you came "followed" you to a new place. First recall a positive experience, then a negative one.

2) *Write the scene in which the narrator tells Hank about her new position. What does she say? How does he react? What changes must be made in their life to deal with the new job?*

3) *Interview a faculty member of color at your school about how, if at all, he or she feels race and/or ethnicity has an impact on the position as a teacher.*

4) *Contact your campus Affirmative Action office to find out the number of faculty and staff of color at your university. How does your university compare to other campuses in your state? How does it compare nationally? Why do you think this is so?*

Open Admission

Shirley Lauro

————————————— 66 —————————————

I'll 'ax' you how come I have been in this here college three months on this here Open Admissions and I don't know nothin more than when I came in here?

————————————— 99 —————————————

Critical thinking points: As you read

1) What kind of person is the teacher? The student? Choose some adjectives that would describe each of them. What details in the play support your opinions?

2) Dialogue often depends as much on what goes unsaid as what is said. Pay attention throughout the play to what the characters don't really say but seem to be talking about. Why do you think that is so?

3) Pay attention to the words the teacher uses as examples of the student's "substandard urban patterns." Do you think that these words are chosen by the teacher (or the author) completely by accident?

The Characters

Professor Alice Miller: Professor of Speech Communications. Started out to be a Shakespearean scholar. Has been teaching Speech at a city college in New York for twelve years. She is overloaded with work and exhausted. Late thirties. Wears skirt, blouse, sweater, coat, gloves. Carries briefcases.

Calvin Jefferson: Eighteen, a Freshman in Open Admissions Program at the college. Black, powerfully built, handsome, big. At first glance a streetperson, but belied by his intensity. Wears jacket, jeans, cap, sneakers. Has been at the college three months, hoping it will work out.

The Place

A cubicle speech office at a city college in New York.

The Time

The present. Late fall. 6 o'clock in the evening.

Shirley Lauro (b. 1933) is a former professor of speech. This play was selected for the *New York Times* "Ten Best Plays [of the Year]" list and was chosen as cowinner of the Fourth Annual Off-Off-Broadway Original Short Play Festival.

The play begins on a very high level of tension and intensity and builds from there. The level of intensity is set by CALVIN who enters the play with a desperate urgency, as though he had arrived at the emergency room of a hospital, needing immediate help for a serious problem. He also enters in a state of rage and frustration but is containing these feelings at first. The high level of tension is set by both ALICE and CALVIN and occurs from the moment CALVIN enters. ALICE wants to leave. She does not want the scene to take place. The audience's experience from the start should be as if they had suddenly tuned in on the critical round of a boxing match.

CALVIN'S speech is "Street Speech" jargon. Run-on sentences and misspellings in the text are for the purpose of helping the actor with the pronunciations and rhythms of the language.

The speech office of Professor Alice Miller in a city college in New York. A small cubicle with partitions going three-quarters of the way up. Windowless, airless, with a cold antiseptic quality and a strong sense of impersonalness and transience. The cubicle has the contradictory feelings of claustrophobia and alienation at the same time. It is a space used by many teachers during every day of the week.

On the glass-windowed door it says:

SPEECH COMMUNICATIONS DEPT.
Prof. Alice Miller, B.A., M.A., Ph.D.

There are other names beneath that.

In the cubicle there is a desk with nothing on it except a phone, a chair with a rain coat on it, a swivel chair and a portable blackboard on which has been tacked a diagram of the "Speech Mechanism." Room is bare except for these things.

At Rise: *Cubicle is in darkness. Muted light filters through glass window on door from hallway. Eerie feeling. A shadow appears outside door. Someone enters, snapping on light.*

It is Alice. She carries a loose stack of essays, a booksack loaded with books and a grade book, one Shakespeare book, two speech books, and a portable cassette recorder. She closes the door, crosses to the desk, puts the keys in her purse, puts purse and booksack down and dials "0."

ALICE: Outside please. *(Waits for this, then dials a number.)* Debbie? Mommy, honey. . . . A "93"? Terrific! Listen, I just got through. I had to keep the class late to finish . . . So, I can't stop home for dinner. I'm going right to the meeting . . . no, I'll be safe . . . don't worry. But you go put the double lock on, ok? And eat the cold meatloaf. *(She puts essays in booksack.)* See you later. Love you too. *(She kisses the receiver.)* Bye.

(She hangs up, puts on coat, picks up purse and booksack, crosses to door and snaps off light. Then opens door to go. CALVIN looms in doorway.)

ALICE: OOHH! You scared me!

CALVIN: Yes ma'am, I can see I scared you okay. I'm sorry.

ALICE: Calvin Washington? 10:30 section?

CALVIN: Calvin Jefferson. 9:30 section.

ALICE: Oh, right. Of course. Well, I was just leaving. Something you wanted?

CALVIN: Yes, Professor Miller. I came to talk to you about my grades. My grade on that Shakespeare project especially.

ALICE: Oh. Yes. Well. What did you get, Calvin? A *B* wasn't it? Something like that?

CALVIN: UMHMM. Thass right. Somethin like that . . .

ALICE: Yes. Well, look, I don't have office hours today at all. It's very dark already. I just stopped to make a call. But if you'd like to make an appointment for a conference, I'm not booked yet next month. Up 'till then, I'm just jammed.

CALVIN: Thass two weeks! I need to talk to you right now!

ALICE: Well what exactly is it about? I mean the grade is self-explanatory — "Good" — *B* work. And I gave you criticism in class the day of the project, didn't I? So what's the problem?

CALVIN: I wanna sit down and talk about *why* I got that grade! And all my grades in point of fact.

ALICE: But I don't have office hours today. It's very late and I have another commitment. Maybe tomor — *(She tries to leave.)*

CALVIN: *(voice rising)* I have to talk to you *now*!

ALICE: Look, tomorrow there's a faculty meeting. I can meet you here afterwards . . . around 12:30. Providing Professor Roth's not scheduled to use the desk.

CALVIN: I got a job tomorrow! Can't you talk to me right now?

ALICE: But what's it about? I don't see the emergen —

CALVIN: *(voice rising loudly)* I jiss *tole* you what it's about! My project and my *grades* is what it's about!

ALICE: *(glancing down the hall, not wanting a commotion overheard)* All right! Just stop shouting out here, will you? *(She snaps on light and crosses to desk.)* Come on in. I'll give you a few minutes now. *(He comes in)* *(She pulls purse and booksack down and sits at desk.)* Okay. Now then. What?

CALVIN: *(Closes door and crosses UC. Silent for a moment looking at her. Then —)* How come all I ever git from you is *B*?

ALICE: *(stunned)* What?

CALVIN: This is the third project I did for you. An all I ever git is *B*.

ALICE: Are you joking? This is what you wanted to talk about? *B* is an excellent grade!

CALVIN: No it's not! *A* is "excellent." *B* is "good."

ALICE: You don't think you deserved an *A* on those projects, do you?

CALVIN: No. But I got to know how to improve myself somehow, so maybe sometime I can try for a *A*. I wouldn't even mind on one of those projects if I got a *C*. Thass average — if you know what I mean? Or a *D*. But all I ever git from you is

B. It don't matter what I do in that Speech Communications Class, seems like. I come in the beginnin a it three months ago? On the Open Admissions? Shoot, I didn't know which end was up. I stood up there and give this speech you assigned on "My Hobby." You remember that?

ALICE: *(Reads note on desk.)* About basketball?

CALVIN: Huh-uh. That was Franklin Perkins give that speech. Sits in the back row?

ALICE: *(Tosses note in wastebasket.)* Oh. Yes. Right. Franklin.

CALVIN: Umhmm. I give some dumb speech about "The Hobby a Makin Wooden Trays."

ALICE: Oh, yes. Right. I remember that.

CALVIN: Except I didn't have no hobby makin wooden trays, man. I made one in high school one time, thass all.

ALICE: *(Leafs through pages of speech books.)* Oh, well, that didn't matter. It was the speech that counted.

CALVIN: Umhmm? Well, that was the sorriest speech anybody ever heard in their lives! I was scared to death and couldn't put one word in front a the other any way I tried. Supposed to be five minutes. Lasted two! And you give me a *B*!

ALICE: *(Rises, crosses to DR table and puts speech books down.)* Well, it was your first time up in class, and you showed a lot of enthusiasm and effort. I remember that speech.

CALVIN: Everybody's firss time up in class, ain't it?

ALICE: Yes. Of course.

CALVIN: *(Crosses DR to ALICE)* That girl sits nex to me, that Jody Horowitz — firss time she was up in class too. She give that speech about "How to Play the Guitar?" And man, she brought in charts and taught us to read chords and played a piece herself an had memorized the whole speech by heart. An you give *her* a *B*.

ALICE: *(Crosses to desk, picks up booksack and puts it on desk.)* Well, Judy's organization and her outline was a little shaky as I recall.

CALVIN: *(Crosses end of desk.)* I didn't even turn no outline in.

ALICE: *(Picks up purse and puts it on desk.)* You didn't?

CALVIN: *(Leans in.)* Huh-uh. Didn't you notice?

ALICE: Of course! It's — just — well, it's been sometime — *(She quickly takes the gradebook from the booksack and looks up his name.)* Let me see, oh, yes. Right. Here, I see. You didn't hand it in . . .

CALVIN: Thass right, I didn'.

ALICE: You better do that before the end of the term.

CALVIN: I can't. Because I don' know which way to do no outline!

ALICE: *(Looks up name in gradebook and marks it with red pencil.)* Oh. Well . . . that's all right. Don't worry about it, okay? *(She puts gradebook away.)* Just work on improving yourself in other ways.

CALVIN: What other ways? Only thing you ever say about anything I ever done in there is how I have got to get rid of my "Substandard Urban Speech!"

ALICE: *(Picks up two files from desk and crosses UCR file cabinet.)* Well, yes, you do! You see, that's your real problem, Calvin! "Substandard Speech." It undercuts your "Positive Communicator's Image!" Remember how I gave a lecture about that? About how all of you here have Substandard Urban Speech because this is a Sub — an *Urban* College. *(She puts on gloves.)* Remember? But that's perfectly okay! It's okay! Just like I used to have Substandard Midwestern Speech when I was a student. Remember my explaining about that? How I used to say "crik" for "creek," and "kin" for "can" and "tin" for "ten"? *(She crosses in back of desk and chuckles at herself.)* Oh, and my breathiness! *(She picks up purse.)* That was just my biggest problem of all: Breathiness. I just about worked myself to death up at Northwestern U. getting it right straight out of my speech. Now, that's what you have to do too, Calvin. *(She picks up booksack and keys.)* Nothing to be ashamed of — but get it right straight out! *(She is ready to leave. She pats CALVIN on the shoulder and crosses UC.)*

CALVIN: *(Pause. Looks at her.)* Thass how come I keep on gittin *B*?

ALICE: "That's."

CALVIN: *(Steps in to ALICE.)* Huh?

ALICE: "That's." Not "Thass." Can't you hear the difference? "That's" one of the words in the Substandard Black Urban Pattern. No final "T's." Undermining your Positive Image . . . labeling you. It's "Street Speech." Harlemese. Don't you re-member? I called everyone's attention to your particular syndrome in class the minute you started talking?

(He looks at her, not speaking.)

ALICE: It's "last," not "lass;" "first," not "firss." That's your friend, that good old "Final T!" Hear *it* when I talk?

CALVIN: Sometimes. When you say i*t*, hi*tt*ing i*t* like tha*t*!

ALICE: Well, you should be going over the exercises on it in the speech book all the time, and recording yourself on your tape recorder. *(She pats booksack.)*

CALVIN: I don't got no tape recorder.

ALICE: Well, borrow one! *(She turns away.)*

CALVIN: *(Crosses in back of ALICE to her right.)* On that Shakespeare scene I jiss did? Thass why I got a *B*? Because of the "Final T's"?

ALICE: *(Backs DS a step.)* Well, you haven't improved your syndrome, have you?

CALVIN: How come you keep on answerin me by axin me something else?

ALICE: And that's the other one.

CALVIN: What "other one"?

ALICE: Other most prevalent deviation. You said: "axing" me something else.

CALVIN: Thass right. How come you keep axin somethin else?

ALICE: "Asking me," Calvin, "asking me!"

CALVIN: I jiss did!

ALICE: No, no. Look. That's classic Substandard Black! Textbook case. *(She puts purse and booksack down and crosses to diagram on blackboard.)* See, the jaw and teeth are in two different positions for the two sounds, and they make two completely different words! (*She writes "ass-king," and "axing" on the blackboard, pronouncing them in an exaggerated way for him to see.*) "ass-king" and "ax-ing." I am "ass-king" you the question. But, the woodcutter is "axing" down the tree. Can't you hear the difference? (*She picks up his speech book from desk.*) Here.

(*CALVIN follows her to desk.*)

ALICE: Go over to page 105. It's called a "Sharp S" problem with a medial position "sk" substitution. See? "skin, screw, scream" — those are "sk" sounds in the Primary Position. "Asking, risking, frisking" — that's medial position. And "flask, task, mask" — that's final position. Now you should be working on those, Calvin. Reading those exercises over and over again. I mean the way you did the Othello scene was just ludicrous: "Good gentlemen, I ax thee —" (*She crosses to the board and points to "ax-ing." She chuckles.*) That meant Othello was chopping the gentlemen down!

CALVIN: How come I had to do the Othello scene anyhow? Didn't git any choice. An Franklin Perkins an Sam Brown an Lester Washington they had to too.

ALICE: What do you mean?

CALVIN: An Claudette Jackson an Doreen Simpson an Melba Jones got themselves assigned to Cleopatra on the Nile?

ALICE: Everyone was assigned!

CALVIN: Uh-huh. But everybody else had a choice, you know what I mean? That Judy Horowitz, she said you told her she could pick outa five, six different characters. And that boy did his yesterday? That Nick Rizoli? Did the Gravedigger? He said he got three, four to choose off of too.

ALICE: (*Crosses to CALVIN.*) Well some of the students were "right" for several characters. And you know, Calvin, how we talked in class about Stanislavsky and the importance of "identifying" and "feeling" the part?

CALVIN: Well how Doreen Simpson "identify" herself some Queen sittin on a barge? How I supposed to "identify" some Othello? I don't!

ALICE: (*Crosses to blackboard, picks up fallen chalk.*) Oh, Calvin, don't be silly.

CALVIN: (*Crosses center.*) Well, I don'! I'm not no kind a jealous husband. I haven't got no wife. I don' even got no girlfriend, hardly! And thass what it's all about ain't it? So what's it I'm suppose to "identify" with anyhow?

ALICE: (*Turns to CALVIN.*) Oh, Calvin, what are you arguing about? You did a good job!

CALVIN: *B* job, right?

ALICE: Yes.

CALVIN: (*Crosses to ALICE.*) Well, what's that *B* standin for? Cause I'll tell you somethin you wanna know the truth: I stood up there didn' hardly know the sense a anythin I read, couldn't hardly even read it at all. Only you didn't notice. Wasn't even listenin, sittin there back a the room jiss thumbin through your book.

(ALICE crosses to desk.)

CALVIN: So you know what I done? Skip one whole paragraph, tess you out — you jiss kep thumbin through your book! An then you give me a *B*! *(He has followed ALICE to desk.)*

ALICE: *(Puts papers in box and throws out old coffee cup.)* Well that just shows how well you did the part!

CALVIN: You wanna give me somethin I could "identify" with, how come you ain' let me do that other dude in the play . . .

ALICE: Iago?

CALVIN: Yeah. What is it they calls him? Othello's . . .

ALICE: Subordinate.

CALVIN: Go right along there with my speech syndrome, wouldn' it now? See, Iago has to work for the Man. I identifies with him! He gits jealous man. Know what I mean? Or that Gravedigger? Shovelin dirt for his day's work! How come you wouldn't let me do him? Thass the question I wanna ax you!

ALICE: *(Turns to CALVIN.)* "Ask me," Calvin, "Ask me!"

CALVIN: *(Steps SR.)* "Ax you?" Okay, man. *(Turns to ALICE.)* Miss Shakespeare, Speech Communications 1! *(Crosses US of ALICE.)* Know what I'll "ax" you right here in this room, this day, at this here desk right now? I'll "ax" you how come I have been in this here college three months on this here Open Admissions and I don't know nothin more than when I came in here? You know what I mean? This supposed to be some big break for me. This here is where all them smart Jewish boys has gone from the Bronx Science and went an become some Big Time Doctors at Bellevue. An some Big Time Judges in the Family Court an like that there. And now it's supposed to be my turn.

(ALICE looks away and CALVIN crosses R of ALICE.)

CALVIN: You know what I mean? *(He crosses UR.)* An my sister Jonelle took me out of foster care where I been in six homes and five school to give me my chance. *(He crosses DR.)* Livin with her an she workin three shifts in some "Ladies Restroom" give me my opportunity. An she say she gonna buss her ass git me this education I don't end up on the streets! *(Crosses on a diagonal to ALICE.)* Cause I have got brains!

(ALICE sits in student chair. CALVIN crosses in back, to her left.)

CALVIN: You understand what I am communicatin to you? My high school has tole me I got brains an can make somethin outta my life if I gets me the chance! And now this here's supposed to be my chance! High school says you folks gonna bring me up to date on my education and git me even. Only nothin is happenin to me in my head except I am getting more and more confused about what I knows and what I don't know! (*He sits in swivel chair.*) So what I wanna "ax" you is: How came you don't sit down with me and teach me which way to git my ideas down instead of givin me a *B?*

(ALICE rises and crosses UR.)

CALVIN: I don't even turn no outline in? Jiss give me a *B.* (*He rises and crosses R of ALICE.*) An Lester a *B*! An Melba a *B*! and Sam a *B*! What's that *B* standin for anyhow? Cause it surely ain't standin for no piece of work!
ALICE: Calvin don't blame me!

(CALVIN crosses DR.)

ALICE: I'm trying! God knows I'm trying! The times are rough for everyone. I'm a Shakespearean scholar, and they have me teaching beginning speech. I was supposed to have twelve graduate students a class, nine classes a week, and they gave me thirty-five freshman a class, twenty classes a week. I hear 157 speeches a week! You know what that's like? And I go home late on the subway scared to death! In Graduate School they told me I'd have a first-rate career. Then I started here and they said: "Hang on! Things will improve!" But they only got worse . . . and worse! Now I've been here for twelve years and I haven't written one word in my field! I haven't read five research books! I'm exhausted . . . and I'm finished! We all have to bend. I'm just hanging on now . . . supporting my little girl . . . earning a living . . . and that's all . . . (*She crosses to desk.*)
CALVIN: (*Faces ALICE.*) What I'm supposed to do, feel sorry for you? Least you can *earn* a livin! Clean office, private phone, name on the door with all them B.A.'s, M.A.'s, Ph.D.'s.
ALICE: You can have those too. (*She crosses DR to CALVIN.*) Look, last year we got ten black students into Ivy League Graduate Programs. And they were not better than you. They were just *perceived (Points to blackboard.)* as better. Now that's the whole key for you . . . to be perceived as better! So you can get good recommendations and do well on interviews. You're good looking and ambitious and you have a fine native intelligence. You can make it, Calvin. All we have to do is work on improving your Positive Communicator's Image . . . by getting rid of that Street Speech. Don't you see?
CALVIN: See what? What you axin *me* to see?
ALICE: *"Asking"* me to see, Calvin. *"Asking"* me to see!
CALVIN: (*Starts out of control at this, enraged, crosses UC and bangs on file cabinet.*) Ooooeee! Ooooeee! You wanna *see*? You wanna *see*? Ooooeee!
ALICE: Calvin stop it! STOP IT!
CALVIN: "Calvin stop it"? "Stop it"? (*Picks up school books from desk.*) There any black professors here?
ALICE: (*Crosses UR.*) No! They got cut . . . the budget's low . . . they got . . .

CALVIN: *(interrupting)* Cut? *They* got CUT? *(Crosses to ALICE and backs her to the DS edge of desk.)* Gonna *cut you,* lady! Gonna cut you, throw you out the fuckin' window, throw the fuckin' books out the fuckin' window, burn it all mother fuckin' down. FUCKIN' DOWN!!!

ALICE: Calvin! Stop it! STOP IT! YOU HEAR ME?

CALVIN: *(Turns away, center stage.)* I CAN'T!! *YOU* HEAR *ME*? I CAN'T! *YOU* HEAR *ME*? I CAN'T! YOU GOTTA GIVE ME MY EDUCATION! GOTTA TEACH ME! GIVE ME SOMETHING NOW! GIVE ME NOW! NOW! NOW! NOW! NOW! NOW!

(Calvin tears up textbook. He starts to pick up torn pages and drops them. He bursts into a wailing, bellowing cry in his anguish and despair, doubled over in pain and grief. It is a while before his sobs subside. Finally, ALICE speaks.)

ALICE: Calvin . . . from the bottom of my heart . . . I want to help you . . .

CALVIN: *(barely able to speak)* By changin' my words? Thass nothin . . . nothin! I got to know them big ideas . . . and which way to git em down . . .

ALICE: But how can I teach you that? You can't write a paragraph, Calvin . . . or a sentence . . . you can't spell past fourth grade . . . the essay you wrote showed that . . .

CALVIN: *(rises)* What essay?

ALICE: *(Crosses to UL files, gets essay and hands it to CALVIN.)* The autobiographical one . . . you did it the first day . . .

CALVIN: You said that was for *your* reference . . . didn't count . . .

ALICE: Here . . .

CALVIN: *(Opens it up. Stunned.)* F? Why didn't you tell me I failed?

ALICE: *(Crosses to desk, puts essay down.)* For what?

CALVIN: *(Still stunned.)* So you could teach me how to write.

ALICE: *(Crosses DL.)* In sixteen weeks?

CALVIN: *(Still can't believe this.)* You my teacher!

ALICE: That would take years! And speech is my job. You need a tutor.

CALVIN: I'm your job! They outa tutors!

ALICE: *(Turns to him.)* I can't do it, Calvin. And that's the real truth. I'm one person, in one job. And I can't. Do you understand? And even if I could, it wouldn't matter. All that matters is the budget . . . and the curriculum . . . and the grades . . . and how you look . . . and how you talk!

CALVIN: *(Pause. Absorbing this.)* Then I'm finished, man.

(There is a long pause. Finally —)

ALICE: *(Gets essay from desk, refiles it and returns to desk.)* No, you're not. If you'll bend and take what I can give you, things will work out for you . . . Trust me . . . Let me help you Calvin . . . Please . . . I can teach you speech . . .

CALVIN: *(Crosses to UC file cabinet. Long pause.)* Okay . . . all right, man . . . *(Crosses to student chair and sits.)*

ALICE: *(Crosses to desk, takes off rain coat and sits in swivel chair.)* Now, then, we'll go through the exercise once then you do it at home . . . please, repeat after me, slowly . . . "asking" . . . "asking" . . . "asking" . . .

CALVIN: *(long pause)* Ax-ing . . .

ALICE: Ass-king . . .

CALVIN: *(During the following, he now turns from ALICE, faces front, and gazes out beyond the audience; on his fourth word, lights begin to fade to black)* Ax-ing . . . Aks-ing . . . ass-king . . . asking . . . asking . . . asking . . .

BLACKOUT

1983

Critical thinking points: After you've read

1) What are some of the reasons the teacher offers the specific criticism she does? What other types of criticism might she have made? What are some of the reasons you think she did not make other types of criticism?

2) Why does the play end the way it does? What might have been some other possible endings?

3) How would some of the alternative endings you can imagine change what you think and how you feel about the play?

4) Is either character, or both, "right" in this play? What are some of the reasons you believe what you do?

5) It may seem obvious that Alice's job as a teacher requires her to help Calvin learn. Under what kinds of circumstances might that not be so? Why might Alice think that is not always so?

Some possibilities for writing

1) Rewrite two or three pages of this play as if it were a short story. Add character description, setting, and point of view.

2) When we meet them in fiction or drama, characters, like real people, have histories that have made them who they are. Based on your understanding of their respective characters, write a brief biography that goes beyond what is given in the play for both the student and the teacher.

3) Have you ever received a grade higher than you felt you deserved? Why do you think that happened? How did you feel about it?

4) Research Open Admissions programs. What are they? What is the history of such programs? What schools have them? Does yours? Write an essay in which you argue for or against such programs.

Signed, Grateful

Kate Boyes

But thanks, especially, for not changing my life.
Thanks for giving me the chance to talk myself into changing.

Critical thinking points: As you read

1) *This essay is written in the form of a letter. Do you believe Boyes sent it to her professor? Why or why not?*
2) *Boyes finds a college catalogue in a dumpster, which leads her to apply to college. Why did you apply to and decide to enroll at the college you are currently attending?*
3) *How does Boyes change throughout the essay? Map the stages of her progress.*

Dear Professor,

I didn't belong in college. I should have told you that when we first met. My father had dropped out of school after third grade. My mother had finished high school, but her family thought she was a little uppity for doing that. I clerked part-time nights in a food store and worked days as a baby-sitter. My combined salaries from those two jobs fell far below the poverty level, where I'd lived for much of my life. Statisticians said I didn't belong in college. Who was I to argue?

And I came to college for the wrong reason. My health. I needed health insurance, but neither of my jobs included benefits. Every time one of my kids came down with a cold, every time I felt dizzy with flu, I wondered what would happen to us if we were really sick. How could I tell my kids that they would just have to suffer because I couldn't afford to take them to a doctor? How many extra part-time jobs would I need to take on if the kids or I ever rang up an emergency room bill?

One night when I was emptying the trash at the end of my shift, I noticed a brightly colored catalog in the dumpster behind the store. I fished the catalog out, wiped off the mustard and ketchup drips on the front cover, and took it home. Flip-

---

Kate Boyes' poems and essays have been published in several anthologies including *American Nature Writing*. She teaches at Southern Utah University.

ping through the catalog later, I discovered it advertised all the courses available at the local college.

And I discovered something else — taking only one course would make me eligible to sign up for student health insurance. I did some careful calculations. If I took one course each semester for a year, the cost of tuition, books, and fees would still be far lower than the cost for six months of private insurance. My kids would be covered by the student policy, too. What a deal!

Becoming a student was a great scheme. But I knew, when I took my first course from you, that I was an impostor.

We were both coming to college after a long break. You came from a decade of social work. I came from a decade and a half of post-high school marriage, kids, divorce, and minimum-wage jobs. Neither of us had spoken in a classroom for years.

Perhaps you wondered, that first day you taught, if anything you said affected your students. Well, here's how something you said affected me. You announced that each student must give an oral presentation at the end of the semester. When I came home, my youngest daughter, mimicking my voice and posing the same question I asked her every afternoon, said, "How was school today, Honey?" I couldn't answer. Your announcement of the oral presentation had made me so nervous that I rushed past her to the bathroom, where I lost my lunch.

Weeks passed before I sat through class without nausea. I came early each day to claim the only safe seat — the seat on the aisle in the back row. Close to the door. Just in case. Back with the whisperers and the snoozers. I crouched behind the tall man who always read the student newspaper during class, and I chewed the fingernails on one hand while I took notes with the other hand. I talked myself into going to class each day by telling myself, over and over again, that I was doing this for my kids.

I needed three credits. I didn't need the agony of a presentation. Dropping your course and signing up for something — anything — else made sense. But I stayed, even though I didn't know why. Your lectures certainly weren't polished; you gripped the lectern like a shield and your voice sometimes stopped completely in the middle of a sentence.

I think I stayed because your enthusiasm for the subject left me longing to know more. I looked forward to those few quiet hours each week — those rare times when the store was empty or when the babies were napping — that I spent reading, writing, and thinking about what I'd heard in your class.

And one day, while I was thinking, I recalled a fascinating lecture you gave on the importance of defining terms. I noticed on your syllabus that you hadn't defined "oral presentation." I decided oral meant spoken — in any form — rather than written. When the time came for my presentation at the end of the semester, I carried a tape recorder to the front of the room, pushed "play," and returned to my seat, where I listened with the other students to the oral presentation I'd taped the night before.

When I signed up for the next course you taught — a course on women who had shaped American culture and history — I knew you would require another oral presentation. But I figured a little agony while I started a tape recorder wouldn't be so bad. In this second course, you came out from behind the lectern and paced the aisles as you spoke. You often stood at the back of the room when you made an important point, and all heads turned in your direction. Whispering and sleeping ended when you did that, and newspapers dropped to the floor. Your voice stopped only when you asked a question, and you called on us by name.

I was so caught up in the class that a few weeks passed before I read the syllabus carefully. Then I found your long and precise definition of "oral presentation," a definition that excluded the use of tape recorders. To be sure I understood the definition, you stopped by my desk one day after class and said, "This time, I want it *live!*"

Taking college classes was beginning to sharpen my critical thinking skills, and I put those skills to work when choosing the subject for my presentation. I chose to speak about Lucretia Mott, an early Quaker. Why her? At the end of the semester, when my turn came to present, I walked to the front of the room dressed as Lucretia had dressed, in a long skirt and shawl, and with a black bonnet that covered most of my face. I spoke in the first person. Although I was the person standing in front of the other students and moving my lips, it felt to me as if someone else gave that presentation.

By the time we met again in the classroom, I had had to admit to myself that I was in college for more than my health. I'd scraped together enough credits to be one quarter away from graduation. I had an advisor, a major, and a lean program of study that included no frills, no fluff — just the courses I absolutely needed for my degree. They were all I thought I could afford. Your course didn't fit my program, but I decided to take it anyway, and I skipped lunch for weeks to pay for the extra credits.

When you handed back our first exam, mine had a note scribbled alongside the grade. You said you wanted *me* to give the presentation for this course. Not a tape recorder. Not a persona. The same panic that had gripped me during the first course I took from you returned, and I felt my stomach churn with anxiety. My only comfort came from knowing that by the time I fainted — or worse — during my presentation, the quarter would be over and I would have my degree.

You didn't lecture in this course. You pushed the lectern into a corner and arranged our chairs in a circle. You sat with us, your voice one among many. You gave direction to discussions that we carried on long after class periods officially ended. I came early, not to claim an escape seat but to share ideas with other students. I stayed late to be part of the dialogue.

Three can be a magic number, even in real life. At the end of that third course, I stood in front of the class. I spoke in my own voice, just as I had spoken during our discussion circles. You had erased the distinction between the front of the room and the back, between teacher and student, between those who have knowledge and those who seek to gain knowledge. And I remember thinking, as I walked back to my seat, that I wasn't an impostor in the classroom any more. I had just as much right to be in that room as any of the other students.

I was happy when you stopped to speak with me after class. Happy to belong. Happy to have survived the presentation. Happy to know I never had to do anything like that again. I thought you might congratulate me on surviving the presentation or on finishing course work for my bachelors degree. Instead, you asked where I planned to go to graduate school.

You were doing it again! Every time I crept over the line between the familiar and the fearful, you pushed the line a little farther away. I don't remember how I answered your question, but I remember how I felt when I left the room. Miffed. Okay, angry. I steamed out thinking that you'd already forced me to talk in front of people, to grapple with large concepts, to care about ideas. And now you wanted more?

Weeks later — after graduation, after I'd read all the mindless magazines on the rack at work, after I'd thought about life without the stimulation of classes — I cooled down. And applied to graduate school.

I'm sure you knew the only way I could finance my graduate degree would be by teaching classes as a graduate assistant. You knew I would need to stand in front of a class. Day after day. And speak. I'm also sure — now — that your motives were good and pure when you suggested I continue my education. But for a while, when I couldn't sleep nights before I lectured, when I couldn't eat on days I taught, when I couldn't stand in front of the room without feeling dizzy, I wondered if your motives had something to do with revenge.

Perhaps you wonder now if anything you've done as an instructor has affected your students. Here's how something you did affected me. The first time my voice gave out in the middle of a lecture, I remembered you. I realized then that you had felt as nervous while teaching as I had felt while being taught. Every time you'd pushed me, you were also pushing yourself.

I looked over the lectern at a room full of people who felt, more or less, the same way. Nervous, unsure, but anxious to learn. And I stopped the lecture, arranged the chairs in a circle, and gave everyone the opportunity to speak, to add more voices to the dialogue of education.

So . . . I write this letter to say thanks. My graduate degree opened up a great job for me. Yes, you guessed it — I'm teaching at a university. With health insurance.

But thanks, especially, for not changing my life. Thanks for giving me the chance to talk myself into changing.

1998

Critical thinking points: After you've read

1) How does the narrator, as she says, talk herself into changing?

2) Why does Boyes say, "Statisticians said I didn't belong in college. Who was I to argue?" Who, if anyone, does not "belong" in college? What kinds of statistics might she be talking about?

3) How does the professor's teaching style transform as his student transforms? What evidence in the letter supports this?

4) *Do you believe the professor's motives for encouraging his student to go to graduate school have to do with "revenge"? Why or why not? Why might the narrator, at the time, think that?*
5) *Read or reread Jacob Neusner's "Grading Your Professors," and speculate about what grade he might give Boyes' professor. What in the letter leads you to offer that grade?*

Some possibilities for writing

1) *Imagine you are Boyes' professor. Write a response to her in the form of a letter.*
2) *Research the support services offered to returning adult students on your campus. Write a report to be delivered to your class.*
3) *Interview an adult student. What caused that student to return to school? Are the motivations and/or methods for success the same as yours? Why or why not?*
4) *Read or reread Booker T. Washington's excerpt from* Up From Slavery. *In what way is Boyes' story similar to Washington's?*
5) *Contact your Admissions or Dean of Students Office to discover how many non-traditional students are enrolled. What obstacles do non-traditional students face that "traditional" students do not? What support is offered them on your campus? Write a report to be delivered to your class.*

Of This Time, Of That Place

Lionel Trilling

'Tertan I am, but what is Tertan? Of this time, of that place, of some parentage, what does it matter?'

Critical thinking points: As you read

1) Have you ever known a student like Tertan or one that may have been like him?

2) A short story is often made up of a series of conflicts; that is, opposing forces or differing ideas about things. These conflicts may appear as external — between people or between people and things — or internal within one character. Make a list of the conflicts that arise within this story.

3) What is your impression of Dr. Howe the first day of class? Does your impression of him change throughout the story?

4) How would a student with mental illness be handled by a university today? How is that different from what happened to Tertan?

It was a fine September day. By noon it would be summer again but now it was true autumn with a touch of chill in the air. As Joseph Howe stood on the porch of the house in which he lodged ready to leave for his first class of the year he thought with pleasure of the long indoor days that were coming. It was a moment when he could feel glad of his profession.

On the lawn the peach tree was still in fruit and young Hilda Aiken was taking a picture of it. She held the camera tight against her chest. She wanted the sun behind her but she did not want her own long morning shadow in the foreground. She raised the camera but that did not help and she lowered it but that made things worse. She twisted her body to the left then to the right. In the end she had to step out of the

---

Lionel Trilling (1905–1975) was an American educator and influential literary critic who used psychological and sociological methods to elucidate cultural values. Trilling's works include *The Liberal Imagination* (1950), considered perhaps his major contribution; *Freud and the Crisis of Our Culture* (1955); *The Opposing Self* (1955); *Beyond Culture* (1965); and *Mind in the Modern World* (1972).

direct line of the sun. At last she snapped the shutter and wound the film with intense care.

Howe watching her from the porch waited for her to finish and called good morning. She turned startled and almost sullenly lowered her glance. In the year Howe had lived at the Aikens' Hilda had accepted him as one of her family but since his absence of the summer she had grown shy. Then suddenly she lifted her head and smiled at him and the humorous smile confirmed his pleasure in the day. She picked up her bookbag and set off for school.

The handsome houses on the streets to the college were not yet fully awake but they looked very friendly. Howe went by the Bradby house where he would be a guest this evening at the first dinner-party of the year. When he had gone the length of the picket fence the whitest in town he turned back. Along the path there was a fine row of asters and he went through the gate and picked one for his buttonhole. The Bradbys would be pleased if they happened to see him invading their lawn and the knowledge of this made him even more comfortable.

He reached the campus as the hour was striking. The students were hurrying to their classes. He himself was in no hurry. He stopped at his dim cubicle of an office and lit a cigarette. The prospect of facing his class had suddenly presented itself to him and his hands were cold the lawful seizure of power he was about to make seemed momentous. Waiting did not help. He put out his cigarette, picked up a pad of theme paper and went to his classroom.

As he entered the rattle of voices ceased and the twenty-odd freshmen settled themselves and looked at him appraisingly. Their faces seemed gross, his heart sank at their massed impassivity but he spoke briskly.

"My name is Howe," he said and turned and wrote it on the blackboard. The carelessness of the scrawl confirmed his authority. He went on, "My office is 412 Slemp Hall and my office hours are Monday, Wednesday, and Friday from eleven-thirty to twelve-thirty.

He wrote "M., W., F., 11:30-12:30. He said, "I'll be very glad to see any of you at that time. Or if you can't come then, you can arrange with me for some other time."

He turned again to the blackboard and spoke over his shoulder. "The text for the course is Jarman's *Modern Plays*, revised edition. The Co-op has it in stock." He wrote the name, underlined "revised edition" and waited for it to be taken down in the new notebooks.

When the bent heads were raised again he began his speech of prospectus. "It is hard to explain — ," he said, and paused as they composed themselves. "It is hard to explain what a course like this is intended to do. We are going to try to learn something about modern literature and something about prose composition."

As he spoke, his hands warmed and he was able to look directly at the class. Last year on the first day the faces had seemed just as cloddish, but as the term wore on they became gradually alive and quite likable. It did not seem possible that the same thing could happen again.

"I shall not lecture in this course," he continued. "Our work will be carried on by discussion and we will try to learn by an exchange of opinion. But you will soon recognize that my opinion is worth more than anyone else's here."

He remained grave as he said it, but two boys understood and laughed. The rest took permission from them and laughed too. All Howe's private ironies protested the vulgarity of the joke but the laughter made him feel benign and powerful.

When the little speech was finished, Howe picked up the pad of paper he had brought. He announced that they would write an extemporaneous theme. Its subject was traditional, "Who I am and why I came to Dwight College." By now the class was more at ease and it gave a ritualistic groan of protest. Then there was a stir as fountain-pens were brought out and the writing arms of the chairs were cleared and the paper was passed about. At last all the heads bent to work and the room became still.

Howe sat idly at his desk. The sun shone through the tall clumsy windows. The cool of the morning was already passing. There was a scent of autumn and of varnish, and the stillness of the room was deep and oddly touching. Now and then a student's head was raised and scratched in the old elaborate students' pantomime that calls the teacher to witness honest intellectual effort.

Suddenly a tall boy stood within the frame of the open door. "Is this," he said, and thrust a large nose into a college catalogue, "is this the meeting place of English IA? The section instructed by Dr. Joseph Howe?"

He stood on the very sill of the door, as if refusing to enter until he was perfectly sure of all his rights. The class looked up from work, found him absurd and gave a low mocking cheer.

The teacher and the new student, with equal pointedness, ignored the disturbance. Howe nodded to the boy, who pushed his head forward and then jerked it back in a wide elaborate arc to clear his brow of a heavy lock of hair. He advanced into the room and halted before Howe, almost at attention. In a loud clear voice he announced, "I am Tertan, Ferdinand R., reporting at the direction of Head of Department Vincent."

The heraldic formality of this statement brought forth another cheer. Howe looked at the class with a sternness he could not really feel, for there was indeed something ridiculous about this boy. Under his displeased regard the rows of heads dropped to work again. Then he touched Tertan's elbow, led him up to the desk and stood so as to shield their conversation from the class.

"We are writing an extemporaneous theme," he said. "The subject is, 'Who I am and why I came to Dwight College.'"

He stripped a few sheets from the pad and offered them to the boy. Tertan hesitated and then took the paper but he held it only tentatively. As if with the effort of making something clear, he gulped, and a slow smile fixed itself on his face. It was at once knowing and shy.

"Professor," he said, "to be perfectly fair to my classmates" — he made a large gesture over the room — "and to you" — he inclined his head to Howe — "this would not be for me an extemporaneous subject."

Howe tried to understand. "You mean you've already thought about it — you've heard we always give the same subject? That doesn't matter."

Again the boy ducked his head and gulped. It was the gesture of one who wishes to make a difficult explanation with perfect candor. "Sir," he said, and made the distinction with great care, "the topic I did not expect but I have given much ratiocination to the subject."

Howe smiled and said, "I don't think that's an unfair advantage. Just go ahead and write."

Tertan narrowed his eyes and glanced sidewise at Howe. His strange mouth smiled. Then in quizzical acceptance, he ducked his head, threw back the heavy dank lock, dropped into a seat with a great loose noise and began to write rapidly.

The room fell silent again and Howe resumed his idleness. When the bell rang, the students who had groaned when the task had been set now groaned again because they had not finished. Howe took up the papers and held the class while he made the first assignment. When he dismissed it, Tertan bore down on him, his slack mouth held ready for speech.

"Some professors," he said, "are pedants. They are Dryasdusts. However, some professors are free souls and creative spirits. Kant, Hegel, and Nietzsche were all professors." With this pronouncement he paused. "It is my opinion," he continued, "that you occupy the second category."

Howe looked at the boy in surprise and said with good-natured irony, "With Kant, Hegel, and Nietzsche?"

Not only Tertan's hand and head but his whole awkward body waved away the stupidity. "It is the kind and not the quantity of the kind," he said sternly.

Rebuked, Howe said as simply and seriously as he could, "It would be nice to think so." He added, "Of course I am not a professor."

This was clearly a disappointment but Tertan met it. "In the French sense," he said with composure. "Generically, a teacher."

Suddenly he bowed. It was such a bow, Howe fancied, as a stage director might teach an actor playing a medieval student who takes leave of Abelard — stiff, solemn, with elbows close to the body and feet together. Then, quite as suddenly, he turned and left.

A queer fish, and as soon as Howe reached his office he sifted through the batch of themes and drew out Tertan's. The boy had filled many sheets with his unformed headlong scrawl. "Who am I?" he had begun. "Here, in a mundane, not to say commercialized academe, is asked the question which from time long immemorably out of mind has accreted doubts and thoughts in the psyche of man to pester him as a nuisance. Whether in St. Augustine (or Austin as sometimes called) or Miss Bashkirtsieff or Frederic Amiel or Empedocles, or in less lights of the intellect than these, this posed question has been ineluctable."

Howe took out his pencil. He circled "academe" and wrote "vocab," in the margin. He underlined "time long immemorably out of mind" and wrote "Diction!" But this seemed inadequate for what was wrong. He put down his pencil and read ahead to discover the principle of error in the theme. "Today as ever, in spite of gloomy prophets of the dismal science (economics) the question is uninvalidated. Out of the starry depths of heaven hurtles this spear of query demanding to be caught on the shield of the mind ere it pierces the skull and the limbs be unstrung."

Baffled but quite caught, Howe read on. "Materialism, by which is meant the philosophic concept and not the moral idea, provides no aegis against the question which lies beyond the tangible (metaphysics). Existence without alloy is the question presented. Environment and heredity relegated aside, the rags and old clothes of practical life discarded, the name and the instrumentality of livelihood do not, as the prophets of the dismal science insist on in this connection, give solution to the interrogation which not from the professor merely but veritably from the cosmos is given. I think, therefore I am (cogito etc.) but who am I? Tertan I am, but what is Tertan? Of this time, of that place, of some parentage, what does it matter?"

Existence without alloy: the phrase established itself. Howe put aside Tertan's paper and at random picked up another. "I am Arthur J. Casebeer Jr." he read. "My father is Arthur J. Casebeer and my grandfather was Arthur J. Casebeer before him. My mother is Nina Wimble Casebeer. Both of them are college graduates and my father is in insurance. I was born in St. Louis eighteen years ago and we still make our residence there."

Arthur J. Casebeer, who knew who he was, was less interesting than Tertan, but more coherent. Howe picked up Tertan's paper again. It was clear that none of the routine marginal comments, no "sent. str." or "punct." or "vocab." could cope with this torrential rhetoric. He read ahead, contenting himself with underscoring the errors against the time when he should have the necessary "conference" with Tertan.

It was a busy and official day of cards and sheets, arrangements and small decisions, and it gave Howe pleasure. Even when it was time to attend the first of the weekly Convocations he felt the charm of the beginning of things when intention is still innocent and uncorrupted by effort. He sat among the young instructors on the platform and joined in their humorous complaints at having to assist at the ceremony, but actually he got a clear satisfaction from the ritual of prayer and prosy speech and even from wearing his academic gown. And when the Convocation was over the pleasure continued as he crossed the campus, exchanging greetings with men he had not seen since the spring. They were people who did not yet, and perhaps never would, mean much to him, but in a year they had grown amiably to be part of his life. They were his fellow townsmen.

The day had cooled again at sunset and there was a bright chill in the September twilight. Howe carried his voluminous gown over his arm, he swung his doctoral hood by its purple neckpiece and on his head he wore his mortarboard with its heavy gold tassel bobbing just over his eye. These were the weighty and absurd symbols of his new profession and they pleased him. At twenty-six Joseph Howe had discovered that he was neither so well off nor so bohemian as he had once thought. A small income, adequate when supplemented by a sizable cash legacy, was genteel poverty when the cash was all spent. And the literary life — the room at the Lafayette or the small apartment without a lease, the long summers on the Cape, the long afternoons and the social evenings — began to weary him. His writing filled his mornings and should perhaps have filled his life, yet it did not. To the amusement of his friends and with a certain sense that he was betraying his own freedom, he had used the last of his legacy for a year at Harvard. The small but respectable reputation of his two volumes of verse had proved useful — he continued at Harvard on a fellowship and when he emerged as Dr. Howe he received an excellent appointment, with prospects, at Dwight.

He had his moments of fear when all that had ever been said of the dangers of the academic life had occurred to him. But after a year in which he had tested every possibility of corruption and seduction he was ready to rest easy. His third volume of verse, most of it written in his first year of teaching, was not only ampler but, he thought, better than its predecessors.

There was a clear hour before the Bradby dinner-party and Howe looked forward to it. But he was not to enjoy it, for lying with his mail on the hall table was a copy of this quarter's issue of *Life and Letters*, to which his landlord subscribed. Its severe cover announced that its editor, Frederic Woolley, had this month contributed an essay called "Two Poets," and Howe, picking it up, curious to see who the two poets might be, felt his own name start out at him with cabalistic power — Joseph Howe. As he continued to turn the pages his hand trembled.

Standing in the dark hall, holding the neat little magazine, Howe knew that his literary contempt for Frederic Woolley meant nothing, for he suddenly understood how he respected Woolley in the way of the world. He knew this by the trembling of his hand. And of the little world as well as the great, for although the literary groups of New York might dismiss Woolley, his name carried high authority in the academic world. At Dwight it was even a revered name, for it had been here at the college that Frederic Woolley had made the distinguished scholarly career from which he had gone on to literary journalism. In middle life he had been induced to take the editorship of *Life and Letters*, a literary monthly not widely read but heavily endowed and in its pages he had carried on the defense of what he sometimes called the older values. He was not without wit, he had great knowledge and considerable taste and even in the full movement of the "new" literature he had won a certain respect for his refusal to accept it. In France, even in England, he would have been connected with a more robust tradition of conservatism, but America gave him an audience not much better than genteel. It was known in the college that to the subsidy of *Life and Letters* the Bradbys contributed a great part.

As Howe read, he saw that he was involved in nothing less than an event. When the Fifth Series of *Studies in Order and Value* came to be collected, this latest of Frederic Woolley's essays would not be merely another step in the old direction. Clearly and unmistakably, it was a turning point. All his literary life Woolley had been concerned with the relation of literature to morality, religion, and the private and delicate pieties, and he had been unalterably opposed to all that he had called "inhuman humanitarianism." But here, suddenly, dramatically late, he had made an about-face, turning to the public life and to the humanitarian politics he had so long despised. This was the kind of incident the histories of literature make much of. Frederic Woolley was opening for himself a new career and winning a kind of new youth. He contrasted the two poets, Thomas Wormser who was admirable, Joseph Howe who was almost dangerous. He spoke of the "precious subjectivism" of Howe's verse. "In times like ours," he wrote, "with millions facing penury and want, one feels that the qualities of the *tour d'ivore* are well-nigh inhuman, nearly insulting. The *tour d'ivore* becomes the *tour d'ivresse* and it is not self-intoxicated poets that our people need." The essay said more: "The problem is one of meaning. I am not ignorant that the creed of the esoteric poets declares that a poem does not and should not *mean* anything, that it is something. But poetry is what the poet makes it, and if he is a true poet he makes what his society needs. And what is needed now is the tradition in which Mr. Wormser writes, the true tradition of poetry. The Howes do no harm, but they do no good when positive good is demanded of all responsible men. Or do the Howes indeed do no harm? Perhaps Plato would have said they do, that in some ways theirs is the Phrygian music that turns men's minds from the struggle. Certainly it is true that Thomas Wormser writes in the lucid Dorian mode which sends men into battle with evil."

It was easy to understand why Woolley had chosen to praise Thomas Wormser. The long, lilting lines of *Corn Under Willows* hymned, as Woolley put it, the struggle for wheat in the Iowa fields and expressed the real lives of real people. But why out of the dozen more notable examples he had chosen Howe's little volume as the example of "precious subjectivism" was hard to guess. In a way it was funny, this multiplication of himself into "the Howes." And yet this becoming the multiform political symbol by whose creation Frederic Woolley gave the sign of a sudden new life, this use of him as a sacrifice whose blood was necessary for the rites of rejuvenation, made him feel oddly unclean.

Nor could Howe get rid of a certain practical resentment. As a poet he had a special and respectable place in the college life. But it might be another thing to be marked as the poet of a willful and selfish obscurity.

As he walked to the Bradbys Howe was a little tense and defensive. It seemed to him that all the world knew of the "attack" and agreed with it. And indeed the Bradbys had read the essay but Professor Bradby, a kind and pretentious man, said, "I see my old friend knocked you about a bit, my boy," and his wife Eugenia looked at Howe with her childlike blue eyes and said, "I shall scold Frederic for the untrue things he wrote about you. You aren't the least obscure." They beamed at him. In their genial snobbery they seemed to feel that he had distinguished himself. He was the leader of Howeism. He enjoyed the dinner-party as much as he had thought he would.

And in the following days, as he was more preoccupied with his duties, the incident was forgotten. His classes had ceased to be mere groups. Student after student detached himself from the mass and required or claimed a place in Howe's awareness. Of them all it was Tertan who first and most violently signaled his separate existence. A week after classes had begun Howe saw his silhouette on the frosted glass of his office door. It was motionless for a long time, perhaps stopped by the problem of whether or not to knock before entering. Howe called, "Come in!" and Tertan entered with his shambling stride.

He stood beside the desk, silent and at attention. When Howe asked him to sit down, he responded with a gesture of head and hand as if to say that such amenities were beside the point. Nevertheless he did take the chair. He put his ragged crammed briefcase between his legs. His face, which Howe now observed fully for the first time, was confusing, for it was made up of florid curves, the nose arched in the bone and voluted in the nostril, the mouth loose and soft and rather moist. Yet the face was so thin and narrow as to seem the very type of asceticism. Lashes of unusual length veiled the eyes and, indeed, it seemed as if there were a veil over the whole countenance. Before the words actually came, the face screwed itself into an attitude of preparation for them.

"You can confer with me now?" Tertan said.

"Yes, I'd be glad to. There are several things in your two themes I want to talk to you about." Howe reached for the packet of themes on his desk and sought for Tertan's. But the boy was waving them away.

"These are done perforce," he said. "Under the pressure of your requirement. They are not significant, mere duties." Again his great hand flapped vaguely to dismiss his themes. He leaned forward and gazed at his teacher.

"You are," he said, "a man of letters? You are a poet?" It was more declaration than question.

"I should like to think so," Howe said.

At first Tertan accepted the answer with a show of appreciation, as though the understatement made a secret between himself and Howe. Then he chose to misunderstand. With his shrewd and disconcerting control of expression, he presented to Howe a puzzled grimace. "What does that mean?" he said.

Howe retracted the irony. "Yes. I am a poet." It sounded strange to say.

"That," Tertan said, "is a wonder." He corrected himself with his ducking head. "I mean that is wonderful."

Suddenly he dived at the miserable briefcase between his legs, put it on his knees and began to fumble with the catch, all intent on the difficulty it presented. Howe noted that his suit was worn thin, his shirt almost unclean. He became aware, even, of a vague and musty odor of garments worn too long in unaired rooms. Tertan conquered the lock and began to concentrate upon a search into the interior. At last he held in his hand what he was after, a torn and crumpled copy of *Life and Letters*.

"I learned it from here," he said, holding it out.

Howe looked at him sharply, his hackles a little up. But the boy's face was not only perfectly innocent, it even shone with a conscious admiration. Apparently nothing of the import of the essay had touched him except the wonderful fact that his teacher was a "man of letters." Yet this seemed too stupid and Howe, to test it, said, "The man who wrote that doesn't think it's wonderful."

Tertan made a moist hissing sound as he cleared his mouth of saliva. His head, oddly loose on his neck, wove a pattern of contempt in the air. "A critic," he said, "who admits prima facie that he does not understand." Then he said grandly, "It is the inevitable fate."

It was absurd, yet Howe was not only aware of the absurdity but of a tension suddenly and wonderfully relaxed. Now that the "attack" was on the table between himself and this strange boy and subject to the boy's funny and absolutely certain contempt, the hidden force of his feeling was revealed to him in the very moment that it vanished. All unsuspected, there had been a film over the world, a transparent but discoloring haze of danger. But he had no time to stop over the brightened aspect of things. Tertan was going on. "I also am a man of letters. Putative."

"You have written a good deal?" Howe meant to be no more than polite and he was surprised at the tenderness he heard in his words.

Solemnly the boy nodded, threw back the dank lock and sucked in a deep anticipatory breath. "First, a work of homiletics, which is a defense of the principles of religious optimism against the pessimism of Schopenhauer and the humanism of Nietzsche."

"Humanism ? Why do you call it humanism?"

"It is my nomenclature for making a deity of man," Tertan replied negligently. "Then three fictional works, novels. And numerous essays in science, combating materialism. Is it your duty to read these if I bring them to you?"

Howe answered simply, "No, it isn't exactly my duty, but I shall be happy to read them."

Tertan stood up and remained silent. He rested his bag on the chair. With a certain compunction — for it did not seem entirely proper that, of two men of letters, one should have the right to blue-pencil the other, to grade him or to question the quality of his "sentence structure" — Howe reached for Tertan's papers. But before he could take them up, the boy suddenly made his bow-to-Abelard, the stiff inclination of the body with the hands seeming to emerge from the scholar's gown. Then he was gone.

But after his departure something was still left of him. The timbre of his curious sentences, the downright finality of so quaint a phrase as "It is the inevitable fate" still rang in the air. Howe gave the warmth of his feeling to the new visitor who stood at the door announcing himself with a genteel clearing of the throat.

"Dr. Howe, I believe?" the student said. A large hand advanced into the room and grasped Howe's hand. "Blackburn, sir, Theodore Blackburn, vice-president of the Student Council. A great pleasure, sir."

Out of a pair of ruddy cheeks a pair of small eyes twinkled good-naturedly. The large face, the large body were not so much fat as beefy and suggested something "typical," monk, politician, or innkeeper.

Blackburn took the seat beside Howe's desk. "I may have seemed to introduce myself in my public capacity, sir," he said. "But it is really as an individual that I came to see you. That is to say, as one of your students to be."

He spoke with an "English" intonation and he went on, "I was once an English major, sir."

For a moment Howe was startled, for the roast-beef look of the boy and the manner of his speech gave a second's credibility to one sense of his statement. Then the collegiate meaning of the phrase asserted itself, but some perversity made Howe say what was not really in good taste even with so forward a student, "Indeed ? What regiment?"

Blackburn stared and then gave a little pouf-pouf of laughter. He waved the misapprehension away. "*Very* good, sir. It certainly is an ambiguous term." He chuckled in appreciation of Howe's joke, then cleared his throat to put it aside. "I look forward to taking your course in the romantic poets, sir," he said earnestly. "To me the romantic poets are the very crown of English literature."

Howe made a dry sound, and the boy, catching some meaning in it, said, "Little as I know them, of course. But even Shakespeare who is so dear to us of the Anglo-Saxon tradition is in a sense but the preparation for Shelley, Keats and Byron. And Wadsworth."

Almost sorry for him, Howe dropped his eyes. With some embarrassment, for the boy was not actually his student, he said softly, "Wordsworth."

"Sir?"

"Wordsworth, not Wadsworth. You said Wadsworth."

"Did I, sir?" Gravely he shook his head to rebuke himself for the error. "Wordsworth, of course — slip of the tongue." Then, quite in command again, he went on. "I have a favor to ask of you, Dr. Howe. You see, I began my college course as an English major," — he smiled — "as I said."

"Yes?"

"But after my first year I shifted. I shifted to the social sciences. Sociology and government — I find them stimulating and very real." He paused, out of respect for reality. "But now I find that perhaps I have neglected the other side."

"The other side?" Howe said.

"Imagination, fancy, culture. A well-rounded man." He trailed off as if there were perfect understanding between them. "And so, sir, I have decided to end my senior year with your course in the romantic poets."

His voice was filled with an indulgence which Howe ignored as he said flatly and gravely, "But that course isn't given until the spring term."

"Yes, sir, and that is where the favor comes in. Would you let me take your romantic prose course? I can't take it for credit, sir, my program is full, but just for background it seems to me that I ought to take it. I do hope," he concluded in a manly way, "that you will consent."

"Well, it's no great favor, Mr. Blackburn. You can come if you wish, though there's not much point in it if you don't do the reading."

The bell rang for the hour and Howe got up.

"May I begin with this class, sir?" Blackburn's smile was candid and boyish.

Howe nodded carelessly and together, silently, they walked to the classroom down the hall. When they reached the door Howe stood back to let his student enter, but Blackburn moved adroitly behind him and grasped him by the arm to urge him over the threshold. They entered together with Blackburn's hand firmly on Howe's bicep, the student inducting the teacher into his own room. Howe felt a surge of temper rise in him and almost violently he disengaged his arm and walked to the desk, while Blackburn found a seat in the front row and smiled at him.

II

The question was, At whose door must the tragedy be laid?

All night the snow had fallen heavily and only now was abating in sparse little flurries. The windows were valanced high with white. It was very quiet, something of the quiet of the world had reached the class and Howe found that everyone was glad to talk or listen. In the room there was a comfortable sense of pleasure in being human.

Casebeer believed that the blame for the tragedy rested with heredity. Picking up the book he read, "The sins of the fathers are visited on their children." This opinion was received with general favor. Nevertheless Johnson ventured to say that the fault was all Pastor Manders' because the Pastor had made Mrs. Alving go back to her husband and was always hiding the truth. To this Hibbard objected with logic enough. "Well then, it was really all her husband's fault. He did all the bad things." De Witt, his face bright with an impatient Idea, said that the fault was all society's. "By society I don't mean upper-crust society," he said. He looked around a little defiantly, taking in any members of the class who might be members of upper-crust society. "Not in that sense. I mean the social unit."

Howe nodded and said, "Yes, of course."

"If the society of the time had progressed far enough in science," De Witt went on, "then there would be no problem for Mr. Ibsen to write about. Captain Alving plays around a little, gives way to perfectly natural biological urges, and he gets a social disease, a venereal disease. If the disease is cured, no problem. Invent salvarsan and the disease is cured. The problem of heredity disappears and li'l Oswald just doesn't get paresis. No paresis, no problem — no problem, no play."

This was carrying the ark into battle and the class looked at De Witt with respectful curiosity. It was his usual way and on the whole they were sympathetic with his struggle to prove to Howe that science was better than literature. Still, there was something in his reckless manner that alienated them a little.

"Or take birth control, for instance," De Witt went on. "If Mrs. Alving had had some knowledge of contraception, she wouldn't have had to have li'l Oswald at all. No li'l Oswald, no play."

The class was suddenly quieter. In the back row Stettenhover swung his great football shoulders in a righteous sulking gesture, first to the right, then to the left. He puckered his mouth ostentatiously. Intellect was always ending up by talking dirty.

Tertan's hand went up and Howe said, "Mr. Tertan." The boy shambled to his feet and began his long characteristic gulp. Howe made a motion with his fingers, as small as possible, and Tertan ducked his head and smiled in apology. He sat down.

The class laughed. With more than half the term gone, Tertan had not been able to remember that one did not rise to speak. He seemed unable to carry on the life of the intellect without this mark of respect for it. To Howe the boy's habit of rising seemed to accord with the formal shabbiness of his dress. He never wore the casual sweaters and jackets of his classmates. Into the free and comfortable air of the college classroom he brought the stuffy sordid strictness of some crowded metropolitan high school.

"Speaking from one sense," Tertan began slowly, "there is no blame ascribable. From the sense of determinism, who can say where the blame lies? The preordained is the preordained and it cannot be said without rebellion against the universe, a palpable absurdity."

In the back row Stettenhover slumped suddenly in his seat, his heels held out before him, making a loud dry disgusted sound. His body sank until his neck rested on the back of his chair. He folded his hands across his belly and looked significantly out of the window, exasperated not only with Tertan but with Howe, with the class, with the whole system designed to encourage this kind of thing. There was a certain insolence in the movement and Howe flushed. As Tertan continued to speak, Howe walked casually toward the window and placed himself in the line of Stettenhover's vision. He stared at the great fellow, who pretended not to see him. There was so much power in the big body, so much contempt in the Greek-athlete face under the crisp Greek-athlete curls, that Howe felt almost physical fear. But at last Stettenhover admitted him to focus and under his disapproving gaze sat up with slow indifference. His eyebrows raised high in resignation, he began to examine his hands. Howe relaxed and turned his attention back to Tertan.

"Flux of existence," Tertan was saying, "produces all things, so that judgment wavers. Beyond the phenomena, what? But phenomena are adumbrated and to them we are limited."

Howe saw it for a moment as perhaps it existed in the boy's mind — the world of shadows which are cast by a great light upon a hidden reality as in the old myth of the Cave. But the little brush with Stettenhover had tired him and he said irritably, "But come to the point, Mr. Tertan."

He said it so sharply that some of the class looked at him curiously. For three months he had gently carried Tertan through his verbosities, to the vaguely respectful surprise of the other students, who seemed to conceive that there existed between this strange classmate and their teacher some special understanding from which they were content to be excluded. Tertan looked at him mildly and at once came brilliantly to the point. "This is the summation of the play," he said and took up his book and read, "'Your poor father never found any outlet for the overmastering joy of life that was in him. And I brought no holiday into his home, either. Everything seemed to turn upon duty and I am afraid I made your poor father's home unbearable to him, Oswald.' Spoken by Mrs. Alving."

Yes, that was surely the "summation" of the play and Tertan had hit it, as he hit, deviously and eventually, the literary point of almost everything. But now, as always, he was wrapping it away from sight. "For most mortals," he said, "there are only joys of biological urgings, gross and crass, such as the sensuous Captain Alving. For certain few there are the transmutations beyond these to a contemplation of the utter whole."

Oh, the boy was mad. And suddenly the word, used in hyperbole, intended almost for the expression of exasperated admiration, became literal. Now that the word was used, it became simply apparent to Howe that Tertan was mad.

It was a monstrous word and stood like a bestial thing in the room. Yet it so completely comprehended everything that had puzzled Howe, it so arranged and explained what for three months had been perplexing him that almost at once its horror became domesticated. With this word Howe was able to understand why he had never been able to communicate to Tertan the value of a single criticism or correction of his wild, verbose themes. Their conferences had been frequent and long but had done nothing to reduce to order the splendid confusion of the boy's ideas. Yet, impossible though its expression was, Tertan's incandescent mind could always strike for a moment into some dark corner of thought.

And now it was suddenly apparent that it was not a faulty rhetoric that Howe had to contend with. With his new knowledge he looked at Tertan's face and wondered how he could have so long deceived himself. Tertan was still talking and the class had lapsed into a kind of patient unconsciousness, a coma of respect for words which, for all that most of them knew, might be profound. Almost with a suffusion of shame, Howe believed that in some dim way the class had long ago had some intimation of Tertan's madness. He reached out as decisively as he could to seize the thread of Tertan's discourse before it should be entangled further.

"Mr. Tertan says that the blame must be put upon whoever kills the joy of living in another. We have been assuming that Captain Alving was a wholly bad man, but what if we assume that he became bad only because Mrs. Alving, when they were first married, acted toward him in the prudish way she says she did?"

It was a ticklish idea to advance to freshmen and perhaps not profitable. Not all of them were following.

"That would put the blame on Mrs. Alving herself, whom most of you admire. And she herself seems to think so." He glanced at his watch. The hour was nearly over. "What do you think, Mr. De Witt?"

De Witt rose to the idea, wanted to know if society couldn't be blamed for educating Mrs. Alving's temperament in the wrong way. Casebeer was puzzled, Stettenhover continued to look at his hands until the bell rang.

Tertan, his brows louring in thought, was making as always for a private word. Howe gathered his books and papers to leave quickly. At this moment of his discovery and with the knowledge still raw, he could not engage himself with Tertan. Tertan sucked in his breath to prepare for speech and Howe made ready for the pain and confusion. But at that moment Casebeer detached himself from the group with which he had been conferring and which he seemed to represent. His constituency remained at a tactful distance. The mission involved the time of an assigned essay. Casebeer's

presentation of the plea — it was based on the freshmen's heavy-duties at the fraternities during Carnival Week — cut across Tertan's preparations for speech. "And so
some of us fellows thought," Casebeer concluded with heavy solemnity, "that we
could do a better job, give our minds to it more, if we had more time."

Tertan regarded Casebeer with mingled curiosity and revulsion. Howe not only
said that he would postpone the assignment but went on to talk about the Carnival
and even drew the waiting constituency into the conversation. He was conscious of
Tertan's stern and astonished stare, then of his sudden departure.

Now that the fact was clear, Howe knew that he must act on it. His course was
simple enough. He must lay the case before the Dean. Yet he hesitated. His feeling
for Tertan must now, certainly, be in some way invalidated. Yet could he, because of
a word, hurry to assign to official and reasonable solicitude what had been, until this
moment, so various and warm? He could at least delay and, by moving slowly, lend
a poor grace to the necessary, ugly act of making his report.

It was with some notion of keeping the matter in his own hands that he went to
the Dean's office to look up Tertan's records. In the outer office the Dean's secretary
greeted him brightly and at his request brought him the manila folder with the small
identifying photograph pasted in the corner. She laughed. "He was looking for the
birdie in the wrong place," she said.

Howe leaned over her shoulder to look at the picture. It was as bad as all the
Dean's-office photographs were, but it differed from all that Howe had ever seen.
Tertan, instead of looking into the camera, as no doubt he had been bidden, had, at
the moment of exposure, turned his eyes upward. His mouth, as though conscious of
the trick played on the photographer, had the sly superior look that Howe knew.

The secretary was fascinated by the picture. "What a funny boy," she said. "He
looks like Tartuffe!"

And so he did, with the absurd piety of the eyes and the conscious slyness of the
mouth and the whole face bloated by the bad lens.

"Is he like that?" the secretary said.

"Like Tartuffe? No."

From the photograph there was little enough comfort to be had. The records
themselves gave no clue to madness, though they suggested sadness enough. Howe
read of a father, Stanislaus Tertan, born in Budapest and trained in engineering in
Berlin, once employed by the Hercules Chemical Corporation — this was one of the
factories that dominated the south end of the town — but now without employment.
He read of a mother Erminie (Youngfellow) Tertan, born in Manchester, educated at
a Normal School at Leeds, now housewife by profession. The family lived on
Greenbriar Street, which Howe knew as a row of once elegant homes near what was
now the factory district. The old mansions had long ago been divided into small and
primitive apartments. Of Ferdinand himself there was little to learn. He lived with
his parents, had attended a Detroit high school and had transferred to the local school
in his last year. His rating for intelligence, as expressed in numbers, was high, his
scholastic record was remarkable, he held a college scholarship for his tuition.

Howe laid the folder on the secretary's desk. "Did you find what you wanted to know?" she asked.

The phrases from Tertan's momentous first theme came back to him. "Tertan I am, but what is Tertan? Of this time, of that place, of some parentage, what does it matter?"

"No, I didn't find it," he said.

Now that he had consulted the sad half-meaningless record he knew all the more firmly that he must not give the matter out of his own hands. He must not release Tertan to authority. Not that he anticipated from the Dean anything but the greatest kindness for Tertan. The Dean would have the experience and skill which he himself could not have. One way or another the Dean could answer the question, "What is Tertan?" Yet this was precisely what he feared. He alone could keep alive — not forever but for a somehow important time — the question, "What is Tertan?" He alone could keep it still a question. Some sure instinct told him that he must not surrender the question to a clean official desk in a clear official light to be dealt with, settled and closed.

He heard himself saying, "Is the Dean busy at the moment? I'd like to see him."

His request came thus unbidden, even forbidden, and it was one of the surprising and startling incidents of his life. Later, when he reviewed the events, so disconnected in themselves or so merely odd, of the story that unfolded for him that year, it was over this moment, on its face the least notable, that he paused longest. It was frequently to be with fear and never without a certainty of its meaning in his own knowledge of himself that he would recall this simple, routine request and the feeling of shame and freedom it gave him as he sent everything down the official chute. In the end, of course, no matter what he did to "protect" Tertan, he would have had to make the same request and lay the matter on the Dean's clean desk. But it would always be a landmark of his life that, at the very moment when he was rejecting the official way, he had been, without will or intention, so gladly drawn to it.

After the storm's last delicate flurry, the sun had come out. Reflected by the new snow, it filled the office with a golden light which was almost musical in the way it made all the commonplace objects of efficiency shine with a sudden sad and noble significance. And the light, now that he noticed it, made the utterance of his perverse and unwanted request even more momentous.

The secretary consulted the engagement pad. "He'll be free any minute. Don't you want to wait in the parlor?"

She threw open the door of the large and pleasant room in which the Dean held his Committee meetings and in which his visitors waited. It was designed with a homely elegance on the masculine side of the eighteenth-century manner. There was a small coal fire in the grate and the handsome mahogany table was strewn with books and magazines. The large windows gave on the snowy lawn and there was such a fine width of window that the white casements and walls seemed at this moment but a continuation of the snow, the snow but an extension of casement and walls. The outdoors seemed taken in and made safe, the indoors seemed luxuriously freshened and expanded.

Howe sat down by the fire and lighted a cigarette. The room had its intended effect upon him. He felt comfortable and relaxed, yet nicely organized, some young diplomatic agent of the eighteenth century, the newly fledged Swift carrying out Sir William Temple's business. The rawness of Tertan's case quite vanished. He crossed his legs and reached for a magazine.

It was that famous issue of *Life and Letters* that his idle hand had found and his blood raced as he sifted through it and the shape of his own name, Joseph Howe, sprang out at him, still cabalistic in its power. He tossed the magazine back on the table as the door of the Dean's office opened and the Dean ushered out Theodore Blackburn.

"Ah, Joseph!" the Dean said.

Blackburn said, "Good morning, Doctor." Howe winced at the title and caught the flicker of amusement over the Dean's face. The Dean stood with his hand high on the doorjamb and Blackburn, still in the doorway, remained standing almost under his long arm.

Howe nodded briefly to Blackburn, snubbing his eager deference. "Can you give me a few minutes?" he said to the Dean.

"All the time you want. Come in." Before the two men could enter the office, Blackburn claimed their attention with a long full "Er." As they turned to him, Blackburn said, "Can you give me a few minutes, Dr. Howe?" His eyes sparkled at the little audacity he had committed, the slightly impudent play with hierarchy. Of the three of them Blackburn kept himself the lowest, but he reminded Howe of his subaltern relation to the Dean.

"I mean, of course," Blackburn went on easily, "when you've finished with the Dean."

"I'll be in my office shortly," Howe said, turned his back on the ready "Thank you, sir," and followed the Dean into the inner room.

"Energetic boy," said the Dean. "A bit beyond himself but very energetic. Sit down."

The Dean lighted a cigarette, leaned back in his chair, sat easy and silent for a moment, giving Howe no signal to go ahead with business. He was a young Dean, not much beyond forty, a tall handsome man with sad, ambitious eyes. He had been a Rhodes scholar. His friends looked for great things from him and it was generally said that he had notions of education which he was not yet ready to try to put into practice.

His relaxed silence was meant as a compliment to Howe. He smiled and said, "What's the business, Joseph?"

"Do you know Tertan — Ferdinand Tertan, a freshman?"

The Dean's cigarette was in his mouth and his hands were clasped behind his head. He did not seem to search his memory for the name. He said, "What about him?"

Clearly the Dean knew something and he was waiting for Howe to tell him more. Howe moved only tentatively. Now that he was doing what he resolved not to do, he felt more guilty at having been so long deceived by Tertan and more need to be loyal to his error.

"He's a strange fellow," he ventured. He said stubbornly, "In a strange way he's very brilliant." He concluded, "But very strange." The springs of the Dean's swivel chair creaked as he came out of his sprawl and leaned forward to Howe. "Do you mean he's so strange that it's something you could give a name to?"

Howe looked at him stupidly. "What do you mean?" he said.

"What's his trouble?" the Dean said more neutrally.

"He's very brilliant, in a way. I looked him up and he has a top intelligence rating. But somehow, and it's hard to explain just how, what he says is always on the edge of sense and doesn't quite make it."

The Dean looked at him and Howe flushed up. The Dean had surely read Woolley on the subject of "the Howes" and the *tour d'ivresse*. Was that quick glance ironical?

The Dean picked up some papers from his desk and Howe could see that they were in Tertan's impatient scrawl. Perhaps the little gleam in the Dean's glance had come only from putting facts together.

"He sent me this yesterday," the Dean said. "After an interview I had with him. I haven't been able to do more than glance at it. When you said what you did, I realized there was something wrong."

Twisting his mouth, the Dean looked over the letter. "You seem to be involved," he said without looking up. "By the way, what did you give him at midterm?"

Flushing, setting his shoulders, Howe said firmly, "I gave him *A*–."

The Dean chuckled. "Might be a good idea if some of our boys went crazy — just a little." He said, "Well," to conclude the matter and handed the papers to Howe. "See if this is the same thing you've been finding. Then we can go into the matter again."

Before the fire in the parlor, in the chair that Howe had been occupying, sat Blackburn. He sprang to his feet as Howe entered.

"I said my office, Mr. Blackburn." Howe's voice was sharp. Then he was almost sorry for the rebuke, so clearly and naively did Blackburn seem to relish his stay in the parlor, close to authority.

"I'm in a bit of a hurry, sir," he said, "and I did want to be sure to speak to you, sir."

He was really absurd, yet fifteen years from now he would have grown up to himself, to the assurance and mature beefiness. In banks, in consular offices, in bro-kerage firms, on the bench, more seriously affable, a little sterner, he would make use of his ability to be administered by his job. It was almost reassuring. Now he was exercising his too-great skill on Howe. "I owe you an apology, sir," he said.

Howe knew that he did but he showed surprise.

"I mean, Doctor, after you having been so kind about letting me attend your class, I stopped coming." He smiled in deprecation. "Extra-curricular activities take up so much of my time. I'm afraid I undertook more than I could perform."

Howe had noticed the absence and had been a little irritated by it after Blackburn's elaborate plea. It was an absence that might be interpreted as a comment on the teacher. But there was only one way for him to answer. "You've no need to apologize," he said. "It's wholly your affair."

Blackburn beamed. "I'm so glad you feel that way about it, sir. I was worried you might think I had stayed away because I was influenced by —" He stopped and lowered his eyes.

Astonished, Howe said, "Influenced by what?"

"Well, by —" Blackburn hesitated and for answer pointed to the table on which lay the copy of *Life and Letters*. Without looking at it, he knew where to direct his hand. "By the unfavorable publicity, sir." He hurried on. "And that brings me to another point, sir. I am secretary of Quill and Scroll, sir, the student literary society, and I wonder if you would address us. You could read your own poetry, sir, and defend your own point of view. It would be very interesting."

It was truly amazing. Howe looked long and cruelly into Blackburn's face, trying to catch the secret of the mind that could have conceived this way of manipulating him, this way so daring and inept — but not entirely inept — with its malice so without malignity. The face did not yield its secret. Howe smiled broadly and said, "Of course I don't think you were influenced by the unfavorable publicity."

"I'm still going to take — regularly, for credit — your romantic poets course next term," Blackburn said.

"Don't worry, my dear fellow, don't worry about it."

Howe started to leave and Blackburn stopped him with, "But about Quill, sir?"

"Suppose we wait until next term? I'll be less busy then."

And Blackburn said, "Very good, sir, and thank you."

In his office the little encounter seemed less funny to Howe, was even in some indeterminate way disturbing. He made an effort to put it from his mind by turning to what was sure to disturb him more, the Tertan letter read in the new interpretation. He found what he had always found, the same florid leaps beyond fact and meaning, the same headlong certainty. But as his eye passed over the familiar scrawl it caught his own name and for the second time that hour he felt the race of his blood.

"The Paraclete," Tertan had written to the Dean, "from a Greek word meaning to stand in place of, but going beyond the primitive idea to mean traditionally the helper, the one who comforts and assists, cannot without fundamental loss be jettisoned. Even if taken no longer in the supernatural case, the concept remains deeply in the human consciousness inevitably. Humanitarianism is no reply, for not every man stands in the place of every other man for this other's comrade comfort. But certain are chosen out of the human race to be the consoler of some other. Of these, for example, is Joseph Barker Howe, Ph.D. Of intellects not the first yet of true intellect and lambent instructions, given to that which is intuitive and irrational, not to what is logical in the strict word, what is judged by him is of the heart and not the head. Here is one chosen, in that he chooses himself to stand in the place of another for comfort and consolation. To him more than another I give my gratitude, with all respect to our Dean who reads this, a noble man, but merely dedicated, not consecrated. But not in the aspect of the Paraclete only is Dr. Joseph Barker Howe established, for he must be the Paraclete to another aspect of himself, that which is driven and persecuted by the lack of understanding in the world at large, so that he in himself embodies the full history of man's tribulations and, overflowing upon others, notably the present writer, is the ultimate end."

This was love. There was no escape from it. Try as Howe might to remember that Tertan was mad and all his emotions invalidated, he could not destroy the effect upon him of his student's stern, affectionate regard. He had betrayed not only a power of mind but a power of love. And however firmly he held before his attention the fact of Tertan's madness, he could do nothing to banish the physical sensation of gratitude he felt. He had never thought of himself as "driven and persecuted" and he did not now. But still he could not make meaningless his sensation of gratitude. The pitiable Tertan sternly pitied him, and comfort came from Tertan's never-to-be comforted mind.

III

In an academic community, even an efficient one, official matters move slowly. The term drew to a close with no action in the case of Tertan, and Joseph Howe had to confront a curious problem. How should he grade his strange student, Tertan?

Tertan's final examination had been no different from all his other writing, and what did one "give" such a student? De Witt must have his *A*, that was clear. Johnson would get a *B*. With Casebeer it was a question of a *B–* or a *C+*, and Stettenhover, who had been crammed by the team tutor to fill half a blue-book with his thin feminine scrawl, would have his *C–* which he would accept with mingled indifference and resentment. But with Tertan it was not so easy.

The boy was still in the college process and his name could not be omitted from the grade sheet. Yet what should a mind under suspicion of madness be graded? Until the medical verdict was given, it was for Howe to continue as Tertan's teacher and to keep his judgment pedagogical. Impossible to give him an *F*: he had not failed. *B* was for Johnson's stolid mediocrity. He could not be put on the edge of passing with Stettenhover, for he exactly did not pass. In energy and richness of intellect he was perhaps even De Witt's superior, and Howe toyed grimly with the notion of giving him an *A*, but that would lower the value of the *A* De Witt had won with his beautiful and clear, if still arrogant, mind. There was a notation which the Registrar recognized — Inc. for Incomplete and in the horrible comedy of the situation, Howe considered that. But really only a mark of M. for Mad would serve.

In his perplexity, Howe sought the Dean, but the Dean was out of town. In the end, he decided to maintain the *A–* he had given Tertan at midterm. After all, there had been no falling away from that quality. He entered it on the grade sheet with something like bravado.

Academic time moves quickly. A college year is not really a year, lacking as it does three months. And it is endlessly divided into units which, at their beginning, appear larger than they are — terms, half-terms, months, weeks. And the ultimate unit, the hour, is not really an hour, lacking as it does ten minutes. And so the new term advanced rapidly and one day the fields about the town were all brown, cleared of even the few thin patches of snow which had lingered so long.

Howe, as he lectured on the romantic poets, became conscious of Blackburn emanating wrath. Blackburn did it well, did it with enormous dignity. He did not stir in his seat, he kept his eyes fixed on Howe in perfect attention, but he abstained from using his notebook. There was no mistaking what he proposed to himself as an atti-tude. His elbow on the writing-wing of the chair, his chin on the curled fingers of his hand, he was the embodiment of intellectual indignation. He was thinking his own thoughts, would give no public offense, yet would claim his due, was not to be in-timidated. Howe knew that he would present himself at the end of the hour.

Blackburn entered the office without invitation. He did not smile, there was no cajolery about him. Without invitation he sat down beside Howe's desk. He did not speak until he had taken the bluebook from his pocket. He said, "What does this mean, sir?"

It was a sound and conservative student tactic. Said in the usual way it meant, "How could you have so misunderstood me?" or "What does this mean for my future in the course?" But there were none of the humbler tones in Blackburn's way of saying it.

Howe made the established reply, "I think that's for you to tell me."

Blackburn continued icy. "I'm sure I can't, sir."

There was a silence between them. Both dropped their eyes to the blue-book on the desk. On its cover Howe had penciled: "*F*. This is very poor work."

Howe picked up the blue-book. There was always the possibility of injustice. The teacher may be bored by the mass of papers and not wholly attentive. A phrase, even the student's handwriting, may irritate him unreasonably. "Well," said Howe, "let's go through it."

He opened the first page. "Now here: you write, 'In *The Ancient Mariner*, Coleridge lives in and transports us to a honey-sweet world where all is rich and strange, a world of charm to which we can escape from the humdrum existence of our daily lives, the world of romance. Here, in this warm and honey-sweet land of charming dreams we can relax and enjoy ourselves.'"

Howe lowered the paper and waited with a neutral look for Blackburn to speak. Blackburn returned the look boldly, did not speak, sat stolid and lofty. At last Howe said, speaking gently, "Did you mean that, or were you just at a loss for something to say?"

"You imply that I was just 'bluffing'?" The quotation marks hung palpable in the air about the word.

"I'd like to know. I'd prefer believing that you were bluffing to believing that you really thought this."

Blackburn's eyebrows went up. From the height of a great and firm-based idea he looked at his teacher. He clasped the crags for a moment and then pounced, craftily, suavely. "Do you mean, Dr. Howe, that there aren't two opinions possible?"

It was superbly done in its air of putting all of Howe's intellectual life into the balance. Howe remained patient and simple. "Yes, many opinions are possible, but not this one. Whatever anyone believes of *The Ancient Mariner*, no one can in reason believe that it represents a — a honey-sweet world in which we can relax."

"But that is what I *feel*, sir."

This was well done too. Howe said, "Look, Mr. Blackburn. Do you really relax with hunger and thirst, the heat and the sea-serpents, the dead men with staring eyes, Life in Death and the skeletons? Come now, Mr. Blackburn."

Blackburn made no answer and Howe pressed forward. "Now you say of Wordsworth, 'Of peasant stock himself, he turned from the effete life of the salons and found in the peasant the hope of a flaming revolution which would sweep away all the old ideas. This is the subject of his best poems.'"

Beaming at his teacher with youthful eagerness, Blackburn said, "Yes, sir, a rebel, a bringer of light to suffering mankind. I see him as a kind of Prothemeus."

"A kind of what?"

"Prothemeus, sir."

"Think, Mr. Blackburn. We were talking about him only today and I mentioned his name a dozen times. You don't mean Prothemeus. You mean —" Howe waited but there was no response.

"You mean Prometheus."

Blackburn gave no assent and Howe took the reins. "You've done a bad job here, Mr. Blackburn, about as bad as could be done." He saw Blackburn stiffen and his genial face harden again. "It shows either a lack of preparation or a complete lack of understanding." He saw Blackburn's face begin to go to pieces and he stopped.

"Oh, sir," Blackburn burst out, "I've never had a mark like this before, never anything below a *B*, never. A thing like this has never happened to me before."

It must be true, it was a statement too easily verified. Could it be that other instructors accepted such flaunting nonsense? Howe wanted to end the interview. "I'll set it down to lack of preparation," he said. "I know you're busy. That's not an excuse but it's an explanation. Now suppose you really prepare and then take another quiz in two weeks. We'll forget this one and count the other."

Blackburn squirmed with pleasure and gratitude. "Thank you, sir. You're really very kind, very kind."

Howe rose to conclude the visit. "All right then — in two weeks."

It was that day that the Dean imparted to Howe the conclusion of the case of Tertan. It was simple and a little anticlimactic. A physician had been called in, and had said the word, given the name.

"A classic case, he called it," the Dean said. "Not a doubt in the world," he said. His eyes were full of miserable pity and he clutched at a word. "A classic case, a classic case." To his aid and to Howe's there came the Parthenon and the form of the Greek drama, the Aristotelian logic, Racine and the Well-Tempered Clavichord, the blueness of the Aegean and its clear sky. Classic — that is to say, without a doubt, perfect in its way, a veritable model, and, as the Dean had been told, sure to take a perfectly predictable and inevitable course to a foreknown conclusion.

It was not only pity that stood in the Dean's eyes. For a moment there was fear too. "Terrible," he said, "it is simply terrible."

Then he went on briskly. "Naturally we've told the boy nothing. And naturally we won't. His tuition's paid by his scholarship and we'll continue him on the rolls until the end of the year. That will be kindest. After that the matter will be out of our control. We'll see, of course, that he gets into the proper hands. I'm told there will be no change, he'll go on like this, be as good as this, for four to six months. And so we'll just go along as usual."

So Tertan continued to sit in Section 5 of English IA, to his classmates still a figure of curiously dignified fun, symbol to most of them of the respectable but absurd intellectual life. But to his teacher he was now very different. He had not changed — he was still the greyhound casting for the scent of ideas and Howe could see that he was still the same Tertan, but he could not feel it. What he felt as he looked at the boy sitting in his accustomed place was the hard blank of a fact. The fact itself was formidable and depressing. But what Howe was chiefly aware of was that he had permitted the metamorphosis of Tertan from person to fact.

As much as possible he avoided seeing Tertan's upraised hand and eager eye. But the fact did not know of its mere factuality, it continued its existence as if it were Tertan, hand up and eye questioning, and one day it appeared in Howe's office with a document.

"Even the spirit who lives egregiously, above the herd, must have its relations with the fellowman," Tertan declared. He laid the document on Howe's desk. It was headed "Quill and Scroll Society of Dwight College. Application for Membership."

"In most ways these are crass minds," Tertan said, touching the paper. "Yet as a whole, bound together in their common love of letters, they transcend their intellectual lacks, since it is not a paradox that the whole is greater than the sum of its parts."

"When are the elections?" Howe asked.

"They take place tomorrow."

"I certainly hope you will be successful."

"Thank you. Would you wish to implement that hope?" A rather dirty finger pointed to the bottom of the sheet. "A faculty recommender is necessary," Tertan said stiffly, and waited.

"And you wish me to recommend you?"

"It would be an honor."

"You may use my name."

Tertan's finger pointed again. "It must be a written sponsorship, signed by the sponsor." There was a large blank space on the form under the heading, "Opinion of Faculty Sponsor."

This was almost another thing and Howe hesitated. Yet there was nothing else to do and he took out his fountain pen. He wrote, "Mr. Ferdinand Tertan is marked by his intense devotion to letters and by his exceptional love of all things of the mind." To this he signed his name which looked bold and assertive on the white page. It disturbed him, the strange affirming power of a name. With a businesslike air, Tertan whipped up the paper, folded it with decision and put it into his pocket. He bowed and took his departure, leaving Howe with the sense of having done something oddly momentous.

And so much now seemed odd and momentous to Howe that should not have seemed so. It was odd and momentous, he felt, when he sat with Blackburn's second quiz before him and wrote in an excessively firm hand the grade of *C*–. The paper was a clear, an indisputable failure. He was carefully and consciously committing a cowardice. Blackburn had told the truth when he had pleaded his past record. Howe had consulted it in the Dean's office. It showed no grade lower than a *B*–. A canvass of some of Blackburn's previous instructors had brought vague attestations to the adequate powers of a student imperfectly remembered and sometimes surprise that his abilities could be questioned at all.

As he wrote the grade, Howe told himself that this cowardice sprang from an unwillingness to have more dealings with a student he disliked. He knew it was simpler than that. He knew he feared Blackburn: that was the absurd truth. And cowardice did not solve the matter after all. Blackburn, flushed with a first success, attacked at once. The minimal passing grade had not assuaged his feelings and he sat at Howe's desk and again the blue-book lay between them. Blackburn said nothing. With an enormous impudence, he was waiting for Howe to speak and explain himself.

At last Howe said sharply and rudely, "Well?" His throat was tense and the blood was hammering in his head His mouth was tight with anger at himself for his disturbance.

Blackburn's glance was almost baleful. "This is impossible, sir."

"But there it is," Howe answered.

"Sir?" Blackburn had not caught the meaning but his tone was still haughty.

Impatiently Howe said, "There it is, plain as day. Are you here to complain again?"

"Indeed I am, sir." There was surprise in Blackburn's voice that Howe should ask the question.

"I shouldn't complain if I were you. You did a thoroughly bad job on your first quiz. This one is a little, only a very little, better." This was not true. If anything, it was worse.

"That might be a matter of opinion, sir."

"It is a matter of opinion. Of my opinion."

"Another opinion might be different, sir."

"You really believe that?" Howe said.

"Yes." The omission of the "sir" was monumental.

"Whose, for example?"

"The Dean's, for example." Then the fleshy jaw came forward a little. "Or a certain literary critic's, for example."

It was colossal and almost too much for Blackburn himself to handle. The solidity of his face almost crumpled under it. But he withstood his own audacity and went on. "And the Dean's opinion might be guided by the knowledge that the person who gave me this mark is the man whom a famous critic, the most eminent judge of literature in this country, called a drunken man. The Dean might think twice about whether such a man is fit to teach Dwight students."

Howe said in quiet admonition, "Blackburn, you're mad," meaning no more than to check the boy's extravagance.

But Blackburn paid no heed. He had another shot in the locker. "And the Dean might be guided by the information, of which I have evidence, documentary evidence," — he slapped his breast pocket twice — "that this same person personally recommended to the college literary society, the oldest in the country, that he personally recommended a student who is crazy, who threw the meeting into an uproar, a psychiatric case. The Dean might take that into account."

Howe was never to learn the details of that "uproar." He had always to content himself with the dim but passionate picture which at that moment sprang into his mind, of Tertan standing on some abstract height and madly denouncing the multitude of Quill and Scroll who howled him down.

He sat quiet a moment and looked at Blackburn. The ferocity had entirely gone from the student's face. He sat regarding his teacher almost benevolently. He had played a good card and now, scarcely at all unfriendly, he was waiting to see the effect. Howe took up the blue-book and negligently sifted through it. He read a page, closed the book, struck out the *C–* and wrote an *F*.

"Now you may take the paper to the Dean," he said. "You may tell him that after reconsidering it, I lowered the grade."

The gasp was audible. "Oh sir!" Blackburn cried. "Please!" His face was agonized. "It means my graduation, my livelihood, my future. Don't do this to me."

"It's done already."

Blackburn stood up. "I spoke rashly, sir, hastily I had no intention, no real intention, of seeing the Dean. It rests with you — entirely, entirely. I hope you will restore the first mark."

"Take the matter to the Dean or not, just as you choose. The grade is what you deserve and it stands."

Blackburn's head dropped. "And will I be failed at mid-term, sir?"

"Of course."

From deep out of Blackburn's great chest rose a cry of anguish. "Oh sir, if you want me to go down on my knees to you, I will, I will."

Howe looked at him in amazement.

"I will, I will. On my knees, sir. This mustn't, mustn't happen."

He spoke so literally, meaning so very truly that his knees and exactly his knees were involved and seeming to think that he was offering something of tangible value to his teacher, that Howe, whose head had become icy clear in the nonsensical drama, thought, "The boy is mad," and began to speculate fantastically whether something in himself attracted or developed aberration. He could see himself standing absurdly before the Dean and saying, "I've found another. This time it's the vice-president of the Council, the manager of the debating team, and secretary of Quill and Scroll."

One more such discovery, he thought, and he himself would be discovered! And there, suddenly, Blackburn was on his knees with a thump, his huge thighs straining his trousers, his hands outstretched in a great gesture of supplication.

With a cry, Howe shoved back his swivel chair and it rolled away on its casters half across the little room. Blackburn knelt for a moment to nothing at all, then got to his feet.

Howe rose abruptly. He said, "Blackburn, you will stop acting like an idiot. Dust your knees off, take your paper and get out. You've behaved like a fool and a malicious person. You have half a term to do a decent job. Keep your silly mouth shut and try to do it. Now get out."

Blackburn's head was low. He raised it and there was a pious light in his eyes. "Will you shake hands, sir?" he said. He thrust out his hand.

"I will not," Howe said.

Head and hand sank together. Blackburn picked up his blue-book and walked to the door. He turned and said, "Thank you, sir." His back, as he departed, was heavy with tragedy and stateliness.

IV

After years of bad luck with the weather, the College had a perfect day for Commencement. It was wonderfully bright, the air so transparent, the wind so brisk that no one could resist talking about it.

As Howe set out for the campus he heard Hilda calling from the back yard. She called, "Professor, professor," and came running to him.

Howe said, "What's this 'professor' business?"

"Mother told me," Hilda said. "You've been promoted. And I want to take your picture."

"Next year," said Howe. "I won't be a professor until next year. And you know better than to call anybody 'professor.'"

"It was just in fun," Hilda said. She seemed disappointed.

"But you can take my picture if you want. I won't look much different next year." Still, it was frightening. It might mean that he was to stay in this town all his life.

Hilda brightened. "Can I take it in this?" she said, and touched the gown he carried over his arm.

Howe laughed. "Yes, you can take it in this."

"I'll get my things and meet you in front of Otis," Hilda said. "I have the background all picked out."

On the campus the Commencement crowd was already large. It stood about in eager, nervous little family groups. As he crossed, Howe was greeted by a student, capped and gowned, glad of the chance to make an event for his parents by introducing one of his teachers. It was while Howe stood there chatting that he saw Tertan.

He had never seen anyone quite so alone, as though a circle had been woven about him to separate him from the gay crowd on the campus. Not that Tertan was not gay, he was the gayest of all. Three weeks had passed since Howe had last seen him, the weeks of examination, the lazy week before Commencement, and this was now a different Tertan. On his head he wore a Panama hat, broad-brimmed and fine, of the shape associated with South American planters. He wore a suit of raw silk, luxurious but yellowed with age and much too tight, and he sported a whangee cane. He walked sedately, the hat tilted at a devastating angle, the stick coming up and down in time to his measured tread. He had, Howe guessed, outfitted himself to greet the day in the clothes of that ruined father whose existence was on record in the Dean's office. Gravely and arrogantly he surveyed the scene — in it, his whole bearing seemed to say, but not of it. With his haughty step, with his flashing eye, Tertan was coming nearer. Howe did not wish to be seen. He shifted his position slightly. When he looked again, Tertan was not in sight.

The chapel clock struck the quarter hour. Howe detached himself from his chat and hurried to Otis Hall at the far end of the campus. Hilda had not yet come. He went up into the high portico and, using the glass of the door for a mirror, put on his gown, adjusted the hood on his shoulders and set the mortarboard on his head. When he came down the steps Hilda had arrived.

Nothing could have told him more forcibly that a year had passed than the development of Hilda's photographic possessions from the box camera of the previous fall. By a strap about her neck was hung a leather case, so thick and strong, so carefully stitched and so molded to its contents that it could only hold a costly camera. The appearance was deceptive, Howe knew, for he had been present at the Aikens' pre-Christmas conference about its purchase. It was only a fairly good domestic camera. Still, it looked very impressive. Hilda carried another leather case from which she drew a collapsible tripod. Decisively she extended each of its gleaming legs and set it up on the path. She removed the camera from its case and fixed it to the tripod. In its compact efficiency the camera almost had a life of its own, but Hilda treated it with easy familiarity, looked into its eye, glanced casually at its gauges. Then from a pocket she took still another leather case and drew from it a small instrument through which she looked first at Howe, who began to feel inanimate and lost, and then at the sky. She made some adjustment on the instrument, then some adjustment on the camera. She swept the scene with her eye, found a spot and pointed the camera in its direction. She walked to the spot, stood on it and beckoned to Howe. With each new leather case, with each new instrument and with each new adjustment she had grown in ease and now she said, "Joe, will you stand here?"

Obediently Howe stood where he was bidden. She had yet another instrument. She took out a tape-measure on a mechanical spool. Kneeling down before Howe, she put the little metal ring of the tape under the tip of his shoe. At her request, Howe pressed it with his toe. When she had measured her distance, she nodded to Howe who released the tape. At a touch, it sprang back into the spool. "You have to be careful if you're going to get what you want," Hilda said. "I don't believe in all this snap-snap-snapping," she remarked loftily. Howe nodded in agreement, although he was beginning to think Hilda's care excessive.

Now at last the moment had come. Hilda squinted into the camera, moved the tripod slightly. She stood to the side, holding the plunger of the shutter-cable. "Ready," she said. "Will you relax, Joseph, please?" Howe realized that he was standing frozen. Hilda stood poised and precise as a setter, one hand holding the little cable, the other extended with curled dainty fingers like a dancer's, as if expressing to her subject the precarious delicacy of the moment. She pressed the plunger and there was the click. At once she stirred to action, got behind the camera, turned a new exposure. "Thank you," she said. "Would you stand under that tree and let me do a character study with light and shade?"

The childish absurdity of the remark restored Howe's ease. He went to the little tree. The pattern the leaves made on his gown was what Hilda was after. He had just taken a satisfactory position when he heard in the unmistakable voice, "Ah, Doctor! Having your picture taken?"

Howe gave up the pose and turned to Blackburn who stood on the walk, his hands behind his back, a little too large for his bachelor's gown. Annoyed that Blackburn should see him posing for a character study in light and shade, Howe said irritably, "Yes, having my picture taken."

Blackburn beamed at Hilda. "And the little photographer," he said. Hilda fixed her eyes on the ground and stood closer to her brilliant and aggressive camera. Blackburn, teetering on his heels, his hands behind his back, wholly prelatical and benignly patient, was not abashed at the silence. At last Howe said, "If you'll excuse us, Mr. Blackburn, we'll go on with the picture."

"Go right ahead, sir. I'm running along." But he only came closer. "Dr. Howe," he said fervently, "I want to tell you how glad I am that I was able to satisfy your standards at last."

Howe was surprised at the hard insulting brightness of his own voice and even Hilda looked up curiously as he said, "Nothing you have ever done has satisfied me and nothing you could ever do would satisfy me, Blackburn."

With a glance at Hilda, Blackburn made a gesture as if to hush Howe — as though all his former bold malice had taken for granted a kind of understanding between himself and his teacher, a secret which must not be betrayed to a third person. "I only meant, sir," he said, "that I was able to pass your course after all."

Howe said, "You didn't pass my course. I passed you out of my course. I passed you without even reading your paper. I wanted to be sure the college would be rid of you. And when all the grades were in and I did read your paper, I saw I was right not to have read it first."

Blackburn presented a stricken face. "It was very bad, sir?"

But Howe had turned away. The paper had been fantastic. The paper had been, if he wished to see it so, mad. It was at this moment that the Dean came up behind

Howe and caught his arm. "Hello, Joseph," he said. "We'd better be getting along, it's almost late."

He was not a familiar man, but when he saw Blackburn, who approached to greet him, he took Blackburn's arm, too. "Hello, Theodore," he said. Leaning forward on Howe's arm and on Blackburn's, he said, "Hello, Hilda dear." Hilda replied quietly, "Hello, Uncle George."

Still clinging to their arms, still linking Howe and Blackburn, the Dean said, "Another year gone, Joe, and we've turned out another crop. After you've been here a few years, you'll find it reasonably upsetting — you wonder how there can be so many graduating classes while you stay the same. But of course you don't stay the same." Then he said, "Well," sharply, to dismiss the thought. He pulled Blackburn's arm and swung him around to Howe. "Have you heard about Teddy Blackburn?" he asked. "He has a job already, before graduation, the first man of his class to be placed." Expectant of congratulations, Blackburn beamed at Howe. Howe remained silent.

"Isn't that good?" the Dean said. Still Howe did not answer and the Dean, puzzled and put out, turned to Hilda. "That's a very fine-looking camera, Hilda." She touched it with affectionate pride.

"Instruments of precision," said a voice. "Instruments of precision." Of the three with joined arms, Howe was the nearest to Tertan, whose gaze took in all the scene except the smile and the nod which Howe gave him. The boy leaned on his cane. The broad-brimmed hat, canting jauntily over his eye, confused the image of his face that Howe had established, suppressed the rigid lines of the ascetic and brought out the baroque curves. It made an effect of perverse majesty.

"Instruments of precision," said Tertan for the last time, addressing no one, making a casual comment to the universe. And it occurred to Howe that Tertan might not be referring to Hilda's equipment. The sense of the thrice-woven circle of the boy's loneliness smote him fiercely. Tertan stood in majestic jauntiness, superior to all the scene, but his isolation made Howe ache with a pity of which Tertan was more the cause than the object, so general and indiscriminate was it.

Whether in his sorrow he made some unintended movement toward Tertan which the Dean checked or whether the suddenly tightened grip on his arm was the Dean's own sorrow and fear, he did not know. Tertan watched them in the incurious way people watch a photograph being taken and suddenly the thought that, to the boy, it must seem that the three were posing for a picture together made Howe detach himself almost rudely from the Dean's grasp.

"I promised Hilda another picture," he announced — needlessly, for Tertan was no longer there, he had vanished in the last sudden flux of visitors who, now that the band had struck up, were rushing nervously to find seats.

"You'd better hurry," the Dean said. "I'll go along, it's getting late for me." He departed and Blackburn walked stately by his side.

Howe again took his position under the little tree which cast its shadow over his face and gown. "Just hurry, Hilda, won't you?" he said. Hilda held the cable at arm's length, her other arm crooked and her fingers crisped. She rose on her toes and said

"Ready," and pressed the release. "Thank you," she said gravely and began to dismantle her camera as he hurried off to join the procession.

1943

Critical thinking points: After you've read

1) *What might be some of the reasons the story begins and ends with Hilda and her camera?*
2) *Do you think Tertan is "mad"? Why or why not?*
3) *The essay on the teacher's poetry says, "The Howes do no harm, but they do no good when positive good is demanded of all responsible men. Or do the Howes indeed do no harm?" Do you think this is true within this story? Why or why not?*
4) *The Dean says, after hearing Tertan's midterm grade, "Might be a good idea if some of our boys went crazy — just a little." What do you think he might mean by that?*
5) *What do you think Trilling meant when he said that in an academic community "offical matters move slowly" and "academic time moves quickly"? In your experience, is this true? Why or why not?*
6) *Read or reread Charles Macomb Flandreau's excerpt from* Diary of a Freshman. *Compare that student's conference with his advisor to Blackburn's conferences with Howe.*
7) *Why do you think Howe "fears" Blackburn? Does he fear him at the end of the story? Why or why not?*

Some possibilities for writing

1) *Howe's first assignment is "Who I am and why I came to Dwight College." We hear some of Tertan's response, but little of the others. Choose another student — Blackburn, De Witt, Casebeer, or Stettenhover — and write at least the beginning of the essay you imagine he turned in.*
2) *The same as above but write an answer the professor himself might give.*
3) *Short stories usually involve one or more characters changing in some significant ways. Which characters in this story seem to change? What is the nature of this change and why does it occur?*
4) *Write a one-page narrative called "Who I am and why I came to this college."*
5) *Compare Blackburn and Tertan as students. Do they seem to stand for certain types? Write an essay about what an "education" means to each of them. What specifically within the story leads you to your conclusions?*

April Inventory

W. D. Snodgrass

"

And one by one the solid scholars
Get the degrees, the jobs, the dollars.

"

Critical thinking points: As you read

1) *What is an "inventory" and why would a person take one? What do people usually take an "inventory" of?*
2) *Look for nature images throughout this poem. Why are they appropriate in a poem about aging?*
3) *At what kind of school does the narrator teach? What details in the poem support this?*

The green catalpa tree has turned
All white the cherry blooms once more.
In one whole year I haven't learned
A blessed thing they pay you for.
The blossoms snow down in my hair;
The trees and I will soon be bare.

The trees have more than I to spare.
The sleek, expensive girls I teach,
Younger and pinker every year,
Bloom gradually out of reach.
The pear tree lets its petals drop
Like dandruff on a tabletop.

William Dewitt Snodgrass (b. 1926) is a recipient of the Pulitzer Prize for Poetry and a Fellow of the Academy of American Poets. His books include *Heart's Needle*; *After Experience*; *The Fuerer Bunker: A Cycle of Poems in Progress*; and *Selected Poems 1957–1987*.

The girls have grown so young by now
I have to nudge myself to stare.
This year they smile and mind me how
My teeth are falling with my hair.
In thirty years I may not get
Younger, shrewder, or out of debt.

The tenth time, just a year ago,
I made myself a little list
Of all the things I'd ought to know,
Then told my parents, analyst,
And everyone who's trusted me
I'd be substantial, presently.

I haven't read one book about
A book or memorized one plot.
Or found a mind I did not doubt.
I learned one date. And then forgot.
And one by one the solid scholars
Get the degrees, the jobs, the dollars.

And smile above their starchy collars.
I taught my classes Whitehead's notions;
One lovely girl, a song of Mahler's.
Lacking a source-book or promotions,
I showed one child the colors of
A luna moth and how to love.

I taught myself to name my name,
To bark back, loosen love and crying
To ease my woman so she came,
To ease an old man who was dying.
I have not learned how often I
Can win, can love, but choose to die.

I have not learned there is a lie
Love shall be blonder, slimmer, younger;
That my equivocating eye
Loves only by my body's hunger;
That I have forces, true to feel,
Or that the lovely world is real.

While scholars speak authority

And wear their ulcers on their sleeves,
My eyes in spectacles shall see
These trees procure and spend their leaves.
There is a value underneath
The gold and silver in my teeth.

Though trees turn bare and girls turn wives,
We shall afford our costly seasons
There is a gentleness survives
That will outspeak and has its reasons.
There is a loveliness exists,
Preserves us, not for specialists.

1957

Critical thinking points: After you've read

1) *Why do you believe this inventory is taken in April? How might it be different if it was taken in some other month, such as December or August?*
2) *What might Snodgrass mean when he says in the second stanza, "The sleek, expensive girls I teach, / Younger and pinker every year, / Bloom gradually out of reach"?*
3) *What might Snodgrass mean when he says in the ninth stanza, "There is a value underneath / The gold and silver in my teeth"? What is another way of saying this?*
4) *Why does the poet mix nature images with images of "girls" throughout the poem?*
5) *Why might the narrator's age be important to your reading of the poem?*

Some possibilities for writing

1) *Take an "inventory" of your own education to this point. What kinds of things have you "learned" so far? What haven't you learned that you wanted and/or expected to by this time? Why do you think this is so?*
2) *Write a dialogue between Snodgrass and Jacob Neusner. The subject is their respective theories of education.*
3) *Rewrite the poem, perhaps even as prose, as if it were set in a different month or season.*
4) *Does the narrator of this poem meet your expectations of what a teacher should be? Why or why not?*
5) *Research British mathematician and metaphysician Alfred North Whitehead (1861–1947) and Austrian composer and conductor Gustav Mahler (1860–1911). Discuss why the poet might refer to them in this poem.*

Further Suggestions for Writing — "Teacher, Teacher"

1) Write an essay on "How to impress a professor."
2) Do you think that students are in the best position to be able to evaluate their teachers? Defend your answer.
3) Compare and contrast the University system in the U.S. to one from some other country.
4) Why do students cheat?
5) Write a brief history of the concept of Tenure on College Campuses.
6) Taking into consideration all the problems and shortcomings of the lecture format, what kinds of alternative teaching methods could be put into place?
7) Argue for or against Tenure on College Campuses.
8) Argue for or against a policy at your school banning Romantic/Sexual Relationships between Teachers and Students.
9) Research and define the terms "passive learning" and "active learning." Which seems to be the way you have learned previously? Which seems to be the dominant style you have encountered so far at your current school?
10) Choose a course that you are currently taking that is taught primarily in the "passive" style and/or in the lecture mode. Make some considered and serious suggestions as to how it might be taught in a more "active" manner.
11) Many colleges have an honor system that requires students to sign a pledge not to cheat and to report others they observe cheating. Does yours? Write an essay in which you advocate or oppose the establishment of an honor system at your college.
12) Students are often uncertain about what constitutes academic dishonesty, especially what qualifies as plagiarism. On what issues of academic dishonesty (definitions, policies, sanctions) do you think there is confusion or ambiguity?
13) Write about a teacher you thought represented one thing but turned out to be much different. For example, the health teacher who you discovered smokes or the dull math teacher who is funny out of class.
14) Public and private lives differ in and out of the classroom for both teachers and students. How are you the same and/or different in the classroom compared to dealing with your friends and family?
15) Can or should professors set out to "change the lives" of students? Why or why not?
16) Research shows that the way an instructor teaches is a reflection of his or her learning style. For instance, if a teacher is a tactile concrete or kinesthetic learner, he or she will build the class around discussion and hands-on learning. Carefully observe one of your teachers for at least three class periods. Does that teacher have a liberal or traditional style? What part of

that teacher's style is a reflection of his or her pedagogy? From your observations, speculate your teacher's learning style.

17) College students who are not self-motivated often look to teachers for constructive guidance and want to "obey" their teachers. Compare a teacher in high school who served as a constant guide and overseer to a teacher in college who does not function in those roles.

18) Write a brief report for your class on the procedures in place for contesting a grade at your school.

19) Interview faculty about "success stories" of some of their students who they have mentored. Can you come up with some generalizations (and support them) that teachers remember about students?

20) Does your school offer distance education courses? Research the pros and cons of distance education courses. Argue for or against distance education courses.

21) Choose one of your responses to "Some possibilities for writing" in this section and do further research on some aspect of the topic you addressed in your narrative. Write about how and why this new information would have improved your previous effort.

Selected Films — "Teacher, Teacher"

Children of a Lesser God (1986, USA). A speech teacher at a school for the deaf finds himself drawn to a tough, headstrong, beautiful janitor. Adapted from the play by Mark Medoff. Romantic drama. 119 min. R

Educating Rita (1983, Great Britain). A bright but unschooled hairdresser hires a tutor (a dissolute, alcoholic Michael Caine) to expand her literary horizons. Drama. 110 min. PG-13

Fast Break (1979, USA). Deli clerk Gabe Kaplan fast-talks his way into a job coaching college basketball. Sports/Comedy. 107 min. PG

The Freshman (1990, USA). Marlon Brando does a Godfather send-up as he gives a young film student (*Ferris Bueller*'s Matthew Broderick) an education in the school of life. Comedy. 102 min. PG

Good Will Hunting (1997, USA) The smartest kid at college turns out to be the janitor. Drama. 126 min. R

Gross Anatomy (1989, USA). A dying professor inspires a bright but lazy medical student. Comedy/Drama. 109 min. PG-13

Lucky Jim (1957, Great Britain). A lowly college lecturer bungles his attempts to impress his department head. Comedy. 95 min.

Oleanna (1994, USA). David Mamet wrote and directed this adaption of his controversial play about collegiate sexual harrassment and sexual politics. Drama. 89 min.

The Paper Chase (1973, USA). First-year law students toughen up to survive the acid wit of their intimidating professor (John Houseman). Comedy/Drama. 111 min. PG

Surviving Desire (1991, USA). A neurotic English professor falls for his student, who, for her part, is using the affair as fuel for her writing. Romantic comedy. 86 min.

For Critical Thinking Points on these films, see Appendix (p. 335).

Chapter Five

Been There, Done That: Looking Forward, Looking Back

Education can change some people or help them recognize how they have stayed the same.

This chapter will explore —

- Imagining life after graduation
- Finding a vocation
- Looking back in order to go forward
- Short-term and long-term goal setting

The Speech the Graduates Didn't Hear

Jacob Neusner

"
We the faculty take no pride in our educational achievements with you. We have prepared you for a world that does not exist.
"

Critical thinking points: As you read

1) Imagine that this speech is being delivered as an actual commencement address at your graduation from college. How would you feel? How would your parents feel? What questions, complaints, and/or cries for action might come from such a speech?

2) Watch for stereotypes concerning students and faculty in Neusner's speech. What are some of them?

3) What is the tone of the speech? Why is tone something to consider in a piece like this? What is Neusner's attitude toward students?

We the faculty take no pride in our educational achievements with you. We have prepared you for a world that does not exist, indeed, that cannot exist. You have spent four years supposing that failure leaves no record. You have learned at Brown that when your work goes poorly, the painless solution is to drop out. But starting now, in the world to which you go, failure marks you. Confronting difficulty by quitting leaves you changed. Outside Brown, quitters are no heroes.

With us you could argue about why your errors were not errors, why mediocre work really was excellent, why you could take pride in routine and slipshod presentation. Most of you, after all, can look back on honor grades for most of what you have done. So, here grades can have meant little in distinguishing the excellent from the ordinary. But tomorrow, in the world to which you go, you had best not defend errors but learn from them. You will be ill-advised to demand praise for what does not deserve it, and abuse those who do not give it.

Jewish scholar and author Jacob Neusner (b. 1932) has written nearly two hundred books on Judaism including several multivolume works; textbooks for children and college students; and, books for the general reader. His impressive level of productivity inspired Roy Bongartz, in *Publishers Weekly*, to liken Neusner to "the inexhaustible pillar of salt that filled the waters of the seven seas in ancient legend." Neusner is currently retired in Florida.

For four years we created an altogether forgiving world, in which whatever slight effort you gave was all that was demanded. When you did not keep appointments, we made new ones. When your work came in beyond the deadline, we pretended not to care.

Worse still, when you were boring, we acted as if you were saying something important. When you were garrulous and talked to hear yourself talk, we listened as if it mattered. When you tossed on our desks writing upon which you had not labored, we read it and even responded, as though you earned a response. When you were dull, we pretended you were smart. When you were predictable, unimaginative, and routine, we listened as if to new and wonderful things. When you demanded free lunch, we served it. And all this why?

Despite your fantasies, it was not even that we wanted to be liked by you. It was that we did not want to be bothered, and the easy way out was pretense: smiles and easy *B's*.

It is conventional to quote in addresses such as these. Let me quote someone you've never heard of: Professor Carter A. Daniel, Rutgers University (*Chronicle of Higher Education*, May 7, 1979):

> College has spoiled you by reading papers that don't deserve to be read, listening to comments that don't deserve a hearing, paying attention even to the lazy, ill-informed, and rude. We had to do it, for the sake of education. But nobody will ever do it again. College has deprived you of adequate preparation for the last fifty years. It has failed you by being easy, free, forgiving, attentive, comfortable, interesting, unchallenging fun. Good luck tomorrow.

That is why, on this commencement day, we have nothing in which to take much pride.

Oh, yes, there is one more thing. Try not to act toward your co-workers and bosses as you have acted toward us. I mean, when they give you what you want but have not earned, don't abuse them, insult them, act out with them your parlous relationships with your parents. This too we have tolerated. It was, as I said, not to be liked by peer-paralyzed adolescents, fools so shallow as to imagine professors care not about education but about popularity. It was, again, to be rid of you. So go, unlearn the lies we taught you. To life!

1983

Critical thinking points: After you've read

1) How is this "speech" similar to and/or different from others you've heard? What specific items that are usually present in a traditional commencement address are missing here?

2) *Is Neusner's speech based on fact or opinion? Is it based on both? Cite examples from the text that support your ideas.*
3) *Commencement speeches are often positive and congratulatory. What lesson might Neusner be trying to offer students with a speech like this?*
4) *In Professor Daniel's quote he says, "We had to do it, for the sake of education." What do you think he might have meant?*
5) *Neusner ends his speech with, "So go, unlearn the lies we taught you. To life!" How might this inspire?*
6) *List the stereotypes of students and faculty in Neusner's speech. Why might some people believe those characteristics are true?*

Some possibilities for writing

1) *Write a speech for your instructors called "The Speech the Faculty Didn't Hear."*
2) *Neusner's speech originally appeared in Brown University's* **The Daily Herald.** *Write a letter to the editor supporting or negating Neusner's speech.*
3) *Compare and contrast the kind of person you think the author of this piece is to the kind of person who may have written "Grading Your Professors." Are they similar or different? Why do you think so? Do you think Neusner's attitude and/ or tone has changed? Why or why not?*
4) *Assume that Neusner is correct in his assumptions. Write an essay that speculates some of the causes of this situation.*
5) *Assume that Neusner is correct in his assumptions. Write a proposal that would begin to remedy this situation.*

The Eighty-Yard Run

Irwin Shaw

How long ago? It was autumn then and the ground was getting hard
because the nights were cold and leaves from the maples around the
stadium blew across the practice fields in gusts of wind and
the girls were beginning to put polo coats over their sweaters when
they came to watch practice in the afternoons. . . . Fifteen years.

Critical thinking points: As you read

1) *What do you associate with the name "Christian Darling"?*
2) *Why does Christian Darling hold onto the memory of the eighty-yard run?
   What details in the story portray that this was a pivotal moment in his life?*
3) *The story takes place from 1925 to 1940. What are some clues to the era?*
4) *What are some stereotypes associated with student athletes, particularly
   football players? Does Christian conform to any of these?*

The pass was high and wide and he jumped for it, feeling it slap flatly against his
hands, as he shook his hips to throw off the halfback who was diving at him. The
center floated by, his hands desperately brushing Darling's knee as Darling picked
his feet up high and delicately ran over a blocker and an opposing linesman in a
jumble on the ground near the scrimmage line. He had ten yards in the clear and
picked up speed, breathing easily, feeling his thigh pads rising and falling against his
legs, listening to the sound of cleats behind him, pulling away from them, watching
the other backs heading him off toward the sideline, the whole picture, the men closing in on him, the blockers fighting for position, the ground he had to cross, all
suddenly clear in his head, for the first time in his life not a meaningless confusion of
men, sounds, speed. He smiled a little to himself as he ran, holding the ball lightly in
front of him with his two hands, his knees pumping high, his hips twisting in the
almost-girlish run of a back in a broken field. The first halfback came at him and he
fed him his leg, then swung at the last moment, took the shock of the man's shoulder

---

Irwin Shaw (1913–1984) was a Brooklyn-born writer whose works are marked by dramatic
intensity and social awareness. His stories are collected in *Five Decades* (1978).

without breaking stride, ran right through him, his cleats biting securely into the turf. There was only the safety man now, coming warily at him, his arms crooked, hands spread. Darling tucked the ball in, spurted at him, driving hard, hurling himself along, his legs pounding, knees high, all two hundred pounds bunched into controlled attack. He was sure he was going to get past the safety man, stiff-armed him, feeling blood spurt instantaneously from the man's nose onto his hand, seeing his face go awry, head turned, mouth pulled to one side. He pivoted away, keeping the arm locked, dropping the safety man as he ran easily toward the goal line, with the drumming of cleats diminishing behind him.

How long ago? It was autumn then and the ground was getting hard because the nights were cold and leaves from the maples around the stadium blew across the practice fields in gusts of wind and the girls were beginning to put polo coats over their sweaters when they came to watch practice in the afternoons. . . . Fifteen years. Darling walked slowly over the same ground in the spring twilight, in his neat shoes, a man of thirty-five dressed in a double-breasted suit, ten pounds heavier in the fifteen years, but not fat, with the years between 1925 and 1940 showing in his face.

The coach was smiling quietly to himself and the assistant coaches were looking at each other with pleasure the way they always did when one of the second stringers suddenly did something fine, bringing credit to them, making their $2,000 a year a tiny bit more secure.

Darling trotted back, smiling, breathing deeply but easily, feeling wonderful, not tired, though this was the tail end of practice and he'd run eighty yards. The sweat poured off his face and soaked his jersey and he liked the feeling, the warm moistness lubricating his skin like oil. Off in a corner of the field some players were punting and the smack of leather against the ball came pleasantly through the afternoon air. The freshmen were running signals on the next field and the quarterback's sharp voice, the pound of the eleven pairs of cleats, the "Dig, now, *dig!*" of the coaches, the laughter of the players all somehow made him feel happy as he trotted back to midfield, listening to the applause and shouts of the students along the sidelines, knowing that after that run the coach would have to start him Saturday against Illinois.

Fifteen years, Darling thought, remembering the shower after the workout, the hot water steaming off his skin and the deep soapsuds and all the young voices singing with the water streaming down and towels going and managers running in and out and the sharp sweet smell of oil of wintergreen and everybody clapping him on the back as he dressed and Packard, the captain, who took being captain very seriously, coming over to him and shaking his hand and saying, "Darling, you're going to go places in the next two years."

The assistant manager fussed over him, wiping a cut on his leg with alcohol and iodine, the little sting making him realize suddenly how fresh and whole and solid his body felt. The manager slapped a piece of adhesive tape over the cut and Darling noticed the sharp clean white of the tape against the ruddiness of the skin, fresh from the shower.

He dressed slowly, the softness of his shirt and the soft warmth of his wool socks and his flannel trousers a reward against his skin after the harsh pressure of the shoulder harness and thigh and hip pads. He drank three glasses of cold water, the liquid reaching down coldly inside of him, soothing the harsh dry places in his throat and belly left by the sweat and running and shouting of practice.

Fifteen years.

The sun had gone down and the sky was green behind the stadium and he laughed quietly to himself as he looked at the stadium, rearing above the trees, and knew that on Saturday when the 70,000 voices roared as the team came running out onto the field, part of that enormous salute would be for him. He walked slowly, listening to the gravel crunch satisfactorily under his shoes in the still twilight, feeling his clothes swing lightly against his skin, breathing the thin evening air, feeling the wind move softly in his damp hair, wonderfully cool behind his ears and at the nape of his neck.

Louise was waiting for him at the road, in her car. The top was down and he noticed all over again, as he always did when he saw her, how pretty she was, the rough blonde hair and the large, inquiring eyes and the bright mouth, smiling now.

She threw the door open. "Were you good today?" she asked.

"Pretty good," he said. He climbed in, sank luxuriously into the soft leather, stretched his legs far out. He smiled, thinking of the eighty yards. "Pretty damn good."

She looked at him seriously for a moment, then scrambled around, like a little girl, kneeling on the seat next to him, grabbed him, her hands along his ears, and kissed him as he sprawled, head back, on the seat cushion. She let go of him, but kept her head close to his, over his. Darling reached up slowly and rubbed the back of his hand against her cheek, lit softly by a street lamp a hundred feet away. They looked at each other, smiling.

Louise drove down to the lake and they sat there silently, watching the moon rise behind the hills on the other side. Finally he reached over, pulled her gently to him, kissed her. Her lips grew soft, her body sank into his, tears formed slowly in her eyes. He knew, for the first time, that he could do whatever he wanted with her.

"Tonight," he said. "I'll call for you at seven-thirty. Can you get out?"

She looked at him. She was smiling, but the tears were still full in her eyes. "All right," she said. "I'll get out. How about you? Won't the coach raise hell?"

Darling grinned. "I got the coach in the palm of my hand," he said. "Can you wait till seven-thirty?"

She grinned back at him. "No," she said.

They kissed and she started the car and they went back to town for dinner. He sang on the way home.

Christian Darling, thirty-five years old, sat on the frail spring grass, greener now than it ever would be again on the practice field, looked thoughtfully up at the stadium, a deserted ruin in the twilight. He had started on the first team that Saturday and every Saturday after that for the next two years, but it had never been as satisfactory as it should have been. He never had broken away, the longest run he'd ever made was thirty-five yards, and that in a game that was already won, and then that kid had come up from the third team, Diederich, a blank-faced German kid from Wisconsin, who ran like a bull, ripping lines to pieces Saturday after Saturday, plowing through, never getting hurt, never changing expression, scoring more points, gaining more ground than all the rest of the team put together, making everybody's All-American, carrying the ball three times out of four, keeping everybody else out of the headlines. Darling was a good blocker and he spent his Saturday afternoon working on the big Swedes and Polacks who played tackle and end for Michigan, Illinois, Purdue, hurling into huge pileups, bobbing his head wildly to elude the great raw hands swinging like meat cleavers at him as he went charging in to open up holes for Diederich coming through like a locomotive behind him. Still, it wasn't so bad. Everybody liked him and he did his job and he was pointed out on the campus and boys always felt important when they introduced their girls to him at their proms, and Louise loved him and watched him faithfully in the games, even in the mud, when your own mother wouldn't know you, and drove him around in her car keeping the top down because she was proud of him and wanted to show everybody that she was Christian Darling's girl. She bought him crazy presents because her father was rich, watches, pipes, humidors, an icebox for beer in his room, curtains, wallets, a fifty-dollar dictionary.

"You'll spend every cent your old man owns," Darling protested once when she showed up at his rooms with seven different packages in her arms and tossed them onto the couch.

"Kiss me," Louise said, "and shut up."

"Do you want to break your poor old man?"

"I don't mind. I want to buy you presents."

"Why?"

"It makes me feel good. Kiss me. I don't know why. Did you know that you're an important figure?"

"Yes," Darling said gravely.

"When I was waiting for you at the library yesterday two girls saw you coming and one of them said to the other, 'That's Christian Darling. He's an important figure.'"

"You're a liar."

"I'm in love with an important figure."

"Still, why the hell did you have to give me a forty-pound dictionary?"

"I wanted to make sure," Louise said, "that you had a token of my esteem. I want to smother you in tokens of my esteem."

Fifteen years ago.

They'd married when they got out of college. There'd been other women for him, but all casual and secret, more for curiosity's sake, and vanity, women who'd thrown themselves at him and flattered him, a pretty mother at a summer camp for boys, an old girl from his hometown who'd suddenly blossomed into a coquette, a friend of Louise's who had dogged him grimly for six months and had taken advantage of the two weeks when Louise went home when her mother died. Perhaps Louise had known, but she'd kept quiet, loving him completely, filling his rooms with presents, religiously watching him battling with the big Swedes and Polacks on the line of scrimmage on Saturday afternoons, making plans for marrying him and living with him in New York and going with him there to the nightclubs, the theatres, the good restaurants, being proud of him in advance, tall, white-teethed, smiling, large, yet moving lightly, with an athlete's grace, dressed in evening clothes, approvingly eyed by magnificently dressed and famous women in theatre lobbies, with Louise adoringly at his side.

Her father, who manufactured inks, set up a New York office for Darling to manage and presented him with three hundred accounts and they lived on Beekman Place with a view of the river with fifteen thousand dollars a year between them, because everybody was buying everything in those days, including ink. They saw all the shows and went to all the speakeasies and spent their fifteen thousand dollars a year and in the afternoons Louise went to the art galleries and the matinees of the more serious plays that Darling didn't like to sit through and Darling slept with a girl who danced in the chorus of *Rosalie* and with the wife of a man who owned three copper mines. Darling played squash three times a week and remained as solid as a stone barn and Louise never took her eyes off him when they were in the same room together, watching him with a secret, miser's smile, with a trick of coming over to him in the middle of a crowded room and saying gravely, in a low voice, "You are the handsomest man I've ever seen in my whole life. Want a drink?"

Nineteen twenty-nine came to Darling and to his wife and father-in-law, the maker of inks, just as it came to everyone else. The father-in-law waited until 1933 and then blew his brains out and when Darling went to Chicago to see what the books of the firm looked like he found out all that was left were debts and three or four gallons of unbought ink.

"Please, Christian," Louise said, sitting in their neat Beekman Place apartment, with a view of the river and prints of paintings by Dufy and Braque and Picasso on the wall, "please, why do you want to start drinking at two o'clock in the afternoon?"

"I have nothing else to do," Darling said, putting down his glass, emptied of its fourth drink. "Please pass the whiskey."

Louise filled his glass. "Come take a walk with me," she said. "We'll walk along the river."

"I don't want to walk along the river," Darling said, squinting intensely at the prints of paintings by Dufy, Braque, and Picasso.

"We'll walk along Fifth Avenue."

"I don't want to walk along Fifth Avenue."

"Maybe," Louise said gently, "you'd like to come with me to some art galleries. There's an exhibition by a man named Klee —"

"I don't want to go to any art galleries. I want to sit here and drink Scotch whiskey," Darling said. "Who the hell hung those goddamn pictures up on the wall?"

"I did," Louise said.

"I hate them."

"I'll take them down," Louise said.

"Leave them there. It gives me something to do in the afternoon. I can hate them." Darling took a long swallow. "Is that the way people paint these days?"

"Yes, Christian. Please don't drink any more."

"Do you like painting like that?"

"Yes, dear."

"Really?"

"Really."

Darling looked carefully at the prints once more. "Little Louise Tucker. The Middle-Western beauty. I like pictures with horses in them. Why should you like pictures like that?"

"I just happen to have gone to a lot of galleries in the last few years. . . ."

"Is that what you do in the afternoon?"

"That's what I do in the afternoon," Louise said.

"I drink in the afternoon."

Louise kissed him lightly on the top of his head as he sat there squinting at the pictures on the wall, the glass of whiskey held firmly in his hand. She put on her coat and went out without saying another word. When she came back in the early evening, she had a job on a woman's fashion magazine.

They moved downtown and Louise went out to work every morning and Darling sat home and drank and Louise paid the bills as they came up. She made believe she was going to quit work as soon as Darling found a job, even though she was taking over more responsibility day by day at the magazine, interviewing authors, picking painters for the illustrations and covers, getting actresses to pose for pictures, going out for drinks with the right people, making a thousand new friends whom she loyally introduced to Darling.

"I don't like your hat," Darling said, once, when she came in in the evening and kissed him, her breath rich with Martinis.

"What's the matter with my hat, Baby?" she asked, running her fingers through his hair. "Everybody says it's very smart."

"It's too damned smart," he said. "It's not for you. It's for a rich sophisticated woman of thirty-five with admirers."

Louise laughed. "I'm practicing to be a rich, sophisticated woman of thirty-five with admirers," she said. He stared soberly at her. "Now, don't look so grim, Baby. It's still the same simple little wife under the hat." She took the hat off, threw it into a corner, sat on his lap. "See? Homebody Number One."

"Your breath could run a train," Darling said, not wanting to be mean, but talking out of boredom, and sudden shock at seeing his wife curiously a stranger in a new hat, with a new expression in her eyes under the little brim, secret, confident, knowing.

Louise tucked her head under his chin so he couldn't smell her breath. "I had to take an author out for cocktails," she said. "He's a boy from the Ozark mountains and he drinks like a fish. He's a Communist."

"What the hell is a Communist from the Ozarks doing writing for a woman's fashion magazine?"

Louise chuckled. "The magazine business is getting all mixed up these days. The publishers want to have a foot in every camp. And anyway, you can't find an author under seventy these days who isn't a Communist."

"I don't think I like you to associate with all those people, Louise," Darling said. "Drinking with them."

"He's a very nice, gentle boy," Louise said. "He reads Ernest Dobson."

"Who's Ernest Dobson?"

Louise patted his arm, stood up, fixed her hair. "He's an English poet."

Darling felt that somehow he had disappointed her. "Am I supposed to know who Ernest Dobson is?"

"No, dear. I'd better go in and take a bath."

After she had gone, Darling went over to the corner where the hat was lying and picked it up. It was nothing, a scrap of straw, a red flower, a veil, meaningless on his big hand, but on his wife's head a signal of something . . . big city, smart and knowing women drinking and dining with men other than their husbands, conversation about things a normal man wouldn't know much about, Frenchmen who painted as though they used their elbows instead of brushes, composers who wrote whole symphonies without a single melody in them, writers who knew all about politics and women who knew all about writers, the movement of the proletariat, Marx, somehow mixed up with five-dollar dinners and the best looking women in America and fairies who made them laugh and half-sentences immediately understood and secretly hilarious and wives who called their husbands "Baby." He put the hat down, a scrap of straw and a red flower, and a little veil. He drank some whiskey straight and went into the bathroom where his wife was lying deep in her bath, singing to herself and smiling from time to time like a little girl, paddling the water gently with her hands, sending up a slight spicy fragrance from the bath salts she used.

He stood over her, looking down at her. She smiled up at him, her eyes half closed, her body pink and shimmering in the warm, scented water. All over again, with all the old suddenness, he was hit deep inside him with the knowledge of how beautiful she was, how much he needed her.

"I came in here," he said, "to tell you I wish you wouldn't call me 'Baby.'"

She looked up at him from the bath, her eyes quickly full of sorrow, half-understanding what he meant. He knelt and put his arms around her, his sleeves plunged heedlessly in the water, his shirt and jacket soaking wet as he clutched her wordlessly, holding her crazily tight, crushing her breath from her, kissing her desperately, searchingly, regretfully.

He got jobs after that, selling real estate and automobiles, but somehow, although he had a desk with his name on a wooden wedge on it, and he went to the office religiously at nine each morning, he never managed to sell anything and he never made any money.

Louise was made assistant editor and the house was always full of strange men and women who talked fast and got angry on abstract subjects like mural painting, novelists, labor unions. Negro short-story writers drank Louise's liquor, and a lot of Jews, and big solemn men with scarred faces and knotted hands who talked slowly but clearly about picket lines and battles with guns and lead pipe at mine-shaft heads and in front of factory gates. And Louise moved among them all, confidently, knowing what they were talking about, with opinions that they listened to and argued about just as though she were a man. She knew everybody, condescended to no one, devoured books that Darling had never heard of, walked along the streets of the city, excited, at home, soaking in all the million tides of New York without fear, with constant wonder.

Her friends liked Darling and sometimes he found a man who wanted to get off in the corner and talk about the new boy who played fullback for Princeton, and the decline of the double wingback, or even the state of the stock market, but for the most part he sat on the edge of things, solid and quiet in the high storm of words. "The dialectics of the situation . . . the theatre has been given over to the expert jugglers . . . Picasso? What man has a right to paint old bones and collect ten thousand dollars for them? . . . I stand firmly behind Trotsky . . . Poe was the last American critic. When he died they put lilies on the grave of American criticism. I don't say this because they panned my last book, but . . ."

Once in a while he caught Louise looking soberly and consideringly at him through the cigarette smoke and the noise and he avoided her eyes and found an excuse to get up and go into the kitchen for more ice or to open another bottle.

"Come on," Cathal Flaherty was saying, standing at the door with a girl, "you've got to come down and see this. It's down on Fourteenth Street, in the old Civic Repertory, and you can only see it on Sunday nights and I guarantee you'll come out of the theatre singing." Flaherty was a big young Irishman with a broken nose who was the lawyer for a longshoreman's union, and he had been hanging around the house for six months on and off, roaring and shutting everybody else up when he got in an argument. "It's a new play, *Waiting for Lefty*, it's about taxi drivers."

"Odets," the girl with Flaherty said. "It's by a guy named Odets."

"I never heard of him," Darling said.

"He's a new one," the girl said.

"It's like watching a bombardment," Flaherty said. "I saw it last Sunday night. You've got to see it."

"Come on, Baby," Louise said to Darling, excitement in her eyes already. "We've been sitting in the Sunday *Times* all day, this'll be a great change."

"I see enough taxi drivers every day," Darling said, not because he meant it, but because he didn't like to be around Flaherty, who said things that made Louise laugh a lot and whose judgment she accepted on almost every subject. "Let's go to the movies."

"You've never seen anything like this before," Flaherty said. "He wrote this play with a baseball bat."

"Come on," Louise coaxed, "I bet it's wonderful."

"He has long hair," the girl with Flaherty said. "Odets. I met him at a party. He's an actor. He's didn't say a goddamn thing all night."

"I don't feel like going down to Fourteenth Street," Darling said, wishing Flaherty and his girl would get out. "It's gloomy."

"Oh, hell!" Louise said loudly. She looked coolly at Darling, as though she'd just been introduced to him and was making up her mind about him, and not very favorably. He saw her looking at him, knowing there was something new and dangerous in her face and he wanted to say something, but Flaherty was there and his damned girl, and anyway, he didn't know what to say.

"I'm going," Louise said, getting her coat. "I don't think Fourteenth Street is gloomy."

"I'm telling you," Flaherty was saying, helping her on with her coat, "it's the Battle of Gettysburg, in Brooklynese."

"Nobody could get a word out of him," Flaherty's girl was saying as they went through the door. "He just sat there all night."

The door closed. Louise hadn't said good-night to him. Darling walked around the room four times, then sprawled out on the sofa, on top of the Sunday *Times*. He lay there for five minutes looking at the ceiling, thinking of Flaherty walking down the street talking in the booming voice, between the girls, holding their arms.

Louise had looked wonderful. She'd washed her hair in the afternoon and it had been very soft and light and clung close to her head as she stood there angrily putting her coat on. Louise was getting prettier every year, partly because she knew by now how pretty she was, and made the most of it.

"Nuts," Darling said, standing up. "Oh, nuts."

He put on his coat and went down to the nearest bar and had five drinks off by himself in a corner before his money ran out.

The years since then had been foggy and downhill. Louise had been nice to him, and in a way, loving and kind, and they'd fought only once, when he said he was going to vote for Landon. ("Oh, Christ," she'd said, "doesn't anything happen inside your head? Don't you read the papers? The penniless Republican!") She'd been sorry later and apologized for hurting him, but apologized as she might to a child. He'd tried hard, had gone grimly to the art galleries, the concert halls, the bookshops, trying to gain on the trail of his wife, but it was no use. He was bored, and none of what he saw or heard or dutifully read made much sense to him and finally he gave it up. He had thought, many nights as he ate dinner alone, knowing that Louise would come home late and drop silently into bed without explanation, of getting a divorce, but he knew the loneliness, the hopelessness, of not seeing her again would be too much to take. So he was good, completely devoted, ready at all times to go anyplace with her, do anything she wanted. He even got a small job, in a broker's office and paid his own way, bought his own liquor.

Then he'd been offered the job of going from college to college as a tailor's representative. "We want a man," Mr. Rosenberg had said, "who as soon as you look at him, you say 'There's a university man.'" Rosenberg had looked approvingly at Darling's broad shoulders and well-kept waist, at his carefully brushed hair and his honest, wrinkleless face. "Frankly, Mr. Darling, I am willing to make you a proposition. I have inquired about you, you are favorably known on your old campus, I understand you were in the backfield with Alfred Diederich."

Darling nodded. "Whatever happened to him?"

"He is walking around in a cast for seven years now. An iron brace. He played professional football and they broke his neck for him."

Darling smiled. That, at least, had turned out well.

"Our suits are an easy product to sell, Mr. Darling," Rosenberg said. "We have a handsome, custom-made garment. What has Brooks Brothers got that we haven't got? A name. No more."

"I can make fifty, sixty dollars a week," Darling told Louise that night. "And expenses. I can save some money and then come back to New York and really get started here."

"Yes, Baby," Louise said.

"As it is," Darling said carefully, "I can make it back here once a month, and holidays and the summer. We can see each other often."

"Yes, Baby." He looked at her face, lovelier now at thirty-five than it had ever been before, but fogged over now as it had been for five years with a kind of patient, kindly, remote boredom.

"What do you say?" he asked. "Should I take it?" Deep within him he hoped fiercely, longingly, for her to say, "No, Baby, you stay right here," but she said, as he knew she'd say, "I think you'd better take it."

He nodded. He had to get up and stand with his back to her, looking out the window, because there were things plain on his face that she had never seen in the fifteen years she'd known him. "Fifty dollars is a lot of money," he said. "I never thought I'd ever see fifty dollars again." He laughed. Louise laughed, too.

Christian Darling sat on the frail green grass of the practice field. The shadow of the stadium had reached out and covered him. In the distance the lights of the university shone a little mistily in the light haze of evening. Fifteen years. Flaherty even now was calling for his wife, buying her a drink, filling whatever bar they were in with that voice of his and that easy laugh. Darling half-closed his eyes, almost saw the boy fifteen years ago reach for the pass, slip the halfback, go skittering lightly down the field, his knees high and fast and graceful, smiling to himself because he knew he was going to get past the safety man. That was the high point, Darling thought, fifteen years ago, on an autumn afternoon twenty years old and far from death, with the air coming easily into his lungs, and feeling deep inside him that he could do anything, knock over anybody, outrun whatever had to be outrun. And the shower after and the three glasses of water and cool night air on his damp head and Louise sitting hatless in the open car with a smile and the first kiss she ever really meant. The high point, an eighty-yard run in the practice, and a girl's kiss and everything after that a decline. Darling laughed. He had practiced the wrong thing, perhaps. He hadn't practiced for 1929 and New York City and a girl who would turn into a woman.

Somewhere, he thought, there must have been a point where she moved up to me, was even with me for a moment, when I could have held her hand, if I'd known, held tight, gone with her. Well, he'd never known. Here he was on a playing field that was fifteen years away and his wife was in another city having dinner with another and better man, speaking with him a different, new language, a language nobody had ever taught him.

Darling stood up, smiled a little, because if he didn't smile he knew the tears would come. He looked around him. This was the spot. O'Connor's pass has come sliding out just to here . . . the high point. Darling put up his hands, felt all over again the flat slap of the ball. He shook his hips to throw off the halfback, cut back inside the center, picked his knees high as he ran gracefully over two men jumbled on the ground at the line of scrimmage, ran easily, gaining speed, for ten yards, holding the ball lightly in his two hands, swung away from the halfback diving at him, ran, swinging his hips in the almost girlish manner of a back in a broken field, tore into the safety man, his shoes drumming heavily on the turf, stiff-armed, elbow locked, pivoted, raced lightly and exultantly for the goal line.

It was only after he had sped over the goal line and slowed to a trot that he saw the boy and girl sitting together on the turf, looking at him wonderingly.

He stopped short, dropping his arms. "I . . . Once I played here."

The boy and the girl said nothing. Darling laughed embarrassedly, looked hard at them sitting there, close to each other, shrugged, turned and went toward his hotel, the sweat breaking out on his face and running down his collar.

1942

Critical thinking points: After you've read

1) Why is it important to the story that Darling's memorable run occurred during practice? What implications does this have on his life?

2) Compare Darling's first eighty-yard run to the one he recreates fifteen years later. What has changed?

3) Does Darling's role as a Big Ten football player prepare him in any way for his life after college? Why or why not?

4) Why is the scene in the bathtub, when Darling says to Louise, "I wish you wouldn't call me 'Baby,'" a turning point in the story? What might Darling mean by his statement? Louise continues to call her husband "Baby," but he doesn't seem to mind after this scene. Why?

5) The traditional male/female roles for this era are reversed in the story. Why do you think this is so?

Some possibilities for writing

1) *Darling's "moment of greatness" affects the rest of his life. Recall one of your own "moments of greatness" even if it is "great" only to you.*

2) *Write the next scene between the young couple who witnessed Darling's run as a 35-year-old. What do they talk about as they walk home from the stadium? Does seeing Christian Darling, a middle-aged man bolting down the football field, affect these two in any way?*

3) *After his 80-yard run, Darling is keenly aware of all the sights, sounds, and textures around him, as if suddenly everything has become important. Have you ever had an experience like this? Describe it. What caused everything to become "important"?*

4) *Shaw says of Darling, "He had practiced the wrong thing, perhaps. He hadn't practiced for 1929 and New York City and a girl who would turn into a woman." How might Darling have "practiced" for such events? Was "practicing" even a possibility for him? Why or why not? What in his character supports your opinion?*

Reunion

Dawn Karima Pettigrew

I see Ollie Panther in the grandmother's cheekbones, / and that young guy might as well be Thomas Crow. / Probably could see the whole Cherokee nation, / if I sit here and study them all long enough.

Critical thinking points: As you read

1) Why might the title be read as ironic? Is it sarcastic? If so, to whom?

2) How does Jane Gisgi "reinvest," if at all, in Qualla Boundary Reservation?

3) What are some details that represent the narrator's past life on the Qualla Boundary Reservation? What are some details that represent her current life as an Ivy League student?

4) In what ways is the narrator "white-washed and well-read"? Is she really, or just to other Native Americans?

Jane Gisgi, Ivy League student, reinvests in Qualla Boundary
  Reservation

i endure the air-kisses,
avoid the cellular phones,
wend my way through the basil and hypocrisy
in the brunch-hour air.

Painted and powdered,
white-washed and well-read,
I slide into my seat
boy-girl-boy-girl.

Reverend Dawn Karima Pettigrew (b. 1970) holds a degree in Social Studies, with a focus on Popular Culture and Media, from Harvard University and a Master of Fine Arts degree in Creative Writing from Ohio State University. An ordained minister of Cherokee, Creek, Chickasaw, Choctaw, and other Native descent, she directs Wells of Victory Ministries, Inc., which serves the people of North Carolina's Qualla Boundary Cherokee Reservation.

Three pairs of sky-colored eyes
blink back at me.

I forget to remember to thank the waiter.
My eyes find,
at one table made from two,
earthen hands, clay-colored faces.
Men swing hair they can sit on.
Women balance babies between their knees and the table.

I see Ollie Panther in the grandmother's cheekbones,
and that young guy might as well be Thomas Crow.
Probably could see the whole Cherokee nation,
if I sit here and study them all long enough.

Higher education might hurt less if I know them,
it's no threat to my diploma if I wave.

"Look at that."
My undecided boyfriend sounds like anthro stirred with psych.
I was born in the dark, but it wasn't last night.
I've read enough textbooks to know what's coming.
"Looks like they brought the whole tribe with them."
He might love me, he's so mean without malice.

I should shout,
make a scene,
right out of drama class,
chant or cry,
"We do bring everyone with us.
No one is left behind.
We do not warehouse old people for profit,
or eat without children or raise them in boxes."

That's not what comes out.
After all, I left the mountains.
Tired of tourists, bored with bears,
embarrassed everytime Cousin Jess went chiefing,
I ran to college,
ran from drums,
ran from dulcimers.
It's amazing what'll make you go foolish.

I lift my head,
meet each pair of eyes in pale faces,
"Those people are my family."
My smile is wet sugar.

The eyes across the table drop,
fingers pinch the hearts from artichokes.
Soft "sorry" mixing with talk of Sartre
makes everything in me miss the mountains.

1998

Critical thinking points: After you've read

1) How does the narrator's life in the mountains conflict with the life she adapted to at college? What details in the poem lead you to your conclusions?
2) In what ways do Native American students often leave a way of life behind when they come to college? How might this be similar or different to the kinds of changes other students go through?
3) What might Pettigrew be feeling when she says, "Higher education might hurt less if I know them, / it's no threat to my diploma if I wave"?
4) What might the narrator mean when she says of her boyfriend, "He might love me, he's so mean without malice"? What might be some other ways of saying this?
5) How might the image "fingers pinch the hearts from artichokes" be effective and appropriate in the last stanza?

Some possibilities for writing

1) Recall a time when you were with a group of peers or classmates and you were embarrassed to see someone from your past, such as an ex-boyfriend or ex-girlfriend, a friend from grammar school, or a family member.
2) Rewrite this poem as if it were a screenplay. Add dialogue and descriptions of characters as well as recreate a setting.
3) Create the next scene for Jane and her boyfriend as they leave the restaurant. What might their conversation be like? How might the episode in the restaurant affect their future relationship?
4) Why does the narrator say, "Those people are my family"? Support your conclusions with details from the poem.
5) Read or reread Zitkla-Sa's "Incurring My Mother's Displeasure." What does a comparison of the two stories suggest has changed in the past century for Native American college students? What has remained the same?

Moon June Spoon

Frank Smoot

"

Just one second he thinks life's rolled over him

"

Critical thinking points: As you read

1) *The form of this poem is a "sestina." Even if you don't know what that means, can you guess from reading this poem some of the elements of that form?*
2) *Pay attention to the kinds of changes that occur in the narrator's life from "June to June" during this poem. What are they?*
3) *Watch for examples of wedding traditions in the poem. What are some? Are there any other traditions in the poem?*
4) *What are some of the different types of moons mentioned in the poem? List them as you read.*

It's the "awakening" moon in March, the "feasting" moon
in September, but it's "honey" when it comes in June.
In Wisconsin the young lovers dance the polka, spoon
cake into each other's faces, drink too much and soon
stumble into bed. They wake cotton-mouthed and green at noon
to open presents while someone asks him to sing that tune

he sang for her at church — what was it called? — that tune
that made her father cry. And then they're off, the new moon
a day older, a little to the south, five minutes after noon,
and then ten and then fifteen, growing fatter as the June
holiday they thought stretched out like the sea soon
finds its shore. They make love mornings, sleep like spoons

In addition to poems and short stories, Frank Smoot (b. 1961) has published some two hundred articles, including editorials, essays, features, interviews, and critiques of art, dance, film, food, literature, and music. He is currently at work on a biography of 1940s film star Carole Landis.

at night, notice every little thing, how she holds a spoon,
how he sings to her, what a smoothie, what a crooner.
It embarrasses their friends. But they're back to work too soon
to really know each other, and then one night the moon
passes over and they haven't watched it. June's
turned August when the world slicks with sweat by noon,

but still they're in the future garden, her thighs noon-slick
as she pulls thistles — his too as he chips another spoonful
of the drought-hard dirt. But with any luck at all, next June
it'll be rich out here, the little peas in rows, their lives in tune
with nature, the Wisconsin country life. August's moon's
the "woodcutters," so another weekend he's out doing it.

Soon a winter's wood, the patio set at the end-of-season sale.
Soon too that baby they've been trying for morning, noon,
and night. He sure likes the process, her straining skin in moonlight,
yet — he doesn't tell her — he's not sure about the spoon-feedings,
diapers, sleepless nights. In time, he thinks, he'll get tuned up for it,
but before he's ready, she's at the doctor's. She's due in June.

Just one second he thinks life's rolled over him, June to June,
born that month, graduated, married, now to be a father, soon
enough he'll die, probably in June. *Oh that same old tune, huh?*
he laughs at himself. So he buys flowers, takes off the afternoon,
makes a gag of her "condition," how he has to spoon her dinner
to her, help her upstairs, guard her from the "wolf" moon.

Teach me those songs, she says in bed, *sing me to sleep,*
that one about the cat in the cradle with the silver spoon,
the one about the cow who jumped over the moon.

1992

Critical thinking points: After you've read

1) *In what ways is this poem tied to a specific time and place? How might the poem be different if it were set in some other geographical area?*
2) *How might the different names of the moons reflect the subject matter of the poem?*
3) *The narrator says, "Just one second he thinks life's rolled over him." What do you think this might mean? In what way might the man feel acted upon, like Martin in Michael Lancaster's "The Eyes of Chickens"?*

4) *One cliché about rhyming poetry is that it tends to read in straight, predictable rhymes and sound like "moon June spoon." How does this poet avoid that cliché?*

5) *Is this a "love" poem? What elements might make it so? Why would some readers not consider this a "traditional" love poem?*

Some possibilities for writing

1) *Why might the poet end with an allusion to a nursery rhyme? Choose one or two other nursery rhymes and rewrite the ending using those rhymes. Then write about why you chose the nursery rhyme you did and how it fits into the theme of the existing poem.*

2) *This poem could be called "A Year in the Life," since it spans exactly one year in the narrator's life. Write a scene about the husband and wife in which they discuss their first year together.*

3) *Research the different types of moons the poet mentions. Find out how and why they got their names. Choose one and write the history of that moon's name.*

4) *The poet indulges himself with a view of the "perfect" future for his characters. Write a scene full of concrete details that shows instead of tells your "perfect" future.*

5) *The same as above but a scene that shows the least perfect future you can imagine for yourself.*

6) *This is a poem about the subject of love as much as it is a love poem. Write a brief essay on the view of love as depicted in this poem.*

Scarlet Ribbons

Michael Perry

66

It's one thing to speak of the heart as a center of emotion, quite another to see it lurching between the lungs like a spasmodic grey slug.

99

Critical thinking points: As you read

1) What makes a "liberal arts" education?

2) What skills do writers and nurses share?

3) Would you prefer a nurse or doctor who was also knowledgeable and interested in fields such as music, art, and literature? Why or not?

The man in the small room with me is a convicted murderer. He is immense and simple, looks as if he was raised on potatoes and homemade biscuits. I'd lay money that before he wound up here, his clothes smelled of bacon grease. He knows I am uneasy. I know he knows, because he looked me square in the eye, grinned, and told me so. Still, *The New York Times Magazine* has given me an assignment, and although I may be edgy in this prison, in this room with concrete blocks close all around, with this bulky killer two feet away, I must complete it.

I am to determine if the prisoner is happy.

The first person to whom I ever administered an intramuscular injection was a cheery wee granny. I see her still, seated on a hospital chair, flannel gown hiked up to expose her left quadriceps, head fluffed with a blessing of fine white curls, smile as sweet and warm as a batch of sugar cookies. The steel needle is cocked an inch from her skin, and she chirps: "Have you ever done this before?"

"Oh yes," I lie. Brightly. Smoothly. Never breaking eye contact.

Heraclitus said you can never step in the same river twice. Jorge Luis Borges said time is forever dividing itself toward innumerable futures — that we choose one alternative at the expense of all others. We can never be who we set out to be, but will

---

Michael Perry (b. 1964) lives and writes in rural Wisconsin. His essays have appeared in *Esquire, The Utne Reader, Orion Magazine,* and *Salon.*

always be who we were. I went to college to become a nurse. I became a writer. We spring from a thicket of tangents. I remember the exact moment I decided to become a nurse. I was reading Sports Illustrated in the high school library. I was supposed to be in World Literature, but the university recruiter was in town, and we were allowed to skip class to catch her pitch. I signed up, but once in the library, headed straight for the magazine rack, lolling through People and Newsweek while the rest of the students joined the recruiter at a long table. Late in her presentation, I overheard her reciting a list of majors: "Biology. Business. Economics. History. Nursing."

"Nursing," I thought. "That sounds interesting."

I filled out the necessary paperwork, and reported for class in the fall.

Nursing is so easily caricatured by white skirts and chilly bed pans. Pills and needles. Shots. But this is like saying painting is about paint. Practiced at its best, nursing is humane art, arisen from intimate observation and expressed through care. Again and again our instructors reminded us that every patient is a point of convergence, an intersection of body, mind and spirit. We were trained to obtain quantifiable data with stethoscopes and sphygmomanometers, but we were also warned not to ignore intuition. We learned to change sheets without removing a bedridden patient, we learned how to prevent decubitus ulcers by monitoring pressure points, we learned to stick lubricated feeding tubes up noses, but we also learned to seek eye contact, percept nonverbal communication, and establish trust so rapidly that within five minutes of meeting a stranger we could quite comfortably inquire after his bowel habits. Facilitate, reflect, and clarify. Employ empathic response. These are the interviewing tools of the nurse. Also eminently functional, as it turns out, in the service of interviewing murderers for *The New York Times*. Every time I filled a syringe, I was filling my writer's pen with ink.

Heraclitus also said we are never being, but becoming, and in between clinical rotations and classes on skin disease, all nursing students were required to enroll in humanity courses. This rankled me. I have never been taken with the concept of a liberal arts education. The idea of lounging around dissecting Tom Jones when I should have been dissecting piglets always struck me as mark-time dawdling along the road to employability. I'd change out of surgical scrubs and hustle off to badminton class, Econ 110, or The United States Since 1877, or Introduction to Film, or Introduction to Creative Writing, or Folk Music in America. I expected the Chemistry 210, the General Zoology, the Developmental Psych and the Survey of Biochemistry, and willingly submitted to the Minnesota Multiphasic Personality Inventory assessment designed to reassure the beehived matron at the helm of the nursing school that I was unlikely to bite my patients or develop perverse affections for iodine swabs, but a .5 credit course in *relaxation?* What did these things have to do with nursing? Peering into the thicket of tangents, I saw nothing but obstruction.

Early one morning during a summer O.R. rotation, long before most people had finished their first cup of coffee, a surgeon inflated and deflated a lung for me. It pressed out of the patient's bisected chest like a greasy trick balloon, then shrunk back and retreated into a cheesy lump beside the patient's writhing heart. The mechanics were fascinating. Here was the corporeal gristle revealed. We tote our organs around not even knowing them. There is nothing abstract about a glistening length of intestine. But by drawing back the curtain, the surgeon managed to reframe the mystery. Now that I had peeked behind the liver, eyed the discrete lumps of organ, I wondered where the spirit might lie. It's one thing to speak of the heart as a center of emotion, quite another to see it lurching between the lungs like a spasmodic grey slug. We were as deep in the body as you can get — exactly where did they keep the soul? The finite, meaty nature of it all blunted my ability to imagine the body as a place for spirits.

When I was a child, my father, a quietly eccentric farmer, would sometimes come in the house after the evening milking, rustle up his blighted trumpet, and play "A Trumpeter's Lullaby." We sat at his feet, and he swayed above us, an overalled gnome, eyes closed, gently triple-tonguing the wistful passages. The notes twined from the brass bell in liquescent amber, settling over our hearts and shoulders, wreathing us in warm, golden light. Many years later I found myself standing at a meds cart in a surgical ward, sorting pills into cups, chafing in my polyester student nurse smock, short of sleep and overwhelmed by my patient care assignments, desperately trying to sort out the drug interactions before my instructor arrived to grill me on the same, when "A Trumpeter's Lullaby" came seeping from the speaker in the ceiling. I was swept with a desperate melancholy. I have never been so lonely. And try as I might, I could not see how the path on which I stood could be backtracked to the feet of my trumpeting father. In more dramatic circumstances, I might have stripped off my smock, gobbled the meds, and run off to join an agrarian brass band, but my instructor appeared and began to ask me if there was any danger in administering Diazepam and Clonidine in tandem. I fidgeted, answered hopefully, and resumed forward motion.

After four years, I took my nursing boards, convinced I'd fail, and passed just fine. Worked as a nurse for a while and liked it. But I kept having trouble remembering all the numbers, and how Demerol interacted with Elavil, and just what it was phagocytes did, and yet I could remember the poem the stunted guy behind me in creative writing wrote about electrical highlines, and what the professor said it lacked, and how I believed the highline guy could have done better, and how I remembered the way the folk music professor crossed his legs and fingered his guitar when he explained that the scarlet ribbons in "Scarlet Ribbons" weren't ribbons at all, but bright blood on a child's fractured head, and I thought of the lung puffing and falling, and I said if I can conjure these things so easily while I stumble over drug interactions and hematocrits, perhaps I ought to write instead. I took to talking about this. Over-frequently, apparently, because one day my girlfriend said, "Why don't you stop talking about it and do it?"

And so I did.

There was much to learn, but much less to unlearn.

I wonder if Heraclitus would dare tell the prisoner he was not stepping in the same river twice. A lifetime of days between those tan concrete blocks? Sounds like the same old river to me. Still, our little visit must have been a diversion. I imagine he chuckled with his roomie later when he described catching me in my unease. It was a fair cop. But as he leaned in and grinned, I slid the needle in and drew out what I needed. When I stepped out of the prison, it was cold and windy, but the waning light seemed to propose an answer.

1999

Critical thinking points: After you've read

1) *Why do you think humanities courses are required of nursing or other "technical" majors?*
2) *What might Perry mean when he says about changing careers, "There was much to learn, but much less to unlearn"?*
3) *The last few words seem to leave the essay quite open-ended. Why do you think Perry chose to close his essay this way? What answer do you think is proposed?*
4) *Which type of degree do you think is more valuable, a technical degree that teaches a specific skill or a liberal arts degree that offers exposure to many different areas of education? Why do you answer the way you do?*
5) *What might it mean to "never step in the same river twice"? Why do you think Perry included this quote from Heraclitus in his essay?*
6) *Why do you think technical colleges do not offer classes to "undeclared" students? What does this say about the goal of technical colleges?*

Some possibilities for writing

1) *Do you know people in jobs or careers they hate? Speculate about what makes them stay.*
2) *Many college faculty and administrators would like to think that the first year of college is one of exploration. Argue for or against first-year students declaring a major.*
3) *Interview at least five upperclass students about how they chose their major. Using the information gathered from your interviews, try to come to some consensus about the most typical way of choosing a major. Is there a "typical" way of choosing a major?*
4) *Research shows that current college graduates will change careers about six times throughout a lifetime. Visit your campus Career Center to gather information about at least five potential careers for yourself. What about your life now makes you believe each of the careers might be appropriate for you? What education and/or skills do you need to acquire for each profession?*

Passion

Monica Coleman

"

Sometimes I think it was easier before I surrendered . . . accepted.

"

Critical thinking points: As you read

1) What is Coleman's definition of a calling? Can it only be religious in nature?

2) Do you typically think of the word "passion" when you think of a career? Why or why not?

3) What are some careers for which passion is a "requirement" more than others? What makes that so?

4) Do you think people can decide on a vocation, or does the calling find them? Explain your answer.

Passion. Something in your heart that you can't let go of. Or more importantly, that won't let go of you. Something that makes your eyes sparkle and the pace of your words increase whenever someone asks you about it. That thing that keeps you up at night. Thinking and wrestling. That thing you do senseless activities for — like turn down good-paying jobs. That thing, that without, you are convinced you will die.

For me, that passion has always been books. I can not remember my life without books. My mother was a reading teacher, so I grew up believing that every room in a house was supposed to have a bookshelf, and every book on it should have been read . . . a couple times. I have been punished for reading — when I stayed up late with a flashlight under the covers instead of going to sleep — but I was usually rewarded. Summer book clubs at the local library, book reviews for the elementary school paper, payment of five dollars for every book I read during the summer — and ten dollars if my father chose the book. When my classmates spent the last weeks of their senior year traveling, gardening, building cars and robots, I read a book and made my first attempt

Monica Coleman, of Ann Arbor, Michigan, is a 1995 magna cum laude graduate of Harvard-Radcliffe College, where she earned a Bachelor of Arts degree in Afro-American Studies. In 1998, she earned a Master of Divinity degree with honors and a Certificate in the Study of Religion, Gender and Sexuality from Vanderbilt Divinity School. An elder in the AME Church, she currently coordinates the ministries that respond to sexual and domestic violence while also a teaching adjunct in the department of Africana Studies at Tennessee State University.

at literary criticism by comparing the folk legend of the flying Africans to Toni Morrison's *Song of Solomon*. In trudging through the stacks at the local university library and sitting for hours in the PS 153 section, I discovered my passion — books.

My craving quickly became particular. After spending an entire high school summer reading through the works of James Baldwin and finding myself depressed, angry, and still inspired, I found my first heroines: Alice Walker, Toni Morrison, Zora Neale Hurston. I read quickly, and absorbed their stories like they were my own. I lived in the bodies of several women, I cursed at my blond-haired dolls, and I walked down the streets of Eatonville, Florida. Soon, my literary journeys became my committed cause: I berated my high school teachers for teaching only the "major works." I demanded more reading of literary criticism. I wanted course credit for writing on Gloria Naylor. I instituted a book club.

So it was like going to heaven the day I changed my economics and mathematics major to African American Studies. No one had ever told me that I could major in that which I loved. I had discovered that I could spend four years of my time and energy reading more, writing about reading, reading more, and writing about reading. The day I met Henry Louis Gates, Jr. was like finding the pot of gold at the end of my rainbow. Not only could I major in African American Studies (focusing on literature), but I could study with the man whose criticisms I read in my spare time. I could learn directly from the mind of someone who had previously been a name I had seen in everyone's bibliography. It's the same feeling I got when I met Nellie McKay, Toni Morrison, Hazel Carby, Deborah McDowell and Arnold Rampersad. They would never remember me, but I put their faces with their names, and my world had suddenly and swiftly become not only real, but attainable. I fell in love with books, their authors, their critics, and I fell in love with academia.

Of course I wanted to write. Don't all lovers of literature secretly want to write?! But the deeper passion was for teaching. I wanted less to become a Nella [Larsen], Jessie [Fauset], Gloria [Naylor], Gayl [Jones], Ntozake [Shange] or Octavia [Butler], than I wanted to nurture others into the love affair I had found with them. I had no desire to write a novel. In fact, I am still certain that I would fail if I tried. I just wanted to see the light in someone else's eyes. I wanted to see the marked up books in the hands of my students. I wanted to be the harsh midwife that Maryemma, Thadious and Jamaica were to me as they watched me labor through thirty-page papers, and still insisted I could do better. Most importantly, I wanted to be paid to spend hours in the libraries, at the computer and know that I was not crazy.

I remember trying to explain to my parents that academia is a career, a job, a joy, even. They sat blank-eyed, as do all from the generation that believes you go to school to get a job. Wanting to be a professor is like never leaving school. It is like never graduating. To them, it was some quirky license I had invented to become "a professional student." I won numerous grants that allowed me to research full time during my summers. I found fellowships that supported term-time research. I bonded with the stacks on campus, in small public libraries and in The Library of Congress. The more I researched without affecting my parents' checkbooks, and the more I convinced them that people do this — that Black people do this — the more support-ive they became. So I was just as surprised as my parents when I found another passion. One I tried to ignore, but could not. One that I tried to escape, but could not. One that meant death, if I did not. It was ministry.

Unlike my passion for books, I had no role models. In my hometown, I had never seen a preacher under the age of 35, let alone a female minister. I didn't even know that there were young ministers or female ministers until I went to college. I came to know many as surrogate mothers and sisters. I simply assumed that I had my passion and they had theirs. I lived for Black women's books, and their authors, while they lived for "The Book" and its Author. I had prayed, and considered academia my calling.

Yet there was another calling on my life. When I had stopped paying attention, the time I once spent reading Barbara Christian and Mary Helen Washington, be-came time I spent on the train to church. The nights that were reserved for reading yet-another-unassigned novel, were spent on my knees, praying for the members of the Bible Study I now led. The courses that I once took in the Department of English, became graduate courses in the Divinity School. My friends were still the aspiring politicians and professors, but some were now aspiring preachers. These things made me a devoted Christian, I told myself, not a minister.

I knew it immediately, and I was outraged. One day my Bible opened to the book of Amos and I read, "But neither was I a prophet, nor was I a prophet's son, but I was a herdsman and a gatherer of sycamore fruit, and the Lord took me as I fol-lowed the flock and said, 'Go prophesy unto my people.' " I immediately called my best friend, and said to her, "Guess what God had the nerve to tell me!" I knew what it meant because I had read it, "But I was not a preacher, nor a preacher's kid, but a student, a scholar-in-training, and the Lord took me ..." Instantly I knew it was a calling to preach — a calling towards ordained ministry —and I didn't want it. I was perfectly happy on my life plan to B.A. by twenty, Ph.D. by twenty-five, book by twenty-nine, tenure by thirty-two — and sometime fall in love, get married, have children. Everyone has dreams. This was mine.

Quiet as it's kept, I didn't want the hassle of being a young woman in the minis-try in the Black church. My new exposure to seminaries, young preachers, and fe-male preachers had quickly informed me of the disbelief and disrespect I would encounter if I woke up one day and said, "I've been called to preach." I didn't want to fight a system that seemed to respect age and male ego just as much as, if not more than, the calling itself. I didn't want to wear the tired look of carrying the burdens of your family, friends and congregation. I didn't want to stand behind a pulpit and be expected to say something important or holy. My disdain quickly became fear when I declared to myself that I would not do this "preaching thing." I heard wrong. I was called to academia. Period.

I soon learned that fighting the culture of ministry, and fighting God were two very different things. They both seemed impossible. I didn't want to do the former, even though victory was possible; and I consistently did the latter when defeat was inevitable. I didn't consciously hear myself asking other ministers about their callings. I didn't really even notice when I applied for scholarships and listed "ministry" as an interest. I didn't realize that I was writing sermons in my head. I was completely caught off guard the morning I prayed, "Okay God, I give up. I'll do this because I love You."

Sometimes I think it was easier before I surrendered . . . accepted. I was happy leading seminars, teaching Bible Study, receiving calls in the middle of the night by friends who would say, "I thought you could get a prayer through." No one really noticed me, and there were no expectations on my personal life — what kind of men I should date, what length of skirts I must wear, what style of hair I must choose. Now, two months before my senior year, I was entering a world about which I knew nothing except "Christ and Him crucified." That didn't seem like enough when I had three months to apply to seminaries, pursue ordination, explain to my professors, mentors, family and friends that "the plan had changed." I barely left time to do my own personal mourning over the dismantling of the dream.

I began to feel how it was actually harder to live without my passion. Everytime I heard a sermon, I secretly wanted to preach — even though I didn't know what to do. Everytime I prayed, something seemed to be blocking communication between God and myself. Everytime I tried to find a Ph.D. program that would fit my needs, something didn't work out. The day I preached my first sermon, I found a comfort in sitting in the pulpit that I had previously only known when sitting down in the African American Studies section of Harvard Book Store. Once again, I was in love.

With the clarity of hindsight, I recognize ministry as a life-long passion as well. I remember the things that I said to family members about my interest in the studying the Bible. I recall the times that I spent more time in church than at home or in school. I reminisce about the summer workshops I held for the children at my home church. It was all so natural, I didn't even notice it. I didn't know the passion was there, until it bubbled up inside me and threatened to erupt if I did not acknowledge it.

I went to seminary Vanderbilt Divinity School. Attending seminary is known as a painful process because it causes one to consider your faith under the microscope of your professors. Sometimes it seems like they take their tools and try to chisel away at your inner core of beliefs. Everything that isn't stone, will fall away. I have discovered the parts of me that are stone, and the parts that are not. I feel a mixture of joy and anguish when I walk into a bookstore. I am reminded that I have left the plan that so quickly became part of my soul. I see the new books, and yearn to buy and read them all. I realize than I am out of the academic loop that once sustained me — I haven't been to conferences, I haven't read The Op-Ed page of The New York Times, I haven't seen a "Call for Papers" since I graduated from undergrad. In my core, I ache for Octavia and J. California — or sometimes, just the thrill of library research and the anticipation of instruction. In the height of those painful moments, I found that both my passions are true. I have discovered a way of have my cake and eat it too.

I first tasted the cake the year I convinced the director of field education at Vanderbilt that teaching can be considered ministry. I arranged to perform a grossly underpaid internship at a local university. As a "teaching assistant" in the department of Africana Studies, I returned to my first love. Every week, I taught twenty-five students about Martin Luther King, Malcolm X and contemporary issues in Black manhood. The class content was more political and sociological than literary, but the educational process was the same. I used excerpts from my favorite poets. I taught my students how to improve their writing and research techniques. I learned that religious questions arose no matter the official nature of the topic. Much to my surprise, I could respond to their inquiries. When their eyes lit up with recognition and understanding after class discussion, I did not feel like a thorough scholar. I felt like a successful minister.

I learned to change "the plan." I still intend to apply to Ph.D. programs, and I make more time to read and write between preaching engagements and seminary assignments. In the delay of one passion, I found joy in another. I have come to enjoy preaching, and the way the spoken word can reach another person. I have fallen in love with my denomination's liturgy, and I revel in small opportunities to read scripture, pray, or line a hymn. I bring my three years of theological education into every church Bible study I attend. I also believe that teaching college students is a valid branch of ministry. After all, it was my professors who ministered to me.

I also found ministry in being a graduate student. My friends in other graduate schools often asked me to pray for them, to find scriptures for them, to tell them something about God, and everything about my calling. The joy comes in telling them about both my callings, and saying, "Well, there are plans and passions. Sometimes they diverge, but sometimes they come together too."

1997

Critical thinking points: After you've read

1) What books or movies have inspired you the way Coleman was inspired by African-American writers?

2) The University of Wisconsin–Madison was nicknamed "Mad Town" in the 1950s because the children of farmers and blue collar workers came home from college to their small towns raving mad, filled with talk of literature and philosophy. In what way does this happen to Coleman?

3) College students are often "forced" into an area of study by their parents or even their peers. How is Coleman's struggle different from that situation? Did you ever feel a particular area of study or a major was forced on you?

4) Many parents, like Coleman's, expect their children to go to college to later find a job, not their passion or calling. What societal factors lead to this?

Some possibilities for writing

1) Write a definition of passion as it pertains to a career. Use concrete details to describe this abstract concept.

2) *Make a list of your interests or passions. For each, write at least a paragraph speculating how you can involve them in your college career. For instance, a sociology major might use his interest in* The Rocky Horror Picture Show *or* Star Wars *for the topic of his senior thesis.*

3) *Read some of the work of at least one of the authors Coleman mentions, such as James Baldwin, Gloria Naylor, Alice Walker, Toni Morrison, or Zora Neale Hurston. What about the pieces you've read would have affected the author so?*

4) *Coleman says, "Well, there are plans and passions. Sometimes they diverge, but sometimes they come together too." Write about a time when a plan you had came together perfectly with one of your passions. Now describe a time when the two did not come together.*

5) *Recall a time when your life plans changed significantly. What led to that change? Was the outcome positive because of or in spite of that change? Was the outcome negative? What made it so?*

6) *Coleman says, "Wanting to be a professor is like never leaving school. It is like never graduating." Interview at least two of your professors about their reasons for finding a career in higher education. How do their stories compare to Coleman's?*

Further Suggestions for Writing — "Looking Forward, Looking Back"

1) No matter where you are in your college career, write an essay titled "Looking Forward/Looking Back."

2) Compare and contrast the life you have known as a college student to the life you might have had if you had made some other choice.

3) Compare and contrast some aspect of your school now to how it was 20 or 40 years ago or more.

4) Human nature is constantly puzzling. Why are people generous one moment and stingy the next? Love a person one moment and hate that same person the next? Explore your thoughts on some apparently contradictory aspect of human behavior that you particularly find on a college campus.

5) Argue that college should or should not prepare students for specific careers.

6) Argue for or against speech codes at your university.

7) Argue for or against the Greek System at your school.

8) Argue for or against a new policy concerning alcohol on your campus.

9) Argue that universities do too much or too little for students.

10) Argue that your school should or should not do away with intramural athletics.

11) Argue that student athletes at major universities are or are not exploited.

12) Argue that too much has been made of technology at your university.

13) Argue that student athletes should be paid.

14) Many people feel student organizations that support political and/or religious beliefs should not be supported by student fees. Argue for or against that proposition.

15) Write a paper titled "A History of Affirmative Action Policies on College Campuses."

16) What do you make of the fact that college grades do not seem to correlate very well with success after graduation? What might be some of the causes and/or implications of this lack of correlation?

17) Compare and contrast the university system in the United States to that in some other country.

18) Interview faculty and staff on your campus about how they found their "niche" in life. Did they have a "calling"? If so, how did they discover it? If not, what did they go through to get to their current positions?

19) Interview someone you know who has a "job" and someone who has a "career." Compare the two concepts of work using their specific examples. What are some generalizations you can make about the differences between a job and a career?

20) Choose a career possibility you are considering and evaluate it.

21) *Working in groups, read and discuss the mission statement and rationale for general studies requirements in your college catalogue. What values do these statements express? Do you agree with them? Why or why not? Do you feel that a person who enrolls in your college has an obligation to endorse and uphold these values? Compare your reactions with those of the other groups.*

22) *Choose one of your responses to "Some possibilities for writing" in this section and do further research on some aspect of the topic you addressed in your narrative. Write about how and why this new information would have improved your previous effort.*

Selected Films —
"Been There, Done That"

Amongst Friends (1993, USA). Three wealthy suburban childhood friends turn to crime as young adults. Written and directed by 26-year-old Rob Weiss. Drama/ Crime. 86 min. R

The Big Chill (1983, USA). An ensemble cast of baby boomers reunite for a long weekend after the suicide of an old college friend. Drama. 103 min. R

Carnal Knowledge (1971, USA). A gritty look at the seedy sex lives of two college pals (Jack Nicholson and Art Garfunkel) through the filter of their partners (among them Candice Bergen and Ann-Margret). Drama. 96 min. R

Class of '63 (1973, USA). An old flame reignites at a class reunion. Drama. 74 min.

Four Friends (1981, USA). Three men who love the same woman find their entwined lives fractured by college, drug abuse, and the Vietnam War. Drama. 115 min. R

The Graduate (1967, USA). Director Mike Nichol's watershed portrait of an aimless college graduate (Dustin Hoffman) whose progression from sex to love finally defines him. Drama/Comedy. 105 min. R

The Heidi Chronicles (1995, USA). Adapted by Wendy Wasserman from her Pulitzer Prize–winning play, the film follows a woman from prep school to Vassar College and on through her adult life and loves. Made for cable. Drama. 94 min. N/R

Kicking and Screaming (1995, USA). Four recent college graduates don't want to face the realities of life on the outside. Comedy. 96 min. R

Marie (1985, USA). True story of a single mother (divorced after her husband battered her) who works her way through school and finally rises to the head of the Tennessee parole board. Sissy Spacek stars. 113 min. PG-13

Poetic Justice (1993, USA). Pop star Janet Jackson plays a creative young woman who gives up her dream of college after her boyfriend is murdered. She becomes a hair stylist but continues writing poetry (penned for the film by Maya Angelou). Sobering cinematography shows post-1992-riot South Central L.A. Drama. 109 min. R

Reality Bites (1994, USA). A bright young cast (Winona Ryder, Ethan Hawke, Ben Stiller, Janeane Garofalo) stumbles into the real world after college. Romantic drama. 94 min. PG-13

Romy and Michele's High School Reunion (1997,USA). Lisa Kudrow and Mira Sorvino play ditzy best friends who attend their 10-year high school reunion, but they first completely remake their styles and identities in order to impress the people who tormented them. Comedy. 92 min. R

She's Having a Baby (1988, USA). After a dismal try at grad school, Peter Pan–ish writer Kevin Bacon jives his way into an ad agency job, while he deals haphazardly with marriage, fidelity, and planning parenthood. Comedy. 106 min. PG-13

St. Elmo's Fire (1985, USA). A loose-knit group of college friends finds that each of them bears a unique burden in facing adulthood. Drama. 108 min. R

When Harry Met Sally (1989, USA). After undergraduate school, Sally (Meg Ryan)

carpools with her friend's boyfriend, Harry (Billy Crystal), to New York. They meet by chance many times over the years and form a bond. Romantic comedy. 96 min. R

For Critical Thinking Points on these films, see Appendix (p. 335).

Appendix

Critical Thinking Points on Selected Films

As you watch

1) How is film, as a genre, different from written genres such as poetry, essays, novels, and short stories? Are you more likely to "interpret" a film or one of the other genres? Why?
2) Many literary scholars believe that the book has been replaced by film. Do you believe this is true? Why or why not? What might have contributed to scholars making such a statement?
3) How is film more accessible to a general audience? Is this positive or negative? In what ways?
4) What stereotypes are apparent in this film? In what ways, if any, does this film attempt to break out of stereotypes?
5) Are there characters and/or scenes in this film that remind you of yourself or your experiences? Why?

After you've watched

1) Which character in the film can you identify with the most? Why? Which character in the film can you identify with the least? Why?
2) In your opinion, does this film offer a realistic depiction of high school or college? Why or why not?
3) In what ways is this film a reflection of its time? If the film is set before its release date, how is the time it was made reflected in the script?
4) What specifically in the film makes this a "coming of age" movie? Could it fall into another category? Can you create a category for this film?
5) Do you believe this film promotes a positive or negative image of students? Why?

6) *Imagine you were your mother or father watching this film, and then answer the following question: Does this film promote a positive or negative image of students? Why? Have your answers changed from the way you answered question 5? If so, speculate about the reasons.*

Some possibilities for writing

1) *Films often cite the original text in the introduction. Is this film based on a play, novel, or short story? If so, read the original and decide what has been added and/or deleted in the transition from print to film. Speculate why those aspects were added and/or deleted. Which did you prefer, the written or film version? Why?*
2) *Choose at least two characters from the film and write a page of original dialogue between them. Extend an existing scene in the film, or create your own.*
3) *Read at least five reviews of this film, and write a research paper comparing and contrasting the reviews.*
4) *Imagine you were asked to film "A Day in the Life of a Freshman" on your campus. What elements of your life would you include? If you have access to a video camera (many university libraries rent them), film your list of scenes.*
5) *Choose one piece in this collection, and write a proposal to a film company about why this piece would make an excellent film.*
6) *Watch at least three films from three different decades, and write a response about how each depicts high school and/or college students. In what ways is that depiction a reflection of the time?*

Credits and Permissions

Page 122 "Who Shall I Be? The Allure of a Fresh Start" by Jennifer Crichton. Reprinted by permission of the author.

Page 134 "Raspberries" by Jennifer Fandel. Reprinted by permission of the author.

Page 136 "First Love," copyright © 1991 by R. A. Sasaki. Reprinted from *The Loom and Other Stories* by permission of Graywolf Press, Saint Paul, MN.

Page 147 "Revision" by John David Rose first appeared in *Upriver 5*, 1995, Upriver Press. Reprinted by permission of the publisher.

Page 149 "Carmen" by Jennifer Sheridan originally published in *Prairie Hearts*, Outrider Press Inc. Reprinted by permission of Outrider Press.

Page 154 "What It's Really Like" by Frank Smoot. Reprinted by permission of the author.

Page 156 "Virginity" by Jane Barnes Casey. Reprinted by permission of the author.

Page 166 "Irreversible Seasons" by Anita Santiago first appeared in *Palm Readings*, PlainView Press, 1998. Reprinted by permission of the author.

Page 178 "No More Kissing — AIDS Everywhere" by Michael Blumenthal. Reprinted by permission of the author.

Page 181 "The Blue-Light System," by Katie Roiphe from "The Morning After," copyright © 1993 by Katherine Anne Roiphe. Reprinted by permission of Little, Brown and Company.

Page 188 "Dancing" by Paul Durica. Reprinted by permission of the author.

Page 207 "The Good Student Apologizes to His Professor and to the Girl in Room 303" by Ron Watson first printed in *New Mexico Humanities Review* 34, 1991. Reprinted by permission of the author.

Page 214 "Teachers: A Primer" by Ronald Wallace from *Time's Fancy* by Ronald Wallace, copyright © 1994. Reprinted by permission of the University of Pittsburgh Press.

Page 226 "Mayday" by William Crawford Woods. Reprinted by permission of the author.

Page 241 "No Immediate Danger" by Mary McLaughlin Slëchta. Reprinted by permission of the author.

Page 249 "Open Admission," copyright © 1983 by Shirley Lauro. Reprinted by permission of the William Morris Agency on behalf of the author.

Page 259 "Signed, Grateful" by Kate Boyes. Reprinted by permission of the author.

Page 264 "Of This Time, Of That Place," copyright © 1979 by Lionel Trilling, first published in *Of This Time, Of That Place and Other Stories*. Reprinted with permission of the Wylie Agency, Inc.

Page 293 "April Inventory" by W. D. Snodgrass from *Heart's Needle*, copyright © 1959 by William Snodgrass. Reprinted by permission of Alfred A. Knopf Inc.

Page 300 "The Speech the Graduates Didn't Hear" by Jacob Neusner. Reprinted by permission of the author.

Page 303 "The Eighty-Yard Run" by Irwin Shaw originally published in *12 Short Stories 5 Decades*, copyright © Irwin Shaw. Reprinted with permission of the estate of Irwin Shaw.

Page 315 "Reunion" by Dawn Karima Pettigrew. Reprinted by permission of the author.

Page 318 "Moon June Spoon" by Frank Smoot. Reprinted by permission of the author.

Page 321 "Scarlet Ribbons" by Michael Perry. Reprinted by permission of the author.

Page 325 "Passion" by Monica Coleman. Reprinted by permission of the author.